SOLD PRICE
REDBRIDGE
PUBLIC LIBRARY

TAX GUIDE
1992-93

TAX GUIDE 1992-93

by

W I Sinclair, FCA

© Fiscal Services Ltd 1992

ISBN 0 85121 8792

Published by

Longman Law, Tax and Finance
Longman Group UK Limited
21–27 Lamb's Conduit Street, London WC1N 3NJ

Associated Offices

Australia, Hong Kong, Malaysia, Singapore, USA

All rights reserved. No part of this publication may be reproduced, stored in a retrieval system, or transmitted, in any form or by any means, electronic, mechanical, photocopying, recording or otherwise, without either the prior written permission of the copyright holder for which application should be addressed in the first instance to the publishers, or a licence permitting restricted copying issued by the Copyright Licensing Agency Limited, 90 Tottenham Court Road, London, W1P 9HE.

No responsibility for loss occasioned to any person acting or refraining from action as a result of the material in this publication can be accepted by the authors or publishers.

The views and opinions of Allied Dunbar may not necessarily coincide with some of the views and opinions expressed in this book which are solely those of the authors and no endorsement of them by Allied Dunbar should be inferred.

The material herein which is Crown Copyright is reproduced with the permission of the Controller of Her Majesty's Stationery Office.

A CIP catalogue record for this book is available from the British Library.

Computerset by Promenade Graphics Ltd, Cheltenham
Printed in Great Britain by
Bath Press, Bath, Avon

Abbreviations

ACT	advance corporation tax
AEI	average earnings index
AVC	additional voluntary contribution
BES	business expansion scheme
CAA	Capital Allowances Act 1990
CGT	capital gains tax
CGTA	Capital Gains Tax Act 1979
CIC	close investment holding company
COMP	contracted out money purchase
DLTA	Development Land Tax Act 1976
EEIG	European economic interest grouping
ESOP	employee share option plan
FA	Finance Act
F2A	Finance (No 2) Act
FIFO	first in, first out
FPCS	fixed profit car scheme
FSAVC	free standing additional voluntary contribution
HMSO	Her Majesty's Stationery Office
ITA	Inheritance Tax Act 1984
LAPR	life assurance premium relief
LEL	lower earnings limit
MIRAS	mortgage interest relief at source
NRE	net relevant earnings
PAYE	pay as you earn

Abbreviations

PEP	personal equity plan
PET	potentially exempt transfer
PHI	permanent health insurance
PIBS	permanent interest bearing share
PPP (PRO)	personal pension plan (protected rights only)
PRAS	pension relief at source
PRP	profit related pay
PSO	Pension Schemes Office
RPI	retail prices index
S (Ss)	section (sections) of an Act
SAYE	save as you earn
Sch (Schs)	schedule (schedules) of an Act
SERPS	state earnings related pension scheme
SFO	Superannuation Funds Office
TA	Income and Corporation Taxes Act
TCGA	Taxation of Chargeable Gains Act 1992
TESSA	tax exempt special savings account
TMA	Taxes Management Act 1970
UEL	upper earnings limit
USM	Unlisted Securities Market
VAT	value added tax
VATA	Value Added Tax Act 1983

About this book

This book has been designed to be used both by the professional and non-professional. Solicitors, accountants and company secretaries will find it especially useful as a concise ready reference. Many others, company directors and executives, partners and sole-traders, employers and employees, will find in it much helpful information and advice when dealing with problems of personal and company taxation.

It illustrates the working of income tax, capital gains tax, corporation tax, inheritance tax and VAT in the UK.

It is intended to revise the book annually in order to keep it up to date in accordance with the annual changes to the law. This is the twenty-first edition and is based on the law as at 1 August 1992, including the two 1992 Finance Acts.

I am most grateful to all those who have written to me with kind and helpful comments concerning the previous editions, some of which have been taken into account in the preparation of this volume.

Because the book concisely covers a very wide field, it has been necessary to omit some of the exemptions and qualifications with which tax law abounds: to adopt a familiar saying, 'When I say never, I mean hardly ever and when I say always, I mean almost always'.

The book is intended to be only a general tax guide. If it cannot solve a problem, the time has come to look at one of the multi-volume tax textbooks or to consult a tax specialist.

I gratefully acknowledge the help given to me on this edition by E B Lipkin, LLB, FCA, ATII of *Kidsons Impey*, P D Silke, BPhil, MSocSc, and A N Homburger, BCom, FCA, ACMA, and also by Simon Arnot, BA, LLB, Barrister, Mark Davies, BA, Solicitor, Margaret Gibbon, LLB, Solicitor, Lily Olisa, LLB, Solicitor,

Stuart Reynolds, LLB, Philippa Terry, LLM, Solicitor, Vince Jerrard, LLB, Solicitor, Sue Phillipson, LLB, D C Vessey, BSc and C M Green all of *Allied Dunbar Assurance plc*.

My special thanks are due to Vince Jerrard for contributing the chapter on Life Assurance taxation.

W I Sinclair

Introduction

This, the twenty-first edition, deals with the tax system at the time of writing for the 1992–93 fiscal year. Every chapter has been amended to reflect the many tax changes which have been made since the previous edition, including those relating to income tax and personal reliefs, investments, National Insurance, capital gains tax, corporation tax, inheritance tax, pensions, VAT and many, many others. To help keep track of the changes, this edition includes, at the end of the Contents section, a summary of the 1992 Finance Acts with references to the relevant paragraphs in the Guide.

Particular changes in this edition include:

- New income tax lower rate.
- Inheritance tax threshold reaches £150,000.
- VAT threshold up and penalties reduced.
- BES ending announced.
- Inheritance tax relief on business assets much increased.
- Taxes on car benefits up.
- Improved reliefs for charitable giving.
- Better scope for investment through PEPs in unit trusts.
- Changes to VAT etc to accommodate the EC.

Because of the volume of changes, it is not possible to retain in each new edition *full* information for previous years. Thus for the tax rules for previous years, reference to past editions is occasionally necessary.

Ideas on tax saving appear throughout the book. However, the *Tax Savings Hints* chapter comes first with many references to the later chapters for easy location of topics. Furthermore, this chapter contains particular reference to future tax planning in a section entitled 'The way ahead' (1.8).

A particular feature to note is that all indexing and cross-referencing uses chapter and topic numbers. Thus **7.6** means the

x   *Introduction*

sixth-numbered topic in Chapter 7. Similarly **7.6.3** would mean the third subsidiary topic within that main heading. Also, a glossary to help with the meanings of certain terms appears at the end of this book.

The 1992–93 Allied Dunbar Tax Guide brings together in a single volume all of the main taxes which are operating at present, enabling their total effect to be borne in mind. In planning for the future, however, account should be taken of the various avenues for further reform indicated by the Government, as well as the longer-term possibilities for capital gains tax, inheritance tax, etc. Furthermore, possible changes by future governments should not be overlooked. As new developments are crystallised, they will be covered in the future annual editions of this book.

Contents

	Page
Abbreviations	v
About this book	vii
Introduction	ix
Finance Acts 1992 — Checklist	xxii
Key Rates and Allowances — 1992–93	xxv

1 Tax saving hints   1

1.1	Tax planning	1
1.2	Income tax saving	3
1.3	Capital gains tax saving	12
1.4	Inheritance tax planning	15
1.5	Change of residence and domicile	22
1.6	Year-end planning	23
1.7	The seven ages of tax planning	24
1.8	The way ahead	28

2 The basis of your tax liability   31

2.1	Who is taxable?	31
2.2	The taxes payable	31
2.3	What income is taxable?	32
2.4	Deduction of tax at source and tax credits	32
2.5	The distinction between capital and revenue profits	33
2.6	Revenue and capital expenses	34
2.7	Bank and building society interest	35
2.8	Year of assessment	36
2.9	Period of assessment less than full year	36

3 Personal reliefs   37

3.1	Earned and unearned income	38
3.2	Personal allowances	38
3.3	Indexation of personal reliefs	45

4 Annual payments and interest   47

4.1	Annual payments apart from interest	47
4.2	What are annual payments?	48
4.3	Interest payments	48
4.4	Interest paid for business purposes	49
4.5	Tax relief for interest payments	49
4.6	Loans for purchase and improvement of buildings and land	50
4.7	Deduction of tax from mortgage interest payments	52

5 Computing your income tax bill   55

5.1	Indexation of income tax bands	55
5.2	What is total income?	56
5.3	Total income — Deductions	57
5.4	Charges on income	58
5.5	Deductions from tax payable	59
5.6	Investment income surcharge (additional rate)	59
5.7	The assessment and payment of your income tax	60
5.8	Interest on overdue tax	62
5.9	Fluctuating income	62

6 Husband, wife and children   65

6.1	Independent taxation of husband and wife	65
6.2	When you marry	66
6.3	Separate assessment	67
6.4	Separate taxation of wife's earnings	68
6.5	Deeds of covenant	69
6.6	The income of your children	70
6.7	Death of husband or wife	72
6.8	Divorce or separation	73

7 Income from land and property — 77

7.1	Income falling within Schedule A	77
7.2	Special rules concerning expenses	79
7.3	Losses	79
7.4	Assessment under Schedule A	79
7.5	Furnished lettings	81
7.6	Holiday lettings	81
7.7	The taxation of lease premiums	82
7.8	Woodlands	83
7.9	Dealing in property	84
7.10	Artificial transactions in land	84
7.11	Agricultural land, etc	85
7.12	Land sold and leased back	85
7.13	Development land tax	86
7.14	'Rent a room'	87

8 Income from dividends and interest — 88

8.1	How dividends are taxed	88
8.2	Interest paid on government securities, etc	89
8.3	Bond washing — Accrued income	90
8.4	Interest not taxed at source (Schedule D Case III)	92
8.5	Basis of charge under Schedule D Case III	92
8.6	Building society interest	95
8.7	Bank interest	96
8.8	Deep discount and deep gain securities	97
8.9	Scrip dividend options	98
8.10	Personal Equity Plan	99
8.11	Tax exempt special savings accounts (TESSAs)	100

9 Income from employments and PAYE — 101

9.1	Schedule E Case I	101
9.2	Schedule E Case II	101
9.3	Schedule E Case III	102
9.4	The distinction between Schedule D Case I or II and Schedule E	102
9.5	Employment outside the UK	102
9.6	Amounts included in your income	102
9.7	Expense payments for directors and others (form P11D)	114

	9.8	Deductions you may claim	116
	9.9	Share option and share incentive schemes	117
	9.10	Employee Share Ownership Plans (ESOPs)	124
	9.11	Retirement pension schemes	125
	9.12	Compensation for loss of office	126
	9.13	The assessment basis	128
	9.14	The PAYE system	129
	9.15	Profit Related Pay	134

10 Income from businesses and professions — 135

	10.1	Trades, professions and vocations	135
	10.2	What is trading?	135
	10.3	What business expenses are allowed?	136
	10.4	The computation of your assessable profits for Schedule D Cases I and II	139
	10.5	Stock valuation	141
	10.6	Stock relief	142
	10.7	Basis of assessment	143
	10.8	Capital allowances	146
	10.9	Capital allowances on plant and machinery	147
	10.10	Fixtures — Entitlement to capital allowances	155
	10.11	Industrial buildings	155
	10.12	Enterprise Zones	156
	10.13	Small workshops	156
	10.14	Agricultural buildings allowance	157
	10.15	Hotel buildings	157
	10.16	Assured tenancies	158
	10.17	Scientific research allowance	158
	10.18	Patent rights and 'know how'	159
	10.19	Dredging	159
	10.20	Mineral extraction	160
	10.21	Films etc	160
	10.22	Relief for losses	160
	10.23	Loss in new business	162
	10.24	Terminal losses	163
	10.25	Business Expansion Scheme	163
	10.26	Earnings basis and cash basis	166
	10.27	Post-cessation receipts	166
	10.28	Class 4 National Insurance contributions	167

11 Partnerships — 169

11.1	What is a partnership?	169
11.2	How partnership income is taxed	169
11.3	Partnership losses	171
11.4	Changes of partners	172
11.5	Election for continuation basis	172
11.6	Partnership capital gains	173
11.7	Overseas partnerships	173
11.8	European economic interest groupings	174

12 Companies — 175

12.1	Introduction	175
12.2	Corporation tax on profits, etc	175
12.3	The imputation system	176
12.4	Accounting periods for corporation tax	176
12.5	Repayment supplement	177
12.6	ACT on dividends, etc	178
12.7	Small companies rate	181
12.8	Associated companies	182
12.9	The computation of assessable profits	183
12.10	Special capital allowances rules for companies	184
12.11	Losses	184
12.12	Reconstructions	185
12.13	Group loss relief	185
12.14	Terminal losses	186
12.15	Companies' capital gains and capital losses	187
12.16	Groups of companies	189
12.17	Close companies	190
12.18	Close investment holding companies (CICs)	193
12.19	Non-resident companies trading in the UK	194
12.20	UK companies with overseas income	194
12.21	Controlled foreign companies	195
12.22	Stock relief for companies	196
12.23	Demergers	196
12.24	Unquoted company purchasing its own shares	197
12.25	Future administrative changes	198

13 Miscellaneous aspects — 201

13.1	Miscellaneous profits — Schedule D Case VI	201

13.2	Tax-free organisations	202
13.3	Patent holders	205
13.4	Authors' copyright sales and royalties	205
13.5	Sub-contractors	206
13.6	Farming	207
13.7	Building society arrangements	209
13.8	Insolvents	209
13.9	Anti-avoidance provisions	210

14 Returns, assessments and repayment claims 219

14.1	Your tax return	219
14.2	The Tax Inspectors and Collectors	224
14.3	Appeals against assessments	227
14.4	The Special and General Commissioners	228
14.5	Investigatory powers of the Revenue	229
14.6	Repayment claims	232
14.7	The collection of tax	235
14.8	Back duty investigations	238

15 Domicile and residence 243

15.1	The importance of domicile and residence	243
15.2	What is domicile?	244
15.3	What is residence?	245
15.4	How to change your domicile and residence	249

16 Tax on foreign income 251

16.1	Overseas income from investments and businesses	251
16.2	The basis of assessment under Schedule D Cases IV and V	254
16.3	Professions conducted partly abroad	257
16.4	Relief for overseas trading by individuals	257
16.5	Earnings from overseas employments	257
16.6	Double taxation relief	259

17 Non-residents, visitors and immigrants 263

17.1	On what income are non-residents liable to UK tax?	263

Contents xvii

17.2	Interest paid to non-residents in respect of certain UK government securities	266
17.3	Rules for taxation of visitors' income	266
17.4	When does a habitual visitor become a UK resident?	266
17.5	The position of visiting diplomats	267
17.6	Visiting entertainers and sportsmen	268
17.7	The entitlement of certain non-residents to UK tax reliefs	268
17.8	Immigrants	269

18 Capital gains tax 271

18.1	Introduction	271
18.2	What is a chargeable gain?	271
18.3	Who is liable?	271
18.4	Capital gains tax rates from 6 April 1988	272
18.5	Relief for moderate total gains before 6 April 1980	273
18.6	Annual exemptions from 6 April 1980	273
18.7	What assets are liable?	275
18.8	What assets are exempted?	275
18.9	What constitutes a disposal?	276
18.10	How your chargeable gains are computed	277
18.11	Re-basing to 31 March 1982 values	278
18.12	Indexation allowance	279
18.13	Capital losses	283
18.14	Losses on unquoted shares in trading companies	284
18.15	Assessment and payment of capital gains tax	284
18.16	Valuations	286
18.17	Relief on sales of assets owned on 6 April 1965	287
18.18	Quoted shares and securities	288
18.19	Exemption for corporate bonds	295
18.20	Unquoted shares	296
18.21	Part disposals	297
18.22	A series of disposals	297
18.23	Private residences	297
18.24	Chattels sold for £6,000 or less	299
18.25	Replacement of business assets — roll-over relief	300
18.26	Gifts of business assets	301

18.27	General relief for gifts	302
18.28	Gifts relief from 14 March 1989	303
18.29	Business retirement relief	303
18.30	Traded options	306
18.31	Commodity and financial futures	306
18.32	Overseas aspects	306

19 The taxation of trusts and estates — 309

19.1	Trusts	309
19.2	Trusts where the settlor or testator is deceased	309
19.3	Trusts where the settlor is still living	310
19.4	Accumulation settlements for the benefit of the settlor's children	312
19.5	Income of discretionary trusts, etc	313
19.6	Trusts' capital gains tax	313
19.7	Trusts' capital gains tax — business assets, gifts, etc	314
19.8	Trusts' capital gains tax — disposals of interests and distributions	315
19.9	Foreign trusts	316
19.10	Estates of deceased persons	318

20 Inheritance tax — 321

20.1	Introduction	321
20.2	Property chargeable	322
20.3	Potentially exempt transfers	322
20.4	Deemed domicile	323
20.5	Rate scale	323
20.6	Tapering relief	325
20.7	The ten year cumulation period	325
20.8	The seven year cumulation period	325
20.9	Indexation of rate bands	326
20.10	Valuation	326
20.11	Quoted securities passing on death	326
20.12	Valuation of related property	327
20.13	Land sold within three years of death	327
20.14	Abolition of estate duty	328
20.15	Inheritance tax on death	328
20.16	Excluded property	330
20.17	Double taxation relief	331
20.18	Exempt transfers	331

20.19	Relief for business property	335
20.20	Waivers of dividends and remuneration	336
20.21	Conditional exemption for certain objects and buildings, etc	336
20.22	Relief for agricultural property	337
20.23	Woodlands	338
20.24	Quick succession relief	338
20.25	Administration and collection	339
20.26	Payment by instalments of tax on death	340
20.27	Payment of tax on lifetime gifts by instalments	341
20.28	Inheritance tax and life assurance	341
20.29	Property outside Great Britain	342
20.30	Miscellaneous points	342
20.31	Settled property	344
20.32	Mutual and voidable transfers	348
20.33	Avoiding double charges	348
20.34	Example: Calculation of inheritance tax payable	349

21 An outline of VAT — 351

21.1	Introduction	351
21.2	VAT in practice	353
21.3	Zero-rating and exemption	356
21.4	Business	357
21.5	Small traders	357
21.6	Zero-rated supplies	358
21.7	Groups and divisions of companies	358
21.8	Local authorities	359
21.9	Charities	359
21.10	Retailers	359
21.11	Special cases	359
21.12	Documentation	362
21.13	Appeals	364
21.14	Zero-rating	365
21.15	Important changes to zero-ratings	367
21.16	Exemptions	367
21.17	Trading within the EC	368
21.18	Optional rate for farmers	369

22 Stamp duty — 371

22.1	Introduction	371
22.2	Exemptions	372

22.3	Capital duty	373
22.4	Relief for take-overs	373
22.5	*Ad valorem* duties	374
22.6	Stamp duty reserve tax	375
22.7	Abolition of stamp duty on shares, etc	375

23 Social security 377

23.1	Introduction	377
23.2	National Insurance contributions	377
23.3	Social security benefits	380
23.4	Statutory sick pay	382
23.5	Class 4 National Insurance contributions	382

24 Tax aspects of life assurance, pensions annuities and PHI 385
by Vince Jerrard

24.1	Types of contract	385
24.2	Life policies	385
24.3	The company's tax position	385
24.4	The tax treatment of your premiums and proceeds	386
24.5	Qualifying policies	387
24.6	Non-qualifying policies	391
24.7	Chargeable events	392
24.8	Inheritance tax and life policies	401
24.9	Pension business	403
24.10	The State pension scheme	405
24.11	Personal pension plans and retirement annuity contracts	408
24.12	Retirement annuity contracts (S226 contracts)	415
24.13	Free-standing AVC schemes	424
24.14	General annuity business	426
24.15	Permanent health insurance (PHI)	428

25 Tax tables 431

25.1	Income tax table for 1992–93	431
25.2	Tax rates and allowances for 1976–77 to 1991–92	432

25.3	Income tax rates:		
	for 1976–77 and 1977–78	434	
	for 1978–79	434	
	for 1979–80	434	
	for 1980–81 and 1981–82	434	
	for 1982–83	435	
	for 1983–84	435	
	for 1984–85	435	
	for 1985–86	435	
	for 1986–87	435	
	for 1987–88	435	
	for 1988–89	435	
	for 1989–90 and 1990–91	436	
	for 1991–92	436	
25.4	Investment income surcharge	436	
25.5	Capital transfer tax rates:		
	before 27 October 1977	436	
	from 28 October 1977 to 25 March 1980	437	
	from 26 March 1980 to 9 March 1981	437	
	from 10 March 1981 to 8 March 1982	438	
	from 9 March 1982 to 14 March 1983	438	
	from 15 March 1983 to 12 March 1984	438	
	from 13 March 1984 to 5 April 1985	438	
	from 6 April 1985 to 18 March 1986	439	
25.6	Inheritance tax rates:		
	from 18 March 1986 to 16 March 1987	439	
	from 17 March 1987 to 14 March 1988	439	
	from 15 March 1988 to 5 April 1989	439	
	from 6 April 1989 to 5 April 1990	440	
	from 6 April 1990 to 5 April 1991	440	
	from 6 April 1991 to 9 March 1992	440	

Glossary 441

Index 445

Finance Acts 1992 — Checklist

FINANCE ACT 1992

Main Subject	Sections	Schedules	References
Customs duties etc	1–5	1	—
Value added tax—			
Payments on account	6		21.2
Penalties	7		21.2
Car tax	8		—
Income tax—			
Lower rate	9		1,2,18 & 5.0.1.
Rates and allowances	10		5.1
Short title etc	11		—

FINANCE (No 2) ACT 1992

Main subject	Sections	Schedules	References
Customs and Excise	1–13	1–2	—
Value added tax—			
Abolition of fiscal frontiers	14	3	21.17
Time for raising and answering inquiries	15		—
Farming—special treatment	16		21.18
Fuel and power—matches	17		—
Car tax—			
Abolition of fiscal frontiers	18	4	—
Income tax—			
Lower rate	19		1.2.18 & 5.0.1
Married couple's allowance etc	20	5	3.2.2 & 6.1
Corporation tax rates	21–22		12.2 & 12.7
Capital gains tax rates	23		18.4
Groups of companies etc	24–25	6	12.13
Charities—			
Donations—minimum limits	26		13.2.1
Covenants	27		13.2.1
Inspection powers	28		—

Finance Acts 1992 — Checklist

Main Subject	Sections	Schedules	References
Interest, dividends etc—			
Returns of interest—banks etc	29		—
Foreign dividends	30		12.20
Equity notes	31		12.6.1
Distributions information	32		8.1.2
Securities and deposits—			
Deep gain securities	33	7	8.8
Rights re deposits	34	8	8.7
Exchange of securities	35		18.32
Employee shares—			
Employee share ownership trusts	36		9.10
Special benefits	37		9.9.4
Business expansion scheme—			
No relief for shares issued after 1993	38		10.25
Private rented housing—property managing companies	39		10.25
Letting to former owner-occupiers	40		10.25
Films—relief for expenditure	41–43		10.21
Transfer of UK and non-UK trades	44–49		12.15 & 18.32
Double tax relief	50–52		12.15 & 18.32
Miscellaneous—			
Car fuel cash equivalents	53		9.6.5
Foreign earnings	54		16.5
Oil extraction	55		—
Friendly societies	56	9	13.2.2.
Rents—connected persons	57		13.9.11
Rents chargeable under Case VI	58		7.5
Furnished accommodation	59	10	7.14
Deductions on account of certain annual payments	60		—
Qualifying maintenance payments—extension to EC etc	61–62		6.8.5
Paying and collecting agents	63	11	—
Reduced and composite rate	64		13.7
Life assurance business	65		23.3
Banks etc in compulsory liquidation	66	12	—
Capital allowances—			
Transfer of a UK trade	67		10.9.4

Main Subject	Sections	Schedules	References
Capital allowances—contd			
Computer software	68		10.9.14
Films	69		10.21
Enterprise zones	70	13	10.12
Expensive motor cars	71		10.9.10
Inheritance tax—			
Increase of rate bands	72		20.5
Business and agricultural property relief	73	14	20.19, 20.22 & 20.26
Petroleum Revenue Tax	74	15	—
General and Special Commissioners—change of name etc	75–76	16	14.4
Miscellaneous and general—			
Northern Ireland Electricity	77	17	—
Restriction of Gas Levy	78		—
Treasury Bills	79		—
Publication of certain interest rates	80		—
General—repeals etc	81–83	18	—

Key Rates and Allowances — 1992–93

(*Companies year to 31 March 1993*)

INCOME TAX *Reference* 5.0.1

Taxable income £	Slice £	Rate %	Total tax £
2,000		20	400
23,700	21,700	25	5,825
Over 23,700		40	

Income tax allowances 3.0.1

Personal allowance — single	£3,445
Additional personal relief for children	£1,720
Age allowance — single	£4,200
Age 75 or over — single	£4,370
income limit	£14,200
Married couple's allowance	
Age — under 65	£1,720
— 65–74	£2,465
— 75 and over	£2,505
Widow's bereavement allowance	£1,720
Life assurance premium relief — only on pre-14 March 1984 policies	$12\frac{1}{2}\%$

Companies

Full corporation tax rate	33%	12.2
Small companies rate	25%	12.7
Advance corporation tax rate	25/75ths	12.6

CAPITAL GAINS TAX

Rate (individuals)	20%/25%/40%	18.1
Annual exemption (individuals etc)	£5,800	18.6
(available separately for husband and wife)		

INHERITANCE TAX

Band £	Death rate %	20.5
0–150,000	Nil	
150,001 upwards	40	
Annual exemption	£3,000	20.18

VAT

Rate	$17\frac{1}{2}$%	21.1
Registration threshold from 11 March 1992	£36,600	21.5

1 Tax saving hints

1.1 Tax planning

The following pages deal with various ways in which you can arrange your affairs to reduce your tax bill. This should not be done by tax evasion which is completely illegal (13.9) and may result in your tax bill being increased by the addition of interest and penalties (14.8.2). You should always fully disclose your taxable income to the Revenue in your income tax return (14.1).

You are fully entitled, however, to arrange your affairs legally in such a way that your tax liability is reduced. This is known as tax avoidance (13.9). There are various anti-avoidance rules (13.9) but providing you are able to steer clear of these provisions you can make substantial tax savings by sensible planning. This chapter covers numerous tax saving hints with references to fuller explanations later in the book.

Tax planning is a very complex subject and many complicated schemes have been evolved. Such schemes are outside the scope of this book and in any event should be treated with great caution, following certain court decisions (*Ramsay, Furniss v Dawson*, etc). If you have substantial income and/or assets you should obtain professional advice on tax planning if you have not already done so.

1.1.1 Tax planning don'ts

(1) DON'T save tax at the expense of commercial benefits. (It is no good losing money in your business just to pay no tax.)
(2) DON'T cause unhappiness to yourself and your family in order to save tax. (Don't emigrate if you know you will not like your new country.)

(3) DON'T enter into tax-saving schemes which run on for a long time. These may be effective when you set them up but could be the target of future anti-avoidance legislation before they are completed.
(4) DON'T jeopardise your future financial security. (Do not give away all of your money just to reduce inheritance tax.)
(5) DON'T make inflexible arrangements. It is always necessary to review your tax planning in the light of changes in your financial position and family. You must also take full account of changes in the tax system, such as the drastic cuts in tax rates.
(6) DON'T forget that the law may change. Particularly remember that with inheritance tax on death it will be the law at your death and not necessarily the law now that will govern the liability.
(7) DON'T rigidly segregate capital and income. Good tax planning sometimes involves saving income and sometimes spending capital. Each has its own taxes and you should aim to maximise both after tax.

1.1.2 A basic plan

Before examining in detail ways of saving income tax, capital gains tax and inheritance tax, the following general guidelines are given, which are applicable to the tax and financial planning of many people:

(1) Buy your own house when you marry, or as soon afterwards as you can afford. If you remain single, house purchase is also desirable in appropriate circumstances. Tax is saved on *mortgage interest payments* (4.7) as explained. Also, your home should prove a good tax-free investment.
(2) Divide your assets and income with your spouse so that the best use is made of the independent taxation rules (6.1). Savings of both income tax and capital gains tax can be made in this way.
(3) Arrange to have the maximum pension cover possible in your particular circumstances. If you are self-employed, etc you should pay *personal pension contributions* (24.11).
(4) Arrange adequate *life cover* (24.2) to protect your family.
(5) If you have spare funds when your children marry, make outright gifts to them. Provided you survive for seven years no inheritance tax (20.3) will be payable, even if the marriage and other exemptions are exceeded.
(6) When your children have married, if your house is larger

than you need, consider selling it and investing part of the proceeds for your retirement.
(7) If you have spare funds over and above your retirement needs you and your wife should each make outright gifts to and settlements on your children and others. In order to cover inheritance tax, which might be payable if you die within seven years (20.3), appropriate term life assurance is advisable.
(8) Subject to there being sufficient funds for your spouse, leave at least £150,000 in your will to others (1.4.5), otherwise the £150,000 *nil rate inheritance tax band* (20.5) may be wasted.

1.2 Income tax saving

1.2.1 Personal reliefs and allowances

Always claim all of the *personal reliefs and allowances* (3.0.1) to which you are entitled. Notify the Revenue as soon as you qualify for an additional allowance such as married couple's allowance (3.2.2) when you marry. If possible, make sure your spouse and yourself have sufficient income to cover your respective personal reliefs.

1.2.2 Businesses

Make sure that you claim all *business expenses* (10.3) to which you are entitled. If you are able to use your *car in your business* (10.9.10) you can claim a reasonable proportion of the running costs (it is sometimes better if your business, etc actually owns the car).

1.2.3 Capital allowances

Do not overlook *capital allowances on plant and machinery* (10.9) and *industrial buildings* (10.11). Bear in mind that 100 per cent initial allowance is still available on buildings in enterprise zones (10.12).

1.2.4 Incorporation

Once your business profits bring your top income tax rate above 25 per cent, consider incorporation. Operating as a limited company will involve the 25 per cent *small companies corporation tax rate* (12.7), until the limit is passed. (An exception would be if your company is a close investment holding company (12.18) when 33 per cent may be payable.) You will probably become a director and thus be employed by your company; the National Insurance burden will change, but on balance, tax savings are likely. Also, you can normally improve your pension cover.

1.2.5 Employments

Make sure you claim all *allowable expenses* (10.3). Try to obtain part of your wages or salary in tax-free ways such as profit related pay (9.15) or luncheon vouchers. Tax savings may result if for example you have a company car or are given an interest-free loan or join your firm's pension scheme. However, watch changing tax rules such as the higher car benefit scales (9.6.5). If you are not covered by an *occupational scheme* (9.11) you should consider effecting a *personal pension scheme* (24.11).

1.2.6 Saving tax for your employees

If you are an employer you can enhance the after-tax income of your employees by various means including the following:

(1) Have a *canteen* for your staff or supply *luncheon vouchers* (9.6.3).
(2) Provide *business cars* (9.6.5) for employees (including wives who are employees) where appropriate.
(3) Grant *interest-free loans* to staff (but see 9.6.8 for restrictions).
(4) Provide *housing accommodation* (9.6.2) if the employees have to live close to their work.
(5) Operate *pension schemes* for staff (9.11). From July 1988, employers can contribute to personal pension schemes.
(6) Provide *recreation facilities* for your staff — the cost is normally a business expense and the employees will not be taxed on the benefit.
(7) In appropriate circumstances, introduce a *profit related pay* scheme (9.15) for your employees. Up to certain limits (9.15) profit related pay is free of income tax.
(8) If appropriate, operate a *share option* scheme (9.9.2).
(9) If you wish to make leaving payments to any employees make the payments in such forms as to qualify for relief from tax under the '*golden handshake*' *provisions* (9.12 and 9.12.1).
(10) Provide *childcare facilities* (9.6.14).

Note that (2), (3) and (4) above are subject to the fringe benefit rules for *directors and employees earning over £8,500 annually* (9.6.2). It is still of considerable value to provide such benefits in most cases, however. For example, normally a *car* will involve the appropriate *scale charge* (9.6.5) and employer's National Insurance contributions (23.2) but the employee may obtain a larger benefit from having the use of the car. This includes its capital value, insurance, car tax, repairs and, subject to an additional scale charge (9.6.5), any petrol bought for him.

1.2.7 Repayment claims

If you are entitled to make any income tax *repayment claim* (14.6), make sure that you do so at your earliest opportunity. In any event you should not allow the relevant time limit to expire. (This is normally six years after the end of the tax year concerned but is sometimes earlier.)

1.2.8 New businesses and fresh sources of Schedule D income, etc

Plan your starting and accounting dates to minimise your total *assessments for the opening years* (10.7.1). Make sure you make the appropriate claims for assessment on an 'actual' basis in the second and third years if this is beneficial (10.7.2). Similarly employ the *cessation rules* (10.7.3) and *partnership changes provisions* (11.4), to your best advantage. These various provisions which are described elsewhere in this book enable useful tax savings to be made by skilful timing and use of the relevant elections regarding, for example, business commencements, changes and new sources of income assessable under Schedule D Cases III, IV and V. However, the scope for tax savings concerning partnership changes was reduced in 1985.

If you make a *loss in a new business* (10.23), make the best use of it, not forgetting the option of relieving general income going back up to three years before you started to trade. This is particularly useful where income tax rates fall, since your new business losses might be offset against more highly taxed income for previous years.

1.2.9 Wife's earnings

If you have a business, pay your husband or wife properly for any work that he or she does for it. Up to 5 April 1990, this enabled the *wife's earned income allowance* (3.2.4) to be obtained. From 6 April 1990, the rules for independent taxation operate. Thus it remains important that both spouses have adequate income, so as to use their allowances and lower rate (20 per cent) and basic rate income tax bands.

You must be careful that your business does not pay your spouse more than the job is worth, or else the Revenue might seek to disallow part of the spouse's wages and so you will be taxed on the amount as a disallowed business expense. Also note that if the spouse's wage is £54 per week or more, National Insurance contributions must be paid.

Note that from 6 April 1990, the separate taxation of husband and wife is automatic and, as a result, the wife's earnings election (6.4) is no more. However, it is even more advantageous than before for each spouse to have income, because the wife is now taxed on her investment as well as earned income.

A satisfactory arrangement is to form a business partnership with your wife which will give her an entitlement to a share in the profits, normally treated as earned income, and to a personal pension plan. However, note that if your wife's share of the annual profits is over £6,120 the excess is charged at 6.3 per cent (maximum £941.22) under the *Class 4 National Insurance Contribution Scheme* (23.5).

1.2.10 Independent taxation—elections

Make sure that you use the elections under the independent taxation scheme to the best effect (6.1). If you and your spouse jointly own assets, you can elect for the income to be split between you in the ratios that you own them, otherwise the income is split equally for tax purposes.

Joint mortgage interest is divided equally between spouses unless you elect for a different split. These elections enable taxable income to be diverted to the spouse with unused allowances or a lower income tax rate, thus saving tax.

1.2.11 House purchase

By purchasing your house or flat instead of renting it you will normally save income tax. This is because unless you make some business use of your home you obtain no tax relief in respect of rent paid. However, up to the limits (generally £30,000 loan), *mortgage interest* (4.6) (on your main residence) is normally allowable for tax purposes, although, from 6 April 1991, this relief is restricted to the basic rate (25 per cent). If your mortgage is linked with some form of pre-14 March 1984 life assurance your tax bill is effectively reduced by 12.5 per cent of the premiums paid subject to the relevant rules (3.2.8). You must carefully consider the most favourable way to finance your house purchase, particularly since no life assurance relief is due on post-13 March 1984 policies.

As a basic method, you could select the conventional mortgage repayments system. Under this you will normally make monthly payments to the building society etc, partly consisting of the capital advanced to you and partly of interest. Subject to the limits (4.6) you obtain full tax relief for the interest as well as life assurance relief on any mortgage protection life policy which you effected prior to 14 March 1984. Even if you are not liable for tax, you still obtain the benefit of paying the interest net of the basic rate of tax.

If you have a comfortable income you might consider tying your mortgage to a life assurance endowment policy. Under this system you borrow a fixed sum from a building society or insurance company for a given term (20 years, etc).

You effect a life assurance endowment policy for the sum borrowed, the policy being held by the lender as security. Every year you pay the mortgage interest and policy premiums. At the end of the term your life endowment policy matures and the capital sum is paid to the lender in settlement of the mortgage.

Your policy can be with or without profits. The latter is cheaper but the former will generally prove a better investment. Indeed, most building societies will allow an endowment policy for a sum assured that is initially less than the loan, but the maturity proceeds of which will grow to equal or exceed the debt on conservative bonus assumptions. Extra decreasing life assurance covers any shortfall if you die before repayment. This type of endowment has the advantage of being cheaper than one for the full amount of the loan. In some cases, unit-linked endowment policies may be used.

The advantages of this system are that your life is covered automatically so, if you should die, the mortgage is automatically discharged. Also you get basic rate income tax relief on your interest payments each year on up to £30,000 of your mortgage. You also obtain income tax relief in respect of the life assurance policy if taken out before 14 March 1984.

Note, however, that under the endowment system you pay rather more in the earlier years than under a repayment mortgage. Inflation exaggerates this effect because the earlier payments are made in 'dearer' money. Therefore if you are able to invest the difference more profitably, there is a case for choosing a repayment mortgage. A particular instance would be if otherwise you could not afford your total permitted *personal pension* contributions (24.11). Since life assurance relief is not available for post-13 March 1984 policies, the balance has moved away from the endowment system and towards the repayment method or more beneficial personal pension basis (below). However, every case must be considered on its merits.

If you make regular *personal pension* payments you may be able to have an interest only mortgage. The capital sum will then be repaid out of the *cash sum on retirement* (24.11) which you can receive. This method is attractive for tax purposes since the *personal pension* contributions (24.11) which you pay qualify for tax relief at your highest earned income rates, subject to the rules.

A more recent development is the use of personal equity plans (PEPs) to repay the capital element in a mortgage. With the increase in the annual amount allowed to be invested in PEPs to £6,000 (plus £3,000 in single company PEPs from 1 January 1992) (8.10), there is ample scope for continuing schemes to be set up to repay quite substantial mortgages.

1.2.12 Tax-free investments

Various forms of tax-free income are given in a table in Chapter 2 (2.6.1). Avail yourself of the opportunities open to invest in tax-free situations. However, weigh up the interest you might receive tax-free with the after-tax interest on other investments.

Particular investments on which the income is tax-free are PEPs (8.10) and TESSAs (8.11). PEPs (personal equity plans) provide an attractive way to invest in equities, unit trusts, etc and also carry capital gains tax exemption. TESSAs (tax exempt special savings accounts) took effect from 1 January 1991. Their freedom from income tax on the interest, subject to the rules (8.11), makes TESSAs very competitive. You should certainly consider investing all or part of the £9,000 five-year maximum.

1.2.13 Life assurance (24.2)

As well as in connection with house purchase, life assurance provides a valuable method of coupling profitable investment with life cover. Subject to the rules (3.2.8) you obtain 12.5 per cent tax relief on qualifying premiums for policies effected before 14 March

1984. Normally, the 12.5 per cent would be deducted from your premiums on payment. Since relief is not available for policies effected subsequently, any existing at that date should be continued so that relief is obtained on the premiums. (Of course this does not apply to policies no longer appropriate to your needs.)

There are many schemes in which life assurance is linked to property bonds, unit trusts, shares and combinations of these, under which you obtain life cover. Despite the withdrawal of tax relief on premiums, life assurance policies remain attractive as investments (quite apart from the life cover they provide) because of their ability to provide tax-free proceeds and a wide spread of investments for a small outlay, etc.

1.2.14 Personal pensions (24.11.1)

If you have earned income in any year, regarding which you are not in an occupational pension scheme, and on which you pay income tax, you obtain full relief from such tax in respect of any personal pension contributions paid, up to the permitted maximum. The full rules are set out later in this book (24.11.1), subject to which you obtain relief from income tax in respect of the entire contributions paid. Thus you can obtain relief of up to 40 per cent of your contributions if your income is sufficiently high.

You obtain relief at the highest tax rates attributable to your income. Thus suppose on the top £1,000 of your income you pay income tax of £400; if you pay an allowable contribution of £1,000 under a personal pension scheme, you will obtain £400 tax relief and so your net cost is effectively only £600 (£1,000−£400). This will secure for you a pension at retirement when your top tax rate may well be lower. Personal pension annuity contracts provide a very cheap way of obtaining life cover. This is because part of the available limit each year can be applied in *temporary* (term) *life assurance cover* (24.11.1). Again, full tax relief at your top rate is obtained on the contributions paid.

Over the years, the personal pension contributions limits have, in general, been increased, particularly at higher income levels (24.11.1). You should take full advantage of the increased facility particularly bearing in mind that with current trends you will probably need to provide for a higher pension to compensate for inflation. Particularly valuable is the facility of paying contributions in respect of unused relief for the previous six years. This can enable a large contribution to be paid in a year of exceptionally high income.

At least as valuable is the rule allowing contributions paid in one tax year to be treated as paid in the previous one. This is particularly useful if you can elect for contributions to be taken back to a year when your top tax rate was higher than for the year when the contributions are paid.

From 1 July 1988, the personal pensions relief provisions absorbed the old rules for retirement annuities (24.11.1). Also, some improvements have taken place, such as in permitted contribution levels for those in their fifties (as from 6 April 1987). In addition there is the facility for *employees* to pay *personal pension* contributions net of basic rate income tax.

The withdrawal of life assurance relief in 1984 has emphasised the value of maximising your personal pension cover. Remember that it provides a very tax-effective way of covering your life (see above). Also, it may be possible to incorporate your *mortgage* (1.2.11).

The 1989 changes to the personal pension rules have important planning implications. The more beneficial contribution limits ranging up to 40 per cent of earnings at age 61 (24.11.1), should enable all but very high earners to increase their contributions. However, the limit on earnings qualifying for cover may mean that if you come within this category, you would do better to pay increased contributions on existing retirement annuity contracts. You will then only be able to pay up to the old limits ranging up to 27.5 per cent of earnings at age 61 (24.11.1), but you will not be subject to the £75,000 earnings limit (£71,400 for 1991–92).

1.2.15 Pension schemes for controlling directors

If you are a controlling director of a family company, it can implement a *pension scheme* (24.12.1) for you. Contributions paid by the company will enjoy tax relief as a deductible business expense and you can be provided with similar benefits to those of any employee under an occupational pension scheme, such as a pension of up to two-thirds of final salary, or a tax-free cash lump sum and a reduced pension, a pension for your widow in the event of death either before or after retirement and substantial life assurance cover for your family in the event of death in service.

1.2.16 Deeds of covenant (6.5)

Deeds of covenant effected prior to 15 March 1988 to others than your minor unmarried children produce tax savings. Such covenants needed to be capable of exceeding six years (normally seven annual payments).

However, subject to the rules (6.5) deeds of covenant effected after 14 March 1988 in favour of individuals produce no tax savings. This makes it all the more important to keep existing ones in force. (New deeds in favour of charities carry full relief.)

The covenantor who makes the payments under a pre-15 March 1988 deed deducts basic rate income tax and pays the net amount to the beneficiary. If the latter is not liable for income tax because his income is less than his tax allowances, he reclaims the income tax deducted by the covenantor (6.5). With the increase in *personal relief* (3.2.1) to £3,445 this advantage has been further enhanced. Also, the new 20 per cent lower rate band would enable up to £100 (£2,000 × 5 per cent) to be reclaimed in larger cases.

Payments under *deeds of covenant to charities* (13.2.1) are of benefit to them since they reclaim the basic rate income tax which you deduct on payment. Furthermore, charitable covenants qualify if they are capable of exceeding three years; and you obtain higher rate tax relief for any such payments (13.2.1).

1.2.17 Gifts and settlements

If you are a higher rate taxpayer and have more income and capital than you need, you can divest yourself of the surplus altogether and thereby save yourself the income tax on the income concerned. You can probably arrange that the income ends up in the hands of individuals with lower tax rates than yourself. Alternatively the income may be *accumulated* in a *trust* (19.1) where only basic rate income tax and additional rate (10 per cent) is payable. If trusts are created you should take care that the *settlor* is not *taxed on the income* (19.3). Note that inheritance tax may apply in some circumstances (20.31). Similarly watch the effect of *inheritance tax on gifts* (20.1).

This facility for moving income to lower rate taxpayers, such as grandchildren, has become more important with the withdrawal of tax relief on new deeds of covenant (1.2.16). For example, accumulation and maintenance settlements can be used to produce worthwhile income tax savings by making payments for the education and maintenance of beneficiaries. Income tax repayment claims are then likely covering the 10 per cent additional rate; also the 25 per cent basic rate on up to the £3,445 personal relief and an extra 5 per cent on the £2,000 lower rate band.

Gifts to charities which are at least £400 (net) each carry full tax relief. You deduct basic rate tax and the charity reclaims this. At the same time the gross gift carries higher rate tax relief (13.2.1).

1.2.18 Lower rate band

The introduction of a 20 per cent lower rate band for 1992–93, with the promise of widening this in future years, has modestly increased the scope for income tax saving. You should see that your spouse and, where practicable, children have sufficient income to cover their respective £2,000 lower rate bands. If this means transferring your own income to them and you are a 40 per cent tax payer, a maximum of £400 (£2,000 at 20 per cent) could be saved in each case. This depends upon each child being at least 18 years old or married if younger (6.6).

1.2.19 The use of overseas income, taxable on the remittance basis

Generally speaking the *remittance basis* (16.1.1) only applies in certain limited cases. If, however, you obtain any *income overseas* which is taxable here under *Schedule D Case IV or V* (16.1), or under *Schedule E Case III* (16.5.1), and such income is taxed on the remittance basis, do not bring the income into the country unless you need it to cover your living expenses. Note, however, that any *bank deposit interest* (8.7) or other income derived from any investment made with the funds is normally liable to UK tax on an arising basis, if you are *resident and domiciled* in the UK, subject to the detailed rules.

You can use your overseas deposits for spending on holidays abroad, etc (16.1). Furthermore, once your overseas source of income has come to an end you can bring your funds into this country in a subsequent tax year without any charge to income tax.

(If your work takes you overseas, remember that if your period of absence extends to a year, you obtain 100 per cent relief (16.5.1)).

1.3 Capital gains tax saving

A number of simple ways are open to you for saving capital gains tax. Some of these are described below.

1.3.1 £5,800 net gains exemption

Make the best use of this relief. If your sales of chargeable assets produce net gains which are not normally far in excess of £5,800 in any tax year, try to spread your realisations so that your net gains are no more than £5,800 each year — you will then pay no capital gains tax.

Remember that your spouse and each of your minor children can also realise up to £5,800 of net gains each year and pay no capital gains tax. It is thus a good idea to spread any share dealings, etc throughout your family. This is made easier by *capital gains tax gifts relief* (18.28) which now applies in certain circumstances, subject to the necessary election. However, gift elections are no longer normally of use regarding quoted shares, etc (1.3.3).

Under the system for taxing husband and wife from 6 April 1990, you each have a capital gains tax exemption now of £5,800. In order to make full use of both reliefs, split your investments between you.

If your net gains are less than £5,800 in any tax year, realise further profits by means of '*bed and breakfast*' *transactions* involving the sale of shares followed by their subsequent repurchase. In this way, you will be able to make better use of the exempt band. At the same time you will be increasing the base costs of your holdings. In order for 'bed and breakfasting' to be effective for shares, in general you merely need to wait until the next day before you buy them back.

1.3.2 Loss relief

Make sure that you keep a proper record of all your capital losses. These are relievable against any capital gains in the same tax year and any balance is carried forward to be used in future years.

If you make a loss in your non-incorporated trade or profession in 1991–92 or future years, do not overlook claiming to set this against your capital gains. Trading losses can now be offset against capital losses for the same and next tax years (10.22).

1.3.3 Capital gains tax gifts election

Now that the scope for capital gains tax gifts elections has been much restricted (18.28), it is important to structure your gifts to avoid a capital gains tax charge, if possible. For example, make gifts of cash or quoted securities on which you have little or no capital gains, as well as gilts and loan stocks. Also, chattels worth no more than £6,000 each and gifts within your £5,800 annual exemption.

Furthermore, make gifts still within the scope of the election. These include certain unquoted and family company shares and other business assets (18.28); also gifts which involve immediate inheritance tax. This last category includes discretionary settlements and applies even if no tax arises because the nil rate band has not been exceeded.

1.3.4 Husband and wife

Sales and gifts of assets between yourself and your spouse are not normally liable to capital gains tax (18.9). This enables you to redistribute your assets for inheritance tax purposes without paying any capital gains tax.

1.3.5 Retirement relief

If you have a family business or company and are at least 55 years of age, use the *capital gains tax retirement relief* (maximum £150,000, together with £450,000 at 50 per cent relief) to its best advantage. This will mean waiting until you reach the age of 55 before selling your business and also continuing to work in it until that time. Since the entire relief is available at age 55 and there is no longer any tapering relief, it is vital to wait until that age before disposing of your business. If you have not owned it for ten years, more relief will be available if you wait until you have completed ten years of ownership. Remember that, subject to the rules, your wife can also get the relief if she works in the business and owns part of it.

Should you wish to pass your business to your children, a combination of gifts election and retirement relief is very useful, so that you sell them the business (or company) at an undervalue, limiting the capital gain to £150,000.

1.3.6 Timing

Timing your sales of shares or other chargeable assets can have an important bearing on your capital gains tax. If you postpone a sale until after 5 April it means that you delay the payment of your tax for one year. Also if you know that you will be incurring a capital loss during the next tax year you should defer making any potential capital profits until that year because, although capital losses can be carried forward, they cannot be set off against capital profits in earlier tax years.

Similarly if you have already made a lot of capital profits during the current tax year you should consider incurring *capital losses* during the same year which can then be offset. You should not normally sell investments unless it is sound to do so from a commercial point of view. A loss may be established on a shareholding, however, even if you buy it back the next day. Such transactions may be taxable, however, if done by companies (12.15).

1.3.7 Indexation

Pay careful attention to the effects of the *indexation rules* (18.12) on your capital gains tax position. In choosing which investments to sell, have regard to the indexation relief available due to the level of base cost and time held. If you wish to retain an investment it may still be of value to sell it and buy back the next day so as to obtain an enhanced base cost on which future indexation is calculated.

1.3.8 Charities

Gifts made to charities are completely free of capital gains tax. Thus if you wish to make a generous gift to a charity of a capital amount (rather than recurring annual amounts under deed of covenant) you will save yourself future capital gains tax if you gift a chargeable asset on which you have a large potential profit. For example if you wish to give £20,000 to a charity and own shares in A Ltd which cost £4,000 in 1983 and are now worth £20,000 you should gift those shares. (If you sold the shares and donated cash they would only produce £13,600 net of 40 per cent capital gains tax — assuming you are a 40 per cent taxpayer and ignoring indexation and any annual exemption.)

1.3.9 Main private residence

Ensure that you gain the maximum benefit from this exemption (18.23). If you have two residences (even if one is rented), claim within two years of the date of purchase of your second abode which should be treated as your main private residence to be free of capital gains tax. You have a free choice in this matter and so should select the house or flat likely to increase in value the most.

1.4 Inheritance tax planning

The essence of inheritance tax planning is the conservation of wealth. Remember that most lifetime gifts are now free of inheritance tax provided you survive for seven years (20.3). Thus timely action is advisable. Also, bear in mind that a future government could radically change the system and make it much harsher.

In broad terms you should aim to spread assets amongst your family to minimise the effects of these two taxes. Do not make gifts which you cannot afford, however, nor give too much money outright to young or irresponsible children.

1.4.1 Reducing your assets by gifts

Take advantage of the various *exempt transfers* (20.18). By this means you can gift to your children, and others, considerable amounts over a period of years, free of any inheritance tax charge, even if you die within seven years. Gifts to your wife are normally free of inheritance tax in any event (20.18.1).

If you have funds surplus to your requirements, you can make gifts totalling £3,000 in any year (20.18.2). In addition, you can make outright gifts of up to £250 each year to any number of other individuals and, furthermore, if you have surplus after-tax income you can make *normal expenditure gifts out of income* (20.18.2). Do not overlook the reliefs applied to *marriage gifts* (20.18.2) for your children and grandchildren, etc.

By means of all the above transfers you can reduce your estate without risking any inheritance tax liability on your premature death. Furthermore, by making the required election any capital gains tax on the gift (18.28) of certain assets will be held over until the recipient's disposal. However, the scope of capital gains tax gifts relief was much restricted from 14 March 1989. It now mainly applies to gifts of business assets including shares in family companies, etc (18.28). Another important category of gifts qualifying for the relief is those on which inheritance tax may be immediately payable.

Remember that the above exemptions apply to both your wife and yourself. Also, do not forget that unused portions of the £3,000 limit can be carried forward for one year only. Thus your wife should also make gifts, and if her resources are insufficient you should put her in funds. But watch the associated operations rules (20.30.3).

1.4.2 Larger gifts and settlements

If you have a large estate, you should consider making more substantial gifts which will entail the payment of inheritance tax, should you die within seven years. The rate would be nil for the first £150,000 of chargeable transfers, however (20.5). Your relief would effectively be more if *business property relief* (20.19) or *agricultural property relief* (20.22) applies. Subject to the inheritance tax charge if you die within seven years, large gifts are now the most tax-efficient method of passing on wealth in many cases. Provided the recipients are sufficiently mature to look after the money, etc large outright gifts are to be strongly recommended. Unless you are in poor health or of advanced years, the contingent inheritance tax liability can be covered by temporary life assurance (1.4.10) at moderate cost.

For elderly people with smaller estates it is not necessarily advisable, however, to gift the £150,000 tax-free band since this is equally tax-free on death and it could be better to retain this sum for contingencies.

It may be desirable to make larger gifts in the form of settlements, but if these are discretionary the *periodic charge* (20.31.2) would normally apply at some future time, as well as the tax which you pay when you make the settlement and further tax when benefits are paid to the beneficiaries. Also, you are liable for inheritance tax at half the death rates when you set up the trust.

However, *settlements* (20.31) set up within your £150,000 nil rate band are not likely to give rise to significant inheritance tax liability, subject to the detailed rules. *Small* discretionary settlements of this kind are thus useful for passing funds to your dependants whilst maintaining a degree of flexibility. (Note that you should not be a beneficiary under a new settlement.) A further advantage regarding discretionary settlements is that they qualify for capital gains tax gifts relief (1.3.3). This is true whether or not any inheritance is paid on the capital introduced.

Accumulation and maintenance settlements (20.31.1) are useful for the benefit of your minor children and grandchildren. Provided you survive for seven years after establishing the settlement, you pay no inheritance tax. Furthermore, if the beneficiaries obtain fixed interests (eg in the income) which they become entitled to when they are no more than 25 years old, then no subsequent inheritance tax is payable (20.31.1), even if the payment of the ultimate capital is deferred to an older age. (An exception is where a beneficiary with a life interest dies.)

Fixed trusts are also of use if you wish your grown-up children to have income but no capital until a stipulated time. Thus, if you settle money on your 26-year-old son giving him an entitlement to the annual income until he is 35 and then the capital, you are immediately divested of the capital. The amount which you settle is treated as a potentially exempt transfer, so that inheritance tax applies if you die within seven years. Your son eventually gets the capital at age 35 and no more inheritance tax is payable. Your son is fully taxed on the income, however, and if his other income becomes high as he matures, his income tax burden could be heavy.

In establishing settlements unless they are discretionary remember that capital gains tax gifts relief will be limited. Thus either settle cash or assets which will give rise to no capital gains tax, unless you are able to settle assets still qualifying for gifts relief (18.28).

1.4.3 Gifts to charities, etc

Gifts to charities and political parties are completely free from inheritance tax. Thus you should consider making such gifts during your lifetime and bequests in your will. Both will reduce the value of your estate for inheritance tax purposes, and capital gains tax relief applies concerning charitable dispositions (18.29.1).

1.4.4 Equalisation of assets of husband and wife

Provided the recipient is UK domiciled (or deemed domiciled) no inheritance tax is payable on transfers which you make to your wife or she makes to you, either during your lives or on death (20.18.1). But do not keep all of your assets until you die and then leave them to your wife because this may ultimately result in high inheritance tax on her death which is more than the combined tax if your estates were equal and you each left your assets to your children.

Thus, suppose you have £300,000 and your wife has nothing. If you die first, leaving it all to her, no tax is then payable. But if she still has £300,000 when she dies and has made no previous chargeable transfers, the inheritance tax at the present rate will be £60,000 (20.5.1). If you had given or bequeathed your wife £150,000, however, and left your remaining £150,000 to your children, on your death no inheritance tax would be paid. Similarly, on your wife's death nothing would be paid so that altogether £60,000 of inheritance tax would be saved compared with the position where your wife inherits all of your wealth. (Of course the position can be further improved if you both make lifetime gifts to your children.)

If your wife otherwise has insufficient funds, giving her assets will also enable her to make gifts to your children. These will not attract inheritance tax unless she dies within seven years (20.3) and her estate is sufficiently high. This strategy is particularly desirable if your wife is younger and in better health than you are. Note, however, the *associated operations rules* (20.30.3). As mentioned earlier (1.1.2) equalising your assets is likely to produce income tax and capital gains tax savings.

A further point in favour of equalising your estate with your wife's is that wealth tax, if it is ever introduced, would be expected to apply separately to husband and wife at progressive annual rates. Thus less tax is payable on two smaller estates rather than a larger one. Of course, these tax planning considerations must be tempered by practical points, such as making sure your wife has sufficient to maintain her, should you die first. Also, a certain mutual trust is necessary. Your planning should also take account of your respective ages and states of health by arranging for a larger share to be in the hands of the one likely to live longer.

If you are buying a new home, you should ensure that this is put into the joint names of your wife and yourself. Since the matrimonial home often comprises the major part of the assets of a married couple, this is a very useful step towards equalising their respective estates.

1.4.5 Wills

You should think carefully about the preparation of your will and, of course, obtain good legal advice. Substantial inheritance tax savings can result from a well drawn will. For example, you should ensure that both your wife and yourself by your separate wills leave at least £150,000 to other people so that you each get the benefit of the £150,000 nil rate band. (This presupposes the free band has not been exhausted by lifetime gifts and also that the survivor will have adequate funds for his or her old age.) To take full advantage of indexation, instead of £150,000 you could stipulate the amount of your unused nil rate band at death. Also, avoid leaving too much directly to your children if they are already wealthy; it is more beneficial for tax planning purposes to leave money in trust for your grandchildren. Such will trusts, however, should probably not be discretionary, but rather of the accumulation and maintenance variety (20.31.1).

1.4.6 Annuities

If you need to increase your income, annuities provide a means of doing this which at the same time immediately reduces the value of your estate. For example, if you buy an annuity for £10,000 which produces, say, £1,400 yearly until your death, no part of your original capital outlay is charged to inheritance tax on your death. You have thus saved potential tax on your death. Do not overlook the effects of inflation, however; an unindexed annuity which is sufficient for your present needs soon may be worth too little to maintain you.

1.4.7 Using business and agricultural relief

If you have a business, farm or shareholding in an Unlisted Securities Market (USM) company, the improved relief rates (20.19) offer great potential inheritance tax savings. Subject to the rules, 100 per cent or 50 per cent relief will normally be obtained. You should therefore take advantage of the opportunity to create settlements and make gifts with less, or no, inheritance tax, even if you die within seven years. If any capital gains arise, it will normally be possible to obtain holdover relief. However, in cases where death is imminent, it may be better to hold the assets so as to obtain the tax free uplift in base value for capital gains tax purposes.

1.4.8 Protecting family companies

The *'related property' valuation rules* (20.12) may apply if you transfer valuable holdings in your family company to your children, etc. Thus, if you die within seven years, inheritance tax might be payable on the transfers. However, up to 100 per cent *business property relief* (20.19) may be available. The charge (if any) on the shares on your death could be even higher, however, particularly if the rules change and so you should plan to transfer shares to your children before they become too valuable, and your wife should do the same. The best time would be on the formation of a new company or early in its development.

If you are planning a new business venture, then do not put it into your main family company. Form a new company whose shares are owned by your children (or others whom you wish to succeed to your business). The new company should be encouraged to expand as much as possible and you may even let your old company run down. In this way the next generation of your family eventually will be left controlling the major company.

In the case of a partnership, the interest of each partner is valued on the appropriate share of the underlying assets. If, however, the partnership is incorporated into a company, the value of each partner's interest is normally reduced appreciably.

1.4.9 Deeds of family arrangement

Variations or disclaimers made within two years of any death not only effectively change the destination of property left by will (20.30.6), they are effective in changing the inheritance tax position. Property might be diverted from the surviving spouse to other beneficiaries, so as to use fully the nil rate band. Alternatively, substantial legacies may go to others than the surviving spouse, resulting in high inheritance tax. Assets can then be diverted to the surviving spouse, who might in turn pass the assets to others at a later stage, with a good chance of saving tax.

However, if you disclaim your legacy, it will revert to the estate and be re-allocated according to the will (or rules on intestacy if there is no will). Thus whether or not inheritance tax can be saved will depend on the facts in each case. Deeds of variation are effective in changing wills after death, provided that those involved take the necessary steps. However, it is better to ensure that your will is effectively drawn up so as to minimise inheritance tax. In this way, you will be more certain that your estate is passed on in accordance with your wishes. Then regular review is essential.

1.4.10 Providing the funds to pay inheritance tax on death

You may not be able, or indeed wish, to avoid leaving a large estate when you die. In this case you should ensure that sufficient funds are available for paying the inheritance tax. This avoids forced realisations of assets and, for example, the sale of shares in a family company which it might be desirable to keep.

Life assurance provides one of the best means of providing money to pay inheritance tax arising on your death, as well as being a very suitable vehicle for exempt gifts. Ensure, however, that the policy proceeds themselves are not subject to the tax, which could happen if the policy were taken out (with no trust provisions) by you on your own life. Consider taking out policies in trust for your children where you leave assets to them; this will put cash into their hands to pay the tax. They should be 'whole of life' policies, under which capital sums, with or without profits, or unit-linked to combat inflation, are payable when you die.

If both you and your wife have large estates then you should each insure your respective lives in trust for your children, assuming that you each leave your estates to them. If, however, you each leave your estate to the other by your will, then a joint life last survivor policy could be useful, under which a payment is made only on the second death. If the policy is correctly drawn (in trust for the eventual heirs on the second death) it will not attract inheritance tax. Further, the premium rate for such a policy is usually substantially lower than for two individual policies.

The policy can be written in trust for your heirs, under the Married Women's Property Acts or otherwise. Take care that there is at least one trustee other than you so that the proceeds may be claimed without delay on your death.

Temporary life assurance may be used to cover the five-year period following a gift or settlement on which you have paid tax at the lifetime rate. The amount covered should be the additional tax payable on that transfer should you die within five years (20.6). Temporary life assurance written in trust is also most useful for covering any inheritance tax payable on a gift (potentially exempt transfer (PET)) if you die within seven years.

1.5 Change of residence and domicile

Reference to the table at the beginning of Chapter 15 will illustrate the importance of residence and domicile in ascertaining whether or not an individual is liable to income tax, capital gains tax and inheritance tax. If you are able to become non-resident for tax purposes you will avoid liability to UK income tax on many classes of income and if you are also not ordinarily resident here you will not be liable for any UK capital gains tax on sales of assets here or abroad.

If you become neither domiciled (15.2) nor *deemed domiciled* (20.4) in this country you will only be liable for UK inheritance tax on assets situated here.

A very effective way of avoiding liability from UK taxes is to emigrate and take all of your assets out of this country. Once you have ceased to be resident and are no longer domiciled nor deemed domiciled here you will be outside the UK tax net regarding all income arising and assets situated abroad. (You should note that if you have shares in a UK company with its registered office here, the shares are treated for inheritance tax purposes as located in this country unless they are bearer securities kept abroad.)

If you have a large potential capital gain you should defer taking this until you have ceased to be resident and ordinarily resident here; in this way you will avoid capital gains tax. (If you wish you may then return to this country in a future tax year.)

As a pure tax-saving exercise, you should only consider emigrating if you are a very wealthy person; and even then you should only go to a country where you feel that you will be happy. If, however, you wish to retire to a 'place in the sun', then in choosing to which country you should go, you should take into account the tax which you would have to pay there. Once you have established your foreign residence and domicile, in order to preserve this situation, you must avoid paying regular visits to the UK (17.4).

1.6 Year-end planning

Towards the end of the tax year (5 April), you should consider various tax-saving opportunities.

The following is a list of reliefs to use up and other things to be done on or before 5 April. Further details are given elsewhere in this book.

(1) Capital gains tax annual exemption (18.6).
(2) 'Bed and breakfasting' (1.3.1).
(3) Inheritance tax annual exemption (20.18.2).
(4) Inheritance tax relief of £250 per gift to one person (20.18.2).
(5) Normal expenditure gifts for inheritance tax (20.18.2).
(6) Nil rate band for inheritance tax (20.5.1).
(7) Take extra dividends and salary for yourself and your spouse from your family company to maximise the benefits of independent taxation (6.1).
(8) Effect charitable deeds of covenant (6.5) or single 'gift aid' donations of at least £400 net (13.2.1), thus getting relief for the current tax year.
(9) Pay personal pension contributions (24.11).
(10) Elect to carry back personal pension (and retirement annuity) premiums to the previous tax year (24.11).
(11) Make investments qualifying for relief under the Business Expansion Scheme (10.25).

(12) Buy plant and machinery to obtain 25 per cent writing down allowance.
(13) Buy industrial and commercial buildings in enterprise zones obtaining 100 per cent initial allowance on the building content (10.12).
(14) Increase your contributions to your company pension scheme (9.11). (Your employer's contributions are geared to the company accounting date.)
(15) Do extra business mileage in your company car, so as to clear the 2,500 or 18,000 mile requirements for lower scale charges (9.6.5).
(16) Ensure you make any necessary tax elections to do with your business and private affairs within the required time limits. A particular instance is trading loss relief (10.22).
(17) Make investments and re-investments in a Personal Equity Plan by 6 April each year (8.10).

1.7 The seven ages of tax planning

Although tax planning is important at all stages of one's life, different features may be relevant at particular times. There follows a summary of particular tax planning points to remember at seven selected 'ages':

(1) Childhood.
(2) Student days.
(3) Early working life.
(4) Newly married.
(5) Parenthood.
(6) Middle age.
(7) Retirement.

Much of the advice given earlier in this chapter applies at most times in your life and thus is not highlighted in what follows; for example, tax planning for businesses (1.2.2), employments (1.2.5), companies (12.1) and capital gains tax (1.3). The points now classified under different 'ages' have particular relevance to certain times in your life. References are given to earlier paragraphs in this chapter, which will in turn refer you to further detail in the text.

1.7.1 Childhood

Tax planning for children normally involves other people such as their parents and grandparents. A chief objective is to provide for education and maintenance in the most tax-efficient way. Educational schemes may have become less attractive in view of, for example, the withdrawal of life assurance relief. However, lump sum school fee payments in advance by grandparents may prove of value in saving higher rate income tax and inheritance tax.

Older children may work in the family business at weekends and during the holidays, in which case a reasonable salary should be paid. This will be tax free to the extent of the unused personal allowance (£3,445). To avoid any National Insurance contributions the salary should be kept below £54 per week. Also, older children might occasionally buy and sell shares and thus make use of their annual capital gains exemption (£5,800).

Other tax planning points to note include:

(1) Changing wills to include new children (1.4.5).
(2) Settlements by grandparents (1.4.2).
(3) Repayment claims for children (1.2.7).
(4) Gifts to children to save inheritance tax (1.4.1).
(5) Accumulation and maintenance settlements (1.4.2).
(6) Discretionary settlements (1.4.2).
(7) Paying income from settlements for maintenance and education with possible tax repayments (1.2.7).

1.7.2 Student days

If you are a student (post-school), you will normally have attained your majority and this facilitates tax planning. In particular, none of your income will be assessed on your parents even though it arises from gifts which they make to you.

Your single personal allowance (£3,445) will normally cover income from jobs, investments, etc, before you pay any tax. Also, income distributions from certain settlements are likely to entitle you to reclaim at least the 10 per cent additional rate if not the entire 35 per cent tax already suffered.

Your parents and grandparents might save inheritance tax by making gifts to you or in trust (1.4.2). If you invest the money given to you directly in stocks and shares you will have the annual exemption (£5,800) to cover any capital gains (1.3.1).

1.7.3 Early working life

In your early working days you may well be able to benefit from some of the tax planning points regarding employments (1.2.5) and businesses (1.2.2), noting particularly new businesses (1.2.8). If you work overseas in a business or employment, some tax benefits may result (1.2.19).

Make sure that you claim all the expenses to which you may be entitled in your employment (1.2.5) or business (1.2.2) including a proportion of your home expenses if relevant.

Whether you are employed or self-employed, you should consider pensions (1.2.15) or personal pension arrangements (1.2.14) as soon as practicable. These provide a very tax-effective way of providing for your security.

1.7.4 Newly married

When you marry, the opportunity arises for the parents and grandparents on both sides to make gifts and settlements (1.4.1 and 1.4.2), using the special inheritance tax marriage exemptions or otherwise. Also they should re-examine their wills.

Particular tax planning matters for you both to consider include:

(1) Wife's salary (1.2.9).
(2) Independent taxation of husband and wife (6.1)—separate rates and allowances for income and capital gains.
(3) House purchase (1.2.11).
(4) Life assurance (1.2.13).
(5) The making of new wills (1.4.5).

1.7.5 Parenthood

This is the time when you are likely to have a growing income but also to incur the largest expenses. Gifts (1.4.1) and accumulation and maintenance settlements (1.4.2) made in favour of your children by their grandparents are tax-efficient ways in which the gap can be bridged.

As you progress in your employment (1.2.5), business (1.2.2) or profession, the relevant tax planning points become even more important. Particular matters to note include new businesses (1.2.8) and incorporation (1.2.4). Also, you will be well advised to improve your life assurance (1.2.13) and pension (1.2.15) or personal pension (1.2.14) cover as appropriate. You may work overseas (1.2.19) or even completely change your domicile and residence (1.5) if, for example, you become extremely well-to-do.

As you become more wealthy, *capital tax planning* will grow in importance, including capital gains tax (1.3). Inheritance tax planning should include an examination of gifts and settlements (1.4.2), charitable gifts (1.4.3) and equalisation (1.4.4); attention to your will (1.4.5); the protection of family companies (1.4.7) and the provision of funds to pay the tax (1.4.10). Furthermore, assets producing income and capital gains should be split between you, so as to maximise the benefits of independent taxation.

1.7.6 Middle age

You will still need to consider the relevant business (1.2.2) or employment (1.2.5) tax planning points as well as life assurance (1.2.13), pensions (1.2.15) and personal pensions (1.2.14). Even if your earlier pension cover was inadequate, there is scope for compensating for this in later life.

As your children come of age, consider passing them income producing assets. When they marry, make use of the appropriate inheritance tax exemptions (1.4.1), thus guarding against tax payable if you die within seven years. Cover larger gifts by life assurance (1.2.13). When they in turn have children, consider accumulation and maintenance settlements in favour of your grandchildren (1.2.17).

Capital tax planning is vital during this period and if you can afford it, you should make gifts and settlements (1.3.3) to pass on your wealth during your lifetime. Also, provide for the payment of any inheritance tax (1.4). If you have a family company try to guard against future heavy inheritance tax on its shares and help succession by passing on shares to the next generation (1.4.8). Should your house be larger than you need, consider selling and re-investing or gifting the proceeds.

1.7.7 Retirement

Take advantage of the tax planning opportunities arising when your pension (1.2.14) becomes due, such as taking your full tax-free lump sum entitlement or deferring your benefits.

If you have a family company or business, maximise your capital gains tax retirement relief (1.3.5) on sale or gift. At the same time, use the limited capital gains tax gifts election (18.29) if appropriate. Also, do not overlook the valuable inheritance tax business relief (20.19) and agricultural relief (20.22). These will eliminate or substantially reduce the inheritance tax payable if you die within seven years of a gift.

Since more of your income is likely to arise from investments, you may be able to claim repayment of the income tax deducted at source (1.2.7). If your respective incomes are sufficiently small, you may both be entitled to age relief (3.2.15), together with a higher married couple's allowance.

With the sale of your business and perhaps house (1.2.11), you will have the chance of reviewing your will (1.4.5) and making gifts (1.4.1), including settlements (1.4.2). If you have surplus funds, then gifts to charity should be considered, being free of inheritance tax and capital gains tax; whilst the purchase of an annuity will increase your income but reduce your estate.

1.8 The way ahead

An important factor in tax planning is the political element. Different Governments may have completely divergent views on the desirable range of taxes and actual tax levels. The result of the Election on 11 June 1987 signalled a period of moderate taxation. Indeed, the first post-Election Budget drastically reduced income tax and inheritance tax rates. At the same time important structural changes were made regarding capital gains tax and husband and wife taxation.

The election result on 9 April 1992 indicates the continuation of the same moderate taxation policy. The 20 per cent lower tax rate has already been introduced with the suggestion that this will be expanded, perhaps eventually to become the basic rate. At the same time, capital taxes may well become less severe.

The effect on tax planning is important, as this can continue to be done with confidence. However, traditional forms of reliefs cannot be guaranteed to stay open, even under the present Government. For example, consider the moves against deeds of covenant, gifts elections and higher-rate mortgage interest relief in recent years. To take advantage of existing openings, sensible tax planning should always be carried out sooner, rather than later.

Other factors increasingly likely to influence our tax system are the closer involvement of the UK in Europe and also developments within the European Community. Thus, changes will originate not only at home, but also abroad.

As ever, tax planning arrangements should be made in a flexible form. As indicated, substantial structural changes are anticipated over the coming years, which may necessitate new tax planning strategies.

2 The basis of your tax liability

2.1 Who is taxable?

Individuals, partnerships, estates, trusts, companies, and certain other organisations that are resident in the UK are taxable on their income arising here. They are also liable on income arising abroad subject to the rules outlined later in this book. The taxation of the income of individuals is covered first; partnerships, estates, trusts and companies being dealt with in later chapters.

The UK income of non-resident individuals, companies and other entities may also be subject to tax here (17.1).

Similarly capital gains tax is payable on certain capital profits made by UK residents anywhere in the world (18.3). Non-residents, however, are not normally liable to UK capital gains tax.

2.2 The taxes payable
(TA 1988 S1 & FA 1992, Ss9 & 10)

From 6 April 1973 a unified system of personal taxation operates under which there is, for 1992–93, a lower rate of 20 per cent, a basic rate of 25 per cent and a higher rate of 40 per cent (5.0.1). Certain different rates apply for previous years (25.2).

From 6 April 1992, the capital gains tax rates for individuals are 20, 25 and 40 per cent. However, the first £5,800 of your net capital gains is not taxed (18.1).

Special rules apply to companies which are taxed on both income and capital gains at corporation tax rates (12.2).

Inheritance tax applies to wealth passing on death and in some other circumstances (Chapter 20).

2.3 What income is taxable?
(TA 1988 Ss1 & 15–20)

The table below summarises the classes of income that are subject to income tax, or corporation tax for companies. The table also shows the 'Schedules' and 'Cases' under which the income is classified and taxed under the law.

2.3.1 Table: Classes of income

Schedule A Income from land and buildings including rents and certain premiums from leases (7.1).

Schedule B The 'assessable value' of woodlands that were managed on a commercial basis (7.8). This Schedule was abolished as from 6 April 1988.

Schedule C Income from 'gilt-edged securities', payable in the United Kingdom as well as certain overseas public revenue dividends that are paid through a banker or other person here (8.2).

Schedule D This is divided into the following separate 'Cases':
Case I   Trades (10.1).
Case II   Professions or vocations (10.1).
Case III   Interest received, annuities and other annual payments (8.4).
Cases IV and V   Overseas income from certain investments, possessions and businesses (16.1).
Case VI   Miscellaneous profits not falling within any of the other Cases of Schedule D (13.1).

Schedule E Wages and salaries from employments (including directorships). There are the following 'Cases':
Case I   This normally applies where the employee is resident in the UK and the work is done here (9.1).
Case II   Work done here by a non-resident, etc (9.2).
Case III   Work done wholly abroad by a UK resident whose salary is sent here during the course of the overseas employment excluding, however, income taxed under Case I or Case II (9.3).

Schedule F Dividends paid by companies and certain other distributions that they make (8.1).

2.4 Deduction of tax at source and tax credits

Tax under Schedules C and F is deducted at source at the basic rate (25 per cent) by the payers and the recipients get the net amount. The former pay the tax over to the Revenue. Company dividend payments, however, are made without any tax deductions although the recipients are 'imputed' with a credit of 25/75ths of the dividend. (The company pays tax of 25/75ths of its dividend payments by way of advance corporation tax (12.6).) Thus suppose you receive a dividend of £75: you will get a tax credit of £25 (£75 × 25/75ths) which you may be able to reclaim if your income is sufficiently low (14.6). If your income is high enough, however, you may be taxed at higher rates (5.0.1) on £100 (75 + 25); but you deduct the £25 tax credit from your total bill.

Tax is also deducted at source in the case of certain annual payments (4.1) and income from wages and salaries under Schedule E (see above). In the former case the payer of the income is entitled in certain circumstances to retain the tax deducted and need not pay it over to the Revenue.

2.5 The distinction between capital and revenue profits

Most of your income is subjected to income tax at the basic and perhaps higher rate, whereas normally, capital profits are liable to capital gains tax or are tax free. The tax rates borne by income and capital gains are now broadly similar. However, the rules and reliefs are very different. The question is then: What is a capital profit?

Generally speaking, a capital profit is a profit which you realise on the sale of an asset where it is clear that you are not making it your business to buy and sell assets of that type. On the other hand, if you conduct a business in such assets your profits will be income.

2.5.1 Examples of capital transactions

The sale of the house in which you live (also normally free of capital gains tax unless used for business) (18.23).
The sale of your private motor car (also free of capital gains tax).
The sale of shares you held as investments.
The sale of a plot of land you inherited.
The sale of the goodwill of your business.
The receipt of an inheritance (also free of capital gains tax).
The sale of a property which you had bought for investment purposes.
The sale of a picture unless you are the artist or a picture dealer.

The receipt of the proceeds of a 'qualifying' life assurance policy (24.5). (This is also normally free of capital gains tax.)

2.5.2 Examples of revenue transactions

The sale of houses and land if you are a property dealer.
The sale of motor cars if you are a car dealer.
The sale of shares if you are a share dealer.
The sale of pictures if you created them or are a picture dealer.
The receipt of salaries, commissions, interest, dividends, rent, royalties, etc.

2.6 Revenue and capital expenses

In the same way as income and capital profits must be distinguished, you must separate revenue and capital expenses for tax purposes. The latter can only be charged against capital profits and the former against income. For example, the commission on the sale of shares acquired for investment is deducted in calculating your capital gains but if you are a share dealer then it is a revenue expense.

Also, in determining the assessable profits of a business, only revenue expenses may be deducted and capital expenses are prohibited as a deduction (10.3.2).

2.6.1 Table: Tax-free income

Certain items in your income may be entirely free of tax. These are listed below.

(1) Casual gambling profits (eg pools, horse racing, etc).
(2) Premium Bond winnings.
(3) Lottery prizes.
(4) Interest on authorised holdings of National Savings Certificates (TA 1988 S46).
(5) Bonuses paid at the end of 'save as you earn' contracts.
(6) Maturity bonuses payable on Defence Bonds, British Savings Bonds and National Development Bonds.
(7) Interest on Post-war Credits.
(8) Wedding and certain other presents from your employer that are in truth not given in return for your services as an employee.
(9) Certain retirement gratuities and redundancy monies paid by your employer (9.12).
(10) Any scholarship or other educational grant that you receive if you are a full-time student at school, college, etc.

The basis of your tax liability 35

(11) War widows' pensions; also comparable payments overseas (TA 1988 S318).
(12) Certain social security benefits (23.3.1) including:
   (a) earnings-related supplement of unemployment benefit (but not unemployment benefit itself)
   (b) sickness benefit (but not statutory sick pay)
   (c) maternity allowance and grant (but not maternity pay)
   (d) attendance allowance
   (e) child benefit
   (f) family income supplement (but retirement pensions under the National Insurance Scheme and family allowances are assessable)
   (g) mobility allowance
   (h) certain payments of income support, family credit or housing benefit; but taxable up to given limits if related to trade disputes or conditional upon availability for employment (TA 1988 S617).
(13) Housing grants paid by local authorities, etc.
(14) German compensation payments to victims of National-Socialist persecution where such amounts are tax exempted by German law. Also certain Austrian and German state pensions paid to such victims from 6 April 1986 (previously 50 per cent taxable).
(15) Wound and disability pensions.
(16) Allowances, bounties and gratuities paid for additional service in the armed forces.
(17) The capital part of a purchased life annuity (but not the interest portion).
(18) Your first £70 of interest each year from National Savings Bank Ordinary Deposits. This exemption from tax applies separately to husband and wife (TA 1988 S325).
(19) Certain allowances paid under job release schemes, as described in the Job Release Act 1977, within a year of pensionable age.
(20) Additional pensions and annuities paid to the holders of certain gallantry awards by virtue of those awards (TA 1988 S317).
(21) Part of your Profit Related Pay under an approved scheme (9.15).
(22) Income from 1 January 1991 on a TESSA (8.11).

2.7 Bank and building society interest

Any bank or building society interest which you receive normally has basic rate income tax deducted from it at source (8.6). If your income is sufficiently high, however, you will be charged to additional tax on the grossed up equivalent of the interest as if you had suffered tax on it at the basic rate (25 per cent). The additional tax payable consists of higher rate income tax on the grossed up equivalent of the income, less tax on it at the basic rate. Thus if you receive building society interest of £75 in the year then £100 (the grossed up equivalent) will be included in your total taxable income. The grossed up equivalent is determined by the formula:

Interest received $\times \dfrac{100}{75}$ (ie, 100 less 25 per cent).

Prior to 6 April 1991, the composite rate scheme (8.7) applied to bank and building society interest. One effect was that the basic rate (25 per cent) element could not be reclaimed. However, that no longer applies.

2.8 Year of assessment

Income tax is an annual tax; thus it is your total income over each 12-month period that is assessed to tax. The year of assessment runs from 6 April to the following 5 April and so the tax year 1992–93 means the year ending 5 April 1993.

The income chargeable to tax for each year of assessment is computed according to the rules relevant to the various Schedules (see 2.3.1) as described later in this book. Sometimes an 'actual' basis is required in which the income received during a particular year is assessable for that year. Sometimes it is the income of the preceding year of assessment or of the accounting year ending in the preceding year of assessment that is assessed. This 'preceding year basis' is normally used for the profits from trades and vocations, as well as interest assessed under Schedule D.

The year to 5 April also forms the year of assessment for capital gains tax.

2.9 Period of assessment less than full year

It is possible for a taxpayer to have a period of assessment of less than 12 months. For example, a baby born during any year has a period of assessment running from the date of its birth until the next 5 April. If a taxpayer dies, his period of assessment runs from 6 April to the date of his death.

Notwithstanding that the period of assessment may be less than a year, the taxpayer receives the personal reliefs applicable to a whole year of assessment. But see 3.2.3 for the restriction of the married couple's allowance in the year of marriage.

3 Personal reliefs

According to your circumstances you can claim certain personal tax reliefs which are deducted from your total income in arriving at the amount on which you pay income tax.

The rules applying for 1990–91 onwards differ from those for earlier years. This is due to the introduction of independent taxation for husbands and wives as from 6 April 1990. The married personal relief was abolished, as were the married age allowances. At the same time, a married couple's allowance was introduced.

3.0.1 Table: Personal reliefs at a glance — 1992–93

Type	Circumstances	Relief
Personal allowance (3.2.1)	Single	£3,445*
Life assurance relief (3.2.7)	Policy effected before 14 March 1984 on your own or wife's life — deduction from premium	$12\frac{1}{2}$% of premiums
Additional personal allowance for children (3.2.12)		£1,720*
Blind person's allowance (3.2.14)		£1,080
Age allowance (3.2.15)	Age 65–74 — Single Age 75 or over — Single Reduced by £1 for every £2 of excess income over £14,200 down to personal reliefs level	£4,200* £4,370*
Married couple's allowance (3.2.2)	Age under 65 Age 65–74 Age 75 and over	£1,720* £2,465* £2,505*
Widow's bereavement allowance (3.2.16)		£1,720*

*Note: These allowances will be increased for future years in line with the retail price index (unless the Treasury otherwise orders).

3.1 Earned and unearned income

For tax purposes income is classified as being either 'earned' or 'unearned'. Earned income includes the following:

(1) The salary or wages from your job including any taxable benefits.
(2) Certain pensions or retirement annuities paid to you, including those under a Revenue approved scheme (9.11.1).
(3) Any income from a trade or profession in which you engage.
(4) Any income from a partnership provided that you work in it and are not merely a sleeping partner.
(5) Old age pensions and widow's pensions received under the National Insurance Act.
(6) Income from a patent or copyright if you actually created the subject matter.
(7) After leaving your employment, trade or profession, any taxable amounts that you receive from that source.
(8) Income from holiday lettings as defined (7.6).

The rest of your income is 'unearned' and includes:

(1) Dividends.
(2) Bank deposit interest.
(3) Building society interest received.
(4) Rents from property investments.
(5) Income from trusts.
(6) Interest from government or local authority stock.

3.2 Personal allowances
(TA 1988 S257 & FA 1989 Ss31 & 33)

For 1992–93 there is a personal allowance of £3,445. This is available to individuals generally. However, a higher allowance may apply to those who have attained their 65th birthdays (3.2.15).

3.2.1 Single personal allowance

Before 6 April 1990, there was a separate personal allowance (£2,785 for 1989–90) for single people. This also applied if you were a widow or widower or were divorced or separated from your husband or wife. If, however, you were separated from your wife but voluntarily wholly maintaining her (6.8) you qualified for the married personal allowance and so neither of you obtained the single personal allowance.

A married couple each only obtained the single allowance if they elected that their earnings should be separately taxed (6.4).

3.2.2 Married couple's allowance
(TA 1988 S257A, FA 1991 S22 & F2A 1992 S20 & Sch 5)

From 6 April 1990, each married couple normally obtains a married couple's allowance, according to their ages attained during the tax year. The following apply for 1992–93:

husband and wife both aged under 65	£1,720
husband or wife aged 65–74	£2,465
husband or wife aged 75 and over	£2,505

The higher allowances for older people are reduced if the husband's income exceeds £14,200 for 1992–93. For every £2 of income received in excess of £14,200, the higher allowances are reduced by £1 until the basic allowance (£1,720) is reached.

Married couple's allowance automatically goes to the husband. However, any unused balance may be transferred to the wife. To do this, an election must be made to your inspector of taxes within six years of the end of the tax year. For example, for 1992–93 Mr A has an income of £4,445. His personal allowance of £3,445 reduces this to £1,000 and this leaves £720, unused, from the married couple's allowance. Provided an election is made by 5 April 1999, £720 will be transferred to Mrs A, to set against her income for 1992–93.

From 6 April 1993, the married couple's allowance is to be split equally between you or go entirely to the wife, if you elect. Otherwise, it will go to the husband.

In the year of marriage, the allowance is reduced by one-twelfth for each complete month from 6 April until your marriage date.

Transitional relief applies for 1990–91 and subsequent years where the husband's income is not sufficient to cover his personal allowance. Prior to 6 April 1990, the unused allowance would be used against any income of the wife. The transitional relief is designed to ensure that the position is no worse than previously.

3.2.3 Married personal allowance (also 6.2)

Prior to 6 April 1990, you obtained the full married man's personal allowance of £4,375 if you were married at the start of the tax year. If you were married during the year, however, for every completed month from 6 April until your date of marriage, your relief was reduced by 1/12th of £1,590 (£4,375 *less* £2,785). Thus if you married on 21 October 1989 your relief was £4,375 *less* 6/12ths × £1,590 = £3,580. You only obtained this allowance (£4,375) if your wife was living with you or if you were wholly maintaining her by voluntary contributions in the event of your being separated.

3.2.4 Wife's earned income allowance
(TA 1988 S257 & FA 1989 S33)

Prior to 6 April 1990, if your wife worked and her earnings were not separately taxed (6.4) she got this relief in respect of her earned income with a maximum of £2,785 for 1989–90. Earned income for this purpose included national insurance pensions where your wife had made her own contributions (but not otherwise) unemployment benefit and invalid care allowance.

Any housekeeping money paid to your wife is not taxable but if she works for your business then her wages are allowed as earned income and before 6 April 1990 qualified for the wife's earned income allowance. Provided that her salary is in line with the work done, you will be able to deduct her wages from your taxable business profits.

3.2.5 Child relief
(TA 1970 S10 & FA 1979 S1)

Income tax child relief no longer operates but prior to 1979–80 was generally available at different rates depending on the age of the child (25.2). Child relief was replaced by child benefit (see below).

3.2.6 Child benefit
(FA 1977 S23)

Tax-free child benefit has applied since 4 April 1977. It applies in respect of your children under age 16 and those under 19 receiving full-time education, satisfying the necessary rules. From 6 April 1992, the weekly rate is £9.65 for the first child and £7.80 for each other child.

3.2.7 Life assurance relief
(FA 1988 Ss266–274 & FA 1988 S29)

Tax relief in respect of pre-14 March 1984 life assurance policies is given based on the premiums paid in the tax year. You now normally deduct the relief from your premium payments (see table below). The relief only applies to policies taken out *prior to 14 March 1984*. Premiums in respect of policies effected after that

Personal reliefs 41

date attract no relief. Similarly, relief is not due on existing policies for which the benefits are enhanced after that date, for example, by exercising an option to increase the policy term.

3.2.8 Table: Rules for life assurance relief — pre-14 March 1984 policies

---

(1) The policy benefits must include a sum payable on death or in certain circumstances provide for a deferred annuity.
(2) The policy must be effected with a UK, Dominion or Irish insurance company or one carrying on business here; or a Lloyd's Underwriter; or a registered friendly society.
(3) The policy must be on your own or your wife's life and either of you may pay the premiums.
(4) Special relief is given for sums paid under an Act of Parliament or under the rules of your employment to secure a deferred annuity for your widow or children after your death. The relief is given according to your income level by deducting the following percentages of the premiums from your tax bill:

Total income	% Relief
Not over £1,000	half of basic rate of income tax.
£1,001–£2,000	three-quarters of basic rate.
over £2,000	basic rate of income tax.

(5) Policies taken out after 19 March 1968 or changed after that date have to be 'qualifying policies' (24.5).
(6) A fixed percentage of each premium is deducted by you on payment and you keep this relief. The premium limit is the larger of 1/6th of your total income (after charges) and £1,500. Any over-deduction by you will be adjusted in your assessment at the end of the tax year or you may be directed by the Revenue to pay premiums without the deduction of tax relief.
(7) From 6 April 1981 to 5 April 1989 the relief percentage was 15% and for 1979–80 and 1980–81 it was $17\frac{1}{2}\%$.
(8) From 6 April 1989 the relief is $12\frac{1}{2}\%$.

3.2.9 Example: Life assurance relief restrictions for 1992–93

			Date effected	1992–93 premium
Policy A —	Sum assured	£10,000	1.1.80	£1,000
Policy B —	"	£20,000	5.4.82	£1,500
Policy C —	"	£25,000	1.5.84*	£2,000

*Policy C was effected after 13 March 1984 and thus does not qualify for relief. If total income for year = £12,000
 Premiums eligible for relief restricted to
 1/6th × £12,000   = £2,000

Life assurance relief for year = £250 ($12\frac{1}{2}\%$ × £2,000)

3.2.10 Dependent relative relief
(TA 1988 S263 & FA 1988 S25)

(1) This relief of normally £100 applied for many years up to 5 April 1988. However, it was withdrawn for 1988–89 and subsequent years.
(2) You obtained the relief for each of your own or your wife's relatives whom you maintained. The relative needed either to be incapacitated by old age or infirmity or be your own or your wife's widowed, divorced or separated mother.
(3) If the relative's own income exceeded the basic retirement pension, your relief was reduced by £1 for each £1 of the excess.
(4) If you were a woman, your relief for each dependent relative was increased to £145. This increase in the relief did not apply if you were married and living with your husband unless a separate earnings election (6.4) was in force.
(5) Where two or more people maintained a dependent relative, the relief was split between them in proportion to their payments for the relative's keep.

3.2.11 Housekeeper relief
(TA 1988 S258 & FA 1988 S25)

This relief was withdrawn for 1988–89 and future years. Previously, you obtained £100 relief if you were a widow or widower and you had a relative staying with you as your housekeeper. Alternatively, you got the relief if you employed a housekeeper who was not a relative. If the housekeeper was your relative and was married, however, you did not get the relief if her husband was getting the married man's personal allowance. (This relief extended to male as well as female housekeepers.)

3.2.12 Additional personal relief for children
(TA 1988 S259 & FA 1988 S30)

(1) This relief of £1,720 applies to widows, widowers and others, such as single parents, not entitled to married couple's allowance. You also get it if you are married but your wife is totally incapacitated for the year.
(2) Legally adopted and legitimated children are included, as are stepchildren. To qualify for relief for 1992–93, the child must be under 16 on 6 April 1992; or a full-time student at school or university, etc; or studying full-time for not less than two years for a profession or trade.
(3) If the child is not your own, he or she must be under 18 on 6 April 1992 in any event and maintained by you at your own expense.

(4) You only get one £1,720 relief no matter how many children reside with you. (After 5 April 1989 this includes any children of your common law husband or wife.)

3.2.13 Son's or daughter's services
(TA 1988 S264 & FA 1988 S25)

Prior to 6 April 1988, if you were aged or infirm and so needed to depend on the services of a son or daughter you got this relief of £55 each year. The son or daughter had to live with you and you needed to maintain him or her. The relief was withdrawn for 1988–89 and future years.

3.2.14 Blind person's relief
(TA 1988 S265 & FA 1990 S18)

(1) The relief is given to registered blind persons.
(2) The relief is £1,080 for the years 1990–91, 1991–92 and 1992–93.
(3) Previously, the relief was £540 per person.
(4) From 6 April 1990, if a spouse cannot use all his or her allowance, it can be transferred to the other spouse even if he or she is not blind.
(5) Anyone who also qualified for son's or daughter's services relief prior to 6 April 1988 (£55) needed to disclaim it or else he was not allowed blind person's relief.

3.2.15 Age allowance
(TA 1988 Ss257 & 257E)

(1) This applies for 1992–93 if you are over 65 by 5 April 1993.
(2) The allowance is £4,200 if your age on 5 April 1993 is between 65 and 74, increasing to £4,370 if you have reached your 75th birthday.
(3) For 1989–90 and previous years, higher age allowance was available for married couples where at least one partner was 65 years of age.
(4) The above allowance figures are restricted if your income exceeds £14,200. The restriction is one-half of the excess of your income over £14,200. Thus if your income is £15,200 your allowance is restricted to £4,200 − £500 = £3,700. Note that the £14,200 restriction is based on your 'total income' (5.2), which is before tax but after certain deductions, such as mortgage interest.
(5) If your income is sufficiently high your personal relief is restricted to the normal rate (£3,445); but not below this.

(6) Previously, if your wife had earned income, she still obtained wife's earned income allowance, even though you got age allowance. This allowance was lost if an election for separate taxation was made (6.4). This no longer applies due to the introduction of independent taxation from 6 April 1990.
(7) After 5 April 1987, a higher level of age allowance applied to those aged 80 and over. From 6 April 1989 the higher allowance applies from age 75. For 1992–93 the rate is £4,370. You qualify for this allowance if you have reached 75 by 5 April 1993. For the extra age allowance for married people, only one of you needs to be 75 by that time.
(8) Transitional relief is available for 1990–91 and subsequent years to cover the situation where a man married to an older wife might have his allowances reduced due to the change to the new system. If the transitional relief is claimed, the husband's personal allowance is replaced by the single age allowance frozen at the 1989–90 level of £3,400, etc. He also gets the higher married couple's allowance appropriate to his wife's age.

3.2.16 Widow's bereavement allowance
(TA 1988 S262)

(1) This allowance applies to certain widows whose husbands die after 5 April 1980.
(2) The relief for 1992–93 is £1,720 which is given if the husband died in the two years to 5 April 1993. (The relief was £1,720 for 1990–91 and 1991–92, £1,590 for 1989–90 and £1,490 for 1988–89.)
(3) The relief is equal to the difference between the married and single personal allowances.
(4) The relief only applies if the husband was entitled to married personal allowance when he died, ignoring the effect of the wife's earnings election (6.4). If the death is after 5 April 1990, the couple must have been entitled to married couple's allowance.
(5) The allowance originally only applied to the tax year of death, but from 1983/84 it applies to the following year also, unless the widow remarries before it begins. It is given in addition to any other available reliefs.

3.2.17 Vocational training
(FA 1991 Ss32–33)

If you pay for your own vocational training, tax relief is available from 6 April 1992, subject to the rules. Relief will be given for training leading to National Vocational Qualifications and Scottish Vocational Qualifications at any level except the highest.

Under Inland Revenue regulations basic rate tax relief is given by deduction at source, even if you pay no income tax. Otherwise, a claim is needed. (The recipient is normally able to reclaim your tax deduction.) Higher rate tax relief is also available where appropriate.

The relief only applies if you are UK resident or a Crown servant serving overseas and you obtain no other tax relief for it, nor public financial assistance.

3.3 Indexation of personal reliefs
(TA 1988 S257)

For 1981–82 and subsequent years, certain personal reliefs are to be increased from their previous levels by not less than the proportionate increase in the retail prices index for the last calendar year. With parliamentary approval, however, a lower increase (or none at all) may be ordered by the Treasury.

The reliefs concerned are single personal allowance (3.2.1), married couple's allowance (3.2.2), additional personal allowance for children (3.2.12), single age allowance (3.2.15), married age allowance (3.2.15) and widow's bereavement allowance (3.2.16).

3.3.1 Example: Personal reliefs — General illustration

Mr A lives with his family at 1 Bridge Street. Their income consists of:

Name	Earned	Unearned
	Income assessable for 1992–93	
Mr A	£13,400	£4,100
Mrs A	4,000	695

Mr A pays £1,095 interest during 1992–93 on a mortgage of 1 Bridge Street. The mortgage was arranged to purchase the house and so the interest is wholly allowable. Mrs A pays an annual premium of £200 on a qualifying life assurance policy on Mr A's life taken out before 14 March 1984. How much income tax is payable by Mr A and Mrs A for 1992–93?

1992–93	*Mr A*	*Mrs A*
Earned income	£13,400	£4,000
Unearned income	4,100	695
	17,500	4,695

Less: Mortgage interest		1,095	–
Total income		16,405	4,695
Less:			
Personal allowance	3,445		3,445
Married couple's allowance	1,720		
		5,165	
		£11,240	£1,250
Income tax payable: at 20% (on £2,000)		400	£250
at 25% (on £9,240)		2,310	
		£2,710	

Notes

(a) On the levels of income shown above Mr A is not liable to higher rate (5.0.1).

(b) Life assurance relief of $12\tfrac{1}{2}\% \times £200 = £25$ will be obtained by deduction from the premium payments.

(c) Relief for the mortgage interest would normally be obtained by Mr A deducting basic rate income tax of £273.75 on payment. He would thus pay £821.25 net mortgage interest. However, his final income tax payments would be increased by £273.75 to £2,983.75.

(d) For 1992–93 independent taxation applies. The married couple's allowance will be allocated to Mr A.

4 Annual payments and interest

4.1 Annual payments apart from interest
(TA 1988 Ss348–350 & FA 1988 Ss36–40)

If you make an annual payment it is normally considered for tax purposes as being the income of the recipient and is usually subject to income tax at the basic rate (25 per cent) by deduction at source. You should therefore deduct this tax in making each payment. You will be allowed to retain all of the tax deducted provided that your income taxed at the basic or higher rate is sufficient to cover the amount of the payment. For example, if you have suffered basic rate income tax of £200 in the tax year and you made an annual payment of £100 you deduct tax from the latter amounting to £25. You thus pay only £75 when making your annual payment. Your effective income tax bill is £200 − £25 = £175. If, however, your taxed income is less than your annual payments you will have to pay to the Revenue income tax at 25 per cent on the difference. So if your taxed income is nil in any tax year, you will have to account to the Revenue for basic rate income tax on your entire annual payments for that year.

The result of this procedure is to give you basic rate income tax relief on your annual payments provided your income taxable at the basic rate exceeds those payments. From 15 March 1988, new deeds of covenant and maintenance payments are covered by different rules. Broadly, no tax relief applies to the payer and the recipient is not taxed on the payments.

Under certain circumstances relief is available against tax at the higher rates as well as the basic rate.

Examples are as follows:

(1) Annual payments under court orders entered into before 15

March 1988 for maintenance or alimony (6.8.3). (Relief also applies if the court order was applied for on or before 15 March 1988 and made by 30 June 1988.)
(2) Annual payments under deeds of covenant to individuals that were entered into before 7 April 1965.
(3) Certain annual payments under partnership agreements to retiring partners or their widows.
(4) Certain annual payments which you make in connection with the purchase of a business where the payments are made to the former owner of the business or his widow or dependants.
(5) Unlimited donations under deeds of covenant to charities (13.2.1).

4.2 What are annual payments?

(1) Examples of annual payments are annuities, alimony payments, maintenance payments to your divorced or separated wife, payments under *deeds of covenant* (6.5) and certain interest payments which are subject to special tax rules (4.3).
(2) They are normally paid under a binding legal obligation such as a contract or deed of covenant.
(3) The payments must be recurrent although repeated gifts (unless under covenant) are not annual payments.
(4) In the hands of the recipient an annual payment must neither form part of his trading profits nor consist of a payment for services rendered.
(5) Payments consisting of instalments of capital are not annual payments for tax purposes. In the case of life annuities, however, each payment is split between an income element (which is treated as an annual payment) and a capital element which is tax free.

4.3 Interest payments
(TA 1988 Ss353–379)

Subject to the following, you must not deduct income tax from any payments of interest that you make. This means that most types of interest payments made by you personally will be gross without any tax deduction. An important exception concerns mortgage interest (4.7).

If you pay 'annual interest' to anyone who lives outside the UK (unless you get permission to pay gross under a double tax agreement) you must deduct income tax at the basic rate (25 per cent) in making the payment.

If, however, you pay 'annual interest' in this country on an advance from an overseas bank carrying on business in the UK, you should not deduct income tax.

'Annual interest' is interest paid on a loan which is capable of continuing for a period exceeding one year. If, at the start of a loan, you agree that it should last for a stated period of less than one year then any interest arising will not be 'annual interest'.

Companies and local authorities must normally deduct income tax in making 'annual interest' payments and this applies to a partnership of which a company is a member. Interest paid by a bank in the normal course of its business was normally paid without any deduction for income tax. However, different rules apply from 1985–86 (8.7).

Subject to the rules which are outlined in the following pages, certain interest payments are allowed as deductions in computing your total income for income tax at basic and higher rate.

4.4 Interest paid for business purposes

Note that interest paid for business purposes is allowable against your taxable business profits provided the loan is used wholly and exclusively for the purposes of your business, profession or vocation. This basic rule includes interest on bank overdrafts as well as that on other loans.

4.5 Tax relief for interest payments
(TA 1988 Ss353–379 & FA 1989 Ss47–48)

In order to obtain relief for interest paid you must show that it is 'eligible for relief'. This term specifically excludes bank overdraft or credit card interest.

50 *Allied Dunbar Tax Guide*

4.5.1 Table: Tax relief for interest payments

Your interest is 'eligible for relief' if it is paid on loans raised for the following purposes:

(1) Subject to various restrictions, the purchase and improvement of buildings and land in the UK or Eire (4.6).

(2) Buying plant and machinery for use in a partnership which gets capital allowances on it where you are one of the partners.

(3) Buying plant and machinery (eg a motor car) which is used in connection with an office or employment that you hold and for which you personally get capital allowances.

(4) Acquiring ordinary shares in a close company (12.17) or lending it money for use in its business. (This does not apply to a close investment company, nor for shares bought after 13 March 1989 on which BES relief is claimed — 10.25.) To qualify for relief you must either own more than 5% of its shares, or own some shares and work for the greater part of your time for the company. Shares owned by 'associates' (12.17) are included in the 5% but not, after July 1989, if owned by an employee trust of which you are a beneficiary.

(5) Purchases by employees of shares in their company as part of an employee buy-out. (Employees and their spouses must together own more than 50% of the company, ignoring excesses over 10% holdings.)

(6) Purchasing a share in a partnership, or lending it money for use in its business if you are a partner. This applies whether or not you work in the partnership and also extends to investing in a co-operative.

(7) Paying inheritance tax or capital transfer tax arising on death or estate duty. The personal representatives of the deceased obtain relief for interest paid within a year of raising the loan. If the interest cannot be relieved wholly in the year of payment it can be spread forward or backwards.

Note: Relief for interest on loans to purchase plant and machinery (see (2) and (3) above) is given for three years after the year of assessment in which the loan is taken out.

4.6 Loans for purchase and improvement of buildings and land
(TA 1988 Ss354–358, FA 1988 Ss42–44, FA 1989 S46 & FA 1991 Ss26–28)

Within the limits mentioned below, any interest which you pay on a loan raised to buy land or buildings, or to improve them, is 'eligible for relief'. This does not include overdraft interest but covers fixed bank loans and building society mortgages, etc. (Improvement loans only qualify for relief if applied for this purpose before 6 April 1988.) When you pay the interest you must still own the property. The interest on any loan that you raise to pay off another loan previously obtained to buy property is also 'eligible for relief'. However, no relief is available on a loan obtained

Annual payments and interest 51

after 5 April 1988 to replace money borrowed to improve property. Land and buildings include caravans, previously of restricted categories before 6 April 1991, but now unrestricted.

'Property improvements' include:

>Central heating installations.
>Garages and garden sheds.
>Garden construction and landscaping.
>Double glazing installations.
>Plumbing improvements (excluding maintenance).
>Conversions of houses into flats.
>Construction of swimming pools, tennis courts, etc.

If, however, you merely carry out repairs to existing property without improving it then any loan interest incurred will not normally be treated as 'eligible for relief'.

The Revenue gives sympathetic consideration to cases where, for example, the husband buys the property and the wife pays the interest — the couple would usually get tax relief.

From April 1983 mortgage interest up to certain limits is normally paid net of basic rate tax (see below).

Concerning a new property loan raised after 26 March 1974, you only obtain tax relief if either (*a*) it is to purchase or improve your only or main residence or (*b*) you let the property at a commercial rent for at least 26 weeks in the year and it is available for letting at other times.

Under (*a*) your interest is restricted to that on a loan of £30,000 and if your borrowing exceeds this figure your interest relief is proportionately restricted. Before 6 April 1991, relief was available at the basic and higher rates of income tax. However, from that date, higher rate relief is withdrawn and relief is only granted at the basic rate (25 per cent).

You also get relief for interest on a loan which you obtained before 6 April 1988 (but not subsequently) to buy a house for a former or separated spouse, or a dependent relative of your wife or yourself. A dependent relative is broadly defined as an elderly or infirm relative; also your widowed, divorced or separated mother. This interest counts, however, towards the £30,000 limit. Loans obtained for these purposes after 5 April 1988 do not qualify for relief.

Up to 31 July 1988, unmarried people purchasing their own main residence together each obtained relief for the interest on a loan of up to £30,000. However, from 1 August 1988, relief on *new* loans is limited to £30,000 per residence, regardless of the people sharing. Normally, relief would be allocated equally to the borrowers. However, certain transfers of unused relief are allowed.

You obtain relief for interest on a bridging loan of up to £30,000 for normally up to one year (or longer at the discretion of the Inland Revenue) when you change houses. Higher rate relief continued after 5 April 1991 on your existing but not your new bridging loan, if both were in place by that date. This includes where there has been a formal offer and binding contract. This higher rate relief would normally only continue for up to one year, but could be extended at the discretion of the Inland Revenue.

In considering the £30,000 limit, no account is taken of interest which has been added to capital up to £1,000.

Your interest relief is not restricted because you do not reside in your property, if you live in job-related accommodation (9.6.12) and intend to make your property your main residence in due course (TA 1988 S356). A similar rule applies to interest paid on a loan to buy job-related accommodation where you are self-employed.

Under (*b*) (above) you are only allowed interest relief against your income from letting property. You continue to obtain higher rate relief under this category after 5 April 1991.

4.7 Deduction of tax from mortgage interest payments
(TA 1988 Ss369–370)

The current rules relating to mortgage interest payments apply from April 1983. These operate from 1 April 1983 for payments to building societies, other authorised lenders such as certain banks, insurance companies and local authorities; otherwise in general from 6 April 1983. However, if your mortgage is from a private lender, the previous system applies (and so you must pay the interest gross).

Broadly, under the present system, you are able to deduct tax at the basic rate from mortgage interest payments, provided the loan qualifies for relief. If your loan exceeds £30,000, you may deduct income tax from the interest on the £30,000 fraction, provided that you notify the building society, etc they agree and contact the

Revenue. New loans above £30,000 after 5 April 1987 come into the deduction system automatically.

Under the present scheme the lenders will normally arrange for you to deduct the appropriate tax on paying the interest. You may even deduct basic rate tax and keep it if your income is less than your personal allowances or you have none at all.

5 Computing your income tax bill

Your 'total income' (see below) less your allowances for the tax year (3.0.1) will be subjected to income tax at the lower, basic and higher rates according to the following table:

5.0.1 Table: Income tax rates for 1992–93

Slice of income	Rate	Total income (after allowances)	Total tax
2,000 (£0–2,000)	20%	2,000	400
21,700 (£2,000–23,700)	25%	23,700	5,825
Remainder	40%		

5.1 Indexation of income tax bands
(TA 1988 S1 & FA 1992 S10)

Prior to 6 April 1988 there was a basic rate band followed by five higher rate bands. Each of those bands was to be increased in line with the retail price index. The index comparison is made for the previous December each year and the figures rounded up to the next £100.

As with the indexation of personal reliefs (3.3), Parliament has the power to modify the effects of indexing the income tax bands. In fact no indexation increases were made at all for some years, whilst increases above the index were made for others. The 1986–87 and 1987–88 increases were below the index, however this was compensated for in 1988–89; at the same time, one higher rate of 40 per cent replaced the previous five. From 6 April 1992 the 20 per cent lower rate band applies. The starting levels for the income bands continue to be indexed.

5.2 What is total income?
(TA 1988 S835)

Your total income comprises your income for the tax year less specified deductions (5.3). The following classes of income will be included for each tax year:

(1) Income as assessed for the tax year under the following schedules:

Schedule		Details	Para
A		Land and buildings	7.1
B		Woodlands (up to 5 April 1988)	7.8
D	Cases I & II	Trades and professions	10.1
	Case III	Interest, etc	8.4
	Cases IV & V	Overseas securities and possessions	16.2
	Case VI	Miscellaneous	13.1
E		Earnings from employment (see also below)	9.1
F		Dividends	8.1

(2) The gross income actually paid to you in the tax year under the deduction of basic rate income tax (25 per cent) at the source. This will include income taxed at source under Schedules C and F. You will receive the net amount after suffering basic rate income tax (25 per cent) but you will pay the higher rate of tax if appropriate on the gross amount. You will obtain a tax credit for the basic rate tax suffered at source which will be deducted from your tax bill. The following would come within this category:

> The income portion of annuities.
> Interest on certain investments.
> Any annual payments which you receive (4.2).

(3) Income distributions from discretionary and accumulation settlements (19.4). Net payments made to you must be grossed up at 35 per cent and carry with them a tax credit of this amount which represents basic rate income tax (25 per cent) and additional rate tax (10 per cent) effectively suffered by the settlement. Thus if you receive £65 this is included in your total income together with a tax credit of £35. (If you have an interest in possession (20.31), then your income only carries 25 per cent tax in the settlement.)

(4) Dividends received together with the relevant tax credits.

Your dividends from UK companies carry with them tax credits of 25/75ths of the actual payments. Thus if you receive a dividend of £75 during the tax year, this is included in your total income together with the tax credit of £25 (£75 × 25/75ths).
(5) Your gross income taxed at source under PAYE (9.14). This consists of your salary, etc, derived from your employment; it is subjected to basic rate and higher rate income tax at source. The tax suffered at source is naturally deducted from the tax bill on your total income.
(6) The grossed up equivalent of any building society interest received. This income is subject to basic rate income tax deducted at source but must be included in your total income gross. You gross it up by multiplying the income received by $\frac{100}{100-25}$ (ie, $\frac{100}{75}$). You obtain a credit for the tax. For example, if you receive £75 building society interest, your total income will include £75 × $\frac{100}{75}$ = £100 and you obtain a tax credit of £25. Prior to 1991–92, this credit was not repayable (8.6) but effectively exempted you from the first 25 per cent of tax on the grossed interest.
(7) The grossed up equivalent of any bank interest, etc, paid to you (8.7).

5.3 Total income — Deductions

As well as normal business expenses, etc, which are deducted in arriving at the various income tax assessments, the following are deductible:

(1) Loan interest subject to the relevant rules (4.3). Regarding mortgage interest paid after 6 April 1991 in connection with your home, no deduction is allowable for relieving the excess of your higher rate over your basic rate liability (FA 1991 S27).
(2) Business losses and capital allowances.
(3) Annual payments under court orders for maintenance or alimony provided they are made before 16 March 1988 or applied for before that date and made by 30 June 1988. Payments under new arrangements must be gross and are not deductible (6.8.3).
(4) Annual payments under deeds of covenant to individuals

(excluding your infant children) that you entered into before 7 April 1965.
(5) Certain annual payments under partnership agreements to retiring partners or their widows.
(6) Annual payments to individuals under deeds of covenant entered into after 6 April 1965 and before 15 March 1988. In general these are not deductible from your income for higher rate income tax purposes. However, they reduce your total income for the purposes of the life assurance relief one-sixth rule (3.2.8).
(7) Certain annual payments which you make in connection with the purchase of a business where the payments are made to the former owner of the business or his widow or dependants.
(8) Covenanted donations to charities (13.2.1) without limit. (For 1985–86, there was a gross limit of £10,000, with £5,000 for 1983–84 and 1984–85.)
(9) Allowable personal pension contributions, retirement annuity premiums (24.11.1) and additional voluntary contributions (AVCs) (24.12.1).
(10) A proportion of certain transfers to reserves made by underwriters at Lloyd's or other approved underwriters.
(11) Personal reliefs and allowances (see Chapter 3). (These are, strictly speaking, deductions which are made from your total income rather than in its computation.)
(12) Half of your Class 4 National Insurance Contributions (10.28) from 6 April 1985.

5.4 Charges on income
(TA 1988 S276)

The annual payments mentioned above (3)–(8) as well as various other charges on income (4.1) are paid under the deduction of basic rate income tax (25 per cent) (as is your allowable mortgage interest from April 1983 (4.7)). To the extent that your income less allowances is not sufficient to cover your annual charges payments, your personal allowances, etc must be restricted. (This restriction does not apply regarding mortgage interest.)

Thus, if your income for 1992–93 is £3,500 and your personal allowances and reliefs total £2,500, you can pay up to £1,000 annual charges without restriction. The £1,000 is paid by you under deduction of basic rate income tax. Thus you actually pay only £1,000 − 25 per cent × £1,000 = £750. You also pay to the Revenue tax at 25 per cent on £1,000 = £250. If your annual charges were £1,500, your total reliefs would be reduced to £2,000 so that your taxable income after allowances (£1,500) would be sufficient to cover your charges.

The basic rate tax which you deduct from your annual payments must effectively be paid over to the Revenue. This is done by paying basic rate tax on that part of your income which is equal to such annual payments. Where, however, the payments in question are allowed as deductions in computing your total income (eg, (3)–(8) above) you get relief for the excess of your higher rate tax over basic rate tax on income covered by those charges.

5.5 Deductions from tax payable

When your total tax liability is computed certain deductions from the tax payable must be made, either because you have already paid part of it or because of special reliefs. These deductions include the following:

(1) Life assurance relief on policies effected before 14 March 1984 only (3.2.7). Normally $12\frac{1}{2}$ per cent of your qualifying premiums (24.5) (subject to the various rules) is deductible from your tax payable. Before 6 April 1989 the percentage was 15 per cent. You normally obtain this relief by deducting it from each premium payment.
(2) 25/75ths of your building society interest received; similarly 25/75ths of bank deposit interest, etc (8.7). From 6 April 1991 (but not previously), this tax is capable of being repaid.
(3) Tax credits on dividends received (8.1). The tax credit is 25/75ths of each dividend received.
(4) Tax paid under PAYE (9.14).
(5) Basic rate tax deducted at the source on certain investment interest paid to you (such as on company debentures).
(6) Basic rate tax deducted from annual payments made to you during the year which are included in your total income.
(7) Tax at the basic rate (25 per cent) and the additional rate (10 per cent) on income distributions made to you during the tax year by discretionary settlements (19.5). The tax is computed on the gross equivalent of the distributions.

5.6 Investment income surcharge (additional rate)
(TA 1988 S686)

For 1983–84 you were liable to an additional rate of 15 per cent on so much of your investment income as exceeded £7,100 (£6,250 for

60 *Allied Dunbar Tax Guide*

1982–83). For 1984–85 and subsequent years, the additional rate no longer applies to individuals.

Your investment income is sometimes referred to as unearned income (3.1) and for the purposes of ascertaining the amount chargeable to the additional rates, certain special rules applied. (Please refer to previous editions for details.)

Certain discretionary and accumulation settlements (19.5) are subjected to the additional rate (now 10 per cent). In this case, the charge is made on all the income including both that from investments and otherwise. Although the additional rate no longer applies to individuals, it still applies to settlements. Higher rate tax is not normally charged on the trust income, however, unless it is distributed to beneficiaries who are themselves liable to the higher rate of tax. (See Chapter 19, 19.5, for fuller details.)

5.7 The assessment and payment of your income tax
(TA 1988 Ss2–5)

This matter is considered in Chapter 14. *As a general rule* you must pay income tax at the lower, basic and higher rate by 1 January in the year for which the income is assessed, if the income has not already been taxed. If, however, your assessment based on the income has not been agreed in time, then you are due to pay the tax normally 30 days after the assessment is issued. Special rules apply where you appeal (14.3).

An exception to the above rule concerns your tax on business profits (10.1) which is payable in two equal instalments on 1 January in the year of assessment and the following 1 July.

Income tax at higher rates is due for payment by 1 December following the year of assessment on any income from which basic rate tax has been deducted at source. This includes income like building society and bank deposit interest as well as dividends, etc. If the assessment is not issued by 1 November following the year of assessment, you are due to pay the tax no earlier than 30 days after the date of issue, special rules applying if you appeal (14.3).

5.7.1 Example: Income tax computation

Mr B has his own business from which his assessable profit for 1992–93 is £25,000. His other income for 1992–93 consists of £1,125 building society interest and £7,500 dividends received (tax credits £2,500). He pays £1,200 gross interest on a mortgage for the purchase of his house to which MIRAS does not apply. (Mr B is married, and for 1992–93 his wife's income will be taxed separately.) From the above, compute Mr B's income tax liability.

Mr B – Income tax computation for 1992–93

Earned income – business assessment		£25,000
Investment income – building society interest:	£1,125	
Add: Basic rate tax		
£1,125 × 25/75ths	375	
	£1,500	
Dividends	7,500	
Add: Tax credit	2,500	
		11,500
Total income before personal reliefs and allowances		£36,500
Less: Personal allowance	3,445	
Married couple's allowance	1,720	5,165
Taxable balance		£31,335
Tax payable:		
£2,000 at 20%		£400
21,700 at 25%		5,425
7,635 at 40%		3,054
£31,335		
Total tax		8,879
Less: Tax credit on dividends	£2,500	
Tax credit on building society interest	375	
Basic rate tax relief on mortgage interest 25% × £1,200	300	
		3,175
Net further tax payable		£5,704

5.8 Interest on overdue tax
(TMA S86 etc)

If you are late in paying your income tax you may be charged interest at 10 per cent from 6 July 1991 and $9\frac{1}{4}$ per cent from 6 October 1991. Previous recent rates have been:

From	Rate %
1 May 1985	11
6 August 1986	$8\frac{1}{2}$
6 November 1986	$9\frac{1}{2}$
6 April 1987	9
6 June 1987	$8\frac{1}{4}$
6 September 1987	9
6 December 1987	$8\frac{1}{4}$
6 May 1988	$7\frac{3}{4}$
6 August 1988	$9\frac{3}{4}$
6 October 1988	$10\frac{3}{4}$
6 January 1989	$11\frac{1}{2}$
6 July 1989	$12\frac{1}{4}$
6 November 1989	13
6 November 1990	$12\frac{1}{4}$
6 March 1991	$11\frac{1}{2}$
6 May 1991	$10\frac{3}{4}$

This interest is not deductible for income tax purposes. The exact rules are given later (14.7.2).

5.9 Fluctuating income

Because of the graduated nature of income tax rates, if your income fluctuates greatly from year to year you may find that your tax liability is high in some years and low in others. The result is that your total income tax over the years is more than it would have been had your income been spread evenly over those years. Certain special rules exist which have the effect of spreading lump sums of income over the period during which they have been earned. For example, lump sum payments received for the copyright, etc, of artistic works may be taxed as if spread over up to three years, depending on the time taken to produce the work (13.4).

So-called 'top slicing' relief is obtained when you receive certain large taxable sums in one year. You may effectively spread these sums over a stated period and recompute your tax liability on the basis that the income had been paid in this way. (The tax is payable for the year when you receive the income but the rate is normally lower.) What you do is to divide the lump sum (L) by the stated period (P) and calculate the tax payable (T) for the year on your other income plus (L/P). You then calculate the tax payable on your other income by itself and deduct it from (T). This gives the total tax payable on (L/P) and this tax is multiplied by P to give the total tax payable on (L).

A particular example where 'top slicing' applies is regarding the profit element in the proceeds of non-qualifying life assurance policies (24.7.3). Such policy proceeds are taxed at the excess of higher rate income tax over income tax at the basic rate, subject to the relief outlined above.

With effect from 1988–89, two forms of 'top slicing' relief were removed. These related to premiums for certain leases (7.7.1) and relief previously given on the merger of professional firms, resulting in a change in accounting basis.

6 Husband, wife and children

This Chapter deals, in particular, with the taxation of husband and wife. The new system of independent taxation operating from 6 April 1990 is covered. Also, the previous rules are considered, which apply for 1989–90 and earlier years. Thus they are important for open assessments and returns for those years. (Some of the rules for independent taxation have been mentioned in Chapter 3.)

6.1 Independent taxation of husband and wife
(FA 1988 Ss33–35 & Sch 3)

From 6 April 1990, a completely new system for taxing married couples operates. You and your spouse are each taxed separately on all of your income and capital gains. Each has a single person's relief and income tax rates (for 1992–93 the first £2,000 at 20 per cent, the next £21,700 at 25 per cent and the remainder at 40 per cent). Similarly you each have a full capital gains tax annual exemption (£5,800).

There is a new allowance known as the married couple's allowance amounting to £1,720 for 1990–91, 1991–92 and 1992–93. Normally, this goes to the husband. However, if his income is insufficient to use it, part or all can be transferred to the wife. In the year of marriage, the married couple's allowance is reduced by one-twelfth for each month between 6 April and the marriage date. A higher married couple's allowance is given to those entitled to age allowance (3.2.2).

A new rule applies from 6 April 1993. You will be able to elect for the married couple's allowance to be split equally between you or go entirely to the spouse. Otherwise it will be used as at present.

Income from jointly owned property is taken as split equally between husband and wife, subject to the right to make a joint declaration to the contrary. The effect of the election is to split the income in the ratio of the respective shares of husband and wife in the asset. Interest on mortgages in your joint names is split equally between you. However, you can elect for any different split to apply, which could well save tax.

For example, if you and your spouse have a joint mortgage and he or she has no income you should elect to receive all of the mortgage interest relief.

The old-established wife's earnings election (6.4) has no validity for 1990–91 and subsequent tax years. However, as mentioned above, all income will be taxed separately, as will capital gains. As a result, your spouse and yourself will each have the annual capital gains tax exemption (18.6) for 1990–91 and subsequently. Thus each has £5,800 exemption for 1992–93.

An election for transitional relief (3.2.2) is available where a couple might have been worse off in 1990–91, because most of the income belongs to the wife and the husband's personal allowance exceeds his own income. The relief is limited for 1990–91 and future years to the husband's excess personal allowance.

6.2 When you marry

If you marry after 5 April 1990, various new rules will apply to both of you (6.1). However, essentially you will be taxed separately on your income and capital gains, remaining responsible for your own tax returns.

As a married person, prior to 6 April 1990 you were taxed not only on your own income but also normally on that of your wife. You were not taxed, however, on your wife's income for the tax year during which you married. You obtained personal relief at a higher rate (£4,375 for 1989–90) than a single person (£2,785) (3.0.1). If your wife was working then against her earnings was set her (wife's) earned income relief (maximum £2,785).

At the end of the year in which you married both you and your wife had to complete an income tax return. Naturally, this continues under the new system since now you each need to submit your own returns.

In the year of your marriage your wife obtained her own personal relief (£2,785 for 1989–90) but no wife's earned income relief (3.2.4).

6.2.1 Tax returns

Even under the old system, your own return, for the year of marriage, covered the full tax year and needed to include all of your own income for that year but none of your wife's.

Even though you were single for part of the year you were taxed as a married person for the whole of that year. But your personal allowance was restricted by £132.50 (for 1989–90) for every completed month during that tax year prior to your date of marriage (3.2.3), provided your marriage was after 5 April 1989. (For the previous year the figure was £124.17.) A similar rule applies for married couple's allowance (3.2.2) and the monthly restriction is £143.33.

6.3 Separate assessment
(TA 1988 Ss283–285)

Prior to 6 April 1990, despite the fact that it was the husband who was taxed on both his own and his wife's income, it was nevertheless possible for a married couple to be assessed separately and to pay their respective shares of tax separately. However, from 6 April 1990, husband and wife are both taxed and assessed on their own income (6.2).

Separate assessment is not the same as the separate taxation of your wife's earned income (6.4) under which your wife was taxed separately on her earnings as if she were a single person. Separate assessment merely had the effect of apportioning to your wife her share of the total income tax bill so that you each paid your own share according to your own income.

The tax which you each paid was calculated by taking the total tax payable on your combined incomes at the basic, and higher rates. This was then apportioned between your wife and yourself in the ratio of your incomes. You then deducted from the tax share of each the tax equivalent of the personal reliefs attributable to you and your wife. The tax equivalent of the personal reliefs was found by calculating tax on them at your top rate(s). Your personal reliefs were split between you and your wife according to the following rules:

(1) Life assurance relief, if applicable, was given to the payer of the premiums.
(2) The allowances were split in the ratio of the tax on your incomes before allowances.
(3) The allowances allocated to your wife must not have been less than her additional personal relief (maximum £2,785 for 1989–90).
(4) If your wife's allocation of allowances exceeded her taxable income then you got the benefit of her excess allowances and vice versa.

6.4 Separate taxation of wife's earnings
(TA 1988 Ss287 & 288)

Before the introduction of independent taxation from 6 April 1990, it was still possible to elect for the wife to be separately taxed on her earnings up to 5 April 1990 as if she were a single person. The husband was then taxed on the balance of their joint incomes (including the wife's unearned income) as if he also were single.

The necessary joint election was needed not earlier than six months before the start of the year of assessment, nor later than 12 months after the end of the year of assessment; it was then valid for that year of assessment and each subsequent one until revoked. The revocation had to be made jointly by you both not later than 12 months after the end of the year of assessment to which it applied.

For this purpose the wife's 'earnings' means all of her earned income (3.1) apart from:

(1) Any pension or other allowances given in respect of the husband's past employment.
(2) Any National Insurance benefits payable to the wife otherwise than by virtue of her own contributions and apart from invalid care allowance or (from 6 April 1987) unemployment benefit.

The rules for the allocation of your personal reliefs for 1989–90 were as follows:

(1) You obtained the single man's allowance of £2,785 (not £4,375) and your wife also got £2,785 personal allowance.
(2) Reliefs in general were allocated as if you were not married.

For example, mortgage interest relief would go to the wife if she were the borrower.
(3) Certain reliefs were not available to either of you. These include additional personal relief for children and age allowance.

If a joint election was made for the separate taxation of the wife's earnings then any deductions which could normally be directed to be made in priority against the wife's earnings before the husband's could only be set off against her earnings. This applied to items like losses and capital allowances; also deeds of covenant made by her (6.5). For example, trading losses that could normally be set off against the other income of either of you were only usable against the income of the one making the losses. Interest paid by the wife could only be set off against her income.

If an election was made for the wife's earnings to be taxed separately, then she paid the tax or got any tax repayment relative to those earnings. This applied whether or not you had elected for separate assessment (6.3).

6.5 Deeds of covenant
(FA 1988 S36)

Payments under deeds of covenant to charities (13.2.1) provide a most tax-efficient means of passing money regularly to them. Such payments are a class of annual payments (4.1). The deed must be properly drawn up (most charities have prepared forms for covenanted donations) otherwise seek professional advice.

Beneficial treatment also applies to payments under deeds of covenant to individuals, provided the deeds were entered into before 15 March 1988. A further condition is that an Inspector of Taxes must have received the deed by 30 June 1988, otherwise, payments under such deeds are disregarded for tax purposes. The previous beneficial tax treatment which made deeds of covenant so popular for student children and also grandchildren has been withdrawn for new covenants.

The deed needs to provide for payments at annual or more frequent intervals for a period capable of exceeding six years or until your death if earlier. (Note that this also applies to any supplementary deeds.) For 1980–81 and subsequent years, however, deeds of covenant in favour of charities (13.2.1) need only be capable of exceeding three years.

You are required to deduct income tax at 25 per cent from each payment according to the rules for annual payments (4.1). This does not apply to payments made by you under deed of covenant to any of your children who are less than 18 years of age and unmarried. These payments are disregarded for tax purposes as are payments under a reciprocal arrangement.

Payments to individuals under deeds of covenant entered into before 7 April 1965 are allowable deductions for additional and higher rate tax. Deed of covenant payments to charities (13.2.1) are normally deductible from your total income for higher tax rate purposes without limit (FA 1986 S30).

Subject to the above, recipients of payments under deeds of covenant with low incomes can reclaim basic rate tax on them up to the amount of their unused income tax personal relief (£3,445). Thus suppose your grandson has no other income and you pay him £1,500 net under deed of covenant each year, tax of £500 will be reclaimable for him for 1992–93. (This assumes that you entered into the deed of covenant before 15 March 1988.)

6.6 The income of your children

No matter how young they are, there is nothing to prevent your children earning income in their own right and being taxed on that earned income. This also applies to investment income unless the investments were given by your wife or yourself and the child is neither married nor over the age of 18 at the time that the income is paid.

Settlements and arrangements made by you through which your child gets investment income normally result in your being taxed on that income if the child is neither married nor over 18. If the child's investment income which would otherwise be treated as your own is less than £100, however, you will not pay tax on that income (FA 1990 S82). (Prior to 1991–92, this figure was £5.)

You should obtain a tax return each year for each of your minor children who has any income (including trust income). Completing a return will often prove beneficial since if the child has suffered tax at source on any income this may be reclaimable in whole or part depending on its nature and on how much other income there is to set against the child's tax allowances. In such circumstances a repayment claim form can be submitted instead of a normal tax return (14.6).

If the child had little or no other income, then it was of benefit for it to be paid an annual amount under deed of covenant (6.5) by a friend or relative (not its parents, unless the child is over 18 or married). However, there must be no reciprocal arrangement. From 15 March 1988 the rules have been changed (6.5) but existing deeds of covenant attract relief as before. The covenant payments are made under the deduction of income tax at the basic rate (25 per cent). If the child's income is small enough then the tax can be reclaimed on its behalf because he or she has the benefit of the full personal allowance (£3,445) and lower rate (20 per cent) tax band.

6.6.1 Example: Income of child

Mr A has one child, B, aged ten years, whose income for 1992–93 is as follows:

		Gross
(1)	Dividends, including tax credits, on shares given to B by Mr A	£200
(2)	Dividends, including tax credits, on shares given to B by his grandfather	£800
(3)	Annual payment under deed of covenant from B's uncle effected before 15 March 1988	£2,000
(4)	Interest on bank deposit (capital gifted by grandmother)	£1,000

How much income tax is reclaimable on behalf of B for 1992–93?

Item (1) is not treated as B's income for tax purposes because it is regarded as the income of Mr A who gifted the shares to his child B.

The income tax payable by B for 1992–93 is calculated as follows:

		Gross	Income tax deducted or tax credits
(2)	Dividends including tax credits on shares from grandfather	£800	£200
(3)	Annual payment from B's uncle	2,000	500
(4)	Deposit interest	1,000	250
	Total income	£3,800	£950
	Less: Personal allowance of	3,445	
	Taxable amount	£355	
	Income tax due £355 at 20%		£71.00
	Less: Income tax suffered by deduction at source and tax credits		950.00
	Net income tax reclaimable		£879.00

6.7 Death of husband or wife

If you are a widower or widow you are regarded as a single person for tax purposes. This means that the personal reliefs for single persons will apply to your income. You may, however, qualify for the £1,720 additional personal relief for children (3.2.12).

6.7.1 If husband dies

If a husband dies during the tax year his income for the period from 6 April to the date of his death will be subject to tax. A return of this income must be made by his executors who must arrange for payment of tax out of the estate funds. If the date of death is before 6 April 1990, the wife's income must be included.

Even though his period of assessment will be less than a full year, where a husband died during 1989–90 he obtained the full married man's personal allowance (£4,375), and various other reliefs in full including the £2,785 (maximum) earned income allowance for his wife against her earned income.

Where the husband dies after 5 April 1990, he will have the full personal allowance (£3,445 for 1992–93) and married couple's allowance (£1,720). However if his income is not sufficiently large to absorb the full married couple's allowance, the balance will go to his widow.

Where the husband died before 6 April 1990, his widow became a taxpayer in her own right and was taxed on the income derived by her during the period from the date of death to 5 April and she completed a separate tax return for that period. She received the full £2,785 personal allowance as a single person for the period. Also, widow's bereavement allowance was available subject to the rules (3.2.16).

After 5 April 1990, husbands and wives are independently taxed in any event. However, widow's bereavement allowance (£1,720) is available as before.

6.7.2 If wife dies

Where a wife dies after 5 April 1990, she is entitled to the entire personal relief (£3,445 for 1992–93). (Age allowance would alternatively be available in full if she is so entitled.)

If a wife died during the tax year 1989–90 this did not normally affect her husband's tax return. He included with his own income for the full year the income of his wife up to the date of her death. He got personal allowance as a married man for the full year (£4,375) and also £2,785 wife's earned income allowance if appropriate.

6.8 Divorce or separation

If you are divorced or permanently separated you are regarded as a single person for tax purposes. This means that the personal reliefs for single persons will apply to your income. If, however, you were separated but maintained your wife by voluntary maintenance payments for which you got no tax relief, prior to 6 April 1990, you obtained the married man's personal allowance (£4,375). Subsequent to that date, married couple's allowance (£1,720) applies in the tax year of separation only, subject to transitional relief (6.8.3).

You are treated as being permanently separated from your wife if you are separated under a court order or deed of separation; also if you are separated in such circumstances that the separation is likely to be permanent.

6.8.1 Divorce or separation during the tax year

On her divorce or permanent separation prior to 6 April 1990, a woman became a taxpayer in her own right and needed to submit a return from the date of divorce or separation to 5 April. She was then taxed as a single person getting the full 1989–90 personal allowance. Naturally, the independent taxation rules mean that after 5 April 1990, a woman is a taxpayer in her own right in any event.

Where a man is divorced or permanently separated during 1990–91 or later, he obtains the full personal relief (£3,445 for 1992–93) and married couple's allowance for the year.

A man who was divorced or permanently separated during the year 1989–90 still needed to submit a return for the full year in the usual way. He included with his own income for the year that of his wife up to the date of the divorce or separation but not the income derived by her after that date. He got the full married man's personal allowance (£4,375) for that year as well as the wife's earned income relief (maximum £2,785).

6.8.2 Who may claim the additional personal relief?
(TA 1988 S260)

For any tax year only one payment of additional personal relief (£1,720) is normally allowable for your children. If you are separated or divorced from your wife you must agree jointly who should claim the tax relief for your mutual children or you should agree a basis of apportioning the relief between you. If you do not agree a basis, then the relief will be split in proportion to the respective contributions made by you and your ex-wife (or separated wife) towards the children's maintenance and education for the tax year.

As an exception to the general rule, if each parent looks after one or more children of a broken marriage, each can claim additional personal relief of £1,720. However, in the year of separation, only the wife (or ex-wife) is able to claim the relief.

6.8.3 Alimony and maintenance payments
(FA 1988 Ss36–39)

The rules regarding alimony and maintenance payments were changed in 1988. Where payments are made under agreements dated after 14 March 1988, they are to be made without the deduction of tax. At the same time, the recipients are not taxed on the payments. The payer obtains a limited amount of relief, equal to the annual amount paid or, if less, the difference between the married and single reliefs from year to year (£1,720 for 1990–91, 1991–92 and 1992–93).

This applies where one divorced or separated spouse makes payments to the other. If you are separated or divorced and you make any payments under a court order or a binding agreement entered into before 15 March 1988, for the maintenance of your children or your separated or ex-wife, then you should not deduct income tax at the basic rate (25 per cent) from the gross payments. (Such deduction was normally required before 6 April 1989.) The full gross payments up to the level for 1988–89 are deducted from your total income for income tax purposes (5.3).

Purely voluntary payments of maintenance should be paid without any tax deductions and these are not allowable as annual charges against your income; nor are they taxed on the recipient. As indicated, however (6.8), if you maintained your separated wife by voluntary payments only, then prior to 6 April 1990, you obtained the married man's personal allowance. Married couple's allowance normally applies in the tax year of separation only. However, if you separated before 6 April 1990 and the foregoing circumstances apply, you will normally continue to obtain this relief. This does not apply if you are divorced.

Under the previous rules, if maintenance payments under a court order were made direct to the children, then these were treated as their own income. If, however, the payments were made to the mother for the maintenance of the children then the income was treated for tax purposes as her income. This no longer applies under the new provisions.

Regarding agreements made before 15 March 1988, the existing rules continued for 1988–89. This extended to court orders applied for before 16 March 1988 and made by 30 June 1988; also maintenance agreements made before 15 March 1988, provided received by the Inspector of Taxes by 30 June 1988, and variations of such orders or agreements. After 5 April 1989, special rules apply to payments under these agreements. The payer gets tax relief on payments up to the level for which he obtained relief for 1988–89 and the recipient is taxable on no more than was taxable in 1988–89 (taking account of the exemption for a divorced or separated spouse of £1,720 etc). All payments of maintenance due after 5 April 1989 should be made gross.

6.8.4 Small maintenance payments
(TA 1988 S351)

Special rules existed for 'small maintenance payments' made prior to 6 April 1989. These are payments made under a court order to a separated or divorced wife (or husband) or to or for the benefit of a child of a broken marriage under 21 years of age. From 6 April 1986 the amounts could not exceed £48 weekly or £208 monthly; £25 and £108 for certain payments for children. The payments were made without any deduction of tax. They were allowed as deductions from the taxable income of the payer and assessed to tax in the hands of the recipient.

6.8.5 Foreign divorces

If the divorce is effected by a foreign court then different rules relate to the receipt or payment of alimony by residents of this country. Normally no tax will be deductible from the payments by a United Kingdom resident and a recipient resident in this country will be assessed to tax on the amount arising.

However, for 1992–93 and subsequent years, tax relief extends to payments under court orders of countries which are members of the EC; also written agreements enforceable under the law of those countries. Payments must be to a divorced or separated wife or husband for their maintenance, or for the maintenance of a child of the marriage. The relief is limited to £1,720 (F2A 1992 S62).

7 Income from land and property

The amount of income that you derive during the tax year from letting property such as a house, flat, factory or shop, less the deductions you may claim represent your net income from letting property and must be shown separately on your tax return. You must return your gross property income including certain lease premiums and also give full particulars of your expenses. If the income is derived from furnished lettings then the assessment will be under Schedule D Case VI (13.1); otherwise it will generally be under Schedule A.

7.1 Income falling within Schedule A
(TA 1988 S15)

Annual profits or gains (ie, after deducting expenses) in respect of:

(1) Rents under leases of land (and buildings) in the UK.
(2) Rentcharges, ground annual and feu duties, and any other annual payments arising out of land in the UK. (This includes some wayleaves, easements, etc.)
(3) Other receipts arising to a person from the ownership of land in the UK or from rights or interests in such land.

7.1.1 Exceptions

(1) Yearly interest.
(2) Income including royalties from mines, quarries, etc which are charged under Schedule D.
(3) Income from various other sources charged under Schedule D such as ironworks, gasworks, canals, docks, fishing rights, railways, bridges, etc.
(4) Income from furnished lettings (ie, tenant entitled to use of furniture). This is assessed under Schedule D Case VI unless

you elect within two years of the end of the relevant tax year that it should be taxed under Schedule A.

7.1.2 Expenses allowed against Schedule A income
(TA 1988 Ss25–33)

(1) Repairs and maintenance including redecorating the premises during the lease.
(2) Insurance premiums against fire and water damage, etc to the building.
(3) Management costs including costs of rent collection, salaries, advertising for new tenants, legal and accountancy charges, etc. If your wife takes part in the management, consider paying her a salary (1.2.9).
(4) Services that you are obliged to provide for the tenants but for which you get no specific payment.
(5) Any payments that you make for general and water rates.
(6) Any payments that you make for any rent, rentcharge, ground annual, feu duty or other periodical payment in respect of the land.
(7) The cost of lighting any common parts of office blocks or flats and otherwise maintaining them.
(8) The upkeep of gardens of flats, etc where the lease requires you to be responsible for this expense.
(9) Architects' and surveyors' fees in connection with maintenance but not improvements.
(10) Capital allowances (10.9) on any plant or machinery that you might use in the upkeep of your property.
(11) The upkeep of any private roads, drains and ditches, etc, on your land if part or all of the property is let and the expenditure is for the benefit of your tenants.
(12) In the case of an industrial building which is used by the tenant for industrial purposes (eg, manufacturing) you may get capital allowances on the building (10.11). This also applies to some hotels (10.15).
(13) When you live in a part of the premises you let to others you may not deduct the full amount of your expenditure from your income. Instead you must subtract from your expenditure some reasonable proportion because the premises were not wholly used to produce the income. You may calculate this proportion as being, for example:

$$\frac{\text{Area (or rooms) used by you}}{\text{Total area (or rooms)}} \times \text{Expenses}$$

7.2 Special rules concerning expenses

Your expenditure in respect of maintenance and repairs is deductible if incurred by reason of dilapidation attributable to a period falling within the duration of the lease. All other expenditure must be incurred in respect of that period. If, however, you bought the premises subject to a lease, you normally get no relief for your expenses relating to the period prior to the purchase.

Special rules relate to a 'lease at full rent' which is one that produces sufficient income for you to pay for the maintenance, repairs, insurance and management of the premises in accordance with the undertakings in the lease. In that case you can charge expenses relating to a period after your purchase when the premises were empty immediately before they were let at full rent. You can also deduct expenses relating to a previous full rent letting that you made of the premises or a void period between lettings.

If you have a number of 'leases at full rent' that are not 'tenant's repairing leases', then you can set off expenses attributable to one such lease against the rents derived from another (a tenant's repairing lease is one where the lessee (tenant) is under an obligation to maintain the premises).

7.3 Losses

If in any year your expenses for any property exceed the rent and you do not get relief as above then you can carry the resultant loss forward to be set off against future Schedule A income from the same property, or against income from other properties provided that all of the properties concerned are let on 'leases at full rent' that are not 'tenant's repairing leases' (see above). A loss from a property cannot be set off against income derived from a trade or business carried on.

7.4 Assessment under Schedule A
(TA 1988 S22)

Tax under this Schedule is charged by reference to the income to which you become entitled in the tax year. This applies whether or not you actually receive the rents, etc unless:

(1) You did not receive an amount to which you were entitled because of the default of the person who owed you the money and you took reasonable steps to enforce payment; or

(2) you actually waived payment of the rent, etc (without receiving any other benefit) for the purpose of avoiding hardship.

Thus your 1992–93 assessment will be based on the rents, etc to which you are entitled in the year to 5 April 1993 less your allowable Schedule A deductions for that year.

Schedule A income tax is payable on 1 January in the tax year. Thus your 1992–93 demand will be payable on 1 January 1993. Since your income less expenses for that year will not be known until after 5 April 1993 you are first assessed on the basis of the previous year (ie, 1991–92). When your rents, etc and expenses have been computed for the year 1992–93 and agreed with the Revenue, your assessment is adjusted and you will either pay over any additional income tax that is due or receive a repayment.

Income assessable under Schedule A is normally treated as investment income and prior to 6 April 1984 was subjected to the 15 per cent additional rate (5.6), if your investment income was sufficiently high. This still applies for certain trusts and the 1992–93 rate is 10 per cent (5.6).

7.4.1 Example: Assessment under Schedule A

Mr A bought an old house some years ago and divided it into three flats each of which he let unfurnished at an annual rent of £2,000. Taking the expenses shown in the example, assuming that Mr A has already used his personal reliefs and lower rate tax band and that he is not liable for the higher rate of tax, his assessments are as follows:

Year ended 5 April:	1992		1993	
Rents receivable 3 × £2,000		£6,000		£6,000
Less:				
Expenses				
General rates	£900		£1,000	
Water rates	120		130	
Garden upkeep	520		520	
Maintenance, light and heat of hall and stairs	330		350	
Exterior repairs and decorating	400		200	
Fire insurance of structure of building	220		220	
Accountancy	200		220	
Agents' rent collection charges	450		450	
		3,140		3,090
Net Schedule A assessments		£2,860		£2,910
Income tax payable (25%)	1991–92 £715.00	(25%)	1992–93 £727.50	

Note: Income tax will be payable for 1992–93 as follows:

On 1 January 1993 – provisional assessment based on 1991–92 £2,860 at 25%	£715.00
On agreement of 1992–93 assessment – additional demand	12.50
Total income tax liability under Schedule A 1992–93	£727.50

7.5 Furnished lettings

Unless you have elected for Schedule A to apply (7.1), your income from furnished lettings is normally taxed under Schedule D Case VI on the actual income less expenditure for the tax year.

As well as expenses normally allowable for Schedule A purposes (7.1.2), you are also entitled to a deduction to cover depreciation on furniture and furnishings. This may be given to you as a deduction of the entire replacement cost from year to year.

More likely you will obtain a yearly deduction of 10 per cent of your rents less any rates and service costs which you pay. Thus, if your annual rents are £1,000 and you pay £200 in rates, you can deduct £80 yearly to cover the depreciation and replacement of furniture and furnishings.

If, under the terms of a letting, you provide services such as laundry, meals, domestic help, etc then you can charge the cost of these items against your taxable profit. If you provide such services, then your lettings income might possibly be treated as earned income. However, case law has made this less likely. Otherwise it would be unearned income, subject to special rules for holiday lettings (below).

As from 6 April 1992, new relief applies regarding renting a room in your home (7.14). From the same date, the existing practice of including within the furnished lettings rules payments under licences, is confirmed (F2A 1992 S58).

7.6 Holiday lettings
(TA 1988 Ss503–504)

With effect from 6 April 1982, furnished holiday letting businesses which satisfy certain requirements qualify for reliefs only normally available where the activity is a trade for tax purposes. The accommodation must be available for holiday letting for at least 140 days during the year and actually let for at least 70 days (no let to normally exceed 31 days). The income from 6 April 1982 is treated as earned income; also capital gains tax rollover relief (18.25) and retirement relief (18.29) apply. In general, although the income is normally assessed under Schedule D Case VI the letting activity is treated as a trade for the purposes of many tax provisions, including payments by two instalments, loss relief (10.22), capital allowances (10.8), personal pension contracts, etc.

7.6.1 Losses
(TA 1988 S392)

Furnished letting losses can be set off against other Schedule D Case VI profits (from lettings or miscellaneous income) during the tax year. Any losses that are not relieved in this way can be carried forward and set off against future assessments under Schedule D Case VI either in respect of furnished lettings or other income.

7.7 The taxation of lease premiums
(TA 1988 Ss34–39 & Sch 2; FA 1988 S75)

If you obtain a premium in connection with the granting of a lease of not more than 50 years' duration on any property that you own, then you will be assessed to tax (under Schedule A) on part of such premium. The amount to be included in your Schedule A assessment is the premium, reduced by 1/50th of its amount for each complete period of 12 months (other than the first) comprised in the duration of the lease (see 7.7.1). The balance of the premium which is not charged under Schedule A normally attracts capital gains tax (18.1).

If you sell a lease rather than grant one you will normally be assessed to capital gains tax on any profit unless you are a dealer (7.9) or it is an 'artificial transaction' (7.10).

The following are also included with your taxable premiums:

(1) The value of any work that the tenant agreed to do to your premises to the extent that the value of your property is enhanced.
(2) Any premiums paid to you in instalments. You include the aggregate of the instalments in the year that you grant the lease; but you can claim on grounds of hardship to pay the tax

Income from land and property 83

by instalments over a period not exceeding eight years, or ending with your last premium instalment if earlier.
(3) If you are granted a lease at a premium (£P) that is less than its market value (£M) and you then assign the lease at a profit, the amount of your profit is taxed under Schedule D Case VI to the extent that it does not exceed (£M − £P).

7.7.1 Lease premium top slicing relief
(TA 1988 Sch 2 & FA 1988 S75)

Prior to 6 April 1988, having to pay income tax at basic and higher rates on a premium in one tax year might have resulted in a very heavy tax bill. To relieve this situation individuals only were allowed to claim 'top slicing relief'. As a result of such a claim your premium was spread evenly over the term of the lease to give a 'yearly equivalent'. Your allowable expenses were first set against your rents and then any balance was deducted from the 'yearly equivalent'. Tax was then calculated on the latter at your top income tax rates for the tax year. This gave a combined tax rate that was applied to the total premium to give your final tax liability on the premium.

With the cut in income tax rates, top slicing relief on lease premiums was removed for 1988–89 and subsequent years.

7.8 Woodlands
(TA 1988 S16 & FA 1988 S65 & Sch 6)

(1) Prior to 6 April 1988, you were assessed to income tax under Schedule B in respect of woodlands if you occupied them with a view to obtaining a profit and managed them on a commercial basis. Subject to certain transitional provisions, income from woodlands has now been removed from the tax regime.
(2) You were assessed under Schedule B on the 'assessable value' of the woodlands that you occupied in the tax year. The 'assessable value' was one-third of the woodlands' annual value (the annual rent that you would have expected to obtain from letting the woodlands in their natural and unimproved state if you undertook to bear the costs of repairs and insurance, etc).
(3) As an alternative to being assessed under Schedule B you could elect to be assessed under Schedule D Case I on the actual profits derived from your woodlands. The election had to extend to all of the woodlands that you owned on the same

estate. For this purpose, you could treat any area as being a separate estate, if you so elected within ten years of its being planted or replanted. An advantage of making the election was that any losses could then be available against your other income (10.22). Once you made the election you could not normally switch back to Schedule B.
(4) With the ending of Schedule B from 6 April 1988, the Schedule D election has been curtailed. Where already in force, Schedule D treatment broadly continues until 5 April 1993.
(5) The Schedule D election is only available after 15 March 1988 in certain circumstances. These include existing occupiers on that date; also those who had applied for forestry grants or contracted in writing to buy the land by that date. The election must now be made within two years after the chargeable period to which it relates. The 'separate estate' election must be made within two years of planting or replanting.

7.9 Dealing in property

Normally when you sell a property which you acquired as an investment you will be liable to capital gains tax on any profit that you make (18.1). The maximum tax rate would then be 40 per cent.

If, however, you carry out a number of purchases and sales of land and/or buildings you are likely to be treated as dealing in property and you will be taxed accordingly. This means that your profits must be computed as if you were conducting a trade (10.1) and you will be taxed on your adjusted profits under Schedule D Case I. This income will be treated as being earned and you will be charged to income tax at the lower, basic and higher rate where applicable.

7.10 Artificial transactions in land

This is the heading of Section 776 of the 1988 Taxes Act.

The Section may operate wherever you make a capital profit from selling land (or buildings) that you had purchased with a view to selling later at a profit. The Section also applies to sales of land indirectly held as trading stock and the sale of land (and buildings) that had been developed with the intention of selling them at a

Income from land and property 85

profit. However, it does not apply to trading profits from land already taxed as income.

Any capital profit arising in the above circumstances can be treated by the Revenue as being income falling under Schedule D Case VI on which you will be liable to pay income tax instead of capital gains tax. However, this has become less significant now that the top income tax and capital gains tax rates are both 40 per cent.

This Section does not apply to any purchase or sale by you of the house or flat in which you reside provided that it is your principal private residence (18.23).

If you believe that Section 776 might apply to any property sale that you have made or are planning, then you can apply for a clearance to the Inspector of Taxes to whom you submit your annual tax return. You should give the Inspector full written particulars of how the gain has arisen or how it will arise. He must then let you know within 30 days whether or not he is satisfied that your gain is outside the ambit of Section 776. If the Inspector does give you a clearance then provided your transaction proceeds exactly as you have described it to him, you will not be taxed under Section 776 in respect of your gain.

7.11 Agricultural land, etc
(TA 1988 S33)

Basically farmers are chargeable to income tax in the same way as persons who carry on a trade or business (10.1). Certain special rules apply, however (13.6).

If you own any sand or gravel quarries, any rents and royalties to which you are entitled will be payable to you under the deduction at the source of income tax at 25 per cent.

7.12 Land sold and leased back
(TA 1988 S780)

Special provisions may apply when you sell a lease with less than 50 years to run and take a fresh lease on the same premises. If you had been obtaining tax relief for your rent payments under the old lease and your new lease is for a term of less than 15 years, you will be charged to income tax on a proportion of the capital sum that you receive for your old lease.

The proportion is given by the formula $\frac{16-n}{15}$ where n is the term in years of your new lease. Thus if you have, say, a 40-year lease, which you sell for £15,000 and take back a ten-year lease you will be charged to income tax on £15,000 × $\frac{16-10}{15}$ = £6,000.

The balance of £15,000 − £6,000 = £9,000 will be treated as capital on which you may be liable to pay capital gains tax.

The income tax charge is raised under Schedule D Case VI unless the premises are used in your business, in which case your taxable trading profits are correspondingly increased.

The above rules are applicable to trusts and partnerships. They also apply to companies in which case the corporation tax charge (12.2, 12.2.1) may be adjusted.

There are certain rules for treating leases for longer periods than 15 years as being periods shorter than that time. This applies if you sell a lease and take a new one under which the rent for the earlier years of the lease is greater than that for the later years. For example, suppose you sell a 45-year lease for £30,000 and take back one for 20 years at £3,000 annual rent for the first ten years and £1,000 per annum for the remainder. Your new lease will then be treated as being for ten years and you will be charged to income tax on

$$£30,000 \times \frac{16-10}{15} = £12,000.$$

7.13 Development land tax
(DLTA 1976 etc)

For property sales after 31 July 1976 development land tax applied to certain realisations of development value. From 12 June 1979 to 18 March 1985, a single rate of 60 per cent applied with an annual exemption of £75,000 (£50,000 each year from 1 April 1979 to 31 March 1984). Development land tax was withdrawn from 19 March 1985. For full details reference should be made to Chapter 19 in the 1986–87 and earlier editions of this book.

7.14 'Rent a room'
(F2A 1992 Sch 10)

If you let a room in your house, valuable new relief may be available to you for 1992–93 and subsequent years. The relief applies if you are an owner occupier, or a tenant and let furnished accommodation in your only or main home.

The relief covers gross rents of up to £3,250 for any tax year. If the gross rent is higher, you have the option of paying tax on the excess over £3,250, without any relief for expenses, or according to the normal furnished lettings rules (7.5).

For example, suppose that you let a room in your house and your gross rent for 1992–93 is £4,250, with allowable expenses of £1,250. If you are a basic rate tax payer, on the conventional basis, your income tax (ignoring any other allowances) is £750 (£4,250–£1,250 × 25%. However, if you elect for the 'alternative basis', you only pay £250 (£4,250–£3,250) × 25 per cent.

You will need to elect for the 'alternative' basis to apply within one year of the end of the tax year to which it applies. After that, it remains in force until you withdraw it. Note that whilst the election is in force, no capital allowances are available, losses from previous years are carried forward to subsequent ones and balancing charges are added to your gross rental income.

8 Income from dividends and interest

8.1 How dividends are taxed
(TA 1988 S20)

Any dividend paid to you by a United Kingdom company does not have tax deducted. The amount paid to you carries with it a tax credit of currently 25/75ths (12.6). Special rules may apply to any shareholders who live abroad (17.1.5).

United Kingdom companies in turn pay to the Revenue advance corporation tax of currently 25/75ths of the dividends paid. The following are examples of payments by companies to their shareholders (distributions) that are treated in this way:

(1) Dividends on ordinary shares.
(2) Dividends on shares with special rights such as preference and deferred shares.
(3) Capital distributions made in cash, such as dividends, paid out of the capital profits of a company.
(4) Scrip dividend options (8.9).

The gross amounts of your dividends including tax credits (and taxed interest) receivable in the tax year are included with your investment income for total income purposes (5.2).

8.1.1 Dividends, etc and your return

You must enter the amounts of your dividends in your income tax return (14.1). You show, in the separate section provided, details of your dividends from each of your shareholdings with a full description of each holding, as well as the actual payments and relevant tax credits. If there is no room on the form, you should prepare a separate list and submit it with your return.

As well as dividends, etc from companies, you must include in this section of your return the gross amounts of any payments due to

Income from dividends and interest 89

you for taxed interest on government securities, trust income, and the income proportion of annuities, etc. All of these will have been taxed by deduction at the source before you receive them. Also include in this section any loan interest that has been taxed before you receive it and all unit trust dividends including those converted into new units instead of being paid direct to you.

8.1.2 Income tax deduction vouchers

Dividend vouchers show the actual dividend payment made to you together with the tax credit. The vouchers certify that advance corporation tax of an amount equal to the tax credit will be accounted for to the Collector of Taxes. They may be sent to you even though the dividends are credited to your bank account (F2A 1992 S32).

Different certificates are provided for interest payments under deduction of basic rate income tax. These show the gross interest and the basic rate tax which is certified to have been deducted on the payment of the net interest to you. In the case of income distributions from trusts, tax deduction certificates are provided by the trustees (form R185E). All of these tax deduction certificates are accepted by the Revenue in connection with income tax repayment claims (14.6).

8.1.3 Dividends from overseas companies

Any dividends that you receive from overseas companies are normally net of both overseas tax deducted at source and United Kingdom basic rate income tax. The United Kingdom income tax is sometimes at a lower rate than 25 per cent. This is because you have been given some measure of relief from double taxation by the paying agents and collecting agents who are concerned with transmitting to you your overseas dividends. (For a fuller treatment of double tax relief see 16.6.)

You should enter on your tax return the gross amounts of your overseas dividends and also show the amounts of foreign and UK tax deducted at source.

The gross amounts of your overseas dividends are included in your total income (5.2) but you may get some double tax relief in respect of the overseas taxes against your tax liability.

8.2 Interest paid on government securities, etc
(TA 1988 Ss17 & 44–52)

The normal basis of charge to income tax is by deduction at source under Schedule C. This applies to interest payable on certain 'gilt edged securities' of the United Kingdom and overseas governments where the interest is paid here. The tax is assessed on the Bank of England or other paying authority concerned who deduct it from the interest paid to you resulting in your receiving only the net amount. The gross amounts, however, must be entered in your income tax return. No tax deduction is required where paying agents pay foreign dividends into recognised clearing systems.

Certain UK government securities may be held for you on the National Savings Stock Register or Trustee Savings Bank Register in which case the interest will be paid to you gross without any tax deduction. Interest is also paid gross on $3\frac{1}{2}$ per cent War Loan and on holdings of UK government securities which produce less than £2.50 gross interest for you half-yearly. Income tax will then be assessed under Case III of Schedule D (8.4).

Provided that a claim is made to the Revenue on behalf of the individual concerned, the interest on certain specified United Kingdom government securities will be paid gross to any owner who is not ordinarily resident in this country (15.3.1).

8.2.1 Table: UK securities on which interest may be paid gross to non-residents

$2\frac{1}{2}\%$	Treasury Loan, 2024	9%	Treasury Loan, 2008
$3\frac{1}{2}\%$	War Stock 1952 or after	9%	Convertible Loan, 2011
$5\frac{1}{2}\%$	Treasury Stock, 2008–12	$9\frac{1}{2}\%$	Treasury Loan, 1999
6%	Funding Loan, 1993	10%	Treasury Loan, 1994
$6\frac{3}{4}\%$	Treasury Loan, 1995–98	10%	Treasury Loan, 1993
$7\frac{3}{4}\%$	Treasury Loan, 2012–15	$12\frac{1}{4}\%$	Treasury Loan, 1993
8%	Treasury Loan, 2002–06	$12\frac{3}{4}\%$	Treasury Loan, 1995
$8\frac{1}{2}\%$	Treasury Loan, 2000	$13\frac{1}{4}\%$	Treasury Loan, 1997
$8\frac{1}{2}\%$	Treasury Loan, 2007	$13\frac{1}{4}\%$	Exchequer Loan, 1996
$8\frac{3}{4}\%$	Treasury Loan, 1997	$13\frac{3}{4}\%$	Treasury Loan, 1993
9%	Treasury Loan, 1994	$14\frac{1}{2}\%$	Treasury Loan, 1994
9%	Treasury Loan, 1992–96	$15\frac{1}{4}\%$	Treasury Loan, 1996
9%	Conversion Stock, 2000	$15\frac{1}{2}\%$	Treasury Loan, 1998

8.3 Bond washing — Accrued income
(TA 1988 Ss710–728 & FA 1991 Sch 12)

(1) Rules have been introduced to prevent tax saving by selling *securities* with accrued interest and thereby receiving extra capital instead of income. Previously, this would have at most only borne capital gains tax.

Income from dividends and interest 91

(2) The accrued income scheme covers transfers after 27 February 1986. In addition, anti-avoidance rules cover the previous year.
(3) *Securities* excludes shares in a company but covers loan stocks, etc whether issued by the UK or other governments or companies. Thus 'Gilts' are included and 'Corporate Bonds' (18.19). National Savings Certificates and War Savings Certificates are excluded, as are certain securities redeemable at a premium. Certificates of Deposit are also excluded but profits on disposal are assessable under Case VI (13.1).
(4) If after 27 February 1986, you transfer *securities* with accrued interest, so that the purchaser receives the next interest payment, you are taxed under Schedule 'D', Case VI (13.1) on a portion of that interest. The proportion is A/B. 'B' is the total days in the period for which the interest is paid and 'A' is the part of the period during which you held the *securities*.
(5) When the purchaser receives his first interest payment, his taxable amount is reduced by the proportion A/B.
(6) If you transfer *securities* but receive the next interest payment, your taxable amount is reduced by the proportion $(B - A)/B$. The purchaser is taxed on the same proportion, which actually corresponds to his ownership.
(7) For the *year to 27 February 1986,* a modified charge could be made. Details are given in previous editions of this book.
(8) The above rules do not apply if you trade in securities, nor if you are neither UK resident nor ordinarily resident (15.3.1). You are also excluded if the nominal value of your *securities* does not exceed £5,000 at any time in the year of assessment or previous year. A similar rule applies to the estates of deceased persons and trusts for the disabled.
(9) If you sell foreign securities but are not permitted to have the proceeds remitted to you, your tax charge is delayed until they can be sent.
(10) Transactions taxed under these rules are normally excluded from other anti-avoidance provisions.
(11) New rules apply to the issue of securities in tranches after 18 March 1991. Accrued interest included in the issue price qualifies for relief and tax relief for the interest deemed to be paid by the issuer is restricted to the amount taxable in the hands of the subscriber.

8.4 Interest not taxed at source (Schedule D Case III)
(TA 1988 S18)

Subject to the deduction of tax at source (8.6 and 8.7), tax is charged under Schedule D Case III on the following:

(1) Any interest whether receivable yearly or otherwise.
(2) Any annuity or other annual payment received without the deduction of tax.
(3) Discounts.
(4) Income from securities payable out of the public revenue unless already charged under Schedule C (8.2).
(5) Small maintenance payments up to 5 April 1989 (6.8.4).
(6) Various kinds of investment income as specifically directed.
(7) The discount portion of the proceeds of 'deep discount securities' (8.8).

8.4.1 Table: Examples of Schedule D Case III income

> Bank deposit interest generally up to 5 April 1985. (Composite rate rules then applied up to 5 April 1991 — 8.7).
> Discount on treasury bills.
> Interest on $3\frac{1}{2}$% War Loan.
> National or Trustee Savings Bank interest apart from the £70 tax free portion from National Savings Bank Ordinary Deposits (2.6.1).
>
> Income received gross on government securities (8.2):
>
> (*a*) held on post office register.
> (*b*) amount under £2.50 half-yearly.
>
> Gross payment of share and loan interest by a registered industrial and provident society.

8.5 Basis of charge under Schedule D Case III
(TA 1988 S64)

You will normally be assessed to income tax on your Case III income arising during the previous tax year. Special rules must be followed for fresh income and sources that have come to an end (see below). No deductions are allowed in computing the assessable income.

A company is assessed to corporation tax on its actual Case III income for each of its accounting periods (12.6.2).

Income from dividends and interest 93

Your income is normally included when it is due to be paid to you whether or not it is actually paid. For example, if Case III interest is payable for each year ended 31 December, your assessment for 1992–93 would normally be based on the income for the year to 31 December 1991.

8.5.1 Special rules for fresh income
(TA 1988 S66)

If you acquire a new source of Case III income your assessments will be as follows:

(1) For the tax year when the income first arises you are assessed on the income actually arising in that year.
(2) Where the income first arose on 6 April in the preceding tax year your assessment for the second year will be based on the income of the first tax year (subject to (5) below).
(3) Where the income first arose on any day other than 6 April in the preceding tax year your assessment for the second tax year will be based on the income actually arising in that year.
(4) Your assessment for the third tax year will be based on the income arising in the previous tax year (subject to (5) below).
(5) You have the right to elect that your first assessment to be made on the basis of the income for the previous tax year, should be adjusted to the actual income arising in the year of assessment. This would normally apply to the third year of assessment except in (2) above. The election should be made to your Inspector of Taxes within six years of the end of the year of assessment concerned.

8.5.2 Example: Fresh Schedule D Case III income

Mr A opened a National Savings Investment Account on 31 May 1987 when he deposited £1,000. He has varied the amounts in the account since that time but has not yet closed the account. He has obtained interest on his account as follows:

December 1987	£18
1988	50
1989	33
1990	52
1991	60

What are his Schedule D Case III assessments based on the above income?

Mr A – Assessments under Schedule D Case III
1987–88: Actual income arising in year to 5 April 1988   £18

1988–89:	Actual income arising in year to 5 April 1989 (source not held at 6 April 1987)	£50
1989–90: (a)	Normal basis – income arising in preceding tax year, ie year to 5 April 1989	£50
(b)	Optional basis – Actual income in year to 5 April 1990	£33

(Mr A should elect for (b) and his 1989–90 assessment will be the lower amount of £33.)

1990–91:	Preceding year, ie, to 5 April 1990	£33
1991–92:	Preceding year	£52
1992–93:	Preceding year	£60

8.5.3 Special rules where source of income ceases
(TA 1988 S67)

(1) If a source of Case III income ceases during a tax year you will be assessed for that year on the actual income arising from 6 April in that tax year until the closure or disposal of the source.

(2) Your assessment under Schedule D Case III for the tax year preceding that in which the source ceases will be adjusted if the actual income for that year is greater than the assessment already made.

(3) Any adjustment required for the preceding year (see (2)) will be separately assessed on you.

(4) Strictly speaking the cessation rules should be applied to each source but in practice the Revenue did not apply them to the closure of one bank deposit account if you had others that continue.

(5) Special rules applied to bank deposit accounts held at 5 April 1985 (8.7). The source was treated as ceasing so that your 1984–85 assessment was on 'actual' but no adjustment was made for 1983–84.

8.5.4 Example: Cessation of Schedule D Case III source

Mr C, who has held money in a National Savings Investment Account, closed this on 15 January 1992. He received interest as follows:

December 1989	£100
December 1990	£130
December 1991	£150
15 January 1992	£20

What were Mr C's Schedule D Case III assessments on his income?

1990–91: (1) Preceding year, ie, to 5 April 1990 — £100

(2) Actual income arising in year to 5 April 1991 — £130

1991–92: Actual income from 6 April 1991 to 5 April 1992 (£150 + £20) — £170

Note: For 1990–91 Mr C's assessment was first £100, based on the income for the previous tax year. However, on learning of the cessation, the Revenue would normally increase the total 1990–91 assessment to the actual interest received by raising an additional assessment of £130 − £100 = £30.

8.6 Building society interest
(TA 1988 Ss476–8 & 483, FA 1990 S30 & Sch 5 & FA 1991 Ss51–53 & Schs 10 & 11)

Building society interest is normally paid to you less the deduction of basic rate (25 per cent) income tax at source. The system is similar to that which applies for bank interest (8.7). If your income is sufficiently low (8.7) you can request that the interest is paid to you gross.

Any building society interest which you received prior to 6 April 1991 was free of basic rate tax (2.7). You were charged to higher rate tax on the grossed up equivalent as if you had suffered basic rate income tax at 25 per cent on your interest (5.2). This notional 25 per cent basic rate tax was, however, deducted from your tax bill. The reason that building societies were empowered to pay interest to you in this way was that they were assessed to a special composite tax rate on their own profits. By means of this arrangement the Revenue were able to make good the basic rate income tax not charged on the interest (13.7). The composite rate arrangement for building societies and banks (8.7) was abolished as from 6 April 1991. Basic rate income tax is now deducted from the interest, subject to a self-certification arrangement, if you are not liable to tax (8.7).

As an exception, certain certificates of deposit for at least £50,000 issued by building societies after 5 April 1983 carry gross interest. Interest payable after 30 September 1984 on 'qualifying time deposits' (broadly time deposits for at least £50,000 and for less than a year) is paid gross. From 6 April 1986, building societies are able to pay interest gross to non-resident individuals and quoted Eurobond holders; also to charities and registered Friendly Societies.

Certain changes have been introduced in the 1991 Finance Act (13.7). These include provisions dealing with interest paid to investors during the transitional period up to 1986; tax is to be paid by the building societies at 1985–86 rates. Also, rules are introduced to deal with permanent interest bearing shares (PIBS). You will be taxed as if they are 'debt' rather than 'equity'. Thus basic rate income tax will be deducted from your interest. No capital gains tax will arise but the bond washing and accrued income scheme (8.3) will apply.

8.7 Bank interest
(TA 1988 Ss479–485 & FA 1990 S30 & Sch 5)

From 6 April 1991, bank deposit interest is normally paid subject to the deduction of 25 per cent basic rate income tax at source. In contrast to the previous composite rate scheme (below), where appropriate, you are able to reclaim the tax. If your income is sufficiently large, higher rate tax will apply, any assessments being on an actual basis.

There are arrangements under which if you are not liable to tax you may receive the interest gross. You need to complete a certificate enabling each financial institution to pay you gross. You must certify that to the best of your knowledge, you do not expect to be liable to tax and the information which you have given in the form is correct. If you knowingly make a false declaration, you may be subject to penalties. This also applies where you deliberately fail to inform your bank or building society that you have become liable to tax.

From 6 April 1985 until 5 April 1991, the same composite rate as for building societies applied to interest paid by banks and certain other financial institutions. Foreign currency deposits were only included from 6 April 1986, from which date local authority deposits were also within the scheme.

Individuals receiving interest were treated as having suffered basic rate tax, giving rise to a notional tax credit as with building society interest (above).

The institutions covered included recognised banks and licensed deposit takers, the National Giro Bank and Trustee Savings Bank but not National Savings Accounts. The scheme covered individual depositors if ordinarily resident (15.3.1) in the UK, but not companies, charities, pension funds, societies, clubs, associations, churches, etc.

If you were not ordinarily resident in the UK (15.3.1), you could be excluded from the tax deduction and composite rate arrangements, so that deposit interest was paid to you gross. However, you needed to supply the bank, etc with a declaration regarding your residence status and that you would tell them if this changed. Note also that under Extra Statutory Concession B13, if you are not resident in the UK and receive bank interest, etc without the deduction of income tax, in certain circumstances, the Inland Revenue will take no steps to pursue your liability to income tax.

Exclusions from the composite rate included debentures, loans by a deposit taker in the course of business, certain quoted loan stocks, also 'qualifying certificates of deposit' and 'qualifying time deposits', both of which needed to exceed £50,000 when issued and had a life of at least seven days. The income on such deposits is normally payable gross, even if now in 'paperless' form (F2A 1992 Sch 8). Lloyd's premium trust funds and solicitors' and estate agents' undesignated client accounts were also excluded.

8.8 Deep discount and deep gain securities
(TA 1988 Sch 4, FA 1989 Ss93–96 & Schs 10 & 11, FA 1990 Ss56–59 & Sch 10 & FA 1991 Sch 12)

Special rules apply to deep discount securities issued after 13 March 1984. These are securities issued at a discount of more than half of one per cent for each year of their life or more than 15 per cent overall. Effectively the discount is treated as income accruing over the life of the security and when you dispose of your investment, you are normally taxed on the accruals under Schedule D Case III. (Your capital gain (18.1) is correspondingly reduced.)

Exceptionally, you are taxed on the 'income element' arising on certain securities issued after 19 March 1985 from 'coupon stripping operations'. These are where a company acquires securities and issues its own related stocks — normally deep discounted with varying maturity dates.

The company issuing the security gets *annual* relief for the accruing discount. The new rules do not apply to certain securities exchanged for others issued before that date, not of the deep discount type, provided the new redemption date and price do not exceed the original ones.

For disposals after 13 March 1989, the deep discount rules apply to a wider range of investments. Certain variable deep discount securities are now included, but not index-linked bonds satisfying various conditions. These conditions include a limit on capital profits on redemption equal to the rise in the retail price index. Also, the interest rate must be reasonable and commercial; payments being at least annual. The securities must be issued for a period of at least five years.

A security issued after 31 July 1990 is not a 'deep discount security' if under the terms of issue there is more than one date when the holder can require it to be redeemed. Where securities are issued in tranches after 18 March 1991, any accrued interest included in the issue price is excluded from the price used to compute the 'deep discount' or 'deep gain'.

'Deep gain securities' issued after 13 March 1989 are treated in a similar way to deep discount securities. A 'deep gain' means that the redemption price exceeds the issue price by more than 15 per cent or half of one per cent for each completed year. Certain changes take effect from 9 June 1989. For example a security is not to be classed as a 'deep gain security' solely because it may be redeemed early if the issuer fails to comply with the issue terms, is taken over or is unable to pay its debts. Also with effect from that date, 'qualifying convertible securities' are excluded. These are, in general, bonds issued from 9 June 1989 which are convertible into ordinary shares of the issuing company and give the investor an option to 'put' the bond back to the issuer. Bonds issued from 12 November 1991 will not be caught simply through the potential operation of default or event risk clauses (F2A 1992 Sch 7).

8.9 Scrip dividend options
(TA 1988 Ss249–251)

Your taxable dividend income (8.1) includes any shares in UK resident companies (15.3.3) which you obtain by exercising an option to take a dividend in such a form. In this case, you are treated for tax purposes as if you had received the dividend in cash. If, however, the cash equivalent is substantially less than the market value of the shares, on the day when market dealings commence, the Revenue may substitute that market value for the cash value.

8.10 Personal Equity Plan
(TA 1988 S333 & FA 1991 S70)

A scheme to encourage the purchase of shares in UK incorporated companies commenced on 1 January 1987. It is called the Personal Equity Plan (PEP). Substantial changes apply from 6 April 1989, including changing the basis to the fiscal, rather than calendar year.

(1) Provided you are aged over 18, resident and ordinarily resident in the UK (15.3.1) you are eligible.

(2) A maximum of £6,000 can be invested each year from 6 April 1990 (£500 each month if preferred). In addition, from 1 January 1992, you are able to invest £3,000 in a 'single-company PEP' each tax year starting with 1991–92. (Such a PEP is one which invests in the shares of only one company.)

(3) For tax relief, investments needed to be held for at least one complete calendar year from 1 January to 31 December. However, from 6 April 1989 there is no minimum holding period.

(4) The funds must be substantially invested in the ordinary shares of public companies quoted on a UK (or EC) stock exchange or dealt in on the Unlisted Securities Market. However, a unit trust and investment trust element is allowed. From 6 April 1992, the limit is £6,000 and, from 6 April 1990, was £3,000.

(5) From 6 April 1990, the unit or investment trusts themselves must invest at least 50 per cent in UK equities, subject to certain relaxations. For example, unquoted shares and third market shares in UK companies may be included. Also, for schemes existing before 14 March 1989, there is an option to use a limit of £900 from 6 April 1990 and now £1,500, without the 50 per cent rule. From 6 April 1992 the limit of £1,500 applies to all non-qualifying investment trusts, whether established or new. Re-invested dividend income does not count towards the limit.

(6) From 1 January 1992, the requirement that PEPs must invest in UK equities is extended to include those quoted on a recognised stock exchange of any EC member state. A similar extension will apply to the 50 per cent rule for unit trusts.

(7) A manager must look after your PEP investments but they will belong to you and you are able to choose which you buy.

(8) Re-investment of dividends and proceeds is allowed in excess of the limits.

(9) Prior to 6 April 1989, for the year that a plan is started, up to the entire investment limit could be left in cash. After the

first year, broadly 10 per cent could be held in cash. After 5 April 1989, there is no limit on the amount of cash that can be held. However all interest on the cash was subject to tax up to 5 April 1991, but not thereafter, provided the cash is eventually invested in shares, etc.
(10) From 6 April 1989, you are allowed to buy shares through new issue offers and transfer all or part of your allocation into a PEP. This includes privatisation issues and also issues of shares in building societies converting to plc status. This must now be done within six weeks from the day the share allocation is announced and the value at the offer price goes towards your total PEP entitlement for the year.
(11) Subject to the above, re-invested dividends are free of income tax. (Also, tax can be recovered on dividends distributed.) Similarly re-invested capital profits are not subjected to capital gains tax.
(12) Subject to the overall £3,000 limit (see (2) above), employees are able to transfer shares acquired under employee share schemes into 'single-company PEPs'. This applies to savings related share option schemes (9.9.3) and profit sharing schemes (9.9.6). You must transfer the shares within six weeks of getting them from the scheme and no capital gains tax will be charged.

8.11 Tax exempt special savings accounts (TESSAs)
(FA 1990 S28)

(1) You are able to invest in one TESSA only and the accounts have been available from 1 January 1991.
(2) Only individuals aged at least 18 are eligible.
(3) Your TESSA may be with a bank or a building society.
(4) The account must run for a five year period and maximum total deposits of £9,000 are allowed. Of this, up to £3,000 may be invested in the first year and no more than £1,800 in subsequent years, up to the £9,000 maximum.
(5) No capital must be withdrawn before the 5 year period expires, otherwise all tax advantages are lost.
(6) Income may be withdrawn subject to a notional basic rate deduction (25 per cent). Thus if there is £400 of gross income in your TESSA for the year, you will be allowed to withdraw £300.

9 Income from employments and PAYE

Your income from employments or from any office that you hold is normally taxed under Schedule E. From 6 April 1989, a receipts basis broadly applies (9.13). Schedule E is divided into *three cases* as follows (TA 1988 S19 & FA 1989 S34):

9.1 Schedule E Case I

This applies if you are both resident and ordinarily resident (15.3.1) in the UK. Your income tax assessment under this case is usually based on the actual UK income during the tax year.

This case also applies to any work which you do wholly abroad (unless you work for a non-resident employer and are yourself not UK domiciled). If you are absent from this country for a continuous period of 365 days or more, you are not charged to UK tax on your overseas earnings during that period (16.5). (You are allowed to spend up to 1/6th of your time in the UK without losing this relief.)

For 1989–90 and subsequent tax years, tax is due on all earnings, even when the employment is not held at the time they are received. This also applies for Cases II and III (below).

9.2 Schedule E Case II

This applies if you are either not resident in the UK or are resident but not ordinarily resident here. Then you will normally be assessed to tax under this case on your earnings for duties performed here.

9.3 Schedule E Case III

This applies if you are UK resident and do work wholly abroad but remit salary here during the course of your overseas employment. The assessment is based on the actual amounts remitted to this country in the tax year (16.1) but if one of the other cases (see above) applies to the income, then Case III does not operate. This case now normally only applies to non-UK domiciled people.

9.4 The distinction between Schedule D Case I or II and Schedule E

This distinction is sometimes very fine—for instance in the case where you have a number of part-time employments and do some of the work at home. If you can show that you are in fact working on your own account and are self-employed (not an employee) then you will be assessed under Schedule D which normally results in your being able to deduct more of your expenses from your taxable income than if you were assessed under Schedule E. Divers and diving instructors are normally assessable under Schedule D (TA 1988 S314). The Inland Revenue are becoming increasingly insistent that entertainers and journalists should be assessed under Schedule E. When this happens, agents' fees will still be allowable as expenses (FA 1990 S77). These include fees to co-operative agencies (FA 1991 S69).

9.5 Employment outside the UK

If your UK employment involves you in work abroad this is normally treated as being derived from your employment in this country and is included in your taxable income. However, in respect of any work that you do abroad, special rules apply which may result in your paying less tax (16.3).

9.6 Amounts included in your income

Any amount that you derive from your office or employment is normally included in your taxable income. This applies to the value of any payments in kind as well as cash.

9.6.1 Typical items

Normal salary or wage.
Overtime pay.
Salary in lieu of notice (often tax free — see 9.12).
Holiday pay.
Sick pay from your employer, including statutory sick pay.
Sickness insurance benefits paid to you (all sickness benefits are taxable immediately except to the extent that you have paid for these yourself).
The value of luncheon vouchers in excess of 15 pence per day.
Cost-of-living allowance.
Christmas or other gifts in cash excluding personal gifts such as wedding presents.
Annual or occasional bonus.
Commission.
Director's fees.
Director's other remuneration.
Remuneration for any part-time employment.
Salary paid in advance.
Payment for entering into a contract of employment.
Tips from employer or from customers or clients of employer.
Settlement by employer of debts incurred by employee.
Payment by employer of employee's National Insurance contributions.
Value of goods supplied free of cost to employee by employer.
Value of shares or other assets received from employer for no charge, or amount by which their market value exceeds any payment made for them.
Fringe benefits (see below).
Unapproved pension scheme contributions.
Travelling allowances in excess of expenditure incurred for business use (9.6.4).
Share options (9.9.2).
Job release allowances capable of beginning earlier than a year before pensionable age.
Maternity pay.
Payments under *restrictive covenants* including (after 9 June 1988) where separate from the contract of employment (FA 1988 S73).

9.6.2 Fringe benefits
(TA 1988 Ss135–147, 153–168 & Schs 6–10 etc, FA 1989 Ss46–50, FA 1990 Ss21–22 & FA 1991 Ss29–31)

This is a wide term used to describe any tangible benefit which you obtain from your employment that is not actually included in your salary cheque. Fringe benefits are taxable according to the rules outlined below.

If you are an employee earning less than £8,500 each year, including the value of any benefits, then the taxation of your fringe benefits is on a comparatively favourable basis. If, however, you earn over £8,500 or are a director, then you are normally taxed more strictly on the actual value of the benefits obtained. If you fall into this latter class then your employers must submit to the Revenue a form P11D for you every year. This form covers your expenses and benefits (9.7).

You are not caught by the rules as being a *director*, if you own no more than 5 per cent of the company's shares and work full time for it. Any shares owned by relatives and associates count towards your 5 per cent. (In the case of charities, etc you do not need to work full time.) If you work for several companies which are connected, your earnings including benefits must be taken together for the purposes of the rules.

The taxation of certain fringe benefits is summarised in the following table according to whether or not you are a P11D employee (ie, a director or earning over £8,500).

9.6.3 Table: Fringe benefits — Taxation 1992–93

	Details	*Non-P11D employee*	*P11D employee or director*
(1)	Free private use of motor vehicle supplied by your employers. Car mileage allowance.	Tax free (provided some business use is made).	Taxable (9.6.5).
(2)	Company house occupied rent free.	Taxed on annual value of benefit (ie, open market rental and expenses paid) unless you need to occupy house to do your job properly.	Taxed on annual value unless you must live there to perform your duties (9.6.12).
(3)	Board and lodging.	If you receive cash you are taxed on it. Otherwise tax free.	Taxed on cost to employer of board and lodging subject to a limit (9.6.12).

Income from employments and PAYE

(4)	Working clothing, eg, overalls.	Tax free.	Tax free.
(5)	Suits and coats, etc.	Taxed on estimated second-hand value.	Taxed on full cost to employer.
(6)	Private sickness insurance cover.	Tax free.	Taxed on premiums paid by your employer (9.6.10).
(7)	Interest-free loan.	Tax free.	Taxable subject to certain exemptions (9.6.8) — to participator, etc of close company (12.17.3) — employee shareholdings (9.9.5).
(8)	Share options.	Taxable (9.9).	Taxable (9.9).
(9)	Employee's outings.	Tax free.	Normally tax free.
(10)	Luncheon vouchers.	Tax free up to 15p per day — excess taxable.	Tax free up to 15p per day — excess taxable.
(11)	Subsidised staff canteen.	Tax free.	Tax free provided facilities available to all staff.
(12)	Pension and death in service cover.	Normally tax free (9.11).	Normally tax free (9.11).
(13)	Cash vouchers.	Taxable (9.6.11).	Taxable (9.6.11).
(14)	Season tickets and credit cards.	Generally taxable (9.6.11).	Generally taxable (9.6.11).
(15)	Assets at employee's disposal.	Normally tax free.	Taxable (9.6.7).
(16)	Scholarships from employer for children of employee.	Normally tax free.	Taxable with some exceptions (9.6.13).
(17)	Long service awards of articles or employer company shares; after 20 years' service; maximum £20 for each year.	Tax free.	Tax free.
(18)	Security assets and services provided after 5 April 1989 (9.6.7).	Tax free.	Tax free.

(19) Childcare.	Tax free.	Tax free subject to conditions (9.6.14).
(20) Mobile telephones, if privately used.	Tax free.	Tax on £200 per year (9.6.15).

9.6.4 Travelling and entertainment allowances
(TA 1988 S198 & FA 1988 Ss47–49 & 72)

An allowance or advance that you derive from your employer to meet the costs of travelling, entertaining or other services you perform on his behalf is not taxable provided that you actually incur expenditure for these purposes. (Your employer is able to deduct the payments from his taxable profits. Entertaining expenses, however, are not normally deductible, unless in connection with overseas customers and their agents before 15 March 1988 (10.3.1).) Should you incur expenditure of less than the full allowance or advance and are not required to pay back the unexpended portion to your employer, this excess must be included in your taxable income.

If you are a P11D employee (9.6.2) any allowance made to you by your employers for travelling, etc is normally included in your taxable income in full. If you incur travelling expenses, etc in the course of your employment you must make a claim to that effect and you will be allowed to deduct from your taxable income the amount of your expenses. If you are not a P11D employee (or director) any expense allowances or payments on your behalf are not normally included in your taxable income.

You are not in general allowed any deduction for your travelling expenses between your home and your employer's place of business. Thus if your employer makes you any allowance for this expense it is wholly taxable in your hands.

No tax is payable on travel facilities provided for *servicemen* and *servicewomen* going on and returning from *leave* (TA 1988 S197).

If you *travel abroad* in connection with your employer's business, the cost is allowable. If you also have a holiday abroad during the same trip you will be taxed on an appropriate proportion of the cost of your trip as a personal benefit. If your employers pay for your wife to accompany you (and she is not an employee herself) her own trip would normally be taxed as a personal benefit although some allowance could be obtained if, for example, she acted as your secretary during the trip or it was necessary for her to go for reasons of your health.

No benefit is assessed on you if your employer pays for the actual journeys of your family in visiting you, provided you *work abroad* for at least 60 continuous days. This applies to your wife (or husband) and any of your children who are under 18 on the outward journey. Also covered are journeys by your family in accompanying you at the beginning of your overseas period or by you in visiting them at the end. Two return trips for each are covered by the rule, in any tax year (TA 1988 Ss193–5).

Any travel expenses paid by your employer covering journeys to and from the UK will be tax free where you are UK resident and working abroad.

Members of Parliament are allowed no deduction for expenditure incurred to cover staying away from home in London or the constituency. However, the Additional Costs Allowance paid to meet these expenses is not taxable (TA 1988 S200).

From 6 April 1987, certain payments by employers to their employees for travel between work and home are tax-free. Exemption is given by an Inland Revenue concession which covers working until at least 9 pm on no more than 60 occasions in a tax year. Furthermore, there must be no regular pattern. Subject to these points, the cost of a taxi or hired car will not give rise to tax on the employee.

Another concession operating from 6 April 1987 concerns gifts from third parties (ie, not the employer). These are tax-free in an employee's hands providing the cost is no more than £100 in the tax year from any one source. A similar exemption from 6 April 1988 was brought in (FA 1988 Ss47–49) regarding entertainment provided by third parties. Credit tokens and non-cash vouchers are included. There is no limit but the person providing the benefit must not be the employer or anyone connected with him, nor must it be provided in recognition of particular services regarding the employment.

9.6.5 Motor cars
(TA 1988 Ss157–159 & Sch 6, FA 1990 S22, FA 1991 Ss29 & 30 & F2A 1992 S53)

The following rules apply to you if yours is a director's or *higher paid* employment (9.6.2):

108 *Allied Dunbar Tax Guide*

(1) If your employment carries a car but your business use is 'insubstantial', you are assessed on 150 per cent of the scale benefit appropriate to your car (see (2) below). This similarly applies to second cars. 'Insubstantial' is defined as no more than 2,500 miles each year.

(2) If you make *more substantial* business use of your company car, you will be taxed on a benefit figure derived from a scale. The scale is to cover both the capital value and all running costs of your company car. If you are reimbursed for any money which you lay out, you are assessed on the amount and must make an expenses claim for business use. If your business mileage reaches 18,000 for a year your scale benefit is halved.

(3) Provided you do not have the use of a particular car but simply take one from a car pool and do not garage it at home overnight, you will not normally be assessed to any benefit; subject, however, to the further condition that any private use of the car is merely incidental to your business use thereof.

(4) From 1983–84 the provision of petrol for a higher paid employee is taxed by applying an additional scale charge. This only applies if your employer bears any of the cost. If your scale benefit is halved because your business mileage reaches 18,000 (see (2) above), your fuel benefit is also halved.

(5) For 1991–92 and 1992–93 the car scale and fuel benefits are as follows:

Cylinder capacity– original market value (if no cylinder capacity)	Scale benefits assessed Cars under 4 years old		Cars over 4 years old		Fuel Benefit (see (6) below)	
	1991–92	1992–93	1991–92	1992–93	1991–92	1992–93 (Petrol)
1400cc or less (under £6,000)	£2,050	£2,140	£1,400	£1,460	£480	£500
1401cc–2000cc (£6,000–£8,499)	2,650	2,770	1,800	1,880	600	630
Over 2000cc (£8,500–£19,250)	4,250	4,440	2,850	2,980	900	940
£19,251–£29,000	5,500	5,750	3,700	3,870	900*	940
Over £29,000	8,900	9,300	5,900	6,170	900*	940

*provided over 2,000cc

(6) From 6 April 1992, a more favourable car scale applies for diesel vehicles. The scale for 1992–93 is:

Engine size	Scale charge
0–2000cc	£460
2001cc +	590

(7) From 6 April 1988, the provision of *car parking facilities* near to the place of work is not being assessed on an employee as a benefit. Furthermore, any open cases for earlier years are not being pursued by the Inland Revenue, although no repayment will be made of tax already paid.

(8) Special rules apply if you own your car but are paid a mileage allowance (9.6.6).

(9) From 6 April 1991, private use of car telephones is taxed based on a standard £200 annual assessable amount. However, this does not apply if you are required to make good to your employers the full cost of your private use, and do so.

9.6.6 Car mileage allowances
(FA 1990 Ss23 & 87 & Sch 4)

(1) You are entitled to relief for travelling expenses concerning your employment. Mileage allowances paid to you where you use your own car for work are taxable to the extent that they exceed your allowable expenses, including capital allowances (10.9.10).

(2) To reduce the administrative work involved there is the *fixed profit car scheme* (FPCS). Under this, your taxable mileage 'profit' may be calculated using the excess of the mileage rate paid to you over the appropriate FPCS 'tax free' rate. These rates are as follows for 1991–92 and 1992–93:

	Cars up to 1000cc		Cars 1001–1500cc		Cars 1501–2000cc		Cars over 2000cc	
	92–93	91–92	92–93	91–92	92–93	91–92	92–93	91–92
Up to 4,000 miles	25p	24.5p	30p	30p	38p	34p	51p	45p
Over 4,000 miles	14p	11p	17p	13p	21p	16p	27p	20.5p

(3) Capital allowances are available to you if you use your car for work. The allowances are based on the proportion relating to business use. (However travelling to and from work is naturally excluded.) Wider relief is available from 1990–91 since, previously, it was necessary to show that you had no alternative but to use the car in performing your duties. Depreciation is included in the FPCS 'tax free' rates and so if that system applies, you receive no capital allowances.

(4) If you borrow money to buy a car to use for work, interest relief is available on a more general basis since 6 April 1990.

9.6.7 Use of assets
(TA 1988 S156 & FA 1989 Ss50–52)

If your employer places an asset at your disposal for your personal use (eg, a television set) your annual taxable benefit is 20 per cent of its market value when you first began to use it. (For assets placed at your disposal prior to 6 April 1980, the benefit is 10 per cent.) This rule does not apply to cars (see above) nor to land for which 'annual value' is used (S531) and only relates to those in director's or *higher paid* employment (9.6.2).

For assets provided after 5 April 1980 by your employer, a special rule applies if you subsequently become the owner. You will then have a taxable benefit of the excess over what you pay for the asset, of the original market value less the previous annual benefit assessments. This is increased if greater, to the excess of market value over price paid when you obtain the asset from your employers.

From 6 April 1989, employees (and self-employed people) who face a special threat to their *personal physical security* obtain special relief. However, the threat must arise directly out of their particular job or business. The relief extends to services and assets provided by the employer, such as alarm systems, security guards, bullet-resistant windows, etc. In appropriate circumstances, no benefit charge will be made.

9.6.8 Beneficial loan arrangements
(TA 1988 Ss160–161 & Sch 7 & FA 1991 S31 & Sch 6)

(1) If you or a 'relative' have a loan by reason of your director's or *higher paid* employment at no interest or at a lower rate than the 'official' one then you will be taxed on the benefit of your interest saving compared with the official rate, subject to the following rules.

(2) The 'official rate' varies periodically. Recent rates are:

From 6 December 1987	$10\frac{1}{4}$%
From 6 May 1988	$9\frac{1}{2}$%
From 6 August 1988	12%
From 6 October 1988	$13\frac{1}{2}$%
From 6 January 1989	$14\frac{1}{2}$%
From 6 July 1989	$15\frac{1}{2}$%
From 6 November 1989	$16\frac{1}{2}$%
From 6 November 1990	$15\frac{1}{2}$%
From 6 March 1991	$14\frac{1}{2}$%
From 6 April 1991	$13\frac{1}{4}$%
From 6 May 1991	$12\frac{3}{4}$%
From 6 July 1991	$12\frac{1}{4}$%
From 6 August 1991	$11\frac{3}{4}$%

From 6 October 1991	$11\frac{1}{4}$%
From 6 March 1992	$10\frac{3}{4}$%
From 6 June 1992	$10\frac{1}{2}$%

(3) 'Relative' means parent, grandparent, child, grandchild, etc, brother, sister or spouse of yourself or any of the relatives aforementioned.

(4) No charge to tax will be made if the annual cash value of the benefit does not exceed £300 (£200 before 6 April 1991).

(5) No charge to tax will be made if tax relief would have been available for any interest paid on the loan. After 5 April 1991 if you are a higher rate tax payer, the difference between basic rate and higher rate tax (15 per cent) will be charged on a beneficial loan which you have connected with your house purchase. Previously, it would have normally been tax free up to £30,000 but with the abolition of mortgage interest higher rate tax relief, 15 per cent is charged.

9.6.9 Director's PAYE
(TA 1988 S164)

Where a company accounts for PAYE (9.14) to the Inland Revenue from 6 April 1983 in respect of certain directors and this exceeds the amounts which they suffer, the excess is treated as their income. This does not apply to directors owning less than 5 per cent of the company's shares who work full time for it, nor to directors of charities, etc.

9.6.10 Medical insurance
(FA 1989 Ss54–57)

From 1976–77 until 1981–82 all directors and employees were taxed on any medical insurance premiums borne by their employer. (This does not apply, however, to medical insurance covering overseas service.) However, from 1982–83 non-directors earning less than £8,500 annually are not taxed on such premiums.

For 1990–91 and subsequently, relief for private medical insurance is available for those aged 60 and over. The relief is given by deduction of basic rate tax at source. Higher rate relief is given by adjusting PAYE codings, etc.

9.6.11 Vouchers and credit tokens
(TA 1988 Ss141–144)

All employees (and directors) are normally taxed on the value of cash vouchers received as a result of their employment. That value is the money for which the vouchers are capable of being exchanged. The rules include cheque vouchers and credit tokens such as credit and charge cards. However, lower paid employees of transport undertakings are not taxed on transport vouchers provided under arrangements existing at 25 March 1982.

9.6.12 Living accommodation provided for employees
(TA 1988 Ss145 & 146)

In general, living accommodation provided to you because of your employment results in a taxable benefit. You are taxed on the open market rental value of the property, or the actual rent paid by your employer, if this is more. Amounts which you pay towards the cost are deducted.

You are exempted from the charge, however, if any of the following circumstances apply:

(1) You have to live in the accommodation in order to perform your duties properly.
(2) It is customary in your type of employment to have accommodation provided and it helps you to do your job better.
(3) Your employment involves you in a security risk and special accommodation is provided with a view to your safety.

The above exemption also covers rates paid for you, but does not apply in circumstances (1) and (2) if you are a director, unless you have broadly no more than a 5 per cent shareholding and work full time or work for a charity, etc.

If your employment is 'director's or *higher paid*' (9.6.2), you will still be assessed on payments by your employer for your heating, lighting, cleaning, repairs, maintenance and decoration, etc as well as on the value (20 per cent — 9.6.7) of domestic furniture and equipment provided. A limit applies, however, which is 10 per cent of your net emoluments from your job which is after deducting capital allowances, pension contributions and expenses claims, and excludes the expenditure for your benefit.

From 6 April 1984 an additional charge applies to houses costing the employer more than £75,000 or, if purchased more than six years previously, worth more than that figure when first occupied by the employee after 30 March 1983. The additional benefit is broadly based on the excess of the cost, etc over £75,000. This is subjected to the rate of interest in force in relation to beneficial loans (now $10\frac{1}{2}$ per cent) at the start of the year of assessment (9.6.8).

9.6.13 Scholarships
(TA 1988 S165)

You will be assessed on the value of any scholarships awarded by your employer to your children after 14 March 1983, provided you are a director or *higher paid* employee (9.6.2), subject to certain exceptions. However, the scholarships will remain tax-free in the hands of your children.

The above does not normally apply to awards made before 15 March 1983, provided the first payment was before 6 April 1984. However, payments after 5 April 1989 are caught unless the student is still at the same full-time college, school, etc as at 15 March 1983 or when the first payment was made, if later. Another exception is where a scholarship comes from a fund or scheme from which at least 75 per cent by value goes to scholars otherwise than by reason of their parents' employment. From 6 April 1984, but not before, overseas employees who are the parents of scholars are not included in the 75 per cent.

9.6.14 Childcare
(FA 1990 S21)

From 6 April 1990, subject to certain rules, childcare facilities provided by your employer will not give rise to any benefit charge on you. You must either be a parent or foster parent of the child and the care may not be provided on domestic premises. Other conditions include your employer running the nursery at your workplace or elsewhere; or jointly with other employers.

9.6.15 Mobile telephones
(FA 1991 S30)

You will be taxed on a standard amount of £200 yearly, from 6 April 1991 on each mobile phone provided by your employers. (This includes car phones — 9.6.5.) However, if you have no private use, or are required to make good the full cost of such use and do so, there is no tax charge.

There are rules for reducing the charge if the phone is only available to you for part of the year. This applies if you receive or part with the phone during the tax year, or cannot use it for at least 30 consecutive days.

9.6.16 Income from employment and your return

You must enter in your return your occupation and your employer's name and address. Show your total gross earnings before any deductions unless this is not required by the type of return that you are sent by the Revenue. If your duties are performed wholly abroad, this must be indicated.

Include separate details of any director's fees voted by each company before deductions. Also show any part-time or casual earnings. If your spouse has any income of this kind, it must be shown separately in his or her own return. (Prior to 6 April 1990, it was normally all included in the husband's return.)

You must give details of your benefits-in-kind including goods and vouchers received as well as living accommodation. Also show details of any share options granted by your employer (9.9), when these are exercised.

If you are a P11D employee (9.6.2) you must enter the total amount of any expenses payments made to you and the total cost to your employer of any benefits provided for you. If the Inspector has granted a dispensation to your employer, however, you may leave the relevant expenses payments out of your return. (A dispensation will be granted if the Inspector is satisfied that all of the expenses payments are covered by allowable expenses.)

Any leaving payments and compensation must be separately shown (9.12). A separate section in your return is provided for details of your expenses in employment (9.8) including fees or subscriptions to professional bodies and superannuation contributions.

9.7 Expense payments for directors and others (form P11D)

If you have a director's or higher paid employment (9.6.2), your employers must complete a form P11D for each tax year in respect of all benefits in kind and expense payments made to you or on your behalf.

For 1991–92, the following particulars must be entered by your employer on your form P11D regarding any expenses payments made and benefits, etc provided by him, unless covered by a dispensation. (Inland Revenue Pamphlet IR69 explains the procedure under which your employer can request a dispensation from the Inspector of Taxes regarding various business expenses such as scale rate payments for travelling and subsistence.) The amounts entered must include VAT even though this is recovered by the employer.

(1) Cars owned or hired by employer—
  (i) Make, model and whether registered before or after 6 April 1988.
  (ii) Value when new (in bands) and engine capacity.
  (iii) Period for which car available to you in year.
  (iv) Payment by you towards running costs.
  (v) Wages of any driver provided for you.
  (vi) If car is used less than 2,500 miles or more than 18,000 miles in a year for business this must be indicated in boxes provided.
  (vii) Appropriate car fuel scale and other related details.
(2) Cars owned by you—
  (i) Allowances from employer towards your running expenses.
  (ii) Contribution from employer towards purchase price, depreciation or hire.
(3) Entertainment — all payments made exclusively for entertaining including the amount of any round sum allowance, specific allowances, sums reimbursed and sums paid to third persons (entertaining disallowable to your employer must still be included).
(4) General round sum expense allowances not exclusively for entertaining.
(5) Travelling and subsistence — fares, hotels, meals, etc and payments from your employer for travel between your home and work from which no PAYE has been deducted — expenses regarding overseas employments.
(6) Subscriptions.
(7) Private medical and dental attention, treatment and insurance.
(8) Educational assistance for self or family including scholarships awarded to you or your family after 14 March 1983.
(9) Goods and services supplied free or below market value — equivalent cash benefit.
(10) Work done to your own home or other assets by your employer.
(11) Wages and upkeep of personal or domestic staff provided by your employer.
(12) Cost of vouchers and credit cards given to you by your employer.

(13) House, flat, etc, provided by employer — address of property.
(14) The market value of any cars or other assets given to you by your employer (other than personal gifts outside the business).
(15) Home telephone — cost of rental — calls; also mobile telephone.
(16) Nursery places provided for your children.
(17) Other expenses and benefits including your own national insurance contributions (if paid by your employer), holidays, home telephone, etc payments towards cost of your own car.
(18) Beneficial loans — particulars of loans giving rise to benefit assessment (9.6.8).
(19) Income tax paid to the Collector in 1991–92 which was not deducted from your remuneration as a director.

The total of the above items is entered on your P11D and then your employer deducts the following:

(1) The amounts of any of the above expenses that you have repaid to your employer (unless already deducted from the items shown).
(2) Amounts included above from which tax has been deducted under PAYE.

The form P11D also requests details of amounts of remuneration earned for previous years which were paid in 1991–92 (9.14.4).

Prior to 1986–87, employers were required to list on form P11DA all directors and *higher paid* employees (9.6.2) not receiving benefits. Form P11DA has now been abolished and employers merely have to complete a simple confirmation that all necessary forms P11D have been completed and returned to the Revenue.

9.8 Deductions you may claim
(TA 1988 Ss198–201 & 332)

You may claim any expenses which you have to incur wholly, exclusively and necessarily in performing the duties of your employment. These do not include:

(1) The cost of travel between home and work.
(2) The cost of business entertainment except where the expense is disallowed in computing your employer's tax assessment or is reasonable entertainment of an overseas trading customer.

If you are a director or a P11D employee (9.6.2) you should make a claim to the Revenue in respect of any allowable expenses that have been included by your employer in your form P11D. The claim should certify that the expenses covered were incurred 'wholly, exclusively and necessarily' in performing the duties of your employment. You will not then be taxed on payments for such expenses made by your employer whether made to you or third parties.

Any expenses that you personally incur in connection with your employment should be included on your return and these include:

Overalls, clothing and tools.
Travelling.
Business use of your own car including capital allowances (10.9.10).
Home telephone and other expenses.
Professional fees and subscriptions relating to your work.
Your own contributions to any approved superannuation (pension) scheme operated by your employers (9.11).
In certain employments (eg, entertainment industry) such expenses as hairdressing, make-up, clothes cleaning, etc.

9.9 Share option and share incentive schemes
(TA 1988 Ss135–140, 162, 185–187 & Schs 9 & 10, FA 1988 Ss68 & 69 & 77–89 & FA 1991 Ss38–44)

9.9.1 Unapproved share option schemes

As a director or an employee of a company, you may be granted an option to take up shares in the company. When you exercise your option, the notional 'gain' will be included in your Schedule E assessment for the tax year in which you exercise the option. (This does not apply if you exercise your option after 5 April 1984 under an approved scheme — see below.) You thus pay income tax on the 'gain' (as earned income) calculated thus:

Market value of shares on day you exercise option (ie, when you take up the shares)		£A
Less: Price paid by you for the shares	£B	
Price paid by you for the option (if any)	C	D
Assessable 'gain'		£E

(From 19 March 1986 you are liable on gains from omitting to exercise your option; or from granting an option over the shares which are the subject of your option.)

For options *granted* before 6 April 1984 (but not later), if the income tax payable (on E) exceeds £250 then you can elect to pay by five equal instalments. The election must be within sixty days of the end of the tax year and the instalments will cover the next five years. The election only applies if the share price under the option is no less than the market value when it was granted (90 per cent of market value if granted before 6 April 1982).

If you subsequently sell the shares themselves at a profit, subject to the share incentive scheme rules (9.9.4), this will be liable to capital gains tax (18.1) calculated as follows:

Net proceeds obtained on the sale of the shares		£F
Less: Price paid by you for the shares	£B	
Price paid by you for the option (if any)	C	
Gain already assessed under Schedule E	E	A
Capital gain		£G

9.9.2 Approved share option schemes
(TA 1988 S185 & Sch 9, FA 1988 S69, FA 1989 Ss64 & 65 & FA 1991 S39)

Special rules apply to options granted after 5 April 1984 under an approved scheme, which can extend to groups. In particular, the gain will only be taxable when the shares are sold and capital gains tax (not income tax) will apply. The conditions for Inland Revenue approval include the following:

(1) Each participant may hold options over shares with a maximum value at the time of grant of £100,000 or four times his current or previous year's emoluments if greater.
(2) The price to be paid for the shares must not be much lower than market value when the option is granted.
(3) You cannot exercise your option earlier than three years or later than ten years after its grant.
(4) You must be a full-time director or employee when the option is granted to you but may leave before its exercise.

(5) You can only exercise approved options once every three years.
(6) No participant has a 'material interest' (broadly 10 per cent of the shares) in the company or group if close (12.17).
(7) The options must be non-transferable and the shares, fully paid ordinary shares. These shares must form part of the capital of the company (G) granting the option, or its parent, or a consortium company owning at least 5 per cent of the ordinary shares of G.
(8) Shares subject to special restrictions may not be used. However, employees may now be required to sell their shares when their employment ends.
(9) Where a company has two classes of issued ordinary shares, most of the class of shares used in the scheme needed to be held by outsiders. However, a class of shares can now be used of which the majority is held by directors or employees and gives them control of the company.
(10) Redeemable shares cannot be used, except now in the case of registered worker co-operatives.
(11) Where a company with an approved share scheme is taken over by another company, it is now possible for the options to be exchanged for options over shares in that other company. Certain conditions must be satisfied, including having the replacement options governed by the rules of the original scheme.
(12) With retrospective effect back to 1984, where loans are obtained by employees to exercise their options, conditions regarding security and repayment are not regarded as 'restrictions'. Thus the shares are not debarred on this account.
(13) From 1 January 1992, provided a company participates in an approved 'all-employee share scheme', it can grant share options under a discretionary scheme to selected employees at a tax-free discount of up to 15 per cent. 'All-employee share schemes' are profit-sharing schemes (9.9.6) and savings related share option schemes (9.9.3).

9.9.3 Savings related share option schemes
(TA 1988 S185 & Sch 9, FA 1989 S62, FA 1990 S29 & FA 1991 Ss38 & 39)

Any notional or real gains from an approved savings-related share option scheme will be free of income tax. However, some capital gains tax may be payable. Under such a scheme you are given an option to buy shares in the company which employs you or its controlling company. (You would not be eligible if you controlled more than 25 per cent of the shares and it is a close company — 12.17.)

You must save the money to buy the shares through a special SAYE contract set to produce the required cost of the shares on its maturity. (The proceeds from SAYE linked schemes set up under earlier legislation may also be used.) SAYE contracts may now be arranged by banks, as well as building societies and the Department for National Savings, as before.

Early exercise of the option is normally only allowed in special circumstances, such as death, disability, retirement or redundancy. Early exercise is also now allowed if the company or part of its business in which you work leaves the group operating the scheme.

The maximum permitted monthly contribution is £250 and no minimum monthly contribution above £10 can be stipulated. Also, the future purchase price of the shares must not be manifestly less than 80 per cent of the market value of the shares when the option is granted. You must normally exercise the option within six months of reaching pensionable age. However, this becomes an age between 60 and 75 specified for the scheme, where it is approved after 25 July 1991.

9.9.4 Share incentive schemes
(TA 1988 Ss138–139, FA 1988 Ss77–89 & F2A 1992 S37)

These are schemes under which you are allowed to purchase shares in the company where you work because of your employment or directorship and not simply because of a general offer to the public. If you obtain shares under certain incentive schemes, you are broadly assessed to income tax under Schedule E on the increase in the market value of your shares between their acquisition date and the earliest of the following:

(1) seven years from when you bought the shares;
(2) the time when you cease to be a director or an employee of the company;
(3) the time when you sell the shares; and
(4) the time when your shares cease to be subject to any special restrictions.

Your Schedule E assessment is made for the tax year during which the earliest of the above times arises. The above rules apply to shares from incentive schemes acquired before 26 October 1987 and for later acquisitions, subject to certain rules given below.

Income from employments and PAYE 121

(The charge takes account of bonus shares and rights issues which you derive from your scheme shares after 18 March 1986.) Certain *profit sharing schemes* are excluded provided various conditions are satisfied, including the following:

(1) the shares were publicly quoted or are not in one company which was controlled by another or are units in an authorised unit trust which satisfies certain conditions;
(2) the shares were not subject to any special restrictions (excluding stock exchange 'insider dealing' rules);
(3) the scheme was open to all employees of the company aged 25 and over with at least five years' continuous service;
(4) you received your shares as part of your (taxable) emoluments according to a prearranged basis, geared to the profits of the company; and
(5) shares acquired under an approved share option scheme (9.9.2) were also normally excluded.

Special rules operate regarding acquisitions of shares or interests in shares after 25 October 1987. Broadly, the previous rules apply in essence with some changes. However, those not charged under Schedule E Case I in respect of the employment are excluded. Also excluded are acquisitions arising from public offers.

Income tax may be chargeable in certain circumstances, such as the removal or variation of restrictions over the shares; or the creation or variation of rights in the shares owned or other shares in the company. However, this does not apply if the company is employee-controlled because of holdings of shares of the same class, nor if it is a subsidiary (but not a 'dependent subsidiary' — see below); nor if a majority of the shares of the same class are held other than by directors and employees, associated companies, etc. The tax is levied on the value increase resulting from the removal of restrictions, etc.

Special benefits, such as a capital distribution, or the sale of rights in a rights issue may be taxable. However, from 12 November 1991, unless the company is a 'dependent subsidiary' wider exemption applies. Broadly, employee shareholders are not taxed on their special benefits where they are available to at least 90% of shareholders and a majority of the shares are held by non-employees.

A 'dependent subsidiary' is one whose business is mainly carried on with group members. Furthermore, any increase in the value of the company during its accounts period must be limited to 5 per cent. The directors must give the Inland Revenue a certificate within two years of the end of the accounts period. You are liable on shares in a 'dependent subsidiary' in the same way as other shares (see above).

9.9.5 Employee shareholdings
(TA 1988 S162, FA 1988 S68 & FA 1989 S66, FA 1990 S79 & FA 1991 S44)

Special rules apply if you are a director or *higher paid* employee (9.6.2) and you acquire shares at an undervalue by reason of your employment. The shares need not be in the company which employs you.

You are treated as obtaining shares at an undervalue if you pay less than the market value of fully paid shares of the same class at that time. This applies whether or not you are under any obligation to pay more at a future time. You are taxed on the shortfall of what you pay for the shares compared with market value when you bought them. This shortfall is treated as an interest free loan (9.6.8) and you are treated as if your taxable earnings were increased by the benefit of such a loan. This continues until the shortfall is ended or the shares are sold, even if you cease your employment.

If you obtain shares through a priority allocation to the employees of your company, when it offers shares to the public, special rules apply. You will not be assessed on any benefit provided no more than 10 per cent of the offer goes to employees, all entitlements are on similar terms and the arrangement is not exclusively for directors or highly paid employees. In the case of a fixed price issue, the employees must subscribe at that price whilst for a tender issue, the lowest price successfully tendered applies. (The above does not apply before 23 September 1987.)

From 11 October 1988, the foregoing rules apply with certain relaxations. For example, relief is not completely withdrawn if the price is too low; it is simply not to apply to the benefit represented by the difference in price. Also, if there are several offers to the public of shares of the same class, the limit of 10 per cent applies overall but up to 40 per cent of the shares comprised in one offer may go to employees. Furthermore, from August 1990, different directors or employees can obtain a different mix of shares offered to the public at the same time, provided the aggregate benefit is similar. The exemption is further extended from 16 January 1991 to cover a public offer comprising a package of shares in more than one company and also 'special benefits' such as bonus shares.

9.9.6 Profit sharing schemes
(TA 1988 Ss186–187 & Sch 9, FA 1989 Ss63 & 64 & FA 1991 Ss38 & 41)

Tax relief is available for employees participating in a company share scheme which has been approved by the Revenue. Under such a scheme, trustees are allowed to acquire shares in the company to the value of up to £3,000 or 10 per cent of salary, subject to a ceiling of £8,000. For this purpose you take your salary for the current or previous year, whichever is the higher.

From 6 April 1982 to 5 April 1989 there was an annual maximum of £1,250 or 10 per cent of salary (excluding expenses) if higher (maximum £5,000). From 6 April 1989 to 5 April 1991, the limits were £2,000 and £6,000.

A participant must agree to his shares remaining with the trustees for at least two years unless he dies, becomes redundant or reaches normal retirement age. However, for schemes approved after 25 July 1991 an age must be specified between 60 and 75 for all members. The scheme must be open fairly to all employees within the company or group with five years' service or more. The employers may allow those with shorter service to join, however. Any dividends on the shares are paid over to the participants.

When the trustees sell any of a participant's shares after two years, a percentage will be charged to income tax. The percentage is calculated on the original value (less any capital receipts already charged to income tax as below), or the proceeds of the shares if less, as follows:

| | % taxable | |
Period held — years	pre 7.85	post 7.85
2–3	100	100
4	75	75
5	50	Nil
6	25	Nil
7–10	Nil	Nil

The appropriate percentage (see above) of capital receipts less an allowance is charged to income tax. The allowance applicable from August 1982 to 5 April 1986 was £20 for each year until disposal, with a maximum of £140. From 6 April 1986 the maximum is £100. There is a special 50 per cent abatement of the charge for employees leaving due to injury, disability, redundancy or reaching pensionable age.

9.9.7 Setting-up costs of employee share schemes
(FA 1991 S42)

From 1 April 1991, the costs of setting up various types of employee share schemes are allowable for tax purposes. These include all-employee profit sharing schemes (9.9.6), all-employee savings-related share option schemes (9.9.3) and discretionary share option schemes (9.9.2). If Revenue approval is obtained more than 9 months after the end of the period of account when the expenditure was incurred, allowance is given for the period when approval is given.

9.10 Employee Share Ownership Plans (ESOPs)
(FA 1989 Ss67–74 & Sch 5, FA 1990 Ss31–40, FA 1991 S43 & F2A 1992 S36)

Tax relief for ESOPs applies to contributions made to qualifying trusts from 27 July 1989. The main features are:

(1) ESOP trusts may borrow to acquire their shares rather than relying on funds provided by the employer company.

(2) ESOP trusts may provide a market in unquoted shares and may distribute larger amounts of shares than under Profit Sharing Schemes (9.9.6).

(3) All employees of the company and its subsidiaries, who work 20 or more hours weekly and have been employed for at least five years must be beneficiaries of the ESOP trust.

(4) Beneficiaries may also include ex-employees and ex-directors within 18 months of leaving; and employees and directors of at least one year's standing who work at least 20 hours weekly. However, those with a 'material interest' in the company (broadly 5 per cent) must be excluded.

(5) Funds from the company must be used within nine months after the end of the company's accounting period in which they were received. The funds must be used in buying ordinary shares in the company, servicing and repaying borrowings, paying benefits and paying expenses.

(6) The shares must be distributed within seven years of their acquisition to all accepting beneficiaries on similar terms.

(7) Payments to an ESOP trust by the company or a subsidiary are allowed for corporation tax. However, the trust itself is taxable

Income from employments and PAYE 125

on its income and capital gains. Also, employees receiving shares at less than market value will be liable to income tax.
(8) Capital gains tax rollover relief (18.25) is available, subject to certain conditions, for disposals of your company shares to an ESOP trust after 19 March 1990. Replacement assets must be purchased within six months of the sale. (Broadly, your dwelling house and BES shares are not allowed as replacement assets qualifying for relief.) If the replacement assets are disposed of without other assets being acquired, the deferred gain will be brought into charge.
(9) From 1 April 1991, the costs of setting up an ESOP are an allowable deduction for tax purposes.
(10) Prior to 1 January 1992, a tax charge could arise from a share-for-share exchange. Subsequently, there is no tax charge provided the new holding stands in place of the old for capital gains tax purposes (18.18.6).

9.11 Retirement pension schemes
(TA 1988 Ss590–617 & 630–655; FA 1988 Ss54–56, FA 1989 Ss75–77 & Schs 6 & 7 & FA 1991 Ss34–36)

Any national insurance contributions that you pay as an employee are not deductible from your taxable income. Your employer, however, deducts his share of such contributions from his taxable profits. On your retirement your state pension is taxable as earned income, on the basis of the actual amount for the tax year, and any widow's pension payable to your wife is also taxable in this way. There is an Earnings Related component in the State Scheme, out of which you may be contracted (24.12.2). 'Contracting-out' using an occupational scheme relieves you and your employer of the obligation to pay higher rate National Insurance contributions (23.2).

Any pension paid to you out of your employer's own staff superannuation scheme is taxable as earned income. The same applies to any retirement pension paid by your employer that has not been provided for under any scheme.

Retirement schemes are either 'contributory' or 'non-contributory'. In the latter case the employer bears the entire cost and in the former case the employee makes his own regular contributions to the scheme. If you work for a big company it may run its own exempt approved pension scheme which will put aside funds to provide pensions for its employees. A separate pension trust is set up and investments are made on which generally no UK tax is payable either on income or capital gains. The employees' contributions (if any) are deductible from their taxable earnings, subject to certain limits and amounts paid by the company are deductible from its taxable profits. Furthermore no 'benefit in kind' assessments are made on the employees. To qualify for this taxation treatment Revenue approval must be obtained (24.12.1).

Instead of managing their own exempt approved pension scheme many employers arrange for it to be operated by an insurance company. In return for annual premiums paid to it based on the salaries of the employees covered, the insurance company provides retirement pensions and also sometimes lump sum payments in the event of the death in service of any employee. Subject to Revenue approval (see below) the company deducts the contributions that it pays from its taxable profits and the employees deduct their contributions (if any) from their taxable earnings.

From 1 July 1988, *personal pension schemes* (24.11.1) have been available for those not in staff superannuation schemes (or for the purposes of 'contracting-out'). Contributions may be paid by the employer or employee. From October 1987, 'free standing' AVC contracts operate (24.13).

9.11.1 Conditions for Revenue approval of occupational pension schemes

If a new scheme is to obtain Revenue approval it must satisfy various conditions (24.12.1). Existing schemes may have been approved under different conditions but by 6 April 1980 they must have been re-examined by the Revenue and approved under the current rules. If an old scheme is varied it must also be reapproved under the current rules. Separate rules apply to personal pension schemes. For further details please refer to Chapter 24 (24.11.1 and 24.12.1).

9.12 Compensation for loss of office
(TA 1988 Ss148 & 188 & FA 1988 S74)

If a 'golden handshake' payment is made to you on your retirement, resignation, redundancy or removal from that office, etc, at least the first £30,000 will normally be tax free. Prior to 6 April 1988 this figure was £25,000, before 6 April 1981 it was £10,000 and before 6 April 1978 it was £5,000. However, this exemption depends on the payments being not otherwise taxable.

Income from employments and PAYE 127

From 1 November 1991, Inland Revenue practice has changed regarding *ex gratia* payments made on retirement or death. These may now be taxed under the rules relating to pension schemes (Chapter 24). However, Revenue (PSO) approval will be available if the normal retirement benefits scheme requirements are satisfied and the lump sum *ex gratia* payment is the only lump sum relevant benefit potentially payable from your employment. The tax treatment of *ex gratia* termination payments other than on retirement or death is generally unchanged and the excess (if any) over £30,000 will be taxed as your earned income. However, prior to 6 April 1988 certain additional reductions were made apart from the £25,000 exemption (9.12.1).

The employer is usually able to deduct 'golden handshake' payments from his taxable profits unless for example they are abnormally high payments to controlling directors or are made in connection with a sale of the actual business or made just before its cessation.

If you have a service contract that provides for a lump sum payment to be made to you when you leave your employer this payment will not be tax free because it is treated as arising out of your employment. This point should be borne in mind when service contracts are drawn up.

Any payments received by a former employee in the following circumstances are normally tax free:

(1) *Ex gratia* payments on the death or permanent disability of the employee.
(2) Terminal grants to members of HM Forces.
(3) *Ex gratia* payments on the termination of a job where the employee worked abroad either:
    (*a*) for three-quarters of his entire term of service; or
    (*b*) for the whole of the last ten years; or
    (*c*) where the total service is more than 20 years, for half the total service period including any ten of the last 20 years.

9.12.1 Tax treatment — termination after 5 April 1981 and before 6 April 1988

Under the rules which applied for terminations after 5 April 1981 and before 6 April 1988, the first £25,000 which you received was exempt. For 1981–82 the balance was taxed at half your marginal rate on it. This was found by treating the balance as your top slice of income, calculating the income tax on that slice and then halving it to give the tax. After 5 April 1982, the relief was restricted. The first £25,000 was still exempt, but only £25,000 was intended to qualify for 50 per cent relief and then tax on the next £25,000 was to have been reduced by 25 per cent, the remainder being fully taxed.

However, due to faultily drafted legislation, the Inland Revenue now accept that up to 3 June 1986, higher relief was due. The first £25,000 was exempt, for the next £50,000 the tax was reduced by half, and for the next £25,000 the tax was reduced by 25 per cent. From 4 June 1986 legislation took effect which clearly applied the rules as originally intended.

For periods before 6 April 1981, the treatment of 'golden handshake' payments depended on whether they were '*ex gratia*' or compensation payments. Fuller details are given in the 1988–89 and earlier editions of this book.

9.13 The assessment basis
(FA 1989 Ss36–45)

Up to 5 April 1989, many directors and certain others were assessed to income tax on their emoluments on what was known as the 'accounts basis'. This involved paying tax for a tax year based on your director's remuneration, etc, for the accounts year ending therein. Thus, if your remuneration for the year to 31 December 1987 was £25,000, this was assessed for 1987–1988.

From 6 April 1989, the earnings of *all* directors and employees are assessed for the year in which they are received and not for the year for which they were earned. (Certain pensions are to be assessed under Schedule E on an accruals basis.) However, transitional provisions deal with situations where income is either taxed twice or not at all. In general, the earnings are taken out of assessment for the year when earned and taxed only in the year received, provided relief is claimed.

For example, suppose you earned £45,000 for 1988–89, most of this being paid during that tax year. However, fees of £12,000 were not paid to you until the September 1989 AGM. If you made the required claim, your 1988–89 assessment was reduced to £33,000, with £12,000 being assessed for 1989–90. In this way, you avoided £12,000 being assessed twice.

Where the accounts basis has operated, income may escape assessment altogether. This applies to income for 1988–89 relating to that part of the year falling after the accounting date and before 6 April 1989. However, where earnings for 1989–90 or later were received before 6 April 1989, these may have escaped assessment. However, such earnings are taxed as if received on 6 April 1989. For the purposes of the rules, you are regarded as receiving your earnings at the earliest of the following times.

(1) When actual payment is made (in whole or on account).
(2) When you become entitled to be paid.
(3) If you are a director, when sums on account of emoluments are credited to you in the company's books.
(4) The end of a period of account, where your director's emoluments are determined *before* the end of that period.
(5) *When* your director's emoluments are determined, if after the relevant period of account.

Where emoluments for an accounting period ending after 5 April 1989 are paid more than nine months after the end of that period, they must be added back in the employer's tax computations and only allowed as a deduction when paid. This applies where the remuneration relates to any period after 5 April 1989.

9.14 The PAYE system
(TA 1988 S203)

Most of the Schedule E income tax payable on earnings from employments in this country is collected under the 'pay as you earn' system (PAYE), which covers both basic rate and higher rate income tax. Your employer is responsible for administering the PAYE on your own wages and that of your fellow employees. From each wages payment that you receive, whether it be weekly or monthly, your employer must deduct the relevant income tax and National Insurance contributions, paying to you the net amount. (If income tax has been previously over-deducted by your employer or if you suddenly become entitled to higher relief you may be due to receive a repayment which your employer will make to you.)

9.14.1 Payment

Your employer has to pay over to the Collector of Taxes the total PAYE income tax deductions (less refunds) and National Insurance contributions in respect of the previous month. The time limit is by the nineteenth day of the following month. If payment is not made, it is now open to the Collector to send an estimated demand which must be paid within seven days unless:

(1) The correct PAYE is paid.
(2) The Collector is satisfied that nothing further is due.
(3) The Collector is invited to inspect the PAYE records.

After 5 April 1992, employers whose monthly payments of PAYE and national insurance contributions are less than £450 are allowed to pay quarterly. (The figure for 1991–92 was £400.) Payments are then made to the Inland Revenue for the quarters ending 5 July, 5 October, 5 January and 5 April, and each is due within 14 days.

9.14.2 Records

Prior to 6 April 1981, your employer was required to keep a separate tax deduction card for each of his employees (including directors but not partners). From 6 April 1981 he is allowed to use his own records which may be computerised. Otherwise he may use the official Deductions Working Sheet (form P11). This can be used for weekly or monthly paid employees. For a weekly paid person the following particulars are entered and calculated:

(1) National insurance contributions.
(2) Statutory sick pay and statutory maternity pay.
(3) Gross pay for the week.
(4) Cumulative pay for the tax year to date.
(5) Total 'free pay' to date (see below).
(6) Total taxable pay to date (3–4).
(7) Total tax due to date (see below).
(8) Tax to be paid or repaid for the week (see below).

(Similar details for each month are entered for monthly paid employees.) The total 'free pay' to date is obtained from 'Table A' in the tax tables provided by the Revenue. This table shows for each week the 'free pay' applicable to each code number (see below). If your total pay is less than your 'free pay' to date then you pay no more tax for that week and would normally get a refund.

The tax to be paid or repaid for the week (see (7) above) is calculated by subtracting the total tax due to date for the previous week from that for the current week (see (6) above). The total tax due to date is found each week from the tax deduction tables. These show the tax attributable to the relevant total taxable pay to date.

The tax deduction tables in use are designated tables LR, B, C and D. Table LR shows the amount of tax due at the lower rate of 20 per cent. Table B shows tax due at the basic rate. Table C shows for each week or month (see below) the amounts to be taxed at the higher rate.

If you have only one employment your tax is calculated from table B if your earnings are below the higher rates level, unless only the lower rate applies. Should your earnings make you liable for higher rate income tax, however, your PAYE tax payable is calculated from table C which is in fact supplementary to table B.

Where your earnings are substantial and you have more than one employment the Revenue will normally direct that tables B and C are used for your main employment. For your other employments, however, they might issue you with code D0. This means that tax at 40 per cent is applicable to those employments. The 'D' codings merely provide the Revenue with a very approximate method of taxing at source your salaries from employments other than your main one.

The Revenue provide monthly tax deduction tables for use where salary payments are made on a monthly basis. The Deductions Working Sheet has a column in which to enter the amount deductible for earnings-related National Insurance contributions, which are collected through the PAYE system.

9.14.3 Your code number

Your code number is calculated from your income tax allowances and reliefs. It is allocated to you by the Inspector of Taxes and takes into account all the reliefs to which you are entitled against which some of your other income may be set off. Account may also be taken of any Schedule E income tax underpaid or overpaid for the previous year.

Coding notices are only sent to cover changes. Otherwise the code for the previous year must be used. The notice itemises the various allowances and reliefs to which you are entitled (3.0.1). Any other necessary adjustments are also shown on your coding notice which shows at the bottom the adjusted balance of your allowances and also the code number which corresponds to that figure. The Inspector will probably obtain the details for your coding notice from your last income tax return.

In order to convert your total allowances and adjustments into your code number, you simply divide by ten and round down to the nearest whole number. Thus if your allowances, etc for 1992–93 total £3,445, your code number is 344. For administrative purposes, your code number will normally end in L, H, P, T or V depending on your main personal reliefs (single, married couple's, age etc). When these reliefs increase instructions are issued by the Revenue to employers to augment codes ending in L, H, P, T or V accordingly. In these cases revised coding notices are not needed. For 1992–93 the allowance changes became reflected in codings after 17 May 1992.

The above remarks normally apply to your coding in respect of your main employment. If you have other employments and the Revenue consider that your taxable earnings after deductions for the year 1992–93 will not exceed £23,700, you will be coded 'BR' in respect of each of your other employments. This means that table B (9.14.2) is applied to your total earnings from each employment except your main one. No deductions are normally made for your allowances, etc because these are included in your coding for your main employment. If, however, your earnings are likely to exceed £23,700 then the Inspector of Taxes is likely to allocate you with 'D' codings (9.14.2) in respect of your supplementary employments.

From 6 April 1993, a new system of K codes will commence. These will cover car benefits etc which increase your taxable pay. It is hoped that the new arrangement will facilitate the collection of tax on benefits. If you have a K code instead of a normal one, your employer will simply add the appropriate amount to your taxable pay rather than deducting it.

9.14.4 Employers' PAYE returns

At the end of each tax year your employer must complete a form P35 and send this to the Revenue. End of year returns P14 must be completed for each employee and sent with the P35. The P14s are completed from the Deductions Working Sheets (P11) or other records and include National Insurance number, date of birth, final tax code, total pay, tax and National Insurance contributions. Also any forms P11D required for the year (9.7) should be sent to the Revenue.

The form P35 is a summary of the total tax due to be deducted for the tax year in respect of all of the employees. The earnings-related National Insurance contributions are also entered for each employee. The details are obtained from the tax deduction cards. The total income tax due to be paid over for the year by the

Income from employments and PAYE 133

employer is then found by adding up all of the tax entries on the form P35 and from this is deducted the total of the actual payments made. A similar procedure is followed regarding the earnings-related National Insurance contributions except that the amount to be paid over also includes the employer's contributions.

The balances shown by the form P35 represent underpayments or overpayments of PAYE income tax and earnings-related contributions: if the employer has underpaid he should send a cheque with the form and if he has overpaid a repayment will subsequently be received.

There are time limits for submitting the forms which must be carefully watched. Penalties (14.8.4) may arise on forms P14 and P35 not submitted by 19 August 1990 for 1989–90, 19 July 1991 for 1990–91, 19 June 1992 for 1991–92 and 19 May 1993 for 1992–93 (19 May is the actual due date).

At the end of each tax year the employer should issue to each of his employees a form P60 which is a certificate of gross earnings for the year and of income tax deducted under PAYE and now forms part of the P14 pack (P14/P60).

9.14.5 Change of employer

If you leave your employment your old employer should complete for you a form P45 in triplicate showing your name, district reference, code number, week or month number of the last entries on your tax deduction card, total gross pay to date and total tax due to date. Your old employer sends part 1 of the form P45 to his Inspector of Taxes and hands to you parts 2 and 3 which you must give to your new employer. The latter enters your address and date of starting on part 3 and sends it to his Inspector.

Your new employer should prepare for you a tax deduction card in accordance with your form P45 and deduct PAYE tax from your wages in the normal way.

If you are not able to give a form P45 to your new employer, he will normally deduct tax under the 'emergency' system which assumes you are single and gives you no other allowances. If this happens you should make an income tax return to the Inspector of Taxes or supply the necessary details to him, so that he can issue you with your correct code number which your employer will then use, making any necessary tax repayment to you.

Form P46 is available for you to complete if you do not have a P45 when you start a new job. It covers whether you are a school leaver or whether it is your main job or an additional one which you are starting. The P46 enables you to indicate your circumstances so that your employer will know whether to deduct basic rate tax from your salary or use an emergency code. (There is also a coding claim form P15 for use in establishing your coding.)

9.15 Profit Related Pay
(TA 1988 Ss169–184 & Sch 29, FA 1989 S61 & Sch 4 & FA 1991 S37)

Valuable tax relief operates from 6 April 1987 in respect of Profit Related Pay (PRP). The main features are as follows:

(1) For profit periods beginning after 31 March 1991, all of your PRP is free of income tax up to the lower of £4,000 or 20 per cent of your PAYE pay for the year.

(2) For periods of account before 1 April 1991, half of your PRP was free of income tax up to the point where it was 20 per cent of your PAYE pay or £4,000 a year, if lower. (For periods of account before 1 April 1989, this figure was £3,000.)

(3) Relief only applies to PRP payments made under a scheme registered by the Inland Revenue before the start of the first profit period it is to cover. Tax relief is given by your employer through the PAYE system.

(4) PRP schemes can be registered for profitable groups, companies, firms or sub-units of any of these. Also, central (eg, headquarters) units can now be included with PRP based on the profits of the whole undertaking. However, there are certain excluded employers, mainly under the control of central or local government.

(5) The rules of any PRP scheme must provide a clear relationship between PRP and profits. Normally, there is a pool representing a stated percentage of the profits for distribution between eligible employees. Alternatively, a fixed sum might be stipulated which varies in proportion with future profits.

(6) A PRP scheme must exclude controlling directors (with 25 per cent or more interest in the company). Recruits with less than three years' service and part-timers (less than 20 hours per week) may be excluded. Otherwise, the general rule is that at least 80 per cent of the employees in an employment unit at the beginning of each period must be eligible for PRP.

(7) Independent audits are needed for both the registration application and the operation of the scheme.

10 Income from businesses and professions

10.1 Trades, professions and vocations

The profits from trades, professions and vocations are normally assessed under Schedule D Case I (trades) and Schedule D Case II (professions and vocations). There are certain special rules which apply to partnerships (Chapter 11) and companies (Chapter 12).

Trade includes manufacturing, retailing, wholesaling and all kinds of trading ventures.

A profession is defined as an occupation requiring special intellectual skills, sometimes coupled with manual skills (eg, doctor of medicine, architect, accountant, barrister).

A vocation has been defined as the way that a person passes his life (eg, composer, author, actor, singer).

10.2 What is trading?

Your regular business will normally be treated as a trade requiring assessment under Schedule D Case I. There are, however, certain other activities which might constitute trading depending on the circumstances. The following are some general guidelines:

(1) Regular buying and selling normally constitutes trading although this does not usually apply to purchases and sales of shares by an individual.
(2) An isolated transaction might be held to be trading if it is by its very nature commercial. For example, a single purchase and sale of a quantity of unmatured whisky is normally treated as a trading transaction. This is because the ownership of unmatured whisky is mainly for commercial purposes.

136 Allied Dunbar Tax Guide

(3) Isolated transactions involving the purchase and sale of works of art are not normally trading. Here the works of art are owned to be admired and not exclusively (if at all) for commercial purposes. Capital gains tax, however, might be payable on sales of works of art for over £6,000 each (18.24).
(4) Isolated transactions in income producing assets are not usually treated as trading. Capital gains tax would normally apply (18.1).
(5) If you do something to your purchase before selling it the sale might be considered to be trading. For instance, if you buy a ship, convert it and then sell it you will be treated as trading.
(6) Repetition of the same transaction is evidence of trading.
(7) If you deal in property this is likely to be treated as trading (7.9).
(8) The possession of expert business knowledge in connection with a transaction that you carry out will increase your chances of being treated as trading.

10.3 What business expenses are allowed?

In computing the amount of your profits to be charged under Case I or Case II of Schedule D you are allowed to deduct any sums wholly and exclusively incurred for the purposes of the trade, profession or vocation, subject to various special rules (see below). Only expenses of a revenue nature are deductible, however, and these must be distinguished from capital expenditure (2.6).

10.3.1 Table: Allowable business expenses

To the extent that they are incurred wholly and exclusively for business purposes the following are deductible (the list is not exhaustive):

(1) The cost of goods bought for resale and materials used in manufacturing.
(2) Wages and salaries paid to employees, together with National Insurance payments. This includes employees seconded on a temporary basis to charities (TA 1988 S86) and to certain educational bodies including local authorities.
(3) Pensions paid to past employees and their dependants.
(4) Redundancy payments to employees including certain voluntary payments on business cessation, up to three times the statutory amount (TA 1988 S90).
(5) The running costs of any premises used for the business including rent and rates, light and heat, repairs (not capital improvements), insurance, cleaning, etc.

(6) Discounts allowed on sales.
(7) Carriage, packing and delivery costs.
(8) Printing, postage, stationery and telephone.
(9) Repairs to your plant and machinery.
(10) Staff welfare expenses.
(11) Insurance regarding loss of profits, public liability, goods in transit, burglary, etc.
(12) Advertising.
(13) Trade subscriptions.
(14) Professional charges of a revenue nature — eg, audit fees.
(15) Legal charges of a revenue nature, eg, debt collection, preparing trading contracts and settling trading disputes.
(16) If you pay a premium for the lease of your business premises and the recipient is taxed under Schedule A you can claim the cost of the premium as a deduction from your business profits spread over the term of the lease.
(17) VAT on your purchases and expenses if you are not registered for VAT. (If you are registered you set this VAT against that on your sales and only charge your purchases, etc excluding VAT.)
(18) Travelling expenses including hotel bills and fares on business trips but excluding the cost of travelling between your home and business (unless you also do business from home).
(19) The entertaining of overseas customers prior to 15 March 1988 (but not subsequently) and your own staff but not entertaining UK customers.
(20) Gifts which incorporate an advertisement for your business provided that the value for each recipient each year does not exceed £10 (TA 1988 S577).
(21) Bad debts which arose in the course of trading. Also provisions made for specific debtors whom you anticipate may not pay. Special rules limit the relief available for doubtful sovereign debt due from overseas governments, etc, normally to banks. Broadly, the allowable amount for 1990–91 is limited to the 1989–90 level and scaled up by 5 per cent annually thereafter (FA 1990 S74).
(22) A trader's expenses of obtaining patents are normally allowable. The outright purchase of a patent is a capital expense, however, which normally qualifies for capital allowances.
(23) Running expenses of motor vehicles excluding such proportion as is attributable to private use.
(24) Interest payments including hire purchase interest. Relief for bank and other interest is normally given on the basis of payments rather than accruals.
(25) The incidental costs of obtaining loan finance which carries deductible interest (TA 1988 S77). Costs concerning repayment, providing security and abortive exercises are covered; but not stamp duty, foreign exchange losses, issue discounts or repayment premiums. This relief extends to certain convertible loan stocks.
(26) Pre-trading expenditure from 1 April 1980, of a revenue nature, incurred within three years before starting to trade (TA 1988 S401). For trades beginning after 31 March 1989, the period is five years (FA 1989 S114). For companies it is treated as falling on the first day of trading; for individuals it is regarded as a separate loss (10.22).
(27) Contributions before 1 April 1995 to local enterprise agencies approved by the Secretary of State. However, you obtain no relief if

(28) you (or those connected with you) are entitled to benefits from the agencies (TA 1988 S79 & FA 1990 S75).
(28) Similar rules apply to contributions to training and enterprise councils made from 1 April 1990 to 31 March 1995 (FA 1990 S76).
(29) Work training provided by an employer after 6 April 1987 for employees about to leave their current jobs, or who have just left. Training courses must retrain in improved skills or knowledge for use in new jobs or business and the employee is no longer taxed on the benefit. Courses must not exceed one year and must take place within the UK (TA 1988 S588).
(30) Security expenditure (FA 1989 Ss112 & 113). This is allowed for the self-employed (including partners) regarding assets or services to meet personal security threats arising from their businesses.
(31) Certain revenue expenditure incurred concerning waste disposal sites from 6 April 1989 (FA 1990 S78). Expenditure on preparing a site is allowed according to the proportion of its capacity filled with waste in the accounts year. Expenditure on making good a site will be given in the year of payment. However, no allowance is given for expenditure on which capital allowances (10.8) are given.
(32) Certain payments for football ground improvements made by pool promoters (FA 1990 S126).
(33) Gifts of equipment, manufactured, sold or used in the trade, to schools and other educational establishments (FA 1991 S68).
(34) The setting-up costs of certain employee share schemes from 1 April 1991 (9.9.7).

10.3.2 Table: Expenses not deductible from business profits
(TA 1988 S74)

(1) Any payments or expenses not wholly and exclusively laid out for the purposes of the business.
(2) Expenses incurred for the private or domestic purposes of yourself or family.
(3) Where expenses contain some business and some private element the proportion attributable to the latter is not deductible. In the case of a private dwelling house used for business purposes the deductible proportion is not normally allowed to exceed two-thirds of the rent and other costs.
(4) Any capital used for improvements to your business premises.
(5) Any loss not connected with the business.
(6) Any reserves and provisions made for anticipated expenses such as repairs, retirement benefits, etc including general bad debts reserves but not reserves for specific bad debts (nor contributions under approved pension plans).
(7) Any annuity or other annual payment (other than interest) payable out of the profits (4.2).
(8) Payments of income tax, capital gains tax and corporation tax, etc.
(9) Your own drawings as the owner or part owner of the business.
(10) Depreciation and amortisation of plant and machinery, motor vehicles, buildings, etc. Capital allowances are normally available however (10.9).

Income from businesses and professions

(11) Any royalty payment from which you deduct income tax.
(12) Entertaining expenses unless in connection with overseas customers and their agents before 15 March 1988 (FA 1988 S72) or your own staff.
(13) Professional charges of a capital nature. For example legal fees in connection with a new lease, architects' fees for designing a new building, accountants' fees connected with the purchase of a new business. These expenses can often be added to the cost of the assets for capital gains tax purposes (18.10).
(14) Fines for illegal acts and connected legal expenses.
(15) Charitable donations, unless wholly for business purposes (TA 1988 S577). (Note special rules for non-close companies (13.2.1) and gifts each exceeding £400.)
(16) Political donations.
(17) The cost of acquiring capital assets such as plant and machinery, motor vehicles, buildings, etc. Capital allowances are frequently available however (10.9).

10.4 The computation of your assessable profits for Schedule D Cases I and II
(TA 1988 Ss74–112)

If you conduct a business or profession you will normally have annual accounts prepared on a commercial basis including a profit and loss account or an income and expenditure account. Your annual accounts should normally be drawn up to the same date in each year but need not coincide with the tax year (which ends on 5 April).

From April 1990, simpler accounts are permitted from 'small businesses'. These are individuals and partnerships with a turnover less than £10,000 a year. This figure is increased to £15,000 for accounts submitted after 6 April 1992. A simple three line account will be needed showing total turnover, purchases and expenses and net profit. Tax returns from April 1991 allow the three line account to be incorporated therein. However, accurate business records must still be kept.

The profit shown by your annual accounts will form the basis of your assessment under Case I or Case II of Schedule D, but it will normally require adjustment in some or all of the following ways:

(1) Add to your profit any non-deductible expenses that have been charged in your accounts (10.3.2).
(2) Deduct from your profit any items included in your accounts which are not taxed under Cases I and II of Schedule D either

because they are non-taxable or because they are liable to tax under another Case or Schedule. Examples are:
Capital profits liable to capital gains tax (18.1).
Interest receivable taxed under Schedule D Case III (8.4).
Rents receivable taxed under Schedule A (7.1).
Interest received net, income tax having been deducted at source (8.2); also dividends (8.1).
Amounts originally set aside as reserves and now recredited in your accounts provided the original amounts were not allowed against your taxable profits.

(3) Deduct from your profit any allowable expenses not already charged in your accounts.

(4) Exclude from your profits government grants towards the cost of specified capital expenditure or compensation for loss of capital assets. Other grants under the Industries Act 1972, etc are now generally taxable. However, regional development grants under the Industrial Development Act 1982 and certain grants to assist industry in Northern Ireland are normally exempt.

(5) If you have recently left the unemployment register to set up a business you may be receiving Enterprise Allowances. These are paid for one year at a weekly amount and are now taxable under Schedule D Case VI (13.1). They should therefore be eliminated from your profits assessable under Case I or II of Schedule D. (However, Enterprise Allowances are liable to Class 4 National Insurance.)

(6) Add to your profit any trading profits not already included.

(7) From your profits adjusted as above, deduct your capital allowances for the year (10.8).

10.4.1 Example: Schedule D Case I computation

Mr A carries on a manufacturing business. His accounts for the year to 31 December 1991, which show a net profit of £39,000, include the following:

Expenses

Depreciation of motor vehicles	£4,300	Entertaining expenses	£2,250
Depreciation of plant and machinery	6,700		
Bad debts provision (5% × sales debtors)	1,650		
Legal expenses *re* debt collection	200	**Income** Bank deposit interest	£70

Legal expenses *re* new lease (not a renewal)	270	Profit on sale of motor car	1,050
Charitable donations (non business)	90	Bad debts provision no longer required (general)	200

Ignoring capital allowances compute Mr A's adjusted Case I profit.

Mr A — Schedule D Case I computation based on accounts for year ended 31 December 1991

Net profit per accounts		£39,000
Less:		
Bank deposit interest	£70	
Profit on sale of motor car (capital)	1,050	
Bad debts provision no longer required	200	
		1,320
		£37,680
Add: Disallowable expenses:		
Depreciation (£4,300 + £6,700)	£11,000	
General bad debts provision	1,650	
Legal expenses *re* new lease	270	
Charitable donations	90	
Entertaining expenses	2,250	
		15,260
Adjusted profit		£52,940

10.5 Stock valuation

An important factor in the preparation of business accounts is the valuation of stock and work in progress. This is the amount of unsold raw materials, finished goods and work in progress that was owned at the end of the accounts period. The stock, etc must be valued at each accounting date and the profits are augmented by the excess of the closing stock over the opening stock or decreased by the deficit. It is clear that if the closing stock is valued on a more generous basis than the opening stock then the profits shown will be higher than the true profits and vice versa.

The Revenue pay careful attention to the manner in which businesses value their stock and they normally insist that for tax purposes the opening and closing stocks are valued on the same basis. The usual basis adopted is that each item in stock is valued at the lower of its cost or net realisable value. The exact cost to be included may or may not contain an addition for expenses depending on the exact basis adopted. The general rule in ascertaining cost is that identical items should be identified on the basis that the earliest purchases were sold or used first (FIFO). In all cases the method chosen must be used consistently. 'Net realisable value' is what it is estimated will be obtained from disposing of the stock in the ordinary course of business at the balance sheet date, after allowing for all expenses in connection with the disposal.

10.6 Stock relief
(FA 1981 S35, Schs 9 & 10 & FA 1984 Ss48–49)

Stock relief was brought into effect by the Finance Act 1975 and withdrawn for periods of account beginning after 12 March 1984. A brief outline is provided below, with further details in previous editions.

For 'base periods' (normally accounting years) ending after 1974–75, you obtained relief for your stock increase over the period less a deduction of a percentage of your 'relevant income' (excluding investment income and after deducting capital allowances). The percentage was 10 per cent (15 per cent for 'base periods' ending before 6 April 1979). For companies the 15 per cent deduction remained throughout (12.22).

For periods ending between 13 November 1980 and 12 March 1984, relief was based on the opening stock and work in progress at the start of each period of account (normally a year). An 'All Stocks' index was published recording the average price increases of a representative sample of stocks and work in progress on a monthly basis. The percentage increase between the index for the month in which the period of account began and the index for the month when it ended was applied to the opening stock, less £2,000. This gave the stock relief due.

Relief was available for periods beginning before and ending after 12 March 1984, based on the above rules. Any period of account bridging 12 March 1984 was treated as ending on that date and thus the March 1984 index was used. After 12 March 1984, no 'clawback' of stock relief takes place on cessation of trade or in any other circumstances. Stock relief is not available for periods beginning after 12 March 1984.

10.7 Basis of assessment
(TA 1988 S60)

The normal basis of assessment under Cases I and II of Schedule D is the profits of the accounts year ending in the preceding tax year. Thus if a business makes up its annual accounts to 30 September its 1992–93 Schedule D Case I assessment will be based on the profits for the year to 30 September 1991 (ie, ending in the preceding tax year 1991–92). Special rules apply to the opening and closing years (see below) and also where you change your accounting date.

10.7.1 Opening years
(TA 1988 Ss61 & 62)

(1) In the first tax year of a business, profession or vocation the assessment is based on the profits from the starting date until the following 5 April. If accounts have been prepared for the first full year or other period to bridge that date, then the profits must be apportioned on a time basis. Thus if a business started on 6 July 1991 and makes up its accounts to 5 July 1992 showing a profit of £24,000 for that year, the assessment for 1991–92 will be based on the period 6 July 1991 to 5 April 1992, ie, £24,000 × 9/12 = £18,000.

(2) The assessment for the second tax year of a business trade or vocation is normally based on the profits for the first complete 12 months of operations. Thus in the above example the assessment for 1992–93 will be based on the profits for the first complete year, ie, to 5 July 1992 and will therefore be £24,000.

(3) The third year's assessment is normally on the preceding year basis subject to the election option mentioned under (4). In the example above the 1993–94 assessment is thus £24,000 (profits for the accounts year ending in the preceding tax year).

(4) The taxpayer has the option to elect that the assessment for both the second and third tax years (but not only one of them, nor subsequent years) should be based on the actual profits for those years (Example 10.7.2). The election should be made to the Inspector of Taxes within seven years of the end of the second year of assessment.

(5) Special rules apply to commencements following certain partnership changes after 19 March 1985 (11.4).

10.7.2 Example: Schedule D Cases I and II — Assessments for opening years

Mr A started in business on his own account on 1 July 1989 and prepared accounts for an 18-month period to 31 December 1990 producing an adjusted profit of £27,000. He selected 31 December as his regular accounting date and his adjusted profit for the year to 31 December 1991 was £3,600 and for 1992 it was £7,200. What are Mr A's Schedule D Case I assessments based on those profits?

Mr A — Schedule D Case I assessments

Tax year	Basis	Base period	Calculation	Assessment
1989–90	Actual	1.7.89–5.4.90	£27,000 × $9\frac{1}{6}$/18	£13,750
1990–91	First year	1.7.89–30.6.90	£27,000 × 12/18	£18,000
1991–92	Preceding year	1.1.90–31.12.90	£27,000 × 12/18	£18,000
1992–93	Preceding year	1.1.91–31.12.91		£3,600
1993–94	Preceding year	1.1.92–31.12.92		£7,200

The assessments for Mr A's second and third tax year total £36,000 (£18,000 + £18,000). Mr A can effect a saving by electing that his assessments for those years should be on the actual profits made in 1990–91 and 1991–92 as follows:

1990–91	6.4.90–31.12.90	£27,000 × $8\frac{5}{6}$/18	£13,250	
	1.1.91–5.4.91	£3,600 × $3\frac{1}{6}$/12	950	
				£14,200
1991–92	6.4.91–31.12.91	£3,600 × $8\frac{5}{6}$/12	£2,650	
	1.1.92–5.4.92	£7,200 × $3\frac{1}{6}$/12	1,900	
				£4,550

The reduction in the aggregate assessments for 1990–91 and 1991–92 is £17,250 (£36,000 − (£14,200 + £4,550)).

10.7.3 Closing years
(TA 1988 S63)

(1) For the tax year in which a trade, profession or vocation is permanently stopped the assessment under Schedule D Case I or II is based on the actual profits from the previous 6 April until the date of cessation.

(2) Regarding the two years prior to the tax year in which the cessation takes place, assessments normally will have been made on a preceding year basis. The Revenue has the right, however, to make additional assessments to cover any excess

Income from businesses and professions 145

of the actual profits for those two tax years. The adjustment only works in favour of the Revenue and if your profits for the two tax years preceding that in which your business ceases are less than the original assessments for those years, you will not be able to obtain any reduction.

10.7.4 Example: Schedule D Cases I and II — Assessments for closing years

Mr E ceases to trade on 31 July 1992 having made adjusted profits as follows:

Year ended 31 July 1989	£2,500
Year ended 31 July 1990	£2,400
Year ended 31 July 1991	£3,600
Year ended 31 July 1992	£3,000

What are Mr E's final assessments on these profits?

Before it was known that Mr E was ceasing to trade, his assessments would be as follows:

Tax year	Basis	Base period	Schedule D Case I assessment
1990–91	Preceding year	Year to 31.7.89	£2,500
1991–92	Preceding year	Year to 31.7.90	2,400
Total for 1990–91 and 1991–92			£4,900

When cessation on 31.7.92 is notified to the Revenue they will adjust the assessments for 1990–91 and 1991–92 as follows:

1990–91
Actual	6.4.90–31.7.90	£2,400 × $3\frac{5}{6}/12$	767	
	1.8.90–5.4.91	£3,600 × $8\frac{1}{6}/12$	2,450	
				3,217

1991–92
Actual	6.4.91–31.7.91	£3,600 × $3\frac{5}{6}/12$	1,150	
	1.8.91–5.4.92	£3,000 × $8\frac{1}{6}/12$	2,042	
				3,192

Revised total for 1990–91 and 1991–92	£6,409
Less: Already assessed	4,900
Additional assessments 1990–91 and 1991–92	£1,509

1992–93
Actual	6.4.92–31.7.92	£3,000 × $3\frac{5}{6}/12$	£958

10.8 Capital allowances
(CAA etc)

You are not normally allowed to deduct from your taxable profits the cost or depreciation of capital assets. You can, however, deduct capital allowances in respect of the cost of certain assets used in your business or profession including the following:

(1) Plant and machinery (10.9) — this category also includes furniture, fittings, office equipment and motor vehicles, together with the thermal insulation of industrial buildings and of making certain buildings comply with the fire regulations. Other categories of included expenditure relate to safety at sports grounds and stadia (10.9.8) security (10.9.9) and computer software (10.9.14).
(2) Industrial buildings (10.11) — this includes factories and some warehouses, etc.
(3) Agricultural and forestry buildings, etc (10.14).
(4) Hotel buildings, etc (10.15).
(5) Scientific research expenditure (10.17).
(6) Patents and know-how (10.18).
(7) Mines, oil wells, etc (10.20) and dredging (10.19).

If you have expenditure which qualifies for allowances under more than one of the above heads, you will be able to make an irrevocable choice. This applies for accounting periods ending after 27 July 1989 (FA 1989 Sch 13).

10.8.1 Base period
(CAA S160)

For a business, profession or vocation (including partnerships) the capital allowances are computed according to the assets purchased and those used in the annual accounts period (ie, the base period). For these purposes, you must take the date when the expenditure was incurred. This is now generally when the obligation to pay becomes unconditional, unless, for example, part of the capital expenditure is payable more than four months later. A deduction is made from the Schedule D Case I or Case II assessment in respect of the total capital allowances for that tax year. For example, if a business makes up its accounts to 31 December each year then its Schedule D Case I assessment for 1992–93 will be based on its accounts for the year to 31 December 1991 (ending in the preceding tax year). Similarly its 1992–93 capital allowances will be based on the year to 31 December 1991.

In the opening or closing years of a business base periods of less than one year might arise. It is also possible that one base period applies to two tax years in which case the additions during the base period are allocated to the earlier tax year for the purposes of calculating the allowances. If there is a gap between base periods, the gap is added to the second base period unless this marks a cessation of trading — in this case you add the gap to the first period.

10.8.2 VAT Capital Goods Scheme adjustments
(FA 1991 S59)

From 6 April 1990, extra VAT paid under the new VAT Capital Goods Scheme qualifies for capital allowances in the year of payment. Similarly, VAT repaid from that date reduces the appropriate expenditure pool for capital allowances purposes in the year of receipt. This particularly affects businesses which are partly exempt (21.3) from VAT such as those in banking, finance, insurance and property.

The items covered are limited to computers and computer equipment worth at least £50,000 and land and buildings worth at least £250,000. The VAT adjustments generally arise on changes of use.

10.9 Capital allowances on plant and machinery

In general, expenditure after 31 March 1986 only qualifies for 25 per cent writing down allowance each year, however, special rules apply to motor vehicles (10.9.10) and plant which you lease out (10.9.13). Balancing charges and allowances can arise when plant is sold (10.9.4). The main allowances available on plant purchased new or secondhand between 26 October 1970 and 1 April 1986 were normally a first-year allowance for the year of purchase and a writing down allowance for each subsequent year.

10.9.1 First-year allowances
(FA 1971 Ss41–43, FA 1972 S67 & FA 1984 Ss58 & 59 & Sch 12)

Prior to 1 April 1986, for the base year in which you purchased each item of plant or machinery you obtained a first-year allowance based on the cost. You did not get this allowance if the expenditure was incurred in a year during which you permanently ceased to trade nor, in general, if the plant was sold before you brought it into use.

148 Allied Dunbar Tax Guide

For expenditure incurred from 22 March 1972 until 13 March 1984, the first-year allowance rate was 100 per cent and this still applied for expenditure before 1 April 1987 under contracts existing at 13 March 1984. The allowance was then phased out as follows:

Expenditure date	Rate of allowance
After 13.3.84 and before 1.4.85	75%
After 31.3.85 and before 1.4.86	50%
After 31.3.86	nil

Fuller details are given in the 1989–90 and earlier editions of this book.

10.9.2 Writing down allowance
(CAA S24)

Each asset is put into a 'pool' at its cost price (less any first-year allowance obtained) and a writing down allowance of 25 per cent is given on the balance. You can take less than 25 per cent in any year and for accounting periods ending after 13 March 1984, this also applies to companies (12.10). Prior to 1 April 1986, writing down allowance was not normally given for the first year.

Expenditure after 31 March 1986 generally qualifies for no first-year allowance, but writing down allowance runs from the first year. Unlike first-year allowances, writing down allowances only applied when the assets concerned were brought into use. However, from 1 April 1985, they are available from when the expenditure is incurred.

If the base period is less than a year, the rate of writing down allowance is proportionately reduced. Thus, if the base period for a business is only six months for a given year of assessment, then any writing down allowances for that period would be at the rate of $25\% \times 6/12 = 12\frac{1}{2}\%$.

10.9.3 Ships
(CAA Ss30–33)

Free depreciation by postponing first-year allowances is available with regard to new ships. This extends to expenditure on second-hand ships incurred after 31 March 1985. The same principle applies regarding writing down allowances on expenditure on new ships after 13 March 1984 and second-hand ships after 31 March 1985. The allowances can be 'rolled-up' and used at will. These rules do not apply, however, to certain leasing situations where capital allowances are restricted (10.9.13).

10.9.4 Sales of plant and machinery — Balancing allowances and charges
(CAA Ss24, 26, 152 & 161, FA 1990 Sch 13 & F2A 1992 S67)

If you sell an item of plant from your 'pool' of purchases, you simply deduct the sale proceeds from the 'pool' balance. If the proceeds exceed the original cost of the plant, however, you only deduct the cost from the pool and the excess is a capital gain. Should the sale proceeds exceed your 'pool' balance, the excess is treated as a balancing charge and it is added to your assessment for the relevant year. By means of the balancing charge, the Revenue recoup the excess of capital allowances that would otherwise have been given to you.

Note that your time of sale is taken as the earlier of completion or when possession is given. This rule is of general application for most capital allowance purposes regarding sales from 6 April 1990.

Regarding plant, etc (apart from some motor cars) purchased after 26 October 1970, balancing allowances normally only occur in the event of a cessation. If you cease permanently to trade during a period then you receive for that period a 'balancing allowance' equal to the remainder of your 'pool' (of expenditure on assets after 26 October 1970 less allowances already obtained) less its disposal value.

If assets are sold from one person (company, etc) to another, both being under common control, both may elect within two years that the tax written down value is passed from one to the other. The effect is that there is no balancing allowance or charge. A similar election may be made within two years after the succession of a trade between connected persons (for example where a trade passes from one company to another under common control).

With effect from 1 January 1992 balancing charges and other balancing adjustments are not applicable under new legislation relating to certain transfers of UK trades from a company situated in one EC member state to a company situated in another. The consideration must consist of shares or securities and the transfer must be for commercial reasons and not with a main purpose of saving tax.

10.9.5 Example: Capital allowances on plant and machinery

Mr A has been carrying on a manufacturing business for many years and makes up his accounts to 31 December each year. At 31 December 1988 the capital allowances written down value of his plant, etc, was £5,250. Mr A purchased the following new plant:

150 Allied Dunbar Tax Guide

Date	Description	Cost
on 2 February 1989	Typewriters	£1,000
on 1 March 1989	Machinery	5,000
on 30 June 1990	Machinery	8,000
on 30 September 1991	Office furniture	1,925

During the year to 31 December 1989, Mr A sold machinery costing £1,000 for £450.

Compute Mr A's capital allowances from 1990–91 to 1992–93.

		'Pool'	Total allowances
Balance brought forward 1990–91 (base period year to 31 December 1989)		5,250	
Sale proceeds		(450)	
		4,800	
Additions:			
2 February 1989	1,000		
1 March 1989	5,000		
		6,000	
		10,800	
Writing down allowance 25% × £10,800		(2,700)	£2,700
Balance forward 1991–92 (base period year to 31 December 1990)		8,100	
Additions:			
30 June 1990		8,000	
		16,100	
Writing down allowance 25% × £16,100		(4,025)	£4,025
Balance forward		12,075	
1992–93 (base period year to 31 December 1991)			
Additions:			
30 September 1991		1,925	
		14,000	
Writing down allowance 25% × £14,000		(3,500)	£3,500
Balance forward		10,500	

10.9.6 Short-life assets
(CAA Ss37 & 38)

A special rule applies to short-life plant and machinery which you buy for your trade after 31 March 1986. You can elect to have the writing down allowances on that plant calculated separately from your 'pool' (de-pooling). The election must be made within two years of the year of acquisition. De-pooling does not normally apply to assets leased to non-traders, or to cars or ships.

When you sell the assets, there will be a balancing allowance or charge, not normally otherwise arising. However, if the machinery or plant has not been sold within five years, it must be transferred to your 'pool' at its tax written-down value.

10.9.7 Example: Short-life assets — De-pooling

Mr B makes up his business accounts to 31 December and bought plant for £100 on 30 June 1988, for which he made a de-pooling election. The plant is sold for £10 on 15 May 1992. The capital allowances computations are as follows:

Year ended 31 December £

1988	cost	100
	25% writing down allowance	25
		75
1989		19
		56
1990		14
		42
1991		10
		32
1992	Sale proceeds	10
	Balancing allowance	£22

Note: If the plant had not been disposed of by 31 December 1992, the written down value would be transferred to the general plant pool.

10.9.8 Safety at sports grounds
(CAA S70)

If relief is not otherwise available, you can claim capital allowances at 25 per cent on the reducing balance on certain safety expenditure at sports grounds. You must be trading and the grounds designated under the Safety of Sports Grounds Act 1975. From 1 January 1989 this is extended to include 'regulated stands' (broadly providing covered accommodation for 500 or more spectators).

10.9.9 Security assets
(CAA Ss71 & 72)

Expenditure after 5 April 1989 on 'Security assets' may qualify for capital allowances (25 per cent on reducing balance). You must acquire the assets to meet a special threat to your personal security which arises by virtue of your trade or profession. Partnership and sole traders are covered by the rules.

10.9.10 Motor vehicles
(CAA Ss34–36 and 41, FA 1991 S61 & F2A 1992 S71)

If you buy a car for use in your business you will obtain the 25 per cent writing down allowance for every year including the first. Special rules apply, however, to cars costing over £12,000 in which case your allowance for any year is restricted to 25 per cent × £12,000, ie, £3,000. Each car that costs over £12,000 must be treated as a separate 'pool' which, when sold, gives rise to its own balancing allowance or balancing charge. For cars purchased before 11 March 1992 the limit was £8,000.

Cars purchased for no more than £12,000 are all put into a separate pool (CAA S41). This pool also includes assets acquired before 1 April 1986, which you lease out and which did not qualify for first-year allowance (10.9.13). First-year allowances were not given on motor vehicles unless they were designed to carry goods; or were of a type unsuitable for use as private vehicles; or were vehicles for hire to the public such as taxis or certain hire cars; or were provided for the use of the recipients of certain mobility allowances and supplements.

If your car is leased through your business (or company) and its equivalent retail cost price exceeds a given limit, the rental deduction from the taxable business profits is correspondingly restricted. The limit is £12,000 retail cost equivalent if the car was first rented after 10 March 1992 and £8,000 if earlier. This restriction is not to apply to hire purchase arrangements where there is an option to purchase for 1 per cent or less of the original retail cost (FA 1991 S61).

The actual deductible rental is found by multiplying the true rental by $(12,000 + \frac{RP-12,000}{2})$ and dividing it by the RP (retail price of the car when new).

10.9.11 Example: Higher priced motor cars

On 31 January 1992 and 21 June 1992 Mr C purchased for use in his business two cars costing respectively £9,000 and £14,000. The second of these is sold on 30 June 1994 for £7,000. The Revenue direct that 20 per cent of the use of each car should be treated as being for private purposes. Mr C prepares his annual accounts to 31 July each year. Compute the capital allowances available on the cars up to 1995–96.

	(1)	(2)	Total allowances	Allowances available to business (80%)
1993–94				
Additions 31 January 1992	9,000			
21 June 1992		14,000		
Writing down allowance (restricted)	2,000	3,000	£5,000	£4,000
	7,000	11,000		
1994–95 Writing down allowance	1,750	2,750	£4,500	£3,600
	5,250	8,250		
1995–96				
Proceeds 30 June 1994		7,000		
Balancing allowance		£1,250	1,250	
Writing down allowance	1,313		1,313	
			£2,563	£2,050
Carried forward	£3,937			

Notes: (1) Car (1) is subject to the £8,000 restriction being pre-11.3.92 and car (2) to the £12,000 restriction being post 10.3.92.

(2) Because the business use is restricted to 80 per cent the balancing allowance is restricted in this way.

10.9.12 Hire purchase
(CAA S60)

If you buy plant or machinery on hire purchase you are entitled to full capital allowances as soon as you bring it into use in your business. You receive allowances on the capital proportion of the total instalments — the interest proportion is allowed against your business profits in the year that the respective instalments are paid. Thus if you buy under hire purchase a machine whose cash cost would be £1,000 and you are paying a total of £1,600 over three years, you get capital allowances on £1,000 as soon as you start to use the machine (ie, 25 per cent writing down allowance). You would also deduct the interest of £600 from your profits for the three years during which you are paying off the instalments (ie, about £200 each year).

10.9.13 Machinery for leasing
(CAA Ss39–50 & 61)

You are normally able to obtain 25 per cent writing down allowance (10.9.2) on expenditure to buy assets which you lease out. A separate pool is used for all such assets purchased before 1 April 1986 and certain cars (10.9.10). Prior to 1 April 1986 plant purchased for leasing qualified for first year allowance is subject to various rules noted in earlier editions of this book. One requirement was that the assets were used for 'qualifying purposes' for the 'requisite period' (four years of use or earlier disposal).

Where an asset ceased to be used for qualifying purposes during the *requisite period* (above), the capital allowances were recomputed as if no first-year allowance had been given. This normally gave rise to a balancing charge when use for *qualifying purposes* ceased.

Anti-avoidance legislation operates concerning leasing partnerships from which a loss benefit otherwise would be obtained from first-year allowances (13.9.6). Wider provisions prevent your offsetting capital allowances from casual leasing activities against other income (13.9.6). For expenditure incurred after 10 March 1982 on assets leased outside the UK and ships or aircraft let on charter further restrictions apply (13.9.6). Special capital allowances rules also apply to film production costs (10.21).

10.9.14 Computer software
(F2A 1992 S68)

25 per cent writing down allowance is available for capital expenditure on the outright acquisition of computer software. From 10

March 1992, this extends to capital expenditure on software licences and access to electronic transmission.

10.10 Fixtures — Entitlement to capital allowances
(CAA Ss51–59)

Detailed rules apply to clarify who is entitled to capital allowances where machinery or plant is installed in a building or on land and becomes a fixture. The rules may treat the plant as belonging to you for capital allowances purposes even though you are not the owner. Except for payments under certain existing leases or other contracts, the new rules apply to expenditure after 11 July 1984.

If you lease a piece of equipment and it becomes a fixture at a building, you will obtain capital allowances if you jointly elect with the lessee. Where you pay to be granted a lease including a fixture on which the lessor would obtain capital allowances, you can jointly elect that you receive the allowances.

10.11 Industrial buildings
(CAA Ss1–21)

The cost of new industrial buildings that are used in your business (ie factories, warehouses, etc and some repair shops) qualify for industrial buildings allowances. Qualifying expenditure also includes additions and improvements to industrial buildings.

Each year (including the first) a writing down allowance of 4 per cent of the original cost is obtained. (The allowance is 2 per cent if the expenditure was incurred before 6 November 1962.) Up to 25 per cent of the capital cost of an industrial building may relate to a non-qualifying use without restricting the allowances.

Prior to 1 April 1986, expenditure qualified for initial allowance as follows:

Date of expenditure		*Rate*
After	*and before*	
12 November 1974	11 March 1981	50%
10 March 1981	14 March 1984	75%
13 March 1984	1 April 1985	50%
31 March 1985	1 April 1986	25%
31 March 1986		Nil

Building costs after 31 March 1986 normally do not attract initial allowances apart from in Enterprise Zones (10.12). However, expenditure incurred before 1 April 1987 under a binding contract entered into before 14 March 1984, qualified for 75 per cent initial allowance.

If a building on which industrial buildings allowances have been obtained is sold then the sale proceeds must be compared with the balance of original cost less initial allowances and writing down allowances obtained. Any excess proceeds will be assessed as a balancing charge and any deficit will be allowed as a balancing allowance. This now applies even if you had ceased to use the building for industrial purposes. Any excess of the proceeds compared with the original cost must be disregarded for this purpose but may give rise to a capital gain (18.2).

From 6 April 1991, industrial buildings allowance extends to the construction of toll roads (FA 1991 S60).

10.12 Enterprise Zones
(CAA Ss1 & 6, FA 1990 Sch 13 & F2A 1992 Sch 13)

The Government have designated a number of Enterprise Zones. One of their attractions is that expenditure on industrial and commercial buildings including hotels qualifies for 100 per cent initial allowance. Unusually shops and offices are included. Less than the full initial allowance may be claimed in which case 25 per cent writing down allowance (straight line) is available on the original expenditure until used up. These provisions were not changed by the 1984 reforms.

Enterprise Zone allowances are now restricted to exclude expenditure incurred more than ten years after the expiry of the zone. Expenditure payable after 15 December 1991 on an unused building is no longer denied Enterprise Zone allowances because it is bought after the expiry of the zone's ten-year life. Also, allowances are to be available on used buildings sold, within two years of being brought into use after that date. In this case, the purchaser obtains limited relief where part of the expenditure was incurred when the site was in an Enterprise Zone and part was not.

10.13 Small workshops
(FA 1980 S75 & Sch 13, FA 1982 S73, FA 1983 S31 & FA 1984 S58)

Expenditure on small workshops (no more than 2,500 square feet of floor space) incurred after 26 March 1980 and before 27 March

1983 obtained special relief. For small workshops of no more than 1,250 square feet relief extended until 26 March 1985. The reliefs were the same as those available for certain buildings in Enterprise Zones (see above).

10.14 Agricultural buildings allowance
(CAA Ss122–133)

If you are the owner or tenant of any farm or forestry land, you will obtain allowance for your expenditure on certain constructions on that land. These include farmhouses, farm or (generally only up to 19 June 1989) forestry buildings, cottages, and fences, etc.

The allowance is given in the form of an annual writing down allowance of 4 per cent on your original expenditure. For expenditure between 11 April 1978 and 1 April 1986, an initial allowance of up to 20 per cent could also be claimed. The balance was eligible for writing down allowance of 10 per cent of the original cost for each year including the first. For expenditure incurred from 1 April 1986, there is no initial allowance and the writing down allowance is reduced to 4 per cent. (The old rates apply if expenditure is incurred before 1 April 1987 under a contract effected before 14 March 1984.)

Expenditure after 31 March 1986, attracting 4 per cent writing down allowance is generally written off over a 25 year period. However, if you sell or demolish the building within that time, you can elect for a balancing adjustment (ie, balancing allowance or charge — 10.9.4). This also applies if the building is destroyed. The election must be made within two years after the end of the relevant year of assessment (accounting period for a company).

If your expenditure is on a farmhouse, then your allowance will normally be based on only one-third (maximum) of the total cost to take account of the personal benefit.

10.15 Hotel buildings
(CAA Ss6, 7 & 19 & FA 1990 Sch 13)

Expenditure incurred on the construction or improvement of certain hotel buildings qualifies for an annual writing down allowance of 4 per cent of the original cost. If the hotel is in an Enterprise Zone (10.12), expenditure qualifies for relief at special rates (100 per cent initial allowance, etc). To qualify for the allowance, the hotel must have at least ten bedrooms for letting to the public and provide breakfast and an evening meal. Also, it must be open for at least four months in the season from April to October inclusive.

10.16 Assured tenancies
(CAA Ss84–97 & FA 1990 Sch 13)

75 per cent initial allowance followed by 4 per cent writing down allowance was available on qualifying expenditure incurred between 9 March 1982 and 14 March 1984. From 14 March 1984, the initial allowance was phased out in exactly the same way as for industrial buildings (10.11), but the writing down allowance remains for expenditure incurred before 1 April 1992. (The land or property must be acquired under a contract entered into before 15 March 1988.) The allowances are given on dwellings let on assured tenancies by bodies approved by the Secretary of State for the Environment under the Assured Tenancies Scheme. Only approved bodies obtain the allowance.

Although not previously classified as capital allowances for chargeable periods beginning before 6 April 1990, assured tenancies allowances are now included. This enables them to be included in group relief claims (12.13).

The expenditure on each house or flat qualifying for allowance is limited to £40,000 (£60,000 in Greater London). Regarding expenditure after 4 May 1983 (unless under existing contracts) only landlords which are companies qualify for the allowance.

10.17 Scientific research allowance
(CAA Ss136–139 & FA 1990 Sch 13)

Capital expenditure incurred on scientific research for the purposes of your trade is wholly allowed in the year that the expenditure arises. Any revenue expenditure will be allowed as a charge against your taxable profits provided that it is related to your trade or it is medical research related to the welfare of your employees.

Regarding capital expenditure, a full 100 per cent allowance remains after 31 March 1985 subject to some changes. For example, the cost of land and houses is now excluded. At the same time, scientific research allowance and industrial buildings allowance are not given on the same expenditure. Disposal proceeds of scientific research assets are normally treated as taxable trading receipts, to the extent that together with any allowances, they exceed the original cost.

10.18 Patent rights and 'know how'
(TA 1988 Ss520–533 & FA 1989 Sch 13)

The 1985 Finance Act changed the allowance basis for both patent rights and 'know how', so that from 1 April 1986, only a 25 per cent writing down allowance applies.

Prior to 1 April 1986, if you purchased a patent to use in your business then you obtain a writing down allowance of 1/17th of the expenditure for each of the 17 years starting with that in which you made the purchase. If you sell the patent then the excess or deficit of the proceeds compared with the unexpired balance of cost (after writing down allowances) is treated as a balancing charge or allowance (10.9.4). If, however, the proceeds exceed the original cost, then you are assessed to income tax under Schedule D Case VI on this excess (normally spread over six years or the remainder of the patent if less). Note that costs in connection with creating and registering your own patents are treated as deductible revenue expenses (TA 1988 S83).

If you purchase patent rights from a connected person, your allowances may be limited, by reference to the vendor's disposal value for capital allowance purposes. Otherwise, it is necessary to use your capital expenditure, or if smaller, the market value of the rights on your acquiring them, or normally the original acquisition costs of the vendor.

Any payments that you made before 1 April 1986 to obtain 'know how' for your business or profession entitle you to a writing down allowance of one-sixth of such expenditure for each of the first six consecutive years. If you sell 'know how' that had been used in your business, the proceeds are taxed as trading receipts. If, however, you cease to trade within the six years, you may charge the balance of your 'know how' expenditure against the taxable profits of your final trading period.

10.19 Dredging
(CAA Ss134 & 135)

For dredging expenditure after March 1986, an annual writing down allowance of 4 per cent on the original amount is due. Previously an initial allowance of 15 per cent applied, together with writing down allowance at 4 per cent each year on a straight line basis.

10.20 Mineral extraction
(CAA Ss98–121)

Expenditure before 1 April 1986 attracted initial and writing down allowances related to output, etc. These have now been replaced by writing down allowances at 25 per cent or 10 per cent, depending on the nature of the expenditure. Pre-1 April 1986 balances qualify for the new reliefs, but you can claim initial allowances on qualifying expenditure incurred up to 31 March 1987 under a contract entered into before 16 July 1985.

Balancing allowances or charges arise under the present system where mineral deposits cease to be worked or the mine, etc is sold.

10.21 Films, etc
(FA 1982 S72, FA 1983 S32, FA 1984 S62, FA 1985 S48 & F2A 1992 Ss41–43 & 69)

Films, tapes and discs with at least a two-year life normally qualified for full first-year allowances from 1979 (10.9.1). However, this was withdrawn from 10 March 1982 for overseas films but continued for British made films (including those for television). Unless the film, etc is trading stock, the rules provide for the production expenditure not qualifying for capital allowances to be written off over the film's income-producing life. Film investment is sometimes made by means of limited partnerships. However, relief for limited partners' losses after 19 March 1985 was severely restricted (11.3).

The production of qualifying films (those with sufficient EC content) obtains special relief from 11 March 1992. Pre-production costs incurred from that date will attract relief at once, up to a limit of 20 per cent of total budgeted cost; production expenditure on films completed after 10 March 1992 is to be written off as to one-third each year starting with the completion of the film, as is the cost of acquiring qualifying films.

10.22 Relief for losses
(TA 1988 Ss380–390 & 397 & FA 1991 S72)

If the adjusted results for your business, profession or vocation show a deficit of income compared with expenditure for a particu-

Income from businesses and professions   161

lar year then your assessment under Case I or Case II of Schedule D will be nil for the related tax year. Thus, if your accounts run to 31 December and you make an adjusted loss of £1,000 for 1991, your 1992–93 assessment will be nil. The loss of £1,000 for the year to 31 December 1991 should be augmented by your 1992–93 capital allowances (say £600) and the resultant total loss of £1,600 is available for relief. This is first given against (*a*) your other income for the tax year in which you suffer the loss and (*b*) that for the following tax year. ((*a*) includes your business assessment on the profits for the year prior to the loss.)

A new rule was introduced for 1991–92 and future years. If you make a trading loss in the year and have insufficient other income for the year to offset it, you can claim relief against capital gains for that tax year. If there are still unused trading losses after absorbing other income for the following year, relief is available against the capital gains for that year (18.13).

Strictly speaking you should apportion your loss to the actual tax years that span your accounts year: thus, if your loss (excluding capital allowances) for the year to 31 December 1991 is £1,600, this is allocated as follows: £1,600 × 3/12 = £400 to 1990–91 and £1,600 × 9/12 = £1,200 to 1991–92. Except in the first years of trading, however, the Revenue normally allow you to allocate the loss for a given accounts year to the tax year in which it ends. Thus the £1,600 loss for the year to 31 December 1991 is allocated to 1991–92 and your relief is set against other income for 1991–92 and 1992–93.

A strict order of set-off must be followed — the loss is first set against your other earned income for the year, then against your unearned income. Prior to 6 April 1990, it was then possible to set any balance of the loss against your spouse's earned income and then his or her unearned income. However, following the introduction of independent taxation from that date, this is no longer permitted.

The above loss relief is given under TA 1988 S380 and you must claim it by making the required election to your Inspector of Taxes within two years of the end of the tax year to which it relates. If your loss is not entirely relieved as above then you can claim that the balance should be carried forward and set off against future profits from the *same* trade, profession or vocation (TA 1988 S385).

Note that you are not allowed to carry a loss forward from one trade to another. You should remember this if you change businesses. A move to a nearby shop in the same trade may be in order, however.

Your loss in the first year of assessment of a new business includes *pre-trading expenditure* of a revenue nature (10.3.1). This applied to individuals and partnerships regarding such expenditure within three years before trading commences (TA 1988 S401). For trades beginning after 31 March 1989, the period is five years (FA 1989 S113).

Income tax relief is claimable for certain losses on disposals of *unquoted shares in trading companies* by original subscribers (18.14). These losses take precedence over claims under S380.

Loss relief is given before personal reliefs and allowances (3.0.1, etc) which cannot be carried forward. Thus these may be lost through your income being absorbed by losses. If possible, carry the losses forward in these circumstances so that your allowances are not wasted.

10.22.1 Example: Relief for losses

Dr D made a loss of £2,000 in his practice for the year to 31 December 1990 having made a profit of £600 for 1989. In 1991 his profit was £12,000. His only other income is taxed dividends, which including tax credits amount to £500 for 1990–91, £550 for 1991–92 and £600 for 1992–93. What loss relief can Dr D obtain?

Dr D's loss of £2,000 for the year to 31 December 1990 will be allocated to the tax year 1990–91 (10.21).

1990–91 loss relief (S380)	
(1) Against 1990–91 Schedule D Case II assessment	£600
(2) Against 1990–91 dividends	500
	£1,100
1991–92 loss relief (S380)	
Against 1991–92 dividends	£550
1992–93 loss relief (S385)	
Against 1992–93 Schedule D Case II assessment	£350

(Case II assessment for 1992–93 becomes £12,000 − £350 = £11,650)

10.23 Loss in new business
(TA 1988 S381)

If you carry on a business or profession personally or in partnership, a special relief is available. This applies to any loss which you make in your first year of assessment, or in any of the next three years. A written claim is required within two years of the end of the year of assessment.

The losses include capital allowances, and certain pre-trading expenditure (see above). They are offset against your income for the three years of assessment prior to the year in which the losses are made, taking the earliest first.

10.24 Terminal losses

If you cease to carry on a trade, profession or vocation and make an adjusted loss in your last complete year of trading, you get relief for this so-called 'terminal loss'. The relief is augmented by your capital allowances apportionable to your last 12 months of trading. The terminal losses are allowed against your business assessments for the three years prior to that in which you cease to trade.

10.25 Business Expansion Scheme
(TA 1988 Ss289–312, FA 1988 Ss50–53 & Sch 4, FA 1989 S47, FA 1990 S73 & F2A 1992 Ss38–40)

Under the Business Expansion Scheme, subject to the rules, you obtain income tax relief in a year of assessment in respect of amounts subscribed for shares in a qualifying company during that year. A qualifying company exists to carry on one or more *qualifying trades* — broadly, manufacturing, wholesale and retail business but not leasing and financial activities, etc.

The Business Expansion Scheme operates regarding shares issued from 6 April 1983 up to 31 December 1993. Previously, for 1981–82 and 1982–83 the similar but less favourable Business Start-Up Scheme was available.

The following features of the Business Expansion Scheme should be noted:

(1) The life of the scheme was first extended to 5 April 1987 and now to 31 December 1993.
(2) As well as covering investment in new companies, shares issued by established unquoted trading companies satisfying certain conditions are included.

(3) The scheme excludes employees, paid directors and 30 per cent + shareholders.
(4) The annual total investment limit was doubled to £40,000 but the minimum remains at £500 unless made through approved investment funds. There is no restriction on the percentage of the share capital which may be included (but see (15) and (18) below).
(5) Shares on which relief is claimed must in general be held for at least five years.
(6) Claims for relief can be made once the company has carried on its qualifying trade for four months; and normally must be made within two years after the end of the year of assessment to which the claim relates.
(7) The relief does not normally reduce the cost for capital gains tax purposes. Furthermore shares issued after 18 March 1986 are exempt from capital gains tax when first disposed of.
(8) In respect of shares issued after 13 March 1984 and before 19 March 1986, farming is not a qualifying trade (see above).
(9) In general, a trade whose income is mainly from royalties and licence fees does not qualify, but an exception applies for film producing companies. After 16 March 1987, shares issued by companies both producing and distributing films qualify.
(10) From 6 April 1985, companies whose business consists of research and development will, in general, qualify.
(11) Between 19 March 1985 and 19 March 1986, property development was not a qualifying trade where the company doing the development had an interest in the land being developed.
(12) Ship chartering is a qualifying trade for shares issued after 18 March 1986. Charters must not exceed one year and the ships must be UK registered and owned, managed and navigated by the company. (Pleasure craft are excluded.)
(13) After 18 March 1986, wholesaling or retailing goods normally collected or held as investments is not a qualifying trade, unless the company actively tries to sell them. Examples are fine wines and antiques.
(14) Certain parent companies have previously been qualifying companies if all their subsidiaries have been wholly owned. After 18 March 1986, this extends to tiers of companies provided they are each at least 90 per cent owned. Subsidiaries can even be resident abroad if the group's trade is mainly within the UK. (Subject to the rules, a company will not be precluded from the scheme, by having a property management subsidiary.)

(15) Share capital issued in excess of £50,000 in total in any year does not qualify for relief if the company broadly has more than half its assets consisting of land and buildings. This applies regarding shares issued after 18 March 1986 only. The land content test applies at any time within three years after either the issue of the shares, or the commencement of trade if later. In calculating the land and buildings fraction, you deduct from the land liabilities secured on it and certain unsecured long-term liabilities and preference shares. From August 1988 you exclude from the value of buildings any fixed machinery or plant forming part of it.

(16) If you buy qualifying shares after 5 April 1987, half of your investment can be carried back to 1986–87, provided it is made before 6 October 1987. The relief carried back in this way is limited to £5,000. You must elect for this treatment and your total relief for any tax year must not exceed £40,000. Similar relief applies for 1987–88 and future years.

(17) If you invest in an approved BES fund which closes after 15 March 1988, you obtain relief when it becomes closed for investment, rather than when it invests in BES shares. The fund must invest 90 per cent of your investment within six months of the closing date.

(18) Regarding BES shares issued on or after 1 May 1990, a maximum amount of £750,000 capital raised by a company qualifies for relief in any period of 12 months. The limit prior to 1 May 1990 and after 15 March 1988 was £500,000. However, a £5,000,000 limit applies for certain ship chartering and private rented housing (below).

(19) From 29 July 1988, BES relief extends to investment in companies enabling them to buy properties for letting under new-styled *assured tenancies* when this new system started in 1989. (This relief is only available for investment up to 31 December 1993, as with other BES relief.) The company must provide tenancies over at least a four-year period from when the BES shares are issued. Properties valued at over £125,000 in Greater London and otherwise £85,000 are excluded. After 19 March 1990, improvements in the locality are ignored when valuing for this purpose.

(20) From 10 March 1992, BES companies are allowed to buy properties from owner-occupiers and grant qualifying tenancies to the former owners. This helps mortgage rescue schemes to operate without jeopardising BES relief.

(21) Tax relief for interest on loans to buy shares in a close company (12.17) issued after 13 March 1989 is not available if BES relief is available.

10.26 Earnings basis and cash basis

If you are carrying on a trade, you will normally be taxed on an 'earnings basis'. This means that your sales for each accounts period are included as they arise and not when you receive the money. Sales normally arise when they are invoiced. In a retail shop the sales usually arise as the customers pay over the counter. Your expenses are also deductible on an arising basis and the actual date of payment is not relevant.

If you are carrying on a profession or vocation, however, the Revenue may tax you on a 'cash basis', which means by reference to the actual cash received, taking no account of uncollected fees at the end of each accounts period. (Sometimes a mixed earnings and cash basis is allowed.)

The cash basis is usually used for barristers. Other professions must prepare their opening accounts on an earnings basis but have the option of later switching to a cash basis. Often the expenses are calculated on an arising basis but in some small cases the actual expense payments are used ignoring accruals.

10.27 Post-cessation receipts
(TA 1988 Ss103–110)

If, after you permanently cease your trade, profession or vocation, you receive amounts relating to those activities, they are known as 'post-cessation receipts'. An example is a late fee payment that had not been included in your accounts because they are prepared on a cash basis or the fee was not included in your outstandings.

Post-cessation receipts are usually taxed under Schedule D Case VI (13.1). They are normally treated as earned income and you can set off unrelieved losses and capital allowances from before the cessation. You can, however, elect that any post-cessation receipts for the first six years after cessation should be added to your income from the business, etc on its last day of trading.

Relief is available for those born before 6 April 1917 and in business on 18 March 1968 who are taxed on a fraction of their post-cessation receipts varying between 19/20ths and 5/20ths. The latter fraction applies if you were born before 6 April 1903; if you were born before 6 April 1904 the fraction is 6/20ths and so on.

10.28 Class 4 National Insurance contributions
(TA 1988 S617)

You will be liable to pay the contributions if you are self-employed in accordance with the rules in Chapter 23 (23.5). For 1985–86 and subsequent years, you may claim relief for half of your Class 4 contributions. Your total income (5.2) is reduced accordingly.

11 Partnerships

11.1 What is a partnership?

Partnership is the relationship which exists between two persons in business together with the object of making profits. There does not necessarily have to be a written partnership agreement but the partnership must exist in fact. If no partnership is in fact operating then, even though there may be a written agreement, it would not make the partnership exist.

Since the assessment of a partnership differs from that of an individual in certain respects, the Revenue will seek to establish whether a partnership in fact exists. Points to consider include:

(1) Is there a written partnership agreement?
(2) Can the partners close down the business and are they liable for its debts?
(3) Do the partners' names appear on business stationery?
(4) What arrangements exist for dividing the profits (and property on dissolution)?

11.2 How partnership income is taxed
(TA 1988 S111)

A joint assessment to income tax under Case I or Case II of Schedule D (10.1) is made on the partners in respect of the partnership profits. This includes basic rate (25 per cent) and higher rate income tax (if any) on the profits. The rules for the opening (10.7.1) and closing years (10.7.3) are generally followed as for individuals, as are those for capital allowances (10.8). However, there are special rules covering partnership changes (11.4). The 'precedent partner', who is normally the senior partner, must make a joint return of the partnership income each year.

Allied Dunbar Tax Guide

Partnership investment income is split between the partners in their profit-sharing ratios and they personally pay any income tax arising.

When the partnership income has been determined for the purposes of Schedule D Case I or Case II, it must be split between the partners according to the proportions in which they share profits during the tax year. These proportions are not necessarily the same as the profit sharing ratios during the year when the profits were actually made. Thus if A and B made £10,000 in the year to 30 April 1991 when they split their profits 60 : 40 their partnership assessment for 1992–93 is on the preceding year basis, ie, £10,000. This is split in the ratio in which they divide profits for the year to 5 April 1993. Suppose the ratio is altered to 50 : 50 on 1 May 1991 then they will each be assessed on £5,000 for 1992–93. If a partner is remunerated partly by way of a salary and partly by receiving a share of the profits, the salary is normally not assessed under Schedule E but is included in his profit share assessable under Schedule D Case I or Case II.

Interest paid to partners in respect of their capital is also treated as part of the profit share of each partner and is assessed under Schedule D Case I or Case II. Such interest is not an annual payment (4.1), nor is it taxed as investment income (8.1).

11.2.1 Example: Partnership assessments

A, B and C trade in partnership sharing profits equally after the interest and salary allocations shown below. They prepare accounts to 5 April showing the following:

	Profits	Interest A	Interest B	Salary B	Salary C
5 April 1992	£9,000	£500	£500	£1,000	£2,000
1993	£10,000	£400	£600	£1,500	£1,500

The 1992–93 assessment under *Schedule D Case I* is as follows:

	Total	A	B	C
Net profit (preceding year) — year ended 5 April 1992	£9,000			
Add: Interest A	500			
B	500			
Salary B	1,000			
C	2,000			
	£13,000			

					£400		
Less:	Interest	A	400				
		B	600			£600	
	Salary	B	1,500			1,500	
		C	1,500				£1,500
				4,000			
Balance split equally				£9,000	3,000	3,000	3,000
Total assessment				£13,000	£3,400	£5,100	£4,500

Notes:
(1) In addition to the above, the normal Schedule D Case I adjustments must be made (10.4).
(2) The interest and salaries for the year to 5 April 1992 are added back to the profits.
(3) The 1992–93 assessments split includes the interest and salaries for the year to 5 April 1993.

11.3 Partnership losses
(TA 1988 Ss380–381 & 387)

Where a partnership has an adjusted loss for any accounting period, that loss is apportioned between the partners in the same ratio as a profit would have been split. Thus the loss is split according to the profit sharing ratios applying to the year of assessment corresponding to the tax year in which the loss is made. For example, if a loss is made in the year to 5 April 1992 this is split between the partners according to their profit sharing ratios for the tax year 1992–93 (assuming that the preceding year basis of assessment applies).

Each partner can use his partnership losses as he chooses according to the various rules for obtaining loss relief (10.22). Thus he can claim for the loss to be relieved against his other income tax assessments for the tax year in which the loss is actually made or the following year. This means that relief can be obtained against the previous year's partnership profits. Also he can carry forward any unused balance of the loss to be set off against future profit shares from the same partnership; this applies even if the partnership had been treated as discontinued because of a partnership change (see below).

If you are a limited partner, so that your risk is limited to the capital which you have invested, your loss is also restricted in the same way. This applies broadly to losses after 19 March 1985.

11.4 Changes of partners
(TA 1988 Ss61–63 & 113)

If there is any change in the make up of a partnership caused either by a partner leaving or dying or a fresh partner joining, the partnership is treated as ceasing for taxation purposes unless the continuation election described below is made.

The effects of cessation caused by a change of partners are similar to any other Schedule D Case I or Case II cessation (10.7.3). Thus the assessment for the final tax year is based on the actual profits for that year and the Revenue have the option to increase the assessments for the two previous tax years to the actual profits for those years. Also any unrecouped stock relief (10.6) was brought into charge on a change of partners before 13 March 1984, subject to a continuation election (see below).

Up to 19 March 1985, the first years of a changed partnership were assessed in accordance with the normal commencement rules (10.7.1). However, for changes after that date, the first four years are assessed on an actual basis and then the previous year basis applies, unless you elect for years five and six to be on an actual profit basis. This is subject to a continuation election (11.5).

11.5 Election for continuation basis
(TA 1988 Ss113 & 116)

Within two years of the date of a change in the members of a partnership an election can be made to the Revenue that the partnership should be taxed on a continuation basis. This election can be made provided that at least one of the partners in the old partnership remains as a partner in the new partnership. All of the partners in both the old and the new partnership must sign the election.

The effect of the election is that the partnership is not treated as ceasing for taxation purposes at the date of the change. Instead the Schedule D Case I or Case II assessment for the tax year in which the change takes place is apportioned to the date of the change. Then the old partners are assessed on their share of the assessment apportioned up to the change and the new partners are assessed on the proportion after the change.

For example, suppose that the adjusted profits of a professional partnership for the year to 31 December 1991 are £12,000 and until

5 October 1992 there were three equal partners A, B and C. If with effect from that date B and C sell their partnership shares to D and assuming A, B, C and D all make the necessary election before 5 October 1994, the following Schedule D Case II assessments will arise for 1992–93 (on a preceding year basis):

	6 April 1992 – 5 October 1992	6 October 1992 – 5 April 1993	Total
A	£2,000	£2,000	£4,000
B	2,000	—	2,000
C	2,000	—	2,000
D	—	4,000	4,000
	£6,000	£6,000	£12,000

There are some special rules governing partnerships between individuals and a company (TA 1988 Ss114–115).

11.6 Partnership capital gains
(TCGA S59)

When a partnership asset is sold in circumstances that if owned by an individual capital gains tax would have been payable, this tax is assessed on the partners according to their shares in the partnership asset. Thus if a capital gain of £1,000 is made from the sale of a partnership asset on 1 January 1993 and A, B, C and D share equally in the partnership assets, a capital gain of £250 each must be added to the capital gains tax assessments for 1992–93 of A, B, C and D respectively (18.1).

Where a share in a partnership changes hands, a share in all of the partnership assets is treated for capital gains tax purposes as changing ownership and this might give rise to capital gains or capital losses for the partner who is disposing of his share. Thus if A, B and C are equal partners and A sells his share to D, A is treated for capital gains tax purposes as disposing of a one-third share in each of the partnership assets to D.

11.7 Overseas partnerships
(TA 1988 S112)

If you are in partnership carrying on a trade or business and the control and management of the trade or business is outside the UK then the partnership is treated for tax purposes as being non-resident. This follows even if you or some of your other partners are resident here (15.3.4) and some of the business is conducted in this country.

Any profits arising from the partnership trade or business in this country are assessed here under Schedule D Case I. The firm is assessed in the name of any partner resident in the United Kingdom. Regarding the partnership profits earned abroad, these are assessable in respect of any profit shares of the partners resident here under Schedule D Case V according to the special rules outlined in Chapter 16. This now generally applies even if under a double tax agreement, the profits of the overseas partnership arising abroad are exempt from UK tax.

11.8 European economic interest groupings
(FA 1990 S69 & Sch 11)

Tax rules regarding European Economic Interest Groupings (EEIGs) operate from 1 July 1989. Such 'groupings' are business entities set up by two or more European community member states with simpler rules than traditional company law bodies—they are more akin to partnerships in some respects. EEIGs may not be formed to make profits for themselves but rather benefit all of their members. Likely activities are packing, processing, marketing and research.

An EEIG is transparent, so far as tax on income and capital gains is concerned. Thus these will only be charged to tax in the hands of the members. However, this does not apply to the deduction of tax. Thus an EEIG based in the UK is responsible for operating PAYE.

12 Companies

12.1 Introduction

The following is a general outline of the taxation of companies that are resident in the UK or are trading here through a branch or agency. In the latter case it is normally only the profits arising in this country that are taxable here. It must be stressed that the actual provisions are lengthy and many details have been omitted in this summary.

12.2 Corporation tax on profits, etc
(TA 1988 S6 & FA 1991 S23 & F2A 1992 Ss21 & 22)

The tax on the profits, etc of companies is called corporation tax which is charged at the present rate of 33 per cent, subject to special relief for companies with profits under £1,250,000 (12.7). Full corporation tax is now charged both on a company's profits and its capital gains (12.15). (Before 17 March 1987, corporation tax was charged on only a fixed fraction of a company's capital gains — see 12.2.1 below.) Corporation tax applies not only to limited companies, but also to certain associations and unlimited companies. A company's income must be considered for each accounting period (see below). It is charged to corporation tax on the basis of the actual income assessable for each accounting period according to the rules of the various cases of Schedule D (2.3.1) or other Schedules if applicable.

The rate of corporation tax was fixed by Parliament in the Finance Act each year for the preceding 'financial year'. A 'financial year' commences on 1 April and for example the financial year 1992 is the year to 31 March 1993. The Finance Act 1991 retrospectively reduced the rate for 1990 from 35 per cent to 34 per cent often resulting in repayments. The rates for 1991 and 1992 have been fixed at 33 per cent. The following table shows the rates of corporation tax over the years.

12.2.1 Table: Full corporation tax rates

Financial year	Tax rate	Taxable fraction of capital gains
1973–1982	52%	15/26
1983	50%	3/5
1984	45%	2/3
1985	40%	3/4
1986	35%	6/7*
1987–1989	35%	All
1990	34%	All
1991–92	33%	All

* All if gains after 16 March 1987

12.3 The imputation system

If a company pays dividends, these are paid gross to the shareholders, and tax of 25/75ths of the dividend must be paid over to the Revenue as what is known as 'advance corporation tax' (12.6). Before 6 April 1988 the ACT rate was 27/73rds, prior to 6 April 1987 29/71sts, before 6 April 1986 3/7ths and prior to 6 April 1979 33/67ths. This ACT can be deducted from the company's corporation tax bill, so that effectively a lower rate than 33 per cent is paid. The shareholders are 'imputed' with tax of 25/75ths of their dividends, and are only liable for tax at the higher rate.

UK shareholders get a tax credit of 25/75ths of their dividends, but pay the higher rate on their dividends plus tax credits. Thus, if you receive a dividend of £75, you are imputed with a tax credit of 25/75ths × £75 = £25. You pay higher rates of tax on £75 + £25 = £100, but you deduct the £25 tax credit from your total tax bill. The imputation of basic tax rate in the shareholders' hands on their dividends has resulted in the present system being known as the 'imputation system' of corporation tax.

12.4 Accounting periods for corporation tax
(TA 1988 Ss8, 10 & 478 & Sch 30)

Corporation tax is charged in respect of accounting periods. These usually coincide with the periods for which the company prepares its annual accounts but cannot exceed 12 months in duration. Thus, if a company prepares accounts for a period of 18 months, the first 12 months will constitute one accounting period and the remaining six months are treated as another accounting period.

The actual tax is payable nine months after the end of each accounting period, or within 30 days from the date of issue of the assessment if this is later. In the case of a company that traded before April 1965, however, the same interval between the company's accounting date and tax due date as then existed was retained.

The rules for pre-April 1965 companies were changed for accounting periods starting after 16 March 1987. There was first a three-year transitional period, after which corporation tax was to be paid nine months after the end of each accounting period. During the transitional period, the payment interval was reduced to nine months in three equal steps. For example, a company with a payment interval of 21 months and an accounting period ending 31 March had its payment interval reduced as follows:

Accounting period	Payment interval	Payment date
1.4.86 to 31.3.87	21 months	1.1.89
1.4.87 to 31.3.88	17 months	1.9.89
1.4.88 to 31.3.89	13 months	1.5.90
1.4.89 to 31.3.90	9 months	1.1.91

Interest may arise on overdue corporation tax in accordance with the rules (14.7.2). Recent interest rates are 9.75 per cent from 6 October 1991, 10 per cent from 6 July 1991, 10.75 per cent from 6 May 1991 and 11.5 per cent from 6 March 1991. The rates correspond with those for repayment supplements (12.5).

12.5 Repayment supplement
(TA 1988 S825 & FA 1989 S158)

This applies for a company if it receives a tax repayment more than a year after the date that corporation tax is due for the relevant accounting period and after 31 July 1975. Also, prior to 27 July 1989 the repayment needed to be at least £100. The repayment supplement is tax free, and is calculated from the date one year after the due date for paying corporation tax until the end of the tax month (ending fifth day of next month) in which the repayment is made. If the original tax had not been paid, by the anniversary of the due date, the interest runs from the anniversary following the payment of the tax. Where loss relief is claimed (12.11), repayment supplement may arise with reference to the accounting period of the loss, rather than any earlier period when the original profits were made. The rates are as follows:

From	Rate per cent	From	Rate per cent
6 October 1991	$9\frac{1}{4}$	6 May 1988	$7\frac{3}{4}$
6 July 1991	10	6 December 1987	$8\frac{1}{4}$
6 May 1991	$10\frac{3}{4}$	6 September 1987	9
6 March 1991	$11\frac{1}{2}$	6 June 1987	$8\frac{1}{4}$
6 November 1990	$12\frac{1}{4}$	6 April 1987	9
6 November 1989	13	6 November 1986	$9\frac{1}{2}$
6 July 1989	$12\frac{1}{4}$	6 August 1986	$8\frac{1}{2}$
6 January 1989	$11\frac{1}{2}$	1 May 1985	11
6 October 1988	$10\frac{3}{4}$	1 December 1982	8
6 August 1988	$9\frac{3}{4}$	1 January 1980	12

12.6 ACT on dividends, etc
(TA 1988 Ss14, 209, 238 & 239)

Companies have to pay 'advance corporation tax' (ACT) at 25/75ths on their payments of dividends. This tax is also payable on other 'qualifying distributions'. The rate was 3/7ths for 1973–74, 33/67ths to 5 April 1975, 35/65ths to 5 April 1977, 34/66ths to 5 April 1978 and 33/67ths to 5 April 1979, after which it was 3/7ths up to 5 April 1986, then 29/71sts to 5 April 1987 and 27/73rds to 5 April 1988, following which 25/75ths applies (12.3).

12.6.1 Distributions

Under the present system there are two different classes of distribution known as qualifying and non-qualifying distributions. Qualifying distributions are dividends and similar payments. Other examples are interest on certain securities and after 14 May 1992 on Equity Notes (F2A 1992 S32). Non-qualifying distributions are those which are really distributions of special sorts of shares, etc which carry a potential future claim on the company's profits: for example, bonus debentures or bonus redeemable shares. Whereas qualifying distributions are subjected to ACT, in the case of non-qualifying distributions, no ACT is payable by the company. The shareholder gets no tax credit at the basic rate (25 per cent) and is not liable to such tax on the non-qualifying distribution. He is, however, liable to the excess of his higher rate tax over the basic rate on the actual value of the non-qualifying distribution.

12.6.2 Accounting periods for ACT
(TA 1988 Sch 13)

Companies must account to the Revenue for ACT on a three-monthly basis. Returns are made for each three months to 31 March and 30 June, 30 September and 31 December respectively — and so on. Also if the company's accounting period does not end on one of these dates, the period of three months during which it ends is divided into two separate periods for which returns must be submitted. Thus if a company's accounts run to 30 November each year, it submits ACT returns for the period 1 October to 30 November and 1 December to 31 December, as well as for the other three quarters each year.

The ACT return must show for the relevant period the 'franked payments' (see below) and 'franked investment income' received (see below) as well as the amount of ACT payable and certain other details. A cheque in settlement of the ACT due should normally be sent with the return. This is due within 14 days of the return period. In computing the ACT due for payment, companies may deduct tax credits on receipts of 'franked investment income' during the relevant period.

12.6.3 Franked payment
(TA 1988 S238)

This is defined as being a qualifying distribution made by a company together with the relevant ACT. Thus, a qualifying distribution of £7,500 represents a franked payment of £10,000 (ie, £7,500 + £7,500 × 25/75).

12.6.4 Franked investment income
(TA 1988 S238)

This consists of income from a UK resident company (15.3.3) being distributions in respect of which tax credits are obtained. A company's franked investment income is the amount including the relevant tax credits. Thus if a company receives a dividend of £750, this is treated as being franked investment income of £1,000 (ie, £750 + £750 × 25/75).

12.6.5 Setting off ACT against 'mainstream' corporation tax
(TA 1988 Ss238–246)

As its name suggests, advance corporation tax is a pre-payment of the main or mainstream corporation tax bill of a company. The latter is only ascertained when accounts are submitted to the Revenue after the end of the accounting period.

There is a limit to the amount of ACT which can be off-set against a company's 'mainstream' corporation tax liability. This limit is the amount of ACT which would be paid on a full distribution of the company's income excluding capital gains but before the deduction of any tax. In computing this full distribution, account is taken of the notional ACT payable.

For example, if a company makes adjusted revenue profits of £2,000,000 before tax for the year to 31 March 1993, the maximum set-off for ACT is £500,000. Thus, if the company distributed £1,500,000 it would pay ACT of £1,500,000 × 25/75 = £500,000 and so its entire profit would be absorbed. After the end of its accounts year it would be assessed to £2,000,000 × 33 per cent corporation tax (£660,000) from which £500,000 ACT would be deducted leaving a net amount payable of £160,000 (8 per cent). (This is of course an arbitrary calculation because after taking account of all of the corporation tax payable in this example, the distribution would produce a deficit.)

For accounting periods beginning on or after 17 March 1987, but not before, ACT may be set off against corporation tax on capital gains (12.15). Where an accounting period straddled 17 March 1987, only corporation tax on gains after that date qualified for set-off.

A company obtains relief for overseas tax suffered by deducting it from the corporation tax falling on the same income. Previously, this set-off was made after deducting ACT, which resulted in a loss of double tax relief in many cases. However, for accounting periods ending after 31 March 1984, the overseas tax is deducted before any relief is taken for ACT. For accounting periods beginning after 2 June 1986, the rules were changed to ensure that the net corporation tax charge on foreign income, after double tax relief and ACT, is at least the now 8 per cent minimum (see above).

12.6.6 Carry-back and carry-forward of ACT
(TA 1988 S239)

Any ACT which is not relieved against corporation tax payable for the accounting period in which the relevant distribution is made, because of the restriction mentioned above, is known as 'surplus ACT'. This surplus ACT can be carried back and off-set against corporation tax payable for any accounting periods beginning in the six years preceding that in which the relevant distribution is made. (For accounting periods ending before 1 April 1984, the carry-back was confined to accounting periods ending in the previous two years.) A claim to this effect must be made within two years of the end of the period for which the surplus ACT arises.

If a claim as above is made to the Revenue, the surplus ACT will be allocated to one or more earlier periods and a reduction in corporation tax payable or a repayment of corporation tax will result.

Any surplus ACT which is not carried back as above may normally be carried forward without time limit to be set off against future corporation tax payable.

12.7 Small companies rate
(TA 1988 S13 & F2A 1992 S22)

This is the term used to describe the special reduced corporation tax rate which is charged on company profits which do not exceed certain limits for a given accounting period. The profits in question comprise those on which corporation tax is paid together with 'franked investment income' (12.6.4) for the period. The rate is 25 per cent from 1 April 1988. However, small companies rate does not apply to close-investment holding companies for chargeable accounting periods beginning after 31 March 1989 (12.18).

The small companies rate applies to periods after 31 March 1973 and previous rates have been as follows:

	%
6 years to 31 March 1979	42
3 years to 31 March 1982	40
Year to 31 March 1983	38
3 years to 31 March 1986	30
Year to 31 March 1987	29
Year to 31 March 1988	27

The rate is to be charged on the profits of a company with no 'associated companies' (see below) provided these do not exceed £250,000. If the profits are between £250,000 and £1,250,000, some marginal relief is given. These figures have been fixed for the two years to 31 March 1993, prior to which they were £200,000 and £1,000,000 for the year to 31 March 1991, £150,000 and £750,000 for the year to 31 March 1990 and previously £100,000 and £500,000. The tax is then broadly the full corporation tax rate (12.2.1) on the profits less a fixed fraction of the amount by which they fall short of £1,250,000. Recent fractions are 1/50 for financial year 1987 and 1/40 for 1988 and 1989.

For 1990, the fraction was originally set at 1/40 but has been revised to 9/400, with retrospective effect. For 1991 and 1992, the fraction is 1/50. Thus for these years, there is a marginal tax rate of 35 per cent applying within the £250,000–£1,250,000 profit range. This assumes there are no 'associated companies' (see below).

If a company has 'associated companies', then the above-mentioned figures of £250,000 and £1,250,000 must be divided by one plus the number of 'associated companies' connected with the company under consideration. Thus, if five associated companies comprise a group, they will each pay 25 per cent on their profits for the year to 31 March 1993 if these are no more than £50,000 (£250,000/5) each. If any of the companies has profits between £50,000 and £250,000 (£1,250,000/5), some marginal relief is obtained.

12.8 Associated companies
(TA 1988 Ss416 & 417)

These are companies which are either under common control or one controls the other. Control broadly comprises voting power or entitlement to the greater part of either the profits, or the assets on liquidation.

In considering whether two companies are under common control, shares held by a husband and wife and their minor children are considered as one. If, however, one company is controlled by an individual and another company is controlled by a more distant relative such as his brother, the two companies are not normally treated as being 'associated'.

Also 'associated' are the settlor of a trust and its trustees. Furthermore, if you are interested in any shares held by a trust, you are 'associated' with the trustees. Two companies can be associated if both are interested in the same shares.

12.9 The computation of assessable profits
(TA 1988 Ss8–9 & 337–341)

It is strictly speaking necessary to compute the income assessable under each Schedule (and Case of Schedule D) and aggregate these to find the total amount chargeable to corporation tax. All corporation tax assessments are made on an 'actual' basis, however, instead of the preceding year basis that sometimes applies for income tax purposes; for example, Schedule D Case I (10.7.2).

The adjustments to the accounts profits that are required for corporation tax purposes follow with some modifications the normal rules for income tax assessments described earlier in the book. The following are some of the necessary adjustments:

(1) Deduct any franked investment income (12.6.4).
(2) Add back payments made for non-business purposes (10.3.2).
(3) Add back capital losses and payments and deduct capital profits and capital receipts. The capital gain less capital losses of the company must be computed for the accounting period according to the capital gains tax rules (18.1).
(4) Add back legal and other professional charges relating to capital projects.
(5) Add back business entertaining unless in connection with the company's own staff or, before 15 March 1988, overseas customers (10.3.2). Gifts of advertising articles such as diaries, pens, etc of less than £10 value to each customer are also allowable.
(6) Add back depreciation and amortisation charged in the accounts in respect of fixed assets.
(7) Adjust the interest payable and receivable to the actual gross payments and receipts during the accounting period (if this is different from the amount shown in the accounts).
(8) Deduct capital allowances for the accounting period (see below and 10.8).
(9) Add back any balancing charges and deduct any balancing allowances (10.9.4).
(10) Add income tax at the basic rate to any building society interest received. This income tax is calculated by multiplying the actual interest received by 25/75 (2.7). The tax must then be deducted from the total corporation tax payable.
(11) Add accruals of rent from members of the same group of

companies who have already obtained tax relief (13.9.11). This applies to rent accruing on or after 10 March 1992.

12.10 Special capital allowances rules for companies

The normal capital allowances rules for businesses, etc (10.8), apply to companies subject to a number of special rules including the following:
(1) An individual in business can claim that his writing down allowances should be at a lower rate than the normal rate of 25 per cent. Companies have this right (CAA S24) for chargeable periods ending after 13 March 1984.
(2) Where a company obtained first year allowance (10.9.1) in respect of capital expenditure, if this resulted in an adjusted loss for corporation tax purposes such loss may be carried back and set off against profits for the three preceding years (TA 1988 S393). In general, expenditure after 31 March 1986 no longer attracts first year allowance.
(3) Where there is a 'company reconstruction without change of ownership' as a result of which one company takes over all of the assets and business of another company, the former continues to receive exactly the same capital allowances on the assets transferred as the old company would have got. A reconstruction without change of ownership takes place if at any time during the two years following the reconstruction, no less than 75 per cent of the acquiring company belongs to the same people who owned no less than 75 per cent of the old company. (This is treated for all corporation tax purposes as a continuation of the trade (TA 1988 Ss343–344).)
(4) Special rules now apply where a UK trade is transferred in exchange for shares from one EC company to a company in another EC state. Balancing adjustments are not made, subject to certain conditions (10.9.4).

12.11 Losses
(TA 1988 Ss393–396 & FA 1991 S73 & Sch 15)

The loss carry-back rules were improved for accounting periods ending after 31 March 1991. Losses made in such accounting periods can be relieved against profits for the three previous years, provided the same trade has been carried on during that time. Relief is also denied where there is a change of ownership after 13

June 1991 and a major change in the nature or conduct of the trade. Thus if your company has a loss for the year to 30 April 1992, it can claim to offset this against profits going back to the year to 30 April 1989. A claim to the Revenue is needed within generally two years of the end of the accounting period when the loss was incurred. However, the Revenue are empowered to allow extra time.

If, for an accounting period of a company ending before 1 April 1991, a trading loss results after the necessary corporation tax adjustments, then a repayment of the tax on an equal amount of the profits (of any description) for the same period can be obtained. A claim is required and this can also extend to the profits for the previous period. The loss can only be carried back over a period equal in length to that in which it arises. A claim to the Revenue must be made within two years of the end of the accounting period in which the loss occurs.

Alternatively, a repayment of tax deducted at source from interest received and tax credits on dividends can be obtained. Otherwise the losses will be carried forward and relieved against future profits. Losses on shares in qualifying trading companies sold by investment companies can be set off against their surplus franked investment income. This follows the general relief against income now available for such losses made by investment companies (18.14).

12.12 Reconstructions
(TA 1988 Ss343 & 344)

A 'company reconstruction without change of ownership' (12.10(3)) has other advantages apart from capital allowance continuity. In particular where a company takes over the trade and assets of another and they are under at least 75 per cent common ownership, any trading losses are carried over with the trade. A restriction was introduced, however, for transfers of trades after 18 March 1986. The unused tax losses may not be fully available if the original company is insolvent when its trade is transferred.

12.13 Group loss relief
(TA 1988 Ss402–413 & Sch 18 & F2A 1992 S24 & Sch 6)

In a group of companies (ie, parent and subsidiaries) the trading losses (including capital allowances, etc) of respective group members can be offset by way of group relief against the profits of others provided that:

(1) The necessary claim is made within two years of the end of the accounting period.
(2) The group relationship exists throughout the respective accounting periods of the loss making and profit making companies. Otherwise the relief is only obtained for the period during which the group relationship exists; profits and losses being apportioned on a time basis if necessary.
(3) The parent and subsidiary companies are all resident in the UK and the parent has at least a 75 per cent interest in each of the subsidiaries. Also the parent company must be entitled to at least both 75 per cent of the distributable profits of each subsidiary and 75 per cent of the assets available on the liquidation of each subsidiary. Option arrangements etc made after 14 November 1991 are to be taken into account in calculating the percentages, as if they had been exercised.
(4) Subject to certain special rules group relief also applies to a consortium where UK companies own between them ordinary shares of a loss making company or of a holding company which owns 90 per cent of a loss making company. From August 1984 it is necessary for 75 per cent or more of the ordinary shares to be owned by the consortium with no less than 5 per cent held by each member (thus the maximum number is 20). For accounting periods ending after 10 March 1981, losses made by consortium companies can be surrendered down to a company which is jointly owned.
(5) Where a company joins or leaves a group during its accounting period the time apportionment basis (see above) may be set aside if it operates unfairly. A 'just and reasonable method' is then used. A similar rule applies in consortium situations.
(6) For accounting periods commencing after 31 July 1985, subject to certain conditions, a loss can be claimed partly as group relief and partly as consortium relief. Also, consortium relief can flow through to other companies in a consortium member's group.
(7) For accounting periods beginning on or after 1 April 1987, no group relief is available for the losses of dual-resident investment companies (13.9.15).

12.14 Terminal losses
(TA 1988 S394)

These are available to a company in a similar way to an individual who ceases trading (10.24). Thus, a company is entitled to claim to set off a loss incurred in its last 12 months of trading against its profits for the three preceding years.

12.15 Companies' capital gains and capital losses
(Ss267–276 & 278–281, TA 1988 Ss345–347, 400 & 435 & Sch 29, FA 1988 Ss114 & 115 and F2A 1992 Ss44–51)

The capital gains of companies are now charged to corporation tax at the normal rates. This applies for gains realised from 17 March 1987. Thus a gain made by a company with £1.25m profits bears 33 per cent tax. However, a gain of £20,000 made by a company with £50,000 other taxable profits pays the small companies rate on the gain. This is 29 per cent if the gain arose in the period from 17 March to 31 March 1987. Otherwise it will be 27 per cent for the year to 31 March 1988 and 25 per cent subsequently.

An exception concerns the capital gains which life assurance companies make for their policyholders. These remain taxed at 30 per cent. This only applies to the policyholders' funds; any shareholders' profits are now taxable under the new arrangements.

Capital losses in accounting periods may be set off against gains, so that the net gains are taxable. Where an accounting period straddled 17 March 1987, it was regarded as being two separate periods, one before and one starting on that date, for capital gains purposes. Any allowable capital losses in the second period can be carried back and set against gains in the first.

During an accounting period ending prior to 1 April 1983, 15/26ths of any chargeable gains of a company computed according to the normal capital gains tax rules (18.1) were added to the assessable profits of the company and charged to corporation tax at 52 per cent. Even if the lower rate (38 per cent) was applied to the company's profits (12.7), 15/26ths of the capital gains were still subjected to the 52 per cent rate. For periods after 31 March 1983 and before 17 March 1987 the same principles applied, using the appropriate rates and fractions shown in Table 12.2.1. Effectively, companies ended up paying 30 per cent on their capital gains unless they were covered by losses.

Chargeable gains can be relieved by means of capital losses in the same period or those brought forward from previous periods.

Trading losses can be set off against capital profits of the same period or the previous period. Trading losses in accounting periods ending after 31 March 1991 can be set off against gains going back three years (12.11). Capital profits can also be set off by group loss relief claims (12.13). Note that the capital profits before 17 March 1987 were first reduced by the appropriate fraction (2/5ths for financial year 1983, 1/3rd for 1984, 1/4th for 1985, 1/7th for 1986, etc) and the trading losses were deducted from the remainder. Trading losses brought forward from previous periods, however, can only be set off against future trading profits and not against future chargeable gains.

Capital losses (18.13) incurred by a company can only be set off against any capital gains of the company in the same accounting period or a future accounting period. Unused capital losses can be carried forward to future years even if the company has ceased trading whereas a cessation prevents trading losses from being carried forward.

Companies are prevented from manufacturing capital losses by sales from large holdings (2 per cent upwards) of another company's shares and buying them back within a month if quoted and six months otherwise.

Under TCGA S13 UK resident and domiciled shareholders of an overseas company can have its capital gains apportioned to them if the company would have been close if UK resident. This rule also covers overseas trusts with shares in such companies (FA 1981 S85). The effect is that UK beneficiaries of the trusts could then be taxed, if they receive any benefit (18.32).

As from 15 March 1988, the exploitation of capital gains tax indexation allowance through inter-group financing has been countered. From the same date, the rules were amended to ensure that share exchanges by companies in the same group do not result in capital gains or losses being charged or allowed more than once.

As from 1 January 1992, F2A 1992 has introduced various rules concerning capital gains tax where a trade owned by one EC company is transferred to another in exchange for shares or securities. Of particular importance is where a UK trade is transferred in this way from a company resident in one EC country to one resident in another. Under these circumstances, the assets are treated as being transferred at values giving no capital gain or loss, provided certain anti-avoidance provisions are not infringed.

12.16 Groups of companies
(TA 1988 Ss240, 247 & 248 & 402–413, FA 1989 Ss97–102 & 138 & FA 1990 S66)

Various special provisions relate to groups of companies (broadly parent and subsidiaries). A subsidiary company is classified according to the percentage of its ordinary capital owned (directly or indirectly) by its parent. Thus a 51 per cent subsidiary is over 50 per cent owned by its parent; and a 75 per cent subsidiary is not less than 75 per cent owned by its parent. For these purposes, loan financing may play a part in calculating the percentage owned, unless 'normal commercial loans' (TA 1988 Sch 18 & FA 1991 S66).

Some of the main rules relating to groups of companies are as follows:

(1) Group loss relief is available in respect of a parent company and its 75 per cent subsidiaries subject to various rules (12.13).
(2) Provided the necessary election is made to the Revenue, dividend payments from 51 per cent subsidiaries to the parent may be made without having to account for ACT. A similar rule relates to inter-group interest payments. These provisions only apply to companies resident in the UK. Also included are payments from a consortium-owned trading or holding company to the consortium members, where the consortium owns at least 75 per cent of the ordinary shares. Each consortium member must own at least 5 per cent; before 1 January 1985, consortia were limited to five members, but from that date there is no limit apart from the 5 per cent minimum.
From 27 July 1989, there needs to be a group relationship in an economic sense between the companies. For example, one company needs not only more than 50 per cent of the other but also to be entitled to more than 50 per cent of the distributable profits and of the assets in a winding up.
(3) Transfers of assets within a group consisting of a parent and its 75 per cent subsidiaries (all resident in the UK) do not generally give rise to capital gains tax. This excludes certain dual resident companies after 19 March 1990. (From 14 March 1989, the parent must be effectively entitled to over 50 per cent of the profits of the subsidiary and of its assets on winding up.) When the asset leaves the group, however, capital gains tax is paid on the entire chargeable gain on the asset

whilst it was owned by any group company (TA 1970 S273). Rules broadly applying from 14 March 1989 restrict schemes to reduce tax on selling subsidiaries (13.9.18).

(4) Capital gains tax 'roll-over relief' (18.25) applies to a UK group consisting of a parent company and its 75 per cent subsidiaries. The gain on an asset sold by one trading company may be 'rolled over' against the purchase of an asset by another trading company (excluding certain dual resident companies) in the group (TA 1970 S276). (Property holding companies which hold assets used for trade by trading companies in the group are also included.)

(5) If a parent company holds more than 50 per cent of the ordinary shares of a subsidiary and is entitled to more than 50 per cent of its distributable profits and more than 50 per cent of its assets on liquidation, the parent can transfer to its subsidiary relief for ACT. Thus if the parent pays a dividend of £7,500 it gets £7,500 × 25/75 = £2,500 ACT relief, but instead of taking this itself it can surrender the relief to its subsidiary which then deducts £2,500 from its corporation tax bill. If the subsidiary ceases to be owned by the parent, any unused ACT will be lost. However, for accounting periods ending after 13 March 1989, this does not apply if the companies remain in the same overall group.

(6) A special rule applies to interest payments between companies under common control, including a parent and 51 per cent (or more) subsidiaries from 17 March 1987. To prevent relief for the payer occurring in one year and tax being paid the next, the interest is to be treated as received on the day when paid. This rule applies where the paying company obtains relief for the interest as a charge on income and the recipient is taxed under Case III (8.4).

(7) ACT surrendered from one group company to another, which remains unused is lost if there is a major change in the recipient company's business within three years.

12.17 Close companies
(TA 1988 Ss414–430 & Sch 19 & FA 1989 Ss103–107 & Sch 12)

Special provisions relate to 'close' companies, more particularly, for periods beginning before 1 April 1989 and are described in greater depth in previous editions of this book. Close companies are broadly those under the control of five or fewer persons and their 'associates'. The latter term includes close family such as husband, wife, child, father, mother, brother, sister, etc. A quoted company is not 'close', however, if not less than 35 per cent of its voting shares are owned by the general public.

There is also an alternative test by reference to whether five or fewer persons and their 'associates' would receive broadly the greater part of the company's assets on liquidation which would be available for distribution.

A UK subsidiary of an overseas parent company is 'close' if the latter would have itself been 'close' if resident here. It is thus seen that most small or medium companies are likely to be 'close' companies unless they are subsidiaries of non-close companies. The majority of 'family' companies are 'close'.

12.17.1 Apportionment of income under the imputation system
(TA 1988 Ss423–430 & Sch 19 & FA 1989 S103 & Sch 12)

For periods *after 5 April 1973* and beginning *before 1 April 1989*, the Revenue could apportion among the shareholders the excess of the 'relevant income' of a close company over its distributions for that period. In the case of a company which was a trading company or member of a trading group, no apportionment was made if the excess was under £1,001. Also, no apportionment was made on any individual whose share of the total apportioned amount was less than 5 per cent and £1,000. For property investment companies the threshold was £251.

For chargeable accounting periods *ending before 27 March 1980* 'relevant income' consisted of not more than the company's 'distributable investment income' plus 50 per cent of its trading and property income. (This was subject to abatement — 12.17.2.) For periods *ending from that date* the trading income of a trading company was *excluded* from its 'relevant income'. However, 50 per cent of its property income was still included.

The 'relevant income' was reduced below the above maximum if the company could prove that it could not distribute such income because the money was needed for business purposes or could not be legally distributed. Against the 'relevant income' were set dividends paid during the relevant accounting period and within a reasonable time thereafter (not less than 18 months) provided they were stipulated as relating to the accounting period.

12.17.2 Abatement
(TA 1988 Sch 19)

For periods *ending prior to 27 March 1980* in computing 'relevant income' (12.17.1) you excluded a trading company's trading or property income if this was no more than £25,000 after tax and the company had no 'associated companies' (12.8). If the trading or property income after tax of such a company was between £25,000 and £75,000, you reduced this income by half of the difference between it and £75,000.

For periods *ending after 26 March 1980* a proportionate amount of abatement was available. This was found by reducing the limits of £25,000 and £75,000 mentioned above, in the ratio of estate income to estate and trading income ('estate income' refers to property income).

If a company had one or more 'associated companies' (12.8), excluding dormant and non-trading companies, the amounts of £25,000 and £75,000 were reduced by dividing them by one plus the number of the 'associated companies'.

12.17.3 Loans and distributions for close companies
(TA 1988 Ss418–422)

A special provision regarding close companies which remains operative is that if they make loans to their 'participators' (see below) or associates of the latter, the companies are charged tax at 25/75ths of the amounts. Thus if a loan of £7,500 is made to a participator the company will be assessed to tax of 25/75 × £7,500 = £2,500. Loans by companies controlled by or subsequently acquired by close companies are also covered by this rule.

When the loan is repaid to the company, the tax is repaid. If the loan was repaid before any assessment had been raised, no assessment was normally made by the Revenue. However, regarding loans made or repaid after 18 March 1986, the Revenue may now assess loans even if they have been repaid. (The relief on repayment remains.) Should a close company lend money to a participator or his associate and then release the debt, higher rate tax is assessed on the recipient in respect of the grossed up equivalent of the loan. Thus in the above example, if the company releases the participator from his debt he will pay higher rate tax on £10,000 (£7,500 + £2,500). A deduction of £2,500 will be made, however, from the total tax payable.

The meaning of the term 'distribution' (dividend, etc) is extended in the case of close companies to include living expenses and accommodation, etc provided for a 'participator' (or his associate).

A 'participator' means broadly a person having a share or interest in the capital or income of a company, including, for example, a shareholder or loan creditor.

The effect of treating a payment as a distribution is that it is not deductible from the taxable profit of the company. ACT on any 'qualifying distributions' (12.6.1) including the above is paid to the Revenue.

12.17.4 Cessations and liquidations
(TA 1988 S423 & Sch 19)

If a close company ceased to trade, its distribution requirement included all of its trading and property income after abatement (12.17.2) for its final chargeable accounting period and any other chargeable accounting periods ending within a year of the date of cessation and prior to 27 March 1980. For subsequent periods trading income was excluded from the distribution requirement. The company could not claim to retain money for business purposes in these circumstances.

These rules applied to companies in liquidation and extended to income arising after this commenced. However, for accounting periods beginning after 31 March 1989, there is no distribution requirement. The previous close company apportionment rules no longer apply.

12.18 Close investment holding companies (CICs)
(FA 1989 Ss90, 105 & 106 & Sch 12)

(1) New provisions have effect for accounting periods beginning after 31 March 1989 which impose harsher taxation on certain Close Investment Holding Companies (CICs).
(2) A CIC is a close company which is neither a 'trading company' nor a member of a trading group, nor a property investment company (which lets to non-connected persons).
(3) Broadly, a trading company is one which exists wholly or mainly for the purpose of trading on a commercial basis.
(4) Dealing in property or shares does not cause a company to be

a CIC. Similarly, mixed property dealing and investment companies are not CICs.
(5) CICs are subject to 33 per cent corporation tax regardless of their level of profits. They do not obtain the benefit of the 25 per cent small companies rate.
(6) If a shareholder waives, or does not receive a dividend, the extent to which someone else is entitled to be repaid a tax credit may be restricted. The Revenue may request information and make 'just and reasonable' restrictions. This does not apply where, for example, there is only one class of shares.
(7) Where a CIC takes out a life assurance policy after 13 March 1989, profits subsequently realised will be taxed, subject to the rules.

12.19 Non-resident companies trading in the UK
(TA 1988 S11)

Where a non-resident company (15.3.3) carries on a trade in this country through a branch or agency here, corporation tax is charged in respect of the profits of the branch or agency. If those profits are also subject to tax in the country of residence of the company, double tax relief may be available (16.6). (Special rules apply where companies become non-resident (15.3.3).)

12.20 UK companies with overseas income

Any overseas income of a company that is resident in this country is subject to corporation tax on the gross amount of such income. Double tax relief is frequently available in respect of overseas income that is taxed both in the UK and abroad.

If a UK company receives a dividend from an overseas company from which withholding tax has been deducted, the gross dividend is included in the taxable profits subject to corporation tax. Normally, double tax relief for the withholding tax suffered is given against the corporation tax payable. (Withholding tax is tax that is 'withheld' from the dividend when the latter is paid. It is thus a form of tax deducted at source.) In addition, if at least 10 per cent of the voting capital of the overseas company is owned by the UK company, relief is given for the 'underlying tax' (ie, the proportion of the total tax paid by the foreign company attributable to its dividends). Also in these circumstances, in certain cases no basic rate tax is now to be charged on the paying and collecting agents (F2A 1992 S30). In no case, however, can the double tax relief rate exceed the rate of UK corporation tax (33 per cent, etc).

12.21 Controlled foreign companies
(TA 1988 Ss747–756 & Schs 24–26)

From 6 April 1984, the Revenue are able to impose extra tax on UK companies with interests in controlled foreign companies, subject to certain rules including the following:

(1) The overseas company must be under overall UK control.
(2) The overseas company must be subject to tax in its country of residence which is less than half that payable if it were UK resident.
(3) A UK company (together with associates, etc) has at least a 10 per cent interest in the overseas company.
(4) Acceptable dividend payments will exclude the charge (broadly 50 per cent of the available profits of trading companies and 90 per cent for investment companies).
(5) The charge is excluded if the controlled foreign company satisfies an 'exempt activities' test. For this, the company must have a business establishment where it is resident and be managed there. Also it must broadly be a trading or qualifying holding company rather than an investment company.
(6) Exclusion is also available through a motive test. The foreign company's transactions must be carried out for commercial reasons and not for the main purpose of saving UK tax nor diverting profits from the UK.
(7) Certain foreign companies quoted on foreign stock exchanges are also excluded.
(8) There is no charge if the foreign company's profits for the year are less than £20,000.
(9) A list has been published of excluded countries which will not be regarded as low tax countries for the purposes of the above rules. In general, the list excludes tax havens and normally applies where at least 90 per cent is 'local source' income.
(10) Where applicable, the profits of the overseas company are apportioned to any UK companies with at least a 10 per cent interest and corporation tax is charged at the appropriate rate for each. A deduction is then made for any 'creditable tax' (overseas tax etc) which is similarly apportioned. Appropriate relief is then given where dividends are paid by the overseas company.

(11) From 17 March 1987, 'acceptable dividend payments' are only counted if made by a company which is not resident in the UK at the time of payment.
(12) Various anti-avoidance provisions have been introduced (13.9.15). For example, 'controlled foreign companies' can include dual resident companies from 20 March 1990.

12.22 Stock relief for companies
(FA 1976 Sch 5; FA 1984 S48 etc)

Stock relief for companies was based on their accounting periods. The system was similar to that for individuals and partnerships (10.6). For accounting periods ending in the year to 31 March 1974 and subsequently, relief was related to the increase in stock during each period. If stock fell during a period relief could be 'clawed-back'. Important changes were made by the Finance Acts of 1976, 1979 (No 2) and 1980. Reference should be made to previous editions of this book for further details.

The *Finance Act 1981* brought into effect completely new rules which applied for accounting periods ending after 13 November 1980 which began before 13 March 1984. In particular, the relief was found by taking the opening stock (less £2,000) and applying the increase in the 'All Stocks Index' over the accounting period. The *Finance Act 1984* ended stock relief completely for periods of account beginning after 12 March 1984. Where a period bridged 12 March 1984, relief was based on the increase in the 'All Stocks Index' up to March 1984.

12.23 Demergers
(TA 1988 Ss213–218)

Special rules assist two or more trading businesses in 'demerging' where they are carried on by a single company or a group. In demergers, subject to the detailed provisions:

(1) Where a company distributes shares in a 75 per cent subsidiary (12.6.1) to its shareholders this is not treated as a distribution and so no ACT or income tax arises for the company or its shareholders.
(2) Relief also applies where one company transfers a trade to a second company which in turn distributes its shares to the shareholders of the first.

(3) Capital gains tax relief applies to any distribution which you receive in the above circumstances until you sell the actual shares.
(4) There was also certain relief from development land tax and stamp duty in demergers.
(5) The provisions only apply to the genuine splitting off of trades or trading subsidiaries. There are anti-avoidance provisions to counter, for example the extraction of tax-free cash from companies subject to an advance clearance procedure.

12.24 Unquoted company purchasing its own shares
(TA 1988 Ss219–229)

The 1981 Companies Act enabled companies to purchase their own shares and issue redeemable equity shares. If the proceeds exceeded the original cost, the excess would be treated as a distribution under existing law and taxed in the same way as a dividend. Thus the company would pay ACT at 25/75ths on the excess and an individual receiving the payment would pay higher rate tax on the grossed up excess less a tax credit (12.6.5). In order to remove the disincentive of this heavy taxation, relief is provided in certain circumstances so that the company pays no ACT and the shareholder's liability will be restricted to capital gains tax (unless he is a share-dealer, in which case the gain is treated as his income). Stamp duty relief applied up to 27 October 1986, but not subsequently. Broadly, the conditions for relief are as follows:

(1) The company must not be quoted nor be the subsidiary of a quoted company. (Shares dealt with on the Unlisted Securities Market are not treated as quoted.)
(2) The company must be a trading company or the holding company of a trading group.
(3) The purchase or redemption of the shares must be mainly to benefit a trade of the company or its 75 per cent subsidiary.
(4) The shareholder must be UK resident and ordinarily resident, having normally owned the shares for at least five years (three years in specified cases such as inherited shares, where ownership by the deceased is also counted).
(5) If the shareholder keeps part of his shareholding in the company (or its group) his shareholding must be substantially reduced. Broadly, this means reducing his interest by at least 25 per cent and not being 'connected' (ie, holding with 'associates' 30 per cent of the shares, etc).

(6) If the payment is used for capital transfer tax or inheritance tax within two years after a death, (4) and (5) above do not apply and relief is due, provided that to pay the tax out of other funds would have caused undue hardship.
(7) The relieving provisions apply to payments after 5 April 1982 and advance clearance application may be made to the Revenue.
(8) As indicated, the above rules do not apply where a company buys back its shares from a dealer. Instead, the company remains liable for ACT on the excess of the proceeds over the original cost and the dealer is taxed under Schedule D Case I or II (10.4), receiving no tax credit.

12.25 Future administrative changes
(TA 1988 Ss8, 10, 419 & 826, FA 1989 S102 & FA 1990 Ss91 & 93–103 & Schs 15–17)

The Keith Committee made various proposals on filing accounts interest and penalties which were enacted in 1987 but will not take effect until Autumn 1993, at the earliest. The scheme is called the 'pay and file system'. Particular points are:

(1) Companies are to pay corporation tax nine months after their accounting dates, whether or not assessments have been raised.
(2) Tax paid late or repaid by the Revenue will carry interest from the required payment date.
(3) Accounts will be required to be submitted to the Revenue within 12 months from the accounting date.
(4) If accounts are filed late without excuse, penalties will be charged.
(5) In a group of companies, a refund of tax in one company can be set off against liabilities in other companies by election. The object is to avoid companies being penalised by the differential between interest payable and receivable under the new system.
(6) Improved and more flexible procedures will be introduced concerning group relief and capital allowances claims. Losses will be determined by assessment as profits are at present. Claims may be made and be capable of being withdrawn within two years of the end of the accounting period. If later, this is to be extended to the date that the profits and losses for the period are determined, but no more than six years from the end of the period.

(7) Trading losses which have been relieved against the profits of a later period will be allowed to be reallocated and surrendered as group relief.
(8) Companies will be well advised to review their accounting systems, so as to have adequate information available to comply with the new rules, when introduced.

13 Miscellaneous aspects

13.1 Miscellaneous profits — Schedule D Case VI
(TA 1988 Ss18, 69 & 392)

Miscellaneous profits not falling within any of the other cases of Schedule D are charged to income tax under Case VI. Such income includes:

(1) Profits from furnished lettings (7.5).
(2) Income from underwriting (if not a business). Lloyd's underwriting profits, however, are assessed under Schedule D Case I (10.4).
(3) Income from guaranteeing loans.
(4) Income from dealing in futures. However, this is now more likely to be subject to capital gains tax (18.31).
(5) Certain capital sums received from the sale of UK patent rights.
(6) Post-cessation receipts (10.27).
(7) Certain 'anti-avoidance' assessments (13.9).
(8) Enterprise allowance payments after 17 March 1986. Previously Case I or II applied. Case VI also applies to payments before 18 March which continue subsequently (10.4).
(9) Profits on the disposal of certificates of deposit.
(10) Gains on certain life policies held by companies (FA 1989 Sch 9).

The basis of assessment under Schedule D Case VI is the actual income arising in the tax year. Expenses incurred in earning the income can be deducted in ascertaining the assessable profits.

Losses sustained in any Case VI transaction (including furnished lettings) can be set off against Case VI profits of the same or any subsequent year; they cannot, however, be set off against income assessable under any other Case or Schedule (TA 1988, S392).

13.2 Tax-free organisations
(TA 1988 Ss338–339, 505–506 & 683, FA 1990 Ss24–27, FA 1991 Ss71 & 74 & Sch 9 & F2A 1992 Ss26–28)

13.2.1 Charities

Approved charities are exempt from tax on any income that is used only for charitable purposes from:

(1) Land and buildings.
(2) Interest dividends and annual payments.
(3) Trades carried on by the beneficiaries of the charity or trades exercised in the course of executing the actual purposes of the charity.

Approved charities are also exempt from capital gains tax.

Gifts to charity out of both capital and income are often afforded favourable tax treatment as described elsewhere in this book. In particular, note capital gains tax (18.29.1), and inheritance tax (20.1).

Deeds of covenant to charities receive highly favourable tax treatment. As covenantor, you will obtain higher rate tax relief on your gross payments, subject to the rules (6.5). An approved charity (13.2.1) is able to reclaim the basic rate income tax that you will have deducted in making a payment to it under a deed of covenant. Thus if you covenant to pay a charity £100 gross each year, you will deduct income tax at the basic rate (25 per cent) and only pay £75. The charity will then reclaim the income tax amounting to £25. The charity thus gets a total of £100 each year. Even if the basic rate of income tax is changed, the charity will still get a total of £100 each year from your payment. (By way of contrast, if the covenant is 'net', the charity benefits more when the basic rate is higher.)

Deeds of covenant which are written to last four years or until some later event (eg giving up membership of the charity) previously ceased to be effective for tax purposes after four years. (New deeds of covenant were then required.) However, the rules have now changed to allow tax relief for such covenants to run on, provided you are not enpowered to stop payment within the initial four-year period.

From 1 April 1986, single donations by companies which are not close (12.17) are allowable for tax purposes subject to certain conditions. Basic rate income tax (25 per cent) must be deducted on payment which the charity reclaims. The company accounts to the Revenue for this tax but obtains corporation tax relief (normally 33 per cent). Donations qualifying for relief are limited to 3 per cent of ordinary share dividends in the accounting period (TA 1988 Ss338 & 339). A new single-donation relief applies from 1 October 1990 as follows. However, for appropriate companies, the above still applies if more favourable.

Certain charitable gifts after 30 September 1990 qualify for 'Gift Aid'. This is income tax or, for companies, corporation tax relief for charitable donations of at least £600 net each. From 7 May 1992, this limit has been reduced to £400. There was an annual maximum of £5,000,000. (Associated companies shared the £5,000,000 maximum.) However, the maximum was abolished for donations from 19 March 1991. Basic rate income tax is deducted by the donor and reclaimed by the charity. The donor obtains full tax relief at the higher rate, if applicable. Similarly a company deducts the gross donation from its taxable profits and obtains relief at its corporation tax rate (33 per cent etc.).

Thus, suppose you give £800 gross to a charity, you deduct 25 per cent basic rate and pay £600, the charity reclaiming the £200. You will also obtain £120 further relief if you are a higher rate income tax payer. Your net cost will then be £480.

A payroll deduction scheme operates from 1987–88. Employees are able to contribute up to £600 each year to charities (£480 for 1989–90, £240 for 1988–89 and £120 for 1987–88) through an approved agent and obtain tax relief (TA 1988 S202 & FA 1990 S24).

Certain anti-avoidance provisions have been introduced (TA 1988 Ss506–507 & Sch 20). These restrict a charity's tax relief if its *funds* are used for non-charitable purposes, or passed to an overseas body without ensuring that it will use the money for charity. Relief is also restricted if the charity lends or invests the funds for the benefit of the original donor unless for charitable purposes. Note that higher rate relief for covenanted donations may be restricted where the charity's own relief is limited. These rules do not generally apply if a charity's taxable income and gains are no more than £10,000 in a year. If you pay more than £1,000 of donations under covenant in a year to charities whose relief is limited as above, your own higher rate relief may be restricted.

From 14 March 1989, the rules for tax relief on covenanted membership subscriptions to heritage and conservation charities were relaxed. The right to free or cheap entry to view the property of the charity no longer prevents the member from obtaining tax relief (FA 1989 S59).

13.2.2 Other tax-free organisations

Other organisations whose income in certain circumstances may be free of tax include registered and unregistered friendly societies, registered trade unions, mutual associations and pension funds.

Registered friendly societies are exempt from tax on profits from life assurance business subject to certain limits. The current limit is based on annual premiums of £200 (FA 1991 Sch 9). For contracts made from August 1990 to July 1991 the limit is based on annual premiums of £150, whilst from 1 September 1987 to 31 August 1990, the premium limit is £100 (TA 1988 S460 and FA 1990 S49). For contracts issued after 13 March 1984 and before 1 September 1987, the limit is £750 gross assured sums for life or endowment business. There remains a limit of £156 annually for each annuity (TA 1988 S464).

Since 31 May 1984, the life business of friendly societies has been treated for tax purposes as being more akin to that of life assurance companies. The 1992 Friendly Societies Act will allow societies to incorporate. The legislation regarding tax exemption will then extend to incorporated societies (F2A 1992 S56 & Sch 9).

Provident benefits paid by *trade unions* to their members are tax-exempt up to certain limits. (Such payments might cover sickness, injury, etc.) New limits apply from 1 April 1991, being £4,000 for lump sums and £825 for annuities (TA 1988 S467 & FA 1991 S74). (The previous limits were £3,000 and £625.)

Depending on the exact circumstances, tax exemption may apply to government bodies, foreign diplomats and United Nations Organisation officials in this country and the salaries of the members of visiting forces.

13.3 Patent holders
(TA 1988 Ss520–528)

If you own a patent (10.18) and you grant the right to use it to somebody else he will normally pay you a periodical royalty in respect of the patent user. This royalty is normally subject to tax by deduction at source at the basic rate (25 per cent). If, however, the payer does not deduct tax then you would normally be assessed to income tax under Case VI of Schedule D.

The gross equivalent of any patent royalties that you receive must be included in your total income for income tax purposes (5.2), but you get a credit for the basic rate tax already suffered by deduction at source. Where you receive a lump sum payment, in respect of royalties for the past user of your patent, you can spread the payment backwards over the period of use in order to calculate your income tax liability.

If you sell any patent rights for a capital sum, this will normally be chargeable under Case VI of Schedule D provided you are resident in this country. You can, however, spread the payment forward over a period of six years in computing your income tax liability. If, however, you are non-resident, the payer should deduct income tax at 25 per cent in paying you (subject to possible double tax relief and exemptions).

13.4 Authors' copyright sales and royalties
(TA 1988 Ss534–537)

Unlike patent royalties, copyright royalty payments to authors, etc, are made gross without the deduction of any income tax. If you have such receipts and you are an author or composer, etc by profession, then your royalties will be taxed under Schedule D Case II as part of your professional earnings (10.4). Otherwise, any royalties that you receive may be assessed under Schedule D Case VI.

Where you assign the copyright in the whole or a part of a work, any sum that you receive is taxable by reference to the tax year or accounting period in which it is received. If you make the required claim to the Revenue, however, you can normally obtain relief by spreading the payment as follows:

(1) If it took you more than 12 but less than 24 months to prepare the work of art, one half of your proceeds is taxed as if

received when paid to you and the other half of the proceeds is taxed as if received one year earlier. If you took more than 24 months over the writing, composing, etc of the work, then you are taxed on one third of the proceeds as if received when paid to you, another third is taxed as if received one year earlier and the remaining third is taxed one year earlier still. Thus a three-year spread is obtained.
(2) If you are the author of an established work and not less than ten years after the first publication you wholly or partially assign your copyright or grant an interest therein, for a period of at least two years, you can spread any lump sum received. The period over which the sum is spread is the lesser of six years or the duration of the grant or licence.

13.5 Sub-contractors
(TA 1988 Ss559–567 & FA 1988 S28)

If you are an independent or self-employed contractor and are not engaged under a contract of employment, you will be taxed under Schedule D Case I and not under Schedule E. This will normally be advantageous to you because you will be able to deduct various expenses such as travelling from your home or other base of operations to the site, etc where you are working for the time being.

Special rules apply to payments made by a building contractor or similar organisation in the building trade to a sub-contractor in connection with building and construction work. These now extend to non-building firms which spend substantial amounts on construction operations (over £250,000 on average for the last three years).

The contractor must deduct tax at the rate of 25 per cent from each payment made to the sub-contractors who work for him excepting those with exemption certificates (see below). Before 1 November 1988 the tax-deduction rate was 27 per cent. The tax deducted must be paid over to the Revenue. Each sub-contractor then prepares accounts under Schedule D Case I which include the gross equivalents of the payments made to him. Income tax is computed on the basis of the accounts (10.4) and the tax already suffered is deducted. If the income tax liability is less than the tax deducted a repayment is obtained.

From 20 April 1988 interest is charged where formal assessments are made on contractors for under-deductions from payments to sub-contractors. A further change is that companies with a sub-contractor exemption certificate (see below) will need to notify the Revenue of any change in company control.

The scheme also applies to certain companies, whilst other rules require the deduction of tax from payments made to temporary agency workers.

An Inland Revenue consultative document was issued on 19 March 1991 with suggested reforms to the scheme. These are planned for April 1993 and subsequently. Points include the possible increase of the £250,000 threshold for construction operations to £1m and lowering the 25 per cent deduction rate.

If you are a sub-contractor in the building trade you will normally be able to obtain an exemption certificate from your Inspector of Taxes if you complete the necessary application form and can satisfy certain conditions including having a regular place of business in this country. Also you must have been either employed (including full-time education or training) or in business in the UK and made full tax returns for the three years up to your application. Up to six months are allowed in the three-year qualifying period for unemployment, etc at the Inland Revenue's discretion. Relaxations are made to cover periods of working overseas — the three-year qualifying period being allowed to be within the last six years. If you obtain an exemption certificate and show it to a building contractor for whom you do work, then he will be permitted to pay you gross without the tax deduction described above.

13.6 Farming

If you carry on a farming or market gardening business in this country you will be treated as carrying on a trade. You will be assessed to income tax under Schedule D Case I (10.4).

In addition to the normal Schedule D Case I rules, some special ones apply, including the following:

(1) If you have more than one farm they will all be assessed as one business (TA 1988 S53).
(2) You may receive *deficiency payments* from the Government in respect of certain crops, etc. These are by concession included in your taxable profits for the year when they are received rather than when the crop is sold.
(3) If you have an eligible agricultural or horticultural holding,

you may be able to benefit under one of the various Ministry of Agriculture, Fisheries and Food Grant Schemes. Grants received under these schemes are treated as either capital receipts or revenue receipts for tax purposes according to their nature. For example, field husbandry grants are revenue and grants to cover the reclamation of waste land are capital.

(4) Normally all your livestock will be treated for tax purposes as stock-in-trade. If you have any 'production herds', however, you can elect within two years from the end of your first year of assessment that the *herd basis* should apply. 'Production herds' are those kept for the purpose of obtaining products from the living animal (eg, wool, milk, etc). Where a herd basis election has been made the initial cost of the herd is not charged against your profits but is capitalised together with the cost of any additional animals. The cost of rearing the animals to maturity is also capitalised. Any sales proceeds are taxable and the costs of replacement animals are deductible from your taxable profits. If you sell your entire herd you are not charged to tax on the proceeds (TA 1988 S97 & Sch 5).

(5) A special *agricultural buildings allowance* is available (10.14).

(6) If you carry on any farming or market gardening activities without any reasonable expectation of profit on a non-commercial basis you will normally be treated as conducting merely *hobby farming*. The effect of this will be that you will not be granted tax relief for any losses from your farming against your other income. You will, however, be permitted to carry forward any losses from your hobby farming to be set against future taxable profits from the same source (TA 1988 S397). Generally, the restriction applies when you make your sixth consecutive loss.

(7) Relief is available regarding *fluctuating profits* of individual farmers or partnerships. You are able to claim to average the profits of any pair of consecutive years of assessment, provided you do so within two years of the end of the second year. If the taxable profits for either or both years are later adjusted, the original claim is set aside but a new one can be made by the end of the year of assessment following that in which the adjustment is made. Another condition is that the profits in the lower year must be no more than 70 per cent of the profits of the better year. If the lower profits are 70 per cent to 75 per cent of the higher, however, limited spreading is allowed. Where a loss is made in any year, for the purposes of the spreading rules, the profits are treated as nil and the loss is relieved in the usual ways (10.22) (TA 1988 S96).

13.7 Building society arrangements
(TA 1988 S476, FA 1990 S30 & Sch 5 & FA 1991 S53)

From 6 April 1991 building societies (as well as banks, etc) deduct basic rate income tax from interest payments and account for it to the Inland Revenue. Non-taxpayers are able to reclaim tax deducted. In some cases, building societies may be able to pay interest gross (8.6).

Prior to 6 April 1991, if you received any building society interest you were not assessed to basic rate income tax on it. However, you included the grossed up equivalent in your total income for tax purposes (5.2) as if income tax at the basic rate (25 per cent) had been deducted on payment of the interest to you (8.6). This 'notional' tax deduction could not be reclaimed by you, as a general rule. (An exception was made, where a UK resident or ordinarily resident individual (15.3.1) or charity had an absolute interest in the residuary estate of a deceased person (19.10.1) and the income included building society interest.)

From 6 April 1986, building societies may pay interest and dividends gross to individuals ordinarily resident outside the United Kingdom. This also applies to payments to charities, friendly societies and pension funds, etc.

Before 6 April 1991, building societies paid a special composite tax rate based on the interest payable to individual investors, depositors and certain others. This partially compensated the Revenue for the basic rate income tax not directly assessed on the investors in respect of their interest. In fixing the composite rate for a given tax year, the Revenue had regard to the basic rate of tax and personal reliefs for that year together with statistical details concerning building society investors for previous years. For clarification, the composite rates from 1986–87 to 1989–90 were confirmed in F2A 1992 (S64).

13.8 Insolvents

When a person becomes bankrupt, a bankruptcy or interim order is made on a certain date and all income tax and capital gains assessments that have been made by that date for previous years are treated as debts in the bankruptcy. Also any assessments made for the tax year ending on the following 5 April will rank as debts in the bankruptcy provided the assessments were made before the date of the receiving order. PAYE and sub-contractors' deductions made within the previous year will rank as preferential debts. This means that they will be paid in full before any payment is made on the non-preferential debts. The remaining assessments will rank as non-preferential debts.

In the case of VAT (21.11.9) tax payable for the 6 months prior to the date of the order, etc ranks as a preferential debt.

Any future income of the bankrupt individual will be charged to tax in the normal way. Thus any salary would be subjected to PAYE (9.14) — also income tax would be payable on other income.

13.9 Anti-avoidance provisions
(TA 1988 Ss703–787 etc)

There is an important distinction between *tax evasion* and *tax avoidance*. Tax evasion refers to all those activities illegally undertaken by a taxpayer to free himself from tax which the law charges upon his income, eg the falsification of his returns, books and accounts. This is illegal and subject to very heavy penalties (14.8.2). Tax avoidance, on the other hand, denotes that the taxpayer has arranged his affairs in such a way as to reduce his tax liability legally — for example, by investing in tax free securities such as national savings certificates.

Tax avoidance is also attempted in more complicated and devious ways with particular use being made of overseas trusts and companies. In order to prevent abuse of the UK tax rules in this way various anti-avoidance provisions have been introduced. Also, certain Court decisions such as *Ramsay* and *Furniss v Dawson* have barred tax relief from artificial circuitous schemes.

Unfortunately, some of the rules introduced to counter sophisticated avoidance schemes penalise quite innocent commercial activities, not carried out with a view to tax saving. It is thus important to consider the anti-avoidance provisions, particularly when involved in overseas operations and company reorganisations or takeovers. The following are some of the more important provisions to consider.

13.9.1 Transactions in securities
(TA 1988 Ss703–709)

These provisions charge you to income tax under Schedule D Case VI in respect of any 'tax advantage' that you obtain as a result of

Miscellaneous aspects

one or more 'transactions in securities'. For these purposes a 'tax advantage' is a saving of income tax or corporation tax, but it does not apply to capital gains tax. 'Transactions in securities' include the formation and liquidation of companies as well as purchases and sales of shares, etc. A frequent application of this legislation is to prevent tax savings being effected by obtaining the use of the undistributed profits of companies by means of schemes involving 'transactions in securities'.

You can avoid being assessed under these provisions if you can show that the transactions concerned were carried out for commercial purposes and one of your main objects was not tax saving. If you are planning to carry out certain transactions which you fear may be covered by these provisions you have the right to apply for clearance to the Revenue giving all relevant facts and they must let you know within one month whether such clearance is granted.

13.9.2 Transfer of assets abroad
(TA 1988 Ss739–746)

The object of these provisions is to prevent you from avoiding tax by transferring some of your assets abroad. The provisions normally, but not exclusively, apply to transfers of assets made by persons ordinarily resident in this country (15.3.1). If as a result of such transfer of assets, income is payable to persons resident or domiciled abroad (to avoid UK income tax) then if anyone ordinarily resident in the UK has the 'power to enjoy' any of the income, he can be assessed to income tax under Schedule D Case VI on all or part of the income. 'Power to enjoy' the income is widely defined.

There are no provisions under which clearance can be obtained and this particular legislation must be most carefully considered regarding all overseas schemes. You can even be assessed on a benefit if you did not make the original transfer. However, no income can be assessed more than once.

13.9.3 Sales at undervalue or overvalue
(TA 1988 Ss770–774)

It is laid down that where any sale takes place between people who are connected with each other (this can include partnerships and companies) and the price is less than the open market value of the goods, then in calculating the tax liability on the trading income of the seller, the sales proceeds must be adjusted to the true value of the goods if the Revenue so direct. This does not apply if the purchase is made by a taxable business in this country as a part of its trading stock. If the purchaser is an overseas trader, however, the sale is not exempted from these provisions.

A similar adjustment must be made for the buyer if the price is more than the open market value of the goods. Other provisions cover capital gains on sales between connected persons.

13.9.4 Sale of income derived from personal activities
(TA 1988 Ss775, 777 & 778)

The object of these provisions is to prevent you from saving tax by contriving to sell your present or future earnings for a capital sum, thereby paying no tax or only capital gains tax instead of income tax at basic and higher rates. Subject to the precise rules, any such capital sum is to be treated as earned income arising when it is receivable and is chargeable under Case VI of Schedule D. These provisions might apply if you receive a capital sum from the sale of a business which derives part of its value from your personal services. From 6 April 1988, the provisions are not so penal because broadly the same tax rates apply to income and capital gains.

13.9.5 Artificial transactions in land and 'sale and leaseback'
(TA 1988 Ss776–780)

These provisions are considered in detail in the chapter which deals with income from land and property (see 7.10). Note that tax advantages from sales of land with the right to repurchase are also countered.

13.9.6 Capital allowances — leasing
(TA 1988 Ss384 & 395 etc)

Complicated anti-avoidance provisions operate concerning the claiming of relief for capital allowances in certain contrived situations. These provisions were designed to counter certain tax saving schemes involving leasing arrangements in group situations and consortia; also leasing partnerships between individuals and companies.

Wider provisions prevent your setting off losses created through claims for capital allowances on leasing assets, against non-leasing income. The rules cover capital expenditure after 26 March 1980 by individuals and partnerships (unless under previous contracts and the assets are used by 27 March 1982). An exception is made for a leasing trade to which you devote substantially all your time, provided this trade continues for at least six months.

Leasing assets normally qualifies for a 25 per cent writing down allowance (10.9.13). However, the rate is restricted to 10 per cent where the assets are leased to non-residents. Similarly, a writing down allowance of only 10 per cent is available on expenditure after 9 March 1982 where *ships* or *aircraft* were let on charter to non-residents in order to obtain first year allowances.

13.9.7 Group relief restrictions
(TA 1988 Ss409–413 & FA 1989 Ss97–102)

These provisions can act to restrict or prevent group loss relief being available for one group company (12.13) in respect of trading losses of another. A particular point to watch is that if a group of companies has arranged to sell a loss-making company, relief for the losses of that company may not be available to the other group members for periods prior to the accounting period in which the sale actually takes place.

Special rules apply where companies join or leave a group after 13 March 1984 and whose accounting periods began after 7 November 1983. Instead of the normal time apportionment to fit the losses or profits to the respective old and new groups, a just and reasonable basis will be substituted in obviously distorted cases. This could involve separate accounts before and after the date of changing groups.

Modifications of the rules regarding groups took effect during 1989 and are mentioned elsewhere (12.16).

13.9.8 Interest schemes
(TA 1988 S787)

Complicated tax avoidance schemes were developed concerning 'manufactured' interest relief. Anti-avoidance rules operate regarding the interest payments.

13.9.9 Capital gains tax
(TCGA Ss27, 29, 137, 138 & 169)

Various rules were introduced for countering the avoidance of capital gains tax in certain situations. The latter include 'value-shifting' schemes, where an allowable loss has been created artificially by moving value out of one asset and possibly into another.

There are also anti-avoidance rules concerning capital gains tax resulting from company reconstructions, takeovers and amalgamations (18.18.6). A clearance procedure applies, however, which is similar to that applying for transactions in securities (13.9.1). Also, the rules do not apply if you can show that the arrangements were carried out for commercial, rather than tax-saving purposes.

Provisions prevent the artificial creation of capital losses by inflating the purchase price of assets for capital gains tax purposes above their true value, so that by selling for the true worth a capital loss results. This artificial effect sometimes resulted from the rule that transactions between connected persons are treated as being for a consideration equal to market value and sometimes through reorganisations of share capital (18.18.6). After 9 March 1981 the capital gains tax cost of the purchaser will only be increased to the extent that the capital gains tax position of the vendor is affected.

Gifts relief (18.28) does not apply to non-resident donees. This was being avoided by using certain dual-resident trusts, but from 18 March 1986 these are regarded as non-resident for this purpose.

Capital gains tax rollover relief is not available where a non-resident replaces a business asset within the UK charge with one which is outside it. In general, this new rule applies where the old asset is disposed of, or the new one purchased after 13 March 1989.

13.9.10 Commodity futures
(TA 1988 S399)

Losses created by means of certain artificial dealing partnerships may not be relieved against general income. (Note that from 6 April 1985, a commodity deal not forming part of a trade is liable to capital gains tax rather than Case VI income tax as previously.)

13.9.11 Rent between connected persons
(F2A 1992 S57)

A new rule applies to rent accruing after 9 March 1992 between connected persons (broadly close relatives and companies belonging to the same group or under common control). This covers those connected after both that date and when the lease was made. Previously, where the payer obtained tax relief, this was normally on an accruals basis and the recipient was only taxed on the basis of the rent receivable in the period, thus being able to defer tax. Under the new rules, the recipient will be charged on the rent accruing. This applies where the payer obtains tax relief on the rent and this is paid in arrears.

13.9.12 Bank lending, etc
(TA 1988 S798)

Broadly, from April 1982 for new loans and April 1983 for loans existing before 9 March 1982, rules apply to prevent certain tax advantages being obtained by exploiting the double tax relief system. Also, the creation of 'equity loans' where the interest paid is partly dependent on a company's results no longer produces a 'distribution' (previously only causing 30 per cent tax instead of 52 per cent corporation tax). This affects banks and the loss-making companies they were able to lend money to at lower rates. The double taxation rules relate mainly to banks.

13.9.13 Controlled foreign companies
(TA 1988 Ss747–756 & Schs 24–26)

From 6 April 1984, the Revenue are given powers to assess additional tax on certain UK resident companies with interests in controlled foreign companies. Fuller details are given earlier (12.21) but the circumstances where a charge might arise are where a foreign subsidiary in a low tax area is paying insufficient of its profits as dividends, etc, to its UK parent company.

13.9.14 Offshore funds
(TA 1988 Ss757–764 & Schs 27–28 & TCGA S102)

Prior to 1984, you could invest in certain offshore funds in which the income accumulated in a tax haven, suffering little or no tax. When you realised your investment, you only suffered capital gains tax in the UK.

Complicated rules were introduced in 1984 (and slightly modified in 1987). These apply to disposals from 1 January 1984 (1 January 1985 for certain shares, etc, resulting from exchanges). Broadly, if you dispose of an investment in an offshore fund which does not distribute enough of its income, you will be taxed on your entire gain as if it were income under Schedule D Case VI (13.9.2).

Gains made after 13 March 1989 on switches of holdings in offshore 'umbrella' funds by UK investors, attract capital gains tax.

13.9.15 Dual resident companies
(TCGA Ss159, 160 & 188)

Special provisions apply from 1 April 1987 to prohibit a dual resident investment company from surrendering losses to other members of a UK group (12.13). The companies concerned are UK resident and also taxed in another country because of place of incorporation, management or residence. Furthermore, the definition of such dual resident investment companies extends to those which either do not trade or are mainly used to borrow or to purchase or hold shares in another group member.

After 13 March 1989, where an asset of a dual resident company ceases to be within the UK capital gains tax charge due to a double tax agreement, the company is deemed to have disposed of the asset.

Regarding replacements of business assets after 13 March 1989 (either the disposal or replacement) rollover relief is not available if a UK asset within the capital gains tax charge is replaced by an asset which is not.

From 20 March 1990 certain dual resident companies are treated as resident outside the UK for some tax purposes. This is to counter avoidance of tax through controlled foreign companies (12.21) and transfers of assets abroad.

Also from 20 March 1990, rules operate which are designed to prevent a company transferring assets tax-free to a dual resident company in whose hands any gain would be outside the UK tax charge. Similarly, from that date, rollover relief (18.25) is denied on the replacement of business assets where one member of a group disposes of an asset and a dual resident group member replaces it with an asset outside the UK tax charge.

13.9.16 Migration of companies, etc
(TA 1988 S765)

Taxes Act 1988 S765 contains penal provisions to prevent a UK company from becoming non-resident without Treasury consent being obtained. Such consent is also required to transfer part or all of its business to a non-resident and for certain share transactions. From 15 March 1988, such consent is no longer needed (except for certain share transactions) and it is replaced by a tax charge on unrealised gains. Companies intending to emigrate must notify the Inland Revenue in advance providing an estimate of their UK tax commitments including tax on unrealised gains, and details of arrangements to settle such tax. If the tax is not paid, penalties may be charged. Furthermore, former directors and group companies can be held responsible for tax and interest.

After 30 June 1990, Treasury consent is no longer needed regarding certain transactions relating to companies within the European Community. This applies to issues and transfers of shares and debentures of overseas subsidiaries within the EC. Where *special* Treasury consent was previously needed, reporting to the Revenue is now required with non-compliance penalties of up to £3,000.

13.9.17 Lloyd's Underwriters
(TA 1988 S450 & FA 1988 Ss58–61)

The accounts for Lloyd's syndicates are normally drawn up for three-year periods but closed off each year to allow members to join and leave. Each year the members for that year pay those for the following year appropriate insurance premiums and the new year's syndicate members take over the outstanding liabilities. This is known as 'reinsurance to close', and previously has been beyond review by the Revenue.

Starting with the 1985 account, 'reinsurance to close' is tax deductible only to the extent that it is shown not to exceed a fair and reasonable assessment of the liabilities. This means aiming at having neither a profit nor loss accrue to the recipient of the premium. These rules were introduced in 1987 and modified in 1988, but are proving very difficult to apply in practice.

13.9.18 Capital Gains Tax — Sales of subsidiaries
(TCGA Ss31–34)

With effect from 14 March 1989, certain schemes to save tax on capital gains where a group disposes of one or more subsidiaries are curbed. For example, the value of a subsidiary may be reduced before sale by distributing assets to fellow group members at less than market value; such undervalue will be added to the sale proceeds in calculating the capital gain on the sale of the subsidiary. However, the new legislation is not intended to catch distributions which could be made out of normal profits and reserves.

Another situation which has been countered, is where the commercial control of a subsidiary is sold, whilst keeping it within the group for capital gains relief on inter-group transfers etc through using special shares. From 14 March 1989, the benefits of group membership only apply if the parent company of the group has, directly or indirectly, an interest of over 50 per cent in the income and assets of the company.

13.9.19 Capital Gains Tax — Non-resident trusts
(TCGA Ss80–98 & Sch 5)

From 19 March 1991, sweeping changes have effect regarding the capital gains tax rules relating to offshore settlements. The rules (18.32) involve the settlor and beneficiaries. Among other changes, the use of such settlements to delay the onset of capital gains tax has been much curtailed.

14 Returns, assessments and repayment claims

14.1 Your tax return
(TMA S8 & FA 1990 S77 & S90)

The Revenue will normally send to you periodically a tax return for completion. If your income includes Schedule A and/or Schedule D income you will usually have to submit a tax return each year. If, however, all your income is taxed under PAYE (9.14) you may only be required to complete a return about every three years.

For 1990–91 income and subsequently, husbands and wives must submit separate returns. Normally, up to 5 April 1990, your wife's income was included in your return. However, at the same time, wives were being asked to submit returns of their own income for the year 1989–90 in order for them to claim their allowances for 1990–91.

Apart from individuals, trusts, partnerships and companies, etc also have to submit tax returns. In the case of companies, however, provided the Revenue receive the annual accounts and tax computations they do not normally insist on the submission of corporation tax returns. If no return is submitted, sources of income and capital gains must broadly be notified to the Inland Revenue. The time limit is one year from the end of the year of assessment or accounting period and there is a penalty for 1988–89 (accounting periods ending after 31 March 1989 for companies) and subsequently, of up to the amount of the unpaid tax (FA 1988 Ss120–122).

If you have not been sent a tax return for the previous tax year and you have received income for that year apart from your wages or salary, you should request that the Revenue sends you a return form for completion. This request should be made to the Inspector of Taxes who deals with your affairs — if you are employed it will

220 *Allied Dunbar Tax Guide*

be the tax district that handles your employer's PAYE affairs. As well as including details of your income for the previous tax year your tax return also constitutes a claim for income tax allowances and reliefs in respect of the current tax year. Thus your 1992–93 tax return must show your income for the year to 5 April 1992 and the income tax allowances that you are claiming for the year to 5 April 1993.

A further reason for you to request a tax return from your Inspector of Taxes is to ensure that you are granted all of the income tax reliefs and allowances to which you are entitled.

When a tax return is issued to you it normally stipulates that it must be completed and sent back within 30 days but the Revenue usually allow further time if required. (However, if you delay beyond 31 October and have new sources of income unknown to the Inland Revenue, you could be charged interest on the eventual assessment, if this is delayed.)

Your 1992–93 tax return probably will have been sent to you early in April 1992 and has four main headings as follows:

Income: Year ended 5 April 1992
Outgoings: Year ended 5 April 1992
Capital gains: Year ended 5 April 1992
Allowances: Claim for year ending 5 April 1993.

On the first or sometimes last page of your return you must give your private address and also sign the following declaration: 'To the best of my knowledge and belief the particulars given on this form are correct and complete'. (A simplified return issued to certain taxpayers requires your signature at the end and asks you to tick the items of income and allowances which apply, also giving amounts.)

14.1.1 Table: Your 1992–93 tax return — Income

> The following sources of income must be included in your return showing the *amounts* for yourself for the year to 5 April 1992. (The exact detail, order and design of the return may vary for different classes of taxpayer.) Further rules concerning the entries are given elsewhere in this book. Include with your investment income ((4)–(11) below) that on assets given by you to any of your children who are under 18 (6.6).
>
> Joint sources of income held by spouses should be marked 'joint' and the income split equally between you unless a different split has been agreed with the tax office. Only your own share should be entered on your tax return.

Returns, assessments and repayment claims

	Class of Income	Details
(1)	Employments or offices.	Occupation. Employer. Gross earnings (including fees, bonus, commission, tips, etc). Benefits and expense allowances. Leaving payments, etc. Duties performed wholly abroad — state employment, and dates of absence. Whether taxed sum received from approved profit sharing scheme.
(2)	Pensions and social security benefits.	Rates and nature of pensions. National Insurance retirement pension. Old person's pension. Widow's and other benefits. Pension from former employer and other pensions (including war widow's pension). Unemployment benefit/income support.
(3)	Trade, profession or vocation.	Nature. Business name and address. Period. Adjusted profits. Deductions for capital allowances. Enterprise allowance. Other deductions for Class 4 National Insurance purposes. Give turnover and expenses if turnover below £15,000.
(4)	Property (give address, gross income and expenses).	Unfurnished lettings. Furnished lettings and holiday lettings. Ground rents. Land.
(5)	Interest not taxed before receipt.	National and trustee savings interest, deposit or Income Bonds. Other banks (give names). Other sources (including war loan, defence bonds, etc). Banks, building societies etc, to whom you have certified you are not liable to tax.
(6)	Untaxed income from abroad.	
(7)	Interest taxed before receipt.	
	(a) UK banks and deposit takers.	Names and amounts received.
	(b) Interest from UK building societies.	Names of societies, amounts received.
(8)	UK dividends	Show for each source separately, the amounts received, and also the tax credits.
(9)	Interest, trust income, foreign dividends, etc, already taxed.	Enter the gross amounts before deduction of tax.

222 Allied Dunbar Tax Guide

(10)	Income or capital from certain settlements and estates.	Include transfers to be treated as your income — parental gifts — receipts from the estates of deceased persons in administration.
(11)	Any other profit or income.	Maintenance etc received and gains on non-qualifying policies (24.6.2).
(12)	Age and pension details.	Give details of any pension you receive — amounts and frequency of payment. Similar details are required for pensions likely to start before 6 April 1993. Give date of birth if before 6 April 1933.

14.1.2 Table: Your 1992–93 tax return — Outgoings

The amounts of your outgoings for the year ended 5 April 1992 must be shown separately as follows:

Class	Details
Private Medical Insurance for people over 60.	Details, amounts 1991–92 and 1992–93 (net). Enclose certificate to obtain higher rate relief.
Expenses in employment.	Details and amounts including professional subscriptions.

Payroll deductions:
  Superannuation
  Payments to charity
  Profit related pay scheme.
	Indicate if any of these deductions or exemptions have been made from your pay.

Interest on loans (excluding bank overdrafts) for purchase or (on pre-5 April 1988 loans only) improvement of property.	*Only or main residence* To a building society (include loans paid off in 1991–92) — give name and Account No (no amounts needed). To any other person including a bank — give name and account number — enclose certificate. For joint mortgages with your spouse, you may indicate if you wish a special split (6.1). *Let property* — number of weeks let — enclose certificate if further relief claimed.
Interest on other loans (excluding overdrafts).	Qualifying loans — enclose certificates.
Other interest and outgoings.	Covenants and settlements. Alimony or maintenance. UK property rents or yearly interest paid to persons abroad. Net amounts of Gift Aid Donations to charity.

Details of changes in untaxed income or outgoings since 5 April 1991.

Returns, assessments and repayment claims 223

14.1.3 Table: Your 1992–93 tax return — Capital gains

You must give details of the gains for your wife and yourself for the year to 5 April 1992 as follows:

Class	Details
Chargeable assets disposed of (18.9).	Date of disposal, and description. (If your chargeable gains and proceeds are no more than £5,500 and £11,000 respectively, you need only state this fact.)
	Amount of gain for year (also show any losses).

Payments made or benefits provided by non-resident or dual resident settlements (19.9.1).
Chargeable gains of settlements by reference to which you are chargeable as settlor (19.9.1).

14.1.4 Table: Your 1992–93 tax return — Claim for allowances

If you claim any personal reliefs or allowances for 1992–93 (3.0.1) you must enter the required details in the spaces provided on your return. These are summarised below.

Class	Details
Personal allowance.	Indicate if born before 6 April 1928 (possible age allowance entitlement).
Special personal allowance.	Indicate where claimed on account of age allowance previously obtained because of wife's age and no longer due under new system—hence special allowance (3.2.15).
Married couple's allowance (married man living with wife or wholly maintaining her).	Wife's full name. If you married after 5 April 1991: date of marriage. Indicate if higher level claimed because either spouse born before 6 April 1928 (give wife's date of birth).
Additional personal allowance for children.	Does child live with you? Wife's incapacity (if any), and whether likely to continue throughout tax year. Give names, dates of birth and details of school, etc, if child 16 or over on 6 April 1992. Proportions in which relief to be divided between husband and wife.
Blind person's allowance.	Local authority and date of registration.

Personal pension plans (retirement annuity payments) and free-standing additional voluntary contributions as an employee.	Show net payments for 1991–92 and projected amounts for 1992–93. Also, details of schemes, date of birth, etc. (For retirement annuities show gross amounts.) Amount paid by employer for 1991–92 and projected for 1992–93.
Retirement annuity payments and personal pension contributions — self-employed.	Occupation in which non-pensionable earnings arise (employer, etc). Name of insurance company, etc or trust scheme. Contract number, etc. Amount paid (gross) in 1991–92 and to be paid in 1992–93. Date of birth.

14.2 The Tax Inspectors and Collectors
(TMA S1 & FA 1990 S104)

The overall control and management of income tax, corporation tax and capital gains tax is exercised by the Board of Inland Revenue. They are responsible for administering the relevant law as contained in the 1988 Income and Corporation Taxes Act and the various Finance Acts. The latter are normally enacted annually about July, the main items having been announced by the Chancellor of the Exchequer in his budget speech in March or April. It is planned that future budgets will be in December. However, in 1993, there will be a budget in March and one in December.

The Board of Inland Revenue is made up of the Commissioners of Inland Revenue. The day-to-day administration, however, is carried out by various Inspectors of Taxes and Collectors of Taxes who are civil servants, appointed by the Board. Inspectors and collectors may be appointed for general purposes or specific purposes, at the discretion of the Board.

The Inspectors of Taxes are organised into various tax districts to one of which you will have to send your income tax return. A district inspector heads each district under whom are a number of inspectors and clerks, who obtain and verify as they think fit the information that is necessary to raise assessments to income tax, capital gains tax and corporation tax.

The Collectors of Taxes have the responsibility of collecting the tax that has been assessed. They issue demands for the tax that is due (14.7).

The office of the Inspector of Foreign Dividends handles various matters in connection with double tax relief claims.

14.2.1 The assessment mechanism
(TMA S29 & FA 1988 S119)

When you have submitted your income tax return the Inspector of Taxes will issue a 'notice of assessment' to income tax in respect of your various types of income. A separate assessment will be raised in respect of Schedule E earnings. Since the latter normally will have been taxed already under PAYE the assessment will show whether any additional payment of income tax is required or whether a repayment is due (14.6).

Your capital gains tax assessment also will be raised by your Inspector of Taxes (18.15).

If the Revenue have not received sufficient information to raise accurate tax assessments prior to the date on which the tax is due for payment, they will normally make estimated assessments in respect of the taxpayer's sources of income. This practice received confirmation in the 1988 Finance Act. Estimated capital gains tax assessments will also be raised if appropriate.

14.2.2 Due dates for payment of tax
(TA 1988 S5)

The due date for payment of income tax assessed under the various Schedules and Cases (2.3) is normally 1 January in the year of assessment.

Thus your Schedule D Case III income tax for 1992–93 including higher rates is payable on 1 January 1993. Schedule D Case I and Case II assessments on your profits from a trade or profession are payable, however, in two instalments on 1 January in the year of assessment and the following 1 July.

Higher rate income tax on your 'taxed' investment income is payable on 1 December following the year of assessment. This includes tax on interest, etc taxed at source and dividends. Higher rate income tax on other investment income, however (including rents, etc), is normally payable on 1 January in the year of assessment. (For due dates of payment of corporation tax see 12.4.)

If an assessment is issued later than 30 days before the respective date above, however, the date when the tax becomes due and payable is delayed to a later date. This is normally 30 days after the issue of the assessment. Note, however, the effect of appeals (14.3).

14.2.3 Discovery
(TMA S29 (3))

The estimated assessments will be made by the Revenue to as great a degree of accuracy as possible according to any information in their possession such as particulars for previous years. If, however, the Revenue make a *discovery* that:

(1) profits which ought to have been assessed to tax have not been assessed, or
(2) an assessment to tax is or has become insufficient, or
(3) excessive relief has been given

the Revenue may make an assessment in the amount or further amount which ought in their opinion to be charged.

Thus if your business income tax assessment for 1992–93 under Schedule D Case I is estimated at £1,000 and after submitting your accounts it becomes apparent that the correct figure is £2,000, the Inspector of Taxes will raise an additional assessment of £1,000. If, however, you lodged notice of appeal against the assessment (see below), your original assessment for £1,000 will be amended to £2,000.

14.2.4 Time limits for assessments
(TMA Ss34 & 36 & FA 1982 S149)

Normally an assessment to tax may be made at any time not later than six years after the end of the chargeable period to which the assessment relates. This means that any income tax assessment for 1992–93 may be made on or before 5 April 1999.

In cases, however, of any fraudulent or negligent conduct by the taxpayer (14.8.1) the Revenue have more time to make assessments.

A special rule applies to the recovery by the Revenue of excessive repayment claims, etc, made to you after 5 April 1982. The time limit is then six years from the end of the tax year when the original repayment, etc was made.

14.2.5 Tax remission — Official error

If you send in full returns of your taxable income and you receive no assessments, so that you are led to believe that your tax affairs are in order, it is the practice of the Revenue to excuse you the tax, if your income is sufficiently low. Otherwise part of your tax is remitted according to the following table which applies for arrears notified from 14 March 1990.

14.2.6 Table: Tax remission limits from 14 March 1990

Gross income limits		Fraction of arrears collected
Under 65	From 65 or Government pensioners	
£12,000	£15,300	None
14,500	17,800	$\frac{1}{4}$
18,500	21,800	$\frac{1}{2}$
22,000	25,300	$\frac{3}{4}$
32,000	35,300	$\frac{9}{10}$
above 32,000	above 35,300	All

14.3 Appeals against assessments
(TMA S31; F2A 1975 S45 & FA 1982 S68)

If you are not in agreement with an assessment to income tax, capital gains tax or corporation tax you may appeal to the Inspector of Taxes within 30 days of the date of the assessment. Your appeal must be in writing and state the grounds on which you object to the assessment; most frequently these are that 'the assessment is estimated and excessive'. Should you not be able to appeal within 30 days for some good reason such as absence from home or ill-health, the Revenue will normally allow you to make a late appeal.

The majority of appeals are settled by agreement. This normally follows when the accounts and/or returns have been submitted to the Inspector of Taxes and any queries that he raises are answered. If, however, you are not able to agree with the Revenue or if you or your accountants have not submitted all of the required information, the appeal will be listed for personal hearing before the Commissioners (14.3).

All the tax charged by an assessment is treated as due and payable (14.2.2) unless, within 30 days, you estimate how much you are being overcharged and apply to the Inspector for the balance to be postponed.

For assessments issued from August 1982, the 30-day time limit is extended where your circumstances change so that your tax liability reduces. It will then be determined by agreement with the Inspector or otherwise by the Commissioners how much of the tax should be held over with only the balance being collected. This collectable balance is payable within 30 days after the Inspector or Commissioners have dealt with the application for postponement. Any unpaid tax normally becomes due 30 days after the date on which, following the agreement of the assessment, the Inspector issues a notice of the tax payable. An interest charge could run from an earlier date, however (14.7.2), especially in the case of a long drawn out appeal.

14.4 The Special and General Commissioners
(TMA Ss2–6, FA 1984 S127 & Sch 22 & F2A 1992 Ss75, 76 & Sch 16)

The Commissioners before whom tax appeals are heard are of two kinds, General and Special.

The General Commissioners are not normally paid. They are similar to lay magistrates and the majority of them have no special legal or accountancy qualifications. General Commissioners are appointed in England and Wales by the Lord Chancellor. They are appointed for specific districts each of which has a Clerk to the Commissioners, who is usually a solicitor, to assist them.

The Treasury previously appointed the Special Commissioners who usually had practical experience of taxation matters gained either in private practice or with the Inland Revenue. Now, under rules in the 1984 Finance Act, the Lord Chancellor appoints them only from barristers, solicitors or advocates of at least ten years' standing. The Special Commissioners are full-time civil servants.

Appeals will automatically be heard before the General Commissioners in the district which deals with the tax assessment, except that:

(1) When appealing, you may request that any resulting hearing should be in another district which is more convenient to you.

(2) You may elect within 30 days of the assessment that the appeal should be brought before the Special Commissioners. This does not apply, however, to questions regarding personal reliefs and (under the new rules) delay cases which are always dealt with by the General Commissioners.

(3) Appeals against certain income tax assessments are always heard by the Special Commissioners including those on annual payments not covered by income, transactions in securities (TA 1988 S703) valuations of unquoted securities and transfers of assets abroad (TA 1988 S739).

In many cases you will thus have a choice as to whether the Special or General Commissioners should hear your appeal. As a general rule if your case is good in equity and its justice would commend it to average honest men, you should choose the General Commissioners. If you have a good legal case (ie, one sound according to a strict reading of the law) you should choose the Special Commissioners. However, if you elect for your appeal to be heard by the Special Commissioners this can be opposed by the Revenue if they prove you have no case to present.

New rules are planned to take effect from 1 April 1993. These include giving the Special Commissioners powers to publish their decisions and to award costs where either party has acted wholly unreasonably in pursuing a tax appeal.

14.5 Investigatory powers of the Revenue
(TMA S20, FA 1976 S57 & Sch 6, FA 1988 Ss126, 127, FA 1989 Ss142–148 & FA 1990 Ss92–94)

The powers of the Revenue to obtain papers and search premises were strengthened by the 1976 and 1989 Finance Acts. Subject to the consent of the Board of Inland Revenue, the Inspector may require you by notice in writing to supply him with documents in your possession or power, which he considers have a bearing on your tax liability. From 27 July 1990, the Board are not to consent unless you have failed or may have failed to comply with any provisions of the Taxes Acts; and as a result your tax position has been seriously affected.

The Inspector may also require documents from certain other people. These other people include your spouse and any of your children. In general these rules do not apply to pending appeals, nor to development land tax. These rules include access to computer records.

If any of your income comes from a business which you either carried on yourself or you managed, then any person who is or was carrying on a business may be directed to provide documents concerning their dealings with your business. The same applies if your wife carries on a business or manages one.

These rules also apply to a past business and any companies of which you or your spouse are, or were, directors. From August 1988, such companies need not be carrying on business. Furthermore, the Director of Savings is within the net.

In order for your Inspector of Taxes to obtain information about your affairs from other people, he must obtain the consent of a General or Special Commissioner (14.4) and the latter must ensure that the Inspector is justified in his request.

A barrister, advocate or solicitor cannot be compelled to yield up documents without your consent provided these are covered by professional privilege. This even applies to such a lawyer acting as your tax accountant (see below).

From 27 July 1989 various changes took effect including:

(1) the protection of personal records and journalistic material from disclosure;
(2) a requirement for the Inland Revenue to allow not less than 30 days for requested information to be produced;
(3) the putting of written questions to the taxpayer;
(4) it being a criminal offence to falsify, conceal or destroy documents called for under the Revenue powers.

14.5.1 Tax accountants' papers

Your tax accountant is not obliged to reveal his working papers to the Revenue subject to the following.

Where a tax accountant is convicted of an offence in relation to tax by a UK court or has a penalty awarded against him for assisting in making incorrect returns, etc subject to certain rules, an Inspector of Taxes may require him to surrender documents relating to the tax affairs of any of his clients. Notice is required in writing and the permission of a circuit judge, Scottish sheriff or Irish county court judge must be obtained. The power of the Revenue to give this notice generally ceases 12 months after the conviction or penalty award, and does not have effect whilst an appeal is pending.

From 27 July 1989, not less than 30 days must be allowed for a convicted tax accountant to deliver documents required by the Revenue. Also from that time, personal records and journalistic material are protected as are, in general, audit papers and records of tax advice. At the same time, taxpayers must be notified of requests for information from third parties, unless fraud is involved.

14.5.2 Entry warrant to obtain documents

If the Revenue obtain an entry warrant in a case of suspected fraud they may enter specified premises, seizing and removing any documents or other things required as evidence for relevant proceedings. A warrant is valid for 14 days and can only be granted by a circuit judge, etc who is satisfied on information given on oath by an officer of the Board of Inland Revenue, that evidence concerning a tax fraud is to be found on the premises in question.

Under the 1989 Finance Act, the Inland Revenue search powers are broadly restricted to the investigation of 'serious fraud' and are subject to a detailed code of conduct. Also, taxpayers have rights of access to property removed under the search powers.

14.5.3 Returns of information
(TMA Ss13–19 & FA 1988 Ss123–125)

The Revenue are empowered to request returns of certain information from traders and others. For example, you may be required to give particulars of any lodgers you may have.

Your bank may be required to return details of interest paid to you during a tax year, if this exceeds £15 (generally higher in practice). Furthermore, the Revenue are empowered to obtain from any business details of its payments of fees, commissions, royalties, etc exceeding £15 to any person during a tax year.

The 1988 Finance Act introduced a three-year time limit regarding many of the Revenue powers to request information returns. However, they can extend their enquiries to certain government departments and public authorities.

14.5.4 Appeal hearings
(TMA Ss44–59 & FA 1984 Sch 22)

The Clerk to the Commissioners will advise you of the time and place for your appeal hearing. If you are unable to attend for some good reason or if you or your accountants have not completed the required accounts, etc it will normally be possible to have the matter adjourned at least once until a later time. If you would like an adjournment you or your agent should raise the question with your Inspector of Taxes who will usually be prepared to arrange this for you if your reasons are in order.

At the appeal hearing you may represent yourself or be represented by an accountant or a solicitor or barrister. If your appeal is on a point of law which you anticipate may go to the Courts (see below) it is wise to be represented at the outset by a barrister who can act for you in the Courts. The Revenue are normally represented by an Inspector of Taxes but on difficult legal points a person from the Solicitors' Office may act. The proceedings before the Commissioners resemble those in the Courts in many ways — for example, witnesses may be summoned under oath to be examined and cross-examined.

When the hearing has been completed the Commissioners will withdraw to consider their decision. They may confirm or reduce or increase the original assessment. The decision of the Commissioners is final regarding questions of fact. If either the taxpayer or the Revenue are dissatisfied with their decision on a point of law, they should immediately 'express dissatisfaction'. The Commissioners should then be requested to supply a 'case stated' which is a document signed by them setting out their decision. A fee of £25 is now charged. The case will then be taken on appeal to the Courts where it will first be heard before a single judge in the Chancery Division. (It is possible for certain appeals against decisions of the Special Commissioners to be referred direct to the Court of Appeal.) The decision of such a court can be appealed against, following which the case will be heard before the Court of Appeal and on further appeal it may go before the House of Lords.

Before you request a 'case stated' from the Commissioners you should weigh very carefully the strength of your case and the potential tax saving if you succeed in the higher Courts against the high legal costs which would be involved.

14.6 Repayment claims
(TMA Ss42 & 43, TA 1988 S281 & FA 1989 S150)

Repayment claims arise in connection with many different facets of taxation. You will normally, however, find that any income tax repayment to which you become entitled arises in one of the following ways:

(1) Most of your income has been taxed at the source and your personal reliefs and allowances exceed your other income. (Also, you may not have received the full benefit of the £2,000 20 per cent lower rate income tax band for 1992–93.) If your income tax return reveals this position and you send in the required simple repayment claim form together with dividend vouchers, etc in respect of the income tax credits, you will receive an income tax repayment. The repayment will reduce your income tax bill for the tax year to its correct level.

(2) Some of your income has been taxed both in the UK and in another country. You are frequently able to make a double taxation relief repayment claim of either UK tax or overseas tax depending on the circumstances (16.6).

(3) You may have already paid a Schedule A or Schedule D assessment for a tax year and, as described elsewhere in this book, you make an election to the Revenue which results in your assessment for that year being reduced. An example of such an election is where you elect that the second and third years of your business should be assessed on an actual basis (10.7.4).

(4) You make a business loss which you claim to be offset against your other income for the year (10.22). Some of this income has suffered income tax by deduction at the source and on making the required claim and submitting the tax vouchers or receipts you will be repaid an appropriate amount of such tax, as well as tax credits on dividends.

(5) You discover that an 'error or mistake' has been made in a return or statement or schedule that you have previously submitted as a result of which you have been over-assessed to tax. Within six years after the end of the tax year in which the original assessment was made, you may make a claim to your Inspector of Taxes for the repayment of the tax previously overpaid.

(6) Repayment claims often arise in respect of minors (under 18) all of whom are taxpayers in their own right and so are entitled to at least the personal allowance for a single person (£3,445). Thus if a minor's only income for 1992–93 consists of dividends of say £375 and none of the investments were gifted to him by his parents, then he can reclaim all of the relevant tax credits (ie, 25/75 × £375 = £125). Similarly, if the trustees of a settlement apply income for the education and maintenance of a minor, that income is treated as belonging to the child. The income is treated as having suffered basic rate income tax at the source (and additional rate tax if appli-

cable). This enables an income tax repayment claim to be made for the minor unless he has already obtained the full benefit of his tax reliefs and allowances or the settlement had been actually created by one of his parents.

(7) The Revenue may raise an additional assessment and if this is not related to fraud or negligent conduct, you may be able to claim additional reliefs as a result. From 27 July 1989, such claims, elections, etc, even though out of time according to the normal rules, are valid if made within one year of the end of the tax period in which the assessment is made.

The procedure for making repayment claims is normally very simple. If the Revenue have already received a full return of your income, or in the case of a business or company its accounts and tax computations, it will generally only be necessary to sign a short form in which you claim the tax repayment to which you are entitled. You should also send dividend vouchers or tax deduction certificates or receipts to cover the amount of your repayment.

Special forms are usually required for double tax relief claims on which you must enter particulars of the dividends. Special forms are also provided by the Revenue for use in connection with various other repayment claims, for example, concerning minors.

Income tax repayment claims should normally be made to your local Inspector of Taxes. If you are, for example, a British subject resident abroad your repayment claims should be made to the Chief Inspector (Claims) at Bootle. The Inspector of Foreign Dividends, however, deals with applications from those residing abroad for the recovery of United Kingdom tax suffered on overseas dividends, etc. Normally, for years of assessment before 1990–91, most repayments of tax on your wife's income were paid to you. However, her PAYE over-deductions for years of assessment before 1990–91 are repaid direct to her unless she has earnings taxed under Schedule D or you are a higher rate taxpayer.

14.6.1 Example: Income tax repayment claim

Miss A is 24 years of age and during the year to 5 April 1993 she only had occasional employment from which her gross earnings were £1,060, no PAYE being deducted. During 1992–93 she pays allowable loan interest of £125. Miss A's only other income for 1992–93 consists of £1,500 dividends (tax credit £500) and an income distribution of £650 (net) from a discretionary trust. Calculate the amount of the income tax repayment claim of Miss A for 1992–93.

Miss A — Income tax repayment claim 1992–93

Details		Gross income	Tax credits
Earned income		£1,060	
Taxed dividends including tax credit		2,000	£500
Trust income — net	£650		
Grossed up equivalent at 35%	———	1,000	350
		£4,060	
Less: Personal allowance	£3,445		
Loan interest (paid gross)	125		
		3,570	
Taxable amount		£490	
Total tax credits			£850
Less: Income tax liability £490 at 20%			98
Income tax repayable for 1992–93			£752

14.6.2 Repayment supplement
(TA 1988 Ss824–826 & FA 1989 S158)

This applies if you receive a tax repayment more than a year after the end of the year of assessment to which it relates. You also have to be resident in the UK. (Prior to changes brought about by the 1989 Finance Act, the repayment needed to be not less than £25). You will then get interest at $9\frac{1}{4}$ per cent free of tax from normally the later of the end of the assessment year in which the tax was paid or 5 April following the year for which repayment is made, until the end of the tax month when the repayment is made. This rate has applied since 6 October 1991, before which it was 10 per cent and before 6 July 1991 it was $10\frac{3}{4}$ per cent.

Prior to 6 May 1991, the percentage was $11\frac{1}{2}$ and before 6 March 1991, it was $12\frac{1}{4}$. Similar rules and rates apply for companies and a fuller rate scale appears earlier (12.5). Identical rates also apply for interest on overdue tax (14.7.2).

14.7 The collection of tax
(TMA Ss60–68)

The collection of income tax, corporation tax and capital gains tax is done by the Collectors of Taxes (14.2).

On being notified of an assessment by the Inspector of Taxes the Collector will send out a first demand. If this is not paid within about a month of its 'due date' a second demand will be sent and after about another ten days a final demand will follow. The final demand requests payment within seven days under the threat of legal proceedings against the taxpayer concerned. It is usual for the first demand to be integrated with the notice of assessment and the payslip should be detached from the rest of the form when you make your payment.

The Revenue are empowered to take action in Magistrates' Courts for the recovery of tax up to a limit which is currently £250 (FA 1984 S57). Otherwise, action must be in the County Courts (up to the 'County Court limit') or the High Court.

14.7.1 Payments on account

If you receive a large tax demand which you find difficult to meet out of your available funds the Collector of Taxes will in cases of hardship allow you to settle the outstanding tax by instalments payable at say monthly or quarterly intervals. You should contact the Collector of Taxes and explain the position to him. Interest will probably be payable, however (see below).

14.7.2 Interest on overdue tax
(TMA Ss86–92; F2A 1975 S46; FA 1980 Ss61 & 62; FA 1981 S51, F2A 1987 Ss85–89, FA 1988 S128 & FA 1989 Ss156–161)

The following rules apply to assessments issued after 31 July 1975. Assessments issued earlier are covered by different rules (even if still unpaid), and details are given in previous editions. The rules have been clarified and modified by the 1989 Finance Act. For example, the mechanics for altering the interest rate have been made more automatic, rather than needing a statutory instrument, as previously.

Interest is payable at currently $9\frac{1}{4}$ per cent from the 'reckonable date' until the tax is settled. Some recent rates are:

From	Rate per cent
6 October 1991	$9\frac{1}{4}$
6 July 1991	10
6 May 1991	$10\frac{3}{4}$
6 March 1991	$11\frac{1}{2}$
6 November 1990	$12\frac{1}{4}$
6 November 1989	13

From	Rate per cent
6 July 1989	$12\frac{1}{4}$
6 January 1989	$11\frac{1}{2}$
6 October 1988	$10\frac{3}{4}$
6 August 1988	$9\frac{3}{4}$
6 May 1988	$7\frac{3}{4}$
6 December 1987	$8\frac{1}{4}$
6 September 1987	9
6 June 1987	$8\frac{1}{4}$
6 April 1987	9
6 November 1986	$9\frac{1}{2}$
6 August 1986	$8\frac{1}{2}$
1 May 1985	11
1 December 1982	8
1 January 1980	12

The 'reckonable date' is the date when the tax becomes due and payable (14.2.2) unless you appeal and obtain a deferment of tax. In that case the 'reckonable date' is when the tax becomes due and payable or the date given by the following table whichever is earlier:

	Description of tax	Date applicable
(1)	Schedules A or D	1 July following the end of the year of assessment.
(2)	Additional rates of income tax	1 June following the end of the next year of assessment.
(3)	Capital gains tax	1 June following the end of the next year of assessment.
(4)	Corporation tax	Usually 6 months after the normal payment date (12.4).

The above table applies to all amounts, even if not covered by the original assessment if this was issued after July 1982. Otherwise, such additional amounts were only charged to interest from 30 days after the issue of the revised notice of assessment.

The Revenue may excuse at their discretion the payment of interest not exceeding £30 in total for any one assessment. This amount is to be varied following provisions in the 1989 Finance Act which enable the minimum to be updated. No interest paid on overdue tax is allowed as a deduction from your taxable income or business profits nor is it allowed as a deduction for corporation tax or capital gains tax purposes.

From 20 April 1988, interest arises on overdue formal assessments, which have to be raised for PAYE and sub-contractor deductions (13.5). The interest charge runs from 14 days after the end of the tax year to which the assessment relates. At a future date, probably no earlier than 1993, interest will be introduced on late payments to the Revenue of PAYE deductions made by employers.

14.8 Back duty investigations

If you have not disclosed to the Revenue your true income or if you have claimed tax reliefs and allowances to which you were not entitled the discovery of such facts by the authorities might give rise to a 'back duty' case.

It is open to the Revenue to take criminal proceedings against you resulting in a fine and/or imprisonment but this is rare. The normal course will be for the Revenue to obtain full particulars of the income omitted by you and raise assessments on you in respect of the further tax that is due. You will also normally be charged interest on the tax from when it should have been paid if your income had been properly declared. The Revenue may also charge you to penalties (see below) depending upon whether your omissions were due to pure carelessness or ignorance or on the other hand were due to some fraudulent intention.

In order to ascertain the amount of your undisclosed income the Revenue will frequently require that capital statements be drawn up at the beginning and end of the period under review. The increase in your net worth between those two dates is then added to your living expenses for the period to give your total income (subject to adjustments for known capital profits, purchases and sales, betting winnings, etc). Your total income less income already taxed will give your total income requiring still to be taxed. This should be split between the various intervening tax years by considering your assets and living expenses, etc for each tax year.

14.8.1 Fraud, wilful default or neglect; fraudulent or negligent conduct
(TMA S36 & FA 1989 S149)

Tax lost through the 'fraudulent or negligent conduct' of a taxpayer may be assessed up to 20 years after the end of the period to which it relates. This is a new rule introduced by the 1989 Finance Act and it also applies to partners and where agents are culpable. These provisions apply to assessments for 1983–84 onwards and, regarding companies, for accounting periods ending after 31 March 1983.

Returns, assessments and repayment claims 239

For years of assessment prior to 1983–84 and accounting periods ending before 1 April 1983, the normal six-year time limit for making assessments (14.2.2) is extended indefinitely in any case where there is fraud or wilful default. This does not apply, however, in the case of the personal representatives of a deceased person (19.2).

In a case of 'neglect' by a taxpayer, the Revenue are empowered to make assessments for 1982–83 and earlier, for six years prior to a tax year for which an assessment has already been made. The latter must be not more than six years ago and the Revenue must obtain the leave of the Special or General Commissioners. 'Neglect' is defined as 'negligence or a failure to give any notice, make any return or to produce or furnish any document or other information required by or under the Taxes Acts'.

14.8.2 Interest and penalties
(TMA Ss86–107, FA 1988 S129 & FA 1989 Ss156–170)

Where an assessment has been made for the purpose of making good a loss of tax through fraud, wilful default or neglect, interest at 10 per cent is charged on the underpaid tax from the date that the tax should have been paid. This also covers tax lost through 'fraudulent or negligent conduct' and was extended from 27 July 1989 to tax assessed late as the result of an incorrect return. Prior to 6 July 1991, various other interest rates applied as for overdue tax (14.7.2).

The maximum penalties are laid down in the legislation but frequently the Board of the Inland Revenue are prepared to accept less according to the particular facts of each case.

Regarding tax years after 1987–88 (or accounting periods ending after 31 March 1989 for companies), relief is given where more than one penalty arises on the same tax. In no case is the total amount of penalty to exceed the maximum possible amount for any one of the penalties involved.

The 1989 Finance Act introduced a simpler procedure for charging default interest and penalties. The Revenue may make formal determinations of the amounts due rather like assessments. You have full rights of appeal to the Appeal Commissioners and Courts. These new rules do not apply to the initial penalties under the compliance rules which continue to be awarded by the Appeal Commissioners.

14.8.3 Table: Penalties—Previous rules
(TMA Ss93–107 & FA 1988 Ss120–122A)

The following are examples of some of the maximum penalties:

Offence	Penalties
Failure to submit returns.	£50 for each return plus £10 per day after a court declaration.
Failure to submit return continuing beyond tax year following that in which issued.	£50 plus total tax based on return.
Incorrect returns.	£50 plus twice the additional tax in the case of fraud and in other cases £50 plus the additional tax.
Assisting in the preparation of incorrect returns or accounts.	£500.
Supplying incorrect information to the Revenue.	£500 in case of fraud — otherwise £250.
Failure to give notice of liability to tax.	£100. From 6 April 1989 the penalty is the amount of tax if notice is more than one year overdue.
Failure to make when required a return of fees, commissions, etc.	£50 plus £50 for each additional day in default.
False statement made by sub-contractor to obtain exemption from tax deduction (13.5).	£5,000.

14.8.4 Table: Penalties—Current rules
(FA 1989 Ss162–170 & FA 1991 S70)

The following are examples of some of the maximum penalties:

Offence	Penalties
Failure to submit personal tax returns (1).	£300 plus. £60 per day after a court declaration.

Failure to submit return continuing beyond tax year following that in which issued (1).	Additional penalty of up to the amount of tax on income and gain, for year. However, if there is no assessable income or gains, the maximum *total* penalty is £100.
Incorrect returns (2).	100% of tax lost.
Assisting in the preparation of incorrect returns or accounts (2).	£3,000.
Supplying incorrect information to the Revenue (2).	£3,000.
Failure to make (when required) a return of information for the Revenue (2).	£300 plus £60 for each additional day in default.
Late submission of employers' year-end PAYE returns (9.14.4).	Initial penalty of up to £1,200 per 50 employees and £100 per 50 employees per month for further delays up to one year; beyond which up to 100% of tax underpaid or paid late.
Fraudulent or negligent certificate of non-liability to tax re building society or bank deposit (3).	Up to £3,000.

Note: Starting dates:
    (1) 6 April 1989
    (2) 27 July 1989
    (3) 25 July 1991.

15 Domicile and residence

15.1 The importance of domicile and residence

Your domicile and residence have a considerable effect on your liability to UK income tax, capital gains tax and inheritance tax. The position is summarised in the following table and dealt with in more detail in Chapters 16 and 17. (Domicile is defined in 15.2 and residence in 15.3.)

15.1.1 Table: The tax effects of domicile and residence

Tax	Situation of assets or where income arises	Tax treatment depending on taxpayer's residence and domicile		
		Taxed on arising basis	Taxed on remittance basis (16.1.1)	Tax free
Income Tax				
Schedule D				
Cases I & II	UK	All classes		
	Abroad	Not normally applicable		
Case III	UK	Normally all classes		
	Abroad	Not normally applicable		
Cases IV & V other than trades, professions, pensions, etc	UK	Not applicable	Not applicable	Non-resident
	Abroad	UK domiciled resident and ordinarily resident	Non-domiciled, UK domiciled resident but not ordinarily resident	
Case V relating to trades, professions, pensions, etc	UK	Not applicable	Not applicable	Non-resident
	Abroad	UK domiciled resident and ordinarily resident (90% pensions)	Non-domiciled, UK domiciled resident but not ordinarily resident	

Case VI	UK	All classes		
	Abroad	Not normally applicable apart from anti-avoidance rules (13.9)		
Schedule E		See 9.1–9.4		
Capital Gains Tax	UK or Abroad	UK domiciled and resident or ordinarily resident	Non-domiciled but resident or ordinarily resident (UK assets on arising basis)	Neither resident nor ordinarily resident
Inheritance Tax (residence is normally immaterial)	UK	UK domiciled or non-domiciled		
	Abroad	UK domiciled or deemed domiciled (20.4)		Non-domiciled

15.2 What is domicile?

Your domicile is the country which you regard as your natural home. It is your place of abode to which you intend to return in the event of your going abroad. For most people it is their country of birth. Everyone has one domicile only. Unlike dual nationality, it is not possible to have two domiciles under English law. There are three main categories of domicile:

(1) Domicile of origin.
(2) Domicile of choice.
(3) Domicile of dependency.

15.2.1 Domicile of origin

You receive a domicile of origin at birth; it is normally that of your father at the date of your birth. In the case, however, of an illegitimate child or one born after the death of his father, his domicile of origin is that of his mother.

Your domicile of origin can be abandoned and you can take on a domicile of choice (see below). You will quickly revert to your domicile of origin, however, if you take up permanent residence again in that country.

15.2.2 Domicile of choice

If you abandon your domicile of origin and go and live in another country with the intention of permanently living there, the new country will become your domicile of choice. You will normally have to abandon most of your links with your original country of domicile (above).

If you lose or abandon your domicile of choice, your domicile of origin automatically applies once again, unless you establish a new one.

15.2.3 Domicile of dependency

Certain dependent individuals are deemed incapable of choosing a new domicile and the latter is always fixed by the operation of the law. Dependants for this purpose include infants, married women before 1 January 1974 and mental patients.

A child under 16 years of age automatically has the domicile of his father if he is legitimate, and otherwise that of his mother. If, however, a girl of under 16 marries then she takes on her husband's domicile. (Prior to 1 January 1974 the relevant age was 18.) In Scotland a boy has an independent domicile from age 14 and a girl from age 12.

Prior to 1 January 1974 a wife assumed the domicile of her husband while they were married. After the end of the marriage (by death or divorce) the woman kept her former husband's domicile unless she took on a fresh domicile of choice. Since 1 January 1974, however, a wife's domicile is independent of that of her husband. If married before that date, the husband's domicile remains as the wife's deemed domicile of choice until displaced by positive action.

15.3 What is residence?

Your residence for tax purposes is something which is fixed by your circumstances from year to year and you may sometimes be treated as being resident in more than one country at the same time.

Residence depends on the facts of each case and is determined by the individual's presence in a country, his objects in being there and his future intentions regarding his length of stay. The main criterion is the length of time spent in the country during each tax year. Another important point is whether a 'place of abode' is kept in the country (15.3.6).

15.3.1 What is ordinary residence?

If you have always lived in this country you are treated as being ordinarily resident here. Ordinary residence means that the residence is not casual and uncertain but that the individual who resides in a particular country does so in the ordinary course of his life. It implies residence with some degree of continuity, according to the way a person's life is usually ordered.

If you come to this country with the intention of taking up permanent residence here, it is Revenue practice to regard you as being both resident and ordinarily resident in the UK from your date of arrival. If, however, you originally did not intend to take up permanent residence here, you would not be considered ordinarily resident unless you stay here for two complete tax years and keep a place to live in this country.

15.3.2 The residence of an individual
(TA 1988 Ss334–336)

If a person visits this country for some temporary purpose only and not with the intention of establishing his residence here, he is not normally treated as being a UK resident unless he spends at least six months here during the tax year.

An overseas visitor, however, might be treated as acquiring UK residence if he pays habitual substantial visits to this country. The normal requirement would be to come here for at least four consecutive years and stay for an average of at least three months each year. If you wish to remain non-resident you must avoid such habitual visits.

If you pay only short casual visits abroad you will not lose your UK residence, but if an entire tax year is included in any continuous period spent abroad you will normally be treated as being non-resident for at least the intervening tax year (15.3.7).

15.3.3 The residence of a company
(TA 1988 Ss747, 765–767 & FA 1988 Ss66 & 130–132 & Sch 7)

From 15 March 1988, a new rule for determining the residence of a company applies. Subject to transitional provisions (see below), a company which is incorporated in the UK is treated for tax purposes as being resident here. Prior to 15 March 1988, a company was deemed to be resident where its central control and management were carried out. This was not necessarily where the company was registered although normally the central control and management would be exercised in the country in which the company was registered. If, however, a company simply had its registered office here but carried on all its business from offices abroad and held its board meetings abroad, it was non-resident. Such companies will not come within the new rules for determining residence until 15 March 1993, provided they were already non-resident on 14 March 1988 or became non-resident later with Treasury consent. (In general, such companies must continue to carry on business.)

Under the controlled foreign company rules (12.21), where a company is resident abroad, it is necessary to establish in which country. Broadly, it is regarded as resident in the country where it is liable to tax because of its domicile, residence or place of management.

If a company registered abroad transacts some of its business in this country, it will not normally be treated as being UK resident provided its management and control are exercised abroad, which includes all board meetings being held abroad.

Taxes Act 1988 S765 contains certain penal provisions to prevent a UK company from becoming non-resident without Treasury consent being obtained. Fuller details are given earlier (13.9.16).

15.3.4 The residence of a partnership
(TA 1988 S112)

Where any trade or business is carried on by a partnership and the control and management of the trade is situated abroad, the partnership is deemed to be resident abroad. This applies even if some of the partners are resident in this country and some of the trade is carried on here (11.7).

15.3.5 The residence of a trust

A trust is generally treated for capital gains tax purposes as being resident and ordinarily resident in the UK unless its general administration is ordinarily carried on outside this country and a majority of the trustees are neither resident nor ordinarily resident here. Stricter rules generally apply for income tax. For these purposes, broadly from 1989–90 (with some exceptions), special rules apply where at least one trustee is UK resident and one is not, depending on the settlor's status when he created the settlement or introduced further funds. If the settlor was then resident, ordinarily resident or domiciled in the UK, for determining the residence of the trust, all of the trustees are treated as being UK resident.

Otherwise, they are all treated as being resident outside the UK. (A similar rule concerns the residence of executors, etc.) For 1989–90 only, a trust was non-resident if none of the trustees were UK resident from 1 October 1989 to 5 April 1990 (FA 1989 Ss110 & 111).

15.3.6 Place of abode in the UK
(TA 1988 S335)

If you maintain a house or flat in this country available for your occupation this will usually be a factor towards deciding that you are resident here. Your residence position will, however, be decided without regard to any place of abode maintained for your use in the UK in the following circumstances.

(1) You work full-time in a trade, profession or vocation no part of which is carried on in this country.
(2) You work full-time in an office or employment, all the duties of which (ignoring merely incidental duties) are performed outside the UK.

15.3.7 The effect of visits abroad
(TA 1988 S334)

If you are a citizen of the Commonwealth or the Republic of Ireland and your ordinary residence has been in the UK you are still charged to income tax if you have left this country if it is for the purpose of only occasional residence abroad. In order to obtain non-residence for UK tax purposes your overseas residence must be more than merely occasional, it must have a strong element of permanency. The normal Revenue requirements are as follows:

(1) A definite intention to establish a permanent residence abroad.
(2) The actual fulfilment of such intention.
(3) Normally a full tax year should be spent outside this country before you are considered non-resident. Short periods in the UK may be disregarded by the Revenue, however. Thus if you leave the country permanently on 30 September 1989 you will only be confirmed as non-resident after 5 April 1991. If you go abroad for the purposes of employment or to carry on a trade, once you are accepted by the Revenue as being no longer resident here, your non-residence is made retrospective to the day after your date of departure. In other cases of permanent departure, non-residence will normally run from the day after departure, but in some instances may run only

from the following 6 April. In general, the Revenue have less stringent rules regarding those working abroad under contracts of employment.

15.4 How to change your domicile and residence

As has been already indicated, domicile and residence normally run together but domicile is much more difficult to change.

The way in which to change your residence is summarised above. You simply establish a permanent residence abroad and remain out of this country for a complete tax year. (In certain circumstances short visits to the UK are allowed.) After that you must avoid returning to this country for as much as six months in any one tax year, averaging less than three months here every year. If, however, you have a place of abode available for you in the UK you are regarded as being resident here for any tax year during which you pay a visit (no matter how short), unless your residence abroad is for the purpose of an overseas trade or employment (15.3.6).

The general rule is that you will be charged to UK tax for the entire year of assessment as being either resident here or non-resident. However, in certain circumstances, by Inland Revenue Concession, the year of assessment is split for this purpose, namely where:

(1) You come to the UK to take up permanent residence or stay at least three years.
(2) You come to the UK to take up employment expected to last at least two years.
(3) You cease to reside in the UK because you have left for permanent residence abroad.

In order to establish a fresh domicile, you should take as many steps as possible to show that you regard your new country as your permanent home.

The following points are relevant to establishing a particular country as your new domicile:

(1) Develop a long period of residence in the new country.
(2) Purchase or lease a home.
(3) Marry a native of that country.

(4) Develop business interests there.
(5) Make arrangements to be buried there.
(6) Draw up your will according to the law of the country.
(7) Exercise political rights in your new country of domicile.
(8) Arrange to be naturalised (not vital).
(9) Have your children educated in the new country.
(10) Resign from all clubs and associations in your former country of domicile and join clubs, etc in your new country.
(11) Any religious affiliations that you have with your old domicile should be terminated and new ones established in your new domicile.
(12) Arrange for your family to be with you in your new country.

The above are some of the factors to be considered and the more of these circumstances that can be shown to prevail, the sooner you will be accepted as having changed your domicile.

16 Tax on foreign income

16.1 Overseas income from investments and businesses
(TA 1988 Ss18 & 65–67)

If you obtain any income from investments and businesses situated overseas, you will normally be charged to income tax under Case IV or Case V of Schedule D. Case IV applies to income from 'securities' unless the income has already been charged under Schedule C (8.2). Case V applies to income from 'possessions' outside the UK. This includes businesses but does not cover emoluments from any overseas employment (16.5).

Your income assessed under Case IV and V of Schedule D will be included in your total income for tax purposes (5.2).

Frequently your overseas income will have already suffered tax in its country of origin. If you also have to pay UK income tax on this income you will normally be entitled to some relief to limit the extent that you are taxed doubly on the same income (16.6).

The normal basis of assessment under Cases IV and V of Schedule D is the amount of income arising in the tax year preceding the year of assessment. In the opening and closing years of a source of income, however, special rules apply (16.2.1 and 16.2.2).

In certain special circumstances the 'arising basis' is not used and the normally more favourable 'remittance basis' applies. If you are UK domiciled and ordinarily resident, however, your assessments on overseas pensions are based on only 90 per cent of the income arising. Up to 1983–84, only 75 per cent of income from overseas businesses was assessed. For 1984–85, the business percentage was 87.5 per cent with subsequently 100 per cent being taxable.

16.1.1 What is the remittance basis?

Under the remittance basis you are only taxed on the amount of income actually brought into this country in the tax year preceding the year of assessment (whilst you still possess the source of overseas income). If you are assessed on the remittance basis and bring income into the UK in a tax year after the source has come to an end, you are not liable to UK tax on it at all (16.1.2). Remittances can be made in cash or kind (16.1.3).

If you make no remittances you will have no liability to UK tax on your overseas income that is taxable on the remittance basis, no matter how high your income is in any year, although you might well suffer foreign tax.

16.1.2 When does the remittance basis apply?
(TA 1988 S65)

Your Case IV and V assessments will be based not on the 'arising' basis but on the remittance basis:

(1) if you are resident in this country but not domiciled here (15.3.2); or
(2) if you are a British subject or a citizen of the Republic of Ireland and are resident in this country but not ordinarily resident here.

For years of assessment up to and including 1973–74, the remittance basis applied more widely. Any remittances of pre-1974–75 income after 5 April 1974 are not taxed here, even if no tax was payable when it arose.

You may have some overseas income that is taxed on a remittance basis and some that is taxed on an arising basis. In this case you should clearly segregate the two sources of income by using separate bank accounts since income from the latter can be brought into this country without paying any additional tax here because it has already been charged to UK tax.

If you are not resident in this country (15.3.2), you will not normally be charged to tax in respect of your Case IV and Case V income, even if it is remitted here.

16.1.3 What are classed as remittances?
(TA 1988 S65)

Whilst you have any continuing sources of overseas income in respect of which income arising abroad has not been fully transmitted to this country, any sums brought into the UK will normally be first considered to be remittances of overseas income.

The above will not apply if you keep separate bank accounts for income and capital, bringing in funds from the latter only (possibly giving rise to capital gains tax).

As well as cash and cheques, any property imported or value arising here from property not imported will be classed as remittances. Thus if you buy a car abroad out of your overseas profits and bring it into this country this is a remittance (although strictly speaking the second-hand value of the car at the time of importation should be used instead of the cost of the car). Similarly, if you hire an asset abroad out of unremitted overseas income, any use that you get from the asset in this country should be valued and treated as a remittance.

If you borrow money against sums owing to you for overseas income and bring the former into this country, this is a remittance. Similarly, if you borrow money here and repay it abroad out of overseas profits, this is known as a 'constructive remittance' and is taxable. Other forms of 'constructive remittances' include the payment out of overseas income of interest owing in this country, and the repayment out of such income, of money borrowed overseas which was made available to you in this country.

If you use non-remitted overseas income to buy shares in UK companies this is normally treated as a remittance unless a third party abroad actually acts as the principal in the transaction.

You are able to use non-remitted overseas income to cover the costs of overseas visits (including holidays) and provided you bring none of the money back to this country there is no taxable remittance. For this purpose the Revenue allow you to receive traveller's cheques in this country provided they are not cashed here.

If overseas profits are remitted to the Channel Islands or the Isle of Man this is not treated as a taxable remittance since those countries are not regarded as part of the UK for taxation purposes. They were, however, treated as being part of the UK for the purposes of exchange control. This was most important since it was a UK exchange control rule that income earned abroad should be remitted to the UK. This rule was satisfied by sending the money to, say, Jersey or Guernsey without in turn incurring any UK income tax liability. The UK exchange control rules were generally withdrawn from 24 October 1979 and you are now free to keep money in other countries, subject to their own regulations. Furthermore, the legal framework, the Exchange Control Act 1947, was abolished in 1987. However, tax planning should allow for the possible reintroduction of exchange control under a future government.

16.2 The basis of assessment under Schedule D Cases IV and V
(TA 1988 S65 & 391)

As previously mentioned the normal basis of assessment is the amount of income arising in the tax year preceding the year of assessment. In certain cases, however, the assessment is based on the remittances in the previous tax year (16.1.2).

A few deductions are allowed in computing the income arising including the following:

(1) Any annuity paid out of the income to a non-resident of this country.
(2) Any other annual payment (not being interest) out of the income to a non-resident.
(3) Normal trading expenses against the income from any trade, etc which you have abroad.
(4) Normal maintenance costs against rental income arising abroad.
(5) Ten per cent of any pensions.
(6) If you pay any overseas taxes for which you get no form of double tax relief then you can deduct such payments in computing your overseas income arising.
(7) If your overseas pension (or part of it) arises under the German or Austrian law relating to victims of Nazi persecution, the deduction was 50 per cent up to 1985–86. Subsequently such income is totally exempt. This includes cases where refugees from Germany were later credited with unpaid social security contributions thereby getting higher pensions.

16.2.1 Special rules for fresh income
(TA 1988 S66)

If you have a new source of Schedule D Case IV and V income your assessments will be as follows:

(1) For the tax year in which the income first arises on the income for that year.
(2) Unless the income first arose on 6 April, the assessment for the second tax year will also be on the actual income arising in that year.
(3) Your assessment for the third tax year will be based on the income arising in the preceding tax year. Also if income first arose on 6 April your assessment for the second tax year will be based on the income arising in the previous year.
(4) You have the option of electing that your first assessments falling to be made on a preceding year basis as in (3) above should instead be on the income actually arising in the respective tax year.
(5) In case of income assessable on a remittance basis (16.1.1) the above rules are applied by substituting the remittances during the tax year for the income arising during that year.

16.2.2 Special rules where source of income ceases
(TA 1988 S67)

(1) If an overseas source of income ceases in a given tax year then your assessment for that year is on the income arising in it.
(2) Your assessment for the tax year preceding that in which the source ceases is increased to the actual income arising if this is greater than the original 'preceding year' assessment.
(3) If you obtained no income from the terminated source during its last two years then if you so elect within two years after the end of the tax year in which the source ceased, your assessment for the last tax year in which any income arose is adjusted to the actual income for that year. Also the assessment for the following year is cancelled — this would otherwise have been on the preceding year's income.
The assessment for the tax year prior to the one in which income last arose will be increased to the actual amount arising if this is greater than the original 'preceding year' assessment.
(4) If you have obtained no income from an overseas source for six years, you can elect that it should be treated as having ceased in the last tax year in which income arose. Your assessment for that year is then adjusted to 'actual' and the following year's assessment is cancelled. The previous year's assessment may require to be increased to the actual income arising as in (2).
(5) The above rules apply to income assessed on a remittance

basis — you simply consider the remittances during the tax year instead of the income arising. Rules (3) and (4) above are of particular application to situations where the assessments are on a remittance basis since you may choose to make no remittances for a number of years so that you incur no UK tax on the relevant overseas income for those years.

(6) Where you are assessed on the remittance basis (16.1.1) you will not be liable to UK tax on any income that you bring into this country during a tax year later than the one in which your overseas source ceases.

16.2.3 Example: Assessments under Schedule D Cases IV and V

Mr A is resident in the UK but not domiciled here. On 1 July 1979 he opened a bank deposit account in Jersey and made the following remittances of his Jersey bank deposit interest to this country:

31 December 1984	£500
31 December 1985	£1,000
31 December 1986	£750
31 December 1987	£1,100
31 December 1988	£900

No further income remittances were made after 31 December 1988. On 31 January 1994 the Jersey bank deposit account is closed. What will Mr A's income tax assessments be on his Jersey deposit interest?

Because Mr A is not domiciled in this country his assessments under Cases IV and V of Schedule D will be on a remittance basis as follows:

1984–85	First year — actual			£500
1985–86	Second year — actual			£1,000
1986–87	Third year — preceding year basis	£1,000		
	Reduced on claim by Mr A to actual			£750
1987–88	Preceding year basis	£750	adjusted to actual on claim by Mr A	£1,100
1988–89	Preceding year basis	£1,100		£900
1989–90	Preceding year basis	£900		NIL

Note: Since the source is closed during 1993–94 and no interest is remitted during 1992–93 or 1993–94 the assessments for the last years in which remittances were made are adjusted as shown on election by Mr A which results in £750 dropping out of assessment.

Tax on foreign income 257

16.3 Professions conducted partly abroad

If you are engaged in any profession or vocation that is conducted partly within this country and partly overseas, you will normally be assessed on your entire 'global' profits under Case II of Schedule D. It is only if you conduct a separate profession or vocation entirely abroad that Schedule D Case V will apply.

This rule is particularly applicable to actors and entertainers, etc who travel widely in the conduct of their professions. The rule does not apply, however, to income from an office or employment the duties of which are conducted entirely abroad.

16.4 Relief for overseas trading by individuals
(FA 1978 S27 & Sch 4 & FA 1984 S30)

From 1978–79 to 1984–85 inclusive special relief applied against assessments under Schedule D Cases I and II on trades, professions or vocations including partnerships. If you carried on such a trade, etc resided in the UK and were absent from it for at least 30 'qualifying days' in a year of assessment, you were able to claim the relief. The relief consisted of a deduction from your assessment of a percentage of the proportion relating to your total 'qualifying days' working abroad. From 1978–79 to 1983–84, the relief was 25 per cent, for 1984–5 it was $12\frac{1}{2}$ per cent and nil thereafter.

16.5 Earnings from overseas employments
(TA 1988 Ss19, 132, 192 & 193 & F2A 1992 S54)

From 6 April 1974 to 5 April 1984, you were normally assessed to tax under Case I of Schedule E on 75 per cent of your earnings from any overseas employments. For 1984–85, the taxable proportion was 87.5 per cent, after which the relief was totally abolished. However, subject to certain rules, a 100 per cent deduction applies for extended periods of absence (16.5.1).

16.5.1 The 100 per cent deduction

You are not normally liable to UK tax on any income from *overseas employments* which you earn during a 'qualifying period' of absence from this country of at least a year. This does not need to be a tax year and you are allowed to spend here up to one-sixth of the period, but no more than 62 days in any one visit. Otherwise the required continuous 'qualifying period' is broken. This means that you must start reckoning your qualifying period from when you return overseas again.

Also, the one-sixth test is applied to all periods cumulatively from the start of your 'qualifying period' until the end of each overseas visit. Thus if you start your overseas service by being away for 20 days, come back for 20 days and return for 20 days, your 'chain' is broken because you have spent one-third of the 60 days in the UK instead of the maximum of one-sixth.

An *overseas employment* is one the duties of which are performed outside this country. If an employment is performed partly here and partly abroad, you will normally be taxed on the income arising under Case I of Schedule E (9.1). Special rules (17.1.7) apply, however, if you are not domiciled here (15.2). Any duties that you perform in this country which are purely incidental to the performance of your overseas employment are normally disregarded and so the special treatment would apply.

If you work on a ship, from 1988–89 the 62-day period is increased to 90 days and the fraction is one-quarter (FA 1988 S67). Seafarers have longer permitted periods in the UK which apply where at least part of a UK visit between two periods of absence is after 5 April 1991. The new limits are respectively 183 days and half the total period (FA 1991 S43).

There are special rules for *workers in Kuwait or Iraq* who were engaged in an office or employment there at any time during the 62 days to 2 August 1991. Any who returned to the UK after that date but could prove that apart from the Gulf crisis, they would have remained or returned and qualified for the 100 per cent relief, will obtain this (FA 1991 S44).

From 6 April 1992, your overseas earnings must be calculated net for the purposes of the relief. Deductions must be made for appropriate pension contributions, expenses and capital allowances. Previously, faultily drawn legislation allowed gross earnings to be used and the Revenue will agree assessments on that basis for 1990–91, 1991–92 and certain prior assessments which are still open (F2A 1992 S54).

16.5.2 Remittances

The rules concerning the remittance of Schedule E Case III income are exactly the same as for income assessable under Cases

IV and V of Schedule D (16.1.2). The remittance basis now broadly only applies for overseas employments if you are UK resident and not domiciled here and/or not ordinarily resident.

Remittances of income from overseas employments are not taxable here in any of the following circumstances:

(1) If made later than the tax year in which the employment ceases.
(2) If made during a tax year in which you are not resident here (whether or not you are ordinarily resident in this country).
(3) If made when you are UK domiciled and ordinarily resident (normally taxed on an arising basis).

16.5.3 Expenses concerning work overseas
(TA 1988 Ss80–81 & 193–195)

Provided your employer ultimately bears the cost, normally you are not taxed as a benefit on any of the following expenses concerning overseas employments:

(1) Travelling to take up your overseas employment or returning on its termination. (Expense relief is available if you bear the cost yourself).
(2) Board and lodging overseas.
(3) Certain visits by your family (9.6.4).
(4) Unlimited outward and return journeys between your overseas employment and the UK.

Similar rules apply to the travel and subsistence of UK residents with businesses carried on wholly abroad. The rules cover travel between overseas trades as well as between the UK and abroad.

16.6 Double taxation relief
(TA 1988 Ss788–816)

The UK government has entered into agreements with the governments of other countries for the purpose of preventing double taxation under the UK tax law and under the tax law of such other countries in respect of the same income. A further object of certain of those agreements is to render reciprocal assistance in the prevention of tax evasion.

Under particular double taxation conventions certain classes of income are made taxable only in one of the countries who are party to the agreement, for example, that in which the taxpayer resides. Certain other income is taxable in both of the countries concerned but in the case of UK residents, the overseas tax is allowed as a credit against the UK tax.

Double tax relief is restricted for UK banks lending to non-residents to 15 per cent of the gross interest. However, it is now necessary to look at each loan separately. Foreign tax credit relief is only to be offset against the corporation tax on a particular loan.

If there is no double tax convention between this country and another one then 'unilateral relief' may be available. This means that if you are a UK resident and obtain income from the other country, you are normally allowed to set off any overseas tax suffered against your UK tax liability on the same income. If you are not allowed to do so then you can deduct the overseas tax in computing the overseas income taxable in this country.

Double tax agreements may include provisions for the exchange of information about taxpayers, between the UK and overseas country concerned. This is particularly aimed at countering tax evasion.

16.6.1 Table: Double taxation relief — List of countries which have General Agreements with the UK

Antigua	France
Australia	Gambia
Austria	German Federal Republic
Bangladesh	Ghana
Barbados	Gilbert Islands (Kiribati and Tuvalu)
Belgium	Greece
Belize	Grenada
Botswana	Guernsey
Brunei	Hungary
Bulgaria	Iceland
Burma (Myanmar)	India
Canada	Indonesia
China	Irish Republic
Cyprus	Israel
Czechoslovakia	Italy
Denmark	Ivory Coast
Dominica (terminated 1987)	Jamaica
Egypt	Japan
Falkland Islands	Jersey
Faroe Islands	Kenya
Fiji	Korea
Finland	Lesotho

Luxembourg
Malawi
Malaysia
Malta
Isle of Man
Mauritius
Montserrat
Morocco
Netherlands
Netherlands Antilles (ceased 31.3.89)
New Zealand
Nigeria
Norway
Pakistan
Papua New Guinea
Philippines
Poland
Portugal
Romania
Russian Republic
St Christopher & Nevis
St Lucia (terminated 1988)
St Vincent (terminated 1987)
Seychelles (terminated)
Sierra Leone
Singapore
Solomon Islands
South Africa
South West Africa (Namibia)
Spain
Sri Lanka
Sudan
Swaziland
Sweden
Switzerland
Tanzania (terminated)
Thailand
Trinidad & Tobago
Tunisia
Turkey
Uganda
USA
USSR*
Yugoslavia
Zambia
Zimbabwe

* The convention with the USSR has become known as being with the Russian Republic, but also applies to virtually all other states which used to make up the USSR.

Note: In addition to the above general agreements, arrangements of a more restricted kind have been entered into with Argentina, Brazil, Jordan, Lebanon, Venezuela and Zaire covering the double taxation of profits from shipping and air transport. Agreements with Algeria, Cameroon, Ethiopia, Iran and Kuwait cover only air transport.

17 Non-residents, visitors and immigrants

17.1 On what income are non-residents liable to UK tax?

If, for a given tax year, you are not a UK resident (15.3.2) you will normally be liable to UK income tax only on income arising in this country. If your income arising here is also taxed in your country of residence you will in many cases be entitled to double taxation relief (16.6). Should there be a double taxation agreement between your country of residence and the UK (16.6) this agreement may provide that certain categories of income arising in this country should only be taxed in your own country and not here. The following paragraphs cover the position if such relief is not obtained.

17.1.1 Business profits in the UK
(TA 1988 S18)

If you are non-resident but carry on a business in this country you will be charged to tax here on your profits. You will be assessed to income tax under Schedule D Case I (10.2) at the lower rate (20 per cent), basic rate (25 per cent) and higher rate (40 per cent) if your total income liable to UK tax is sufficiently high (2.2).

If your UK business is operated by a manager, etc he is charged to the tax on your behalf but if your only business in this country consists of selling through a broker or agent who acts for various principals, you will not be chargeable.

17.1.2 Income from property and land in the UK
(TA 1988 S15)

Income tax under Schedule A (or Schedule D Case VI) is charged on this income (7.1). If you are non-resident you will nevertheless have to pay UK income tax on this income; the basic rate normally should be deducted at source by the tenant or agent in paying you.

Furthermore such income is frequently not covered by the relevant double taxation agreement.

17.1.3 Interest received from sources in the UK
(TA 1988 Ss18, 66 & 67)

You are liable to income tax under Schedule D Case III on this income (8.5). However, if you are ordinarily resident in the UK, the composite rate scheme might have applied up to 5 April 1991 (8.7).

17.1.4 Interest on UK securities
(TA 1988 Ss44–52)

Income tax at the basic rate (25 per cent) will be withheld from interest payments made to you unless some lower rate (or nil rate) is specified in any double taxation agreement (16.6). (See also exempt gilts, 17.2.)

17.1.5 Dividend payments to non-residents
(TA 1988 Ss232, 811 & 812)

If you are non-resident, your dividends from UK companies normally carry no basic rate tax credits unless you get relief under TA 1988 S278 (17.7), or under certain double taxation arrangements (see below). Thus if you receive a dividend of £75, you will normally pay overseas tax on this amount with no deduction for the £25 tax credit which you would have got, if you were a UK resident. You may be liable, however, to the excess of the higher rate income tax over the basic rate (5.0.1) on the actual dividend payments. Such tax would qualify for relief against your overseas tax subject to the relevant double tax arrangements (16.6).

Provided the relevant double tax agreements have been revised to permit it, special arrangements can be made between UK companies and the Board of Inland Revenue. These enable a UK company, when paying a dividend to an overseas resident, also to pay him an amount representing the excess over his UK tax liability on the dividend, of the UK tax credit to which he is entitled under the relevant double tax agreement (16.6.1). Comparable rules apply to companies. However, from a date to be fixed, the right of certain non-resident companies to payments of tax credits will be subject to withdrawal. This broadly covers various situations involving 'unitary taxation'.

17.1.6 Investment managers acting for non-residents
(TMA S78 & FA 1991 S81)

Investment managers, such as banks and other financial concerns, are exempted from any tax liability as agents for non-residents.

The exemption applies provided, for example, the agent is in the business of providing investment management services to a number of clients, on a normal commercial basis. It extends to stocks and shares, interest on deposits and futures. From 6 April 1991 (1 April for companies), the exemption extends to commodities, financial futures and options contracts (not involving land).

17.1.7 Income from employments in the UK
(TA 1988 S19 etc)

If you are not resident in this country (or if resident if you are not ordinarily resident) you are assessed to UK tax under Case II of Schedule E in respect of any emoluments during the relevant tax year regarding duties performed here. This was modified however regarding 'foreign emoluments', which are those of a person not domiciled in this country from an office or employment with an employer who is not resident here. From 1974–75 to 1986–87 50 per cent of your 'foreign emoluments' were charged to Schedule E income tax, subject to certain rules.

'Foreign emoluments' relief was not available after 1983–84 unless you either held a qualifying employment at any time from 6 April 1983 to 13 March 1984; or took up one before 1 August 1984 under a pre-14 March 1984 obligation. If you qualified, the relief was 50 per cent for 1984–85, 1985–86 and 1986–87; 25 per cent for 1987–88 and 1988–89 following which it was completely withdrawn.

For 1984–85 and subsequently, non-domiciled employees obtain relief for travel expenses between their UK jobs and their countries similar to that afforded to UK personnel working abroad (9.6.4). With effect from 6 April 1986, the relief is only available for five years from the arrival of the employee in the UK (TA 1988 S195).

17.1.8 Higher rate income tax

If you are not resident in this country but are liable to UK income tax on part or all of your income, this may be taxed at the lower, basic and higher rate. This will depend on the amount of your income liable to UK income tax. Thus if for 1992–93 this comes to £24,700 after allowable deductions, you will pay income tax at 20 per cent on £2,000, 25 per cent on £21,700 and 40 per cent on £1,000. Thus your total UK income tax will be £400 + £5,425 + £400 = £6,225 (subject to possible double tax relief).

17.2 Interest paid to non-residents in respect of certain UK government securities
(TA 1988 S47)

The interest on certain specified UK government securities (17.1.4) can be paid to you gross without the deduction of any UK income tax provided the following conditions are satisfied:

(1) You are not ordinarily resident in this country (15.3.1).
(2) A claim has been made on your behalf to the Revenue requesting that payment is made to you without the deduction of any UK income tax.

If the above conditions are satisfied then the Bank of England will be instructed to remit to you overseas the gross amounts of interest as they become payable, without the deduction of any UK income tax at source.

17.3 Rules for taxation of visitors' income
(TA 1988 S336)

If you come to this country as a visitor only and you do not intend to establish your residence here, you will not normally be charged to UK income tax on income arising elsewhere. This applies provided you have not actually been in this country for more than six months during the relevant tax year.

As a general rule you are not subject to UK income tax unless you are chargeable as a person resident here (15.3.2).

Even if you are not resident in this country during a given tax year you will normally be chargeable to UK income tax on your income arising from sources within the UK. However, interest on certain government bonds is exempted if you make the required application to the Revenue (8.2). You may also be entitled to double taxation relief in respect of your income arising in this country (16.6).

17.4 When does a habitual visitor become a UK resident?

If you are a visitor to the UK you are treated as resident here for tax purposes in any year of assessment in which you spend more than six months in this country.

Even if you do not stay for six months in any tax year, you will be regarded as becoming resident if you come here year after year (so that your visits become in effect part of your habit of life) and those visits are for a substantial period or periods of time. The Revenue normally regard an average of three months as being substantial and the visits as having become habitual after four years. Further, if your arrangements indicated from the start that regular visits for substantial periods were to be made the Revenue would regard you as being resident here in and from the first tax year.

If, however, a place of abode is maintained for you in this country, subject to certain specified exceptions, you will be regarded by the Revenue as being resident here for any year in which you pay a visit to the UK (15.3.6).

17.5 The position of visiting diplomats
(TA 1988 Ss320–322)

Special tax exemptions are given to visiting diplomats including agents-general, high commissioners, consuls and official agents. Consular officers and employees of foreign states who visit this country are afforded certain tax exemptions here, even if they stay in the UK for sufficiently long normally to be treated as resident here.

Regarding consular officers and employees of foreign states, the conditions for the exemptions to apply are that:

(1) the individual is not a citizen of the UK or colonies;
(2) he is not engaged in any trade, profession or employment in this country (apart from his diplomatic duties); and
(3) he is either a permanent employee of the foreign state or was not ordinarily resident in the UK immediately before he became a consular officer or employee here.

The tax concessions which apply when appropriate arrangements have been made with the foreign state concerned, include the following:

(1) Any income of the individual which falls under Cases IV and V of Schedule D (16.2) is not subject to income tax here.
(2) Certain overseas dividends and interest on securities are not taxed in this country.
(3) Emoluments of the individual from his consular office or employment are not taxed here.

(4) No capital gains tax (18.3) is payable on disposals of assets situated outside the UK.

17.6 Visiting entertainers and sportsmen
(TA 1988 Ss555–558)

Rules apply from 1 May 1987 under which UK appearances by non-resident sportsmen and entertainers are taxed at once. Payments of £1,000, or more, are subjected to basic rate (25 per cent) income tax at source. However, it is possible to agree a lower or nil rate with the Inland Revenue where it can be established that the eventual UK tax liability will be less than 25 per cent.

17.7 The entitlement of certain non-residents to UK tax reliefs
(TA 1988 S278 & FA 1988 S31)

Unless you are resident here or fall within the categories listed below, you will not obtain any UK personal reliefs and allowances (3.0.1) against your income tax liability in this country.

If you fall within the undermentioned categories, however, you will qualify for personal relief against your income taxable in this country.

(1) Subjects of Great Britain or the Republic of Ireland.
(2) Employees of the Crown or Crown protectorates or missionary societies.
(3) Residents of the Isle of Man or the Channel Islands.
(4) Previous residents of the UK who have gone abroad for reasons of their own health or that of a member of their families.
(5) Widows of Crown servants.

To get this relief, you must submit a claim to the Revenue giving details of your UK and world income. From 6 April 1990 with the introduction of independent taxation of husband and wife, full personal allowances are available for those in the above specified categories.

Prior to 6 April 1990, the relief was restricted, however, so that your UK tax liability was not less than the proportion (A/B) of what it would have been if UK tax had been charged on your world income less UK allowances. (A was your total income subject to

UK tax and B was your total income throughout the world. Any income on which you obtained double tax relief was excluded from A but included in B.)

17.8 Immigrants

If you come from abroad to this country with the intention of taking up permanent residence here the following tax consequences will result:

(1) You will normally get full UK personal reliefs and allowances for income tax for the entire tax year during which you arrive.
(2) If you have any British government securities on which you had been receiving interest gross as a non-resident (8.2) as soon as you arrive here you will be liable to tax on this interest.
(3) You will not be taxed here on any lump sum payment that you receive from a former employer or overseas provident fund in respect of termination of an overseas employment.
(4) If you have any income assessable under Case IV or V of Schedule D on a remittance basis (16.1.1) and the source ceases before you arrive here, you will have no liability on any sums remitted. If the source ceases in your year of arrival but after you take up permanent residence here, your liability is on the lower of your total remittances in the tax year and the income arising from your date of arrival until the date that the source closed.
(5) If you had a source of income outside this country before coming here, this source is not treated as being a fresh one on your arrival. Thus if you had possessed the source for some years the preceding year basis will normally apply.
(6) Subject to the above comments, you will generally be taxed here only in respect of income arising from your date of arrival.

18 Capital gains tax

18.1 Introduction

Subject to the specific rules that are summarised in the following pages, you will be charged to capital gains tax in respect of any chargeable gains that accrue to you on the disposal of assets during a given tax year. You deduct from your capital gains any allowable capital losses (18.13). For individuals, capital gains tax is charged at the same rates as income tax (20 per cent, 25 per cent and 40 per cent). Prior to 6 April 1988, the rate of capital gains tax was 30 per cent. An annual exemption of £5,800 applies for individuals and broadly £2,900 for trusts (19.6). Companies pay corporation tax at corporation tax rates on their capital gains (12.15), subject to special rules for authorised investment trusts and unit trusts (18.18.7).

Most references throughout this chapter are to the Taxation of Chargeable Gains Act 1992 which consolidates the relevant legislation.

18.2 What is a chargeable gain?
(TCGA S15)

A chargeable gain is a gain which accrues after 6 April 1965 to a taxpayer (including a company, trust, partnership, individual, etc) such gain being computed in accordance with the provisions of the relevant legislation. There must, however, be a disposal of an asset in order that there should be a chargeable gain.

18.3 Who is liable?
(TCGA Ss2, 10 & 12)

Any taxpayer (including a company, trust, partnership, individual, etc) is chargeable to capital gains tax on any chargeable gains accruing to him in a year of assessment during any part of which he is: (*a*) resident in this country (15.3), or (*b*) ordinarily resident here (15.3.1).

Also, even if neither resident nor ordinarily resident here, a taxpayer who carries on a trade in the UK through a branch or agency, is generally liable to capital gains tax accruing on the disposal of: (*a*) assets in this country used in his trade, or (*b*) assets held here and used for the branch or agency. For gains accruing from 14 March 1989, this rule extends to professions and vocations, as well as trades (18.32).

If you are resident or ordinarily resident here during a tax year you will be liable to capital gains tax on realisations of assets throughout the world. An exception is made, however, if you are not domiciled in this country (15.2); in that case you are only charged to capital gains tax on your overseas realisations of assets to the extent that such gains are remitted here (16.1). For these purposes, if you are non-domiciled and have a non-sterling bank account, this is treated as located outside the UK unless both the account is held at a UK branch and you are UK-resident (TCGA S275).

18.4 Capital gains tax rates from 6 April 1988
(TCGA Ss4–6 & F2A 1992 S23)

The system of charging capital gains tax by means of a single rate of 30 per cent was changed from 6 April 1988 and further modified from 6 April 1992, with the introduction of the lower rate band:

(1) Individuals now suffer capital gains tax at 20 per cent, 25 per cent and 40 per cent.
(2) The rate for accumulation and maintenance trusts and discretionary settlements is 35 per cent (19.6).
(3) Other trusts in general pay 25 per cent. However if the settlor or his or her spouse has any interest in or rights relating to a settlement, any capital gains will be subjected to his or her rates (19.6).
(4) The capital gains of companies continue to bear corporation tax at the appropriate rate (12.15).
(5) To find the rate or rates payable by an individual, you take the total gains less losses (18.13) for the tax year, deduct capital losses brought forward and the annual exemption, con-

sidering this together with taxable income after reliefs and allowances. (From 1991–92, certain trading losses may also be deducted—18.13.) The first £2,000 is taxed at 20 per cent, the next £21,700 attracts 25 per cent and the remainder 40 per cent. (Your income is taxed at your lower rates first and your capital gains attract your highest rates.)

(6) Thus, if your taxable income after allowances for 1992–93 is £18,700, you have £21,700 − £16,700 = £5,000 of your 25 per cent rate band unused. This means that if your net capital gains for 1992–93 are £15,800, this is reduced to £10,000 by your annual exemption (£5,800). Your capital gains tax is thus:

	£5,000 at 25%	1,250
	£5,000 at 40%	2,000
		£3,250

(7) Husband and wife were considered together for the above rules for 1988–89 and 1989–90, but not subsequently. Now they are treated separately and this represents a substantial improvement which took effect from 6 April 1990.

18.5 Relief for moderate total gains before 6 April 1980
(CGTA S5 & Sch 1 etc)

In calculating your capital gains tax liability for *1977–78 or any earlier tax year*, instead of paying the basic 30 per cent rate you paid a lower amount in certain circumstances. If your capital gains did not exceed £5,000, your tax was limited to broadly your top income tax rates on half your gains less losses. From 1977–78 to 1979–80, if your chargeable gains for a year were no more than £1,000, no tax was charged. The excess over £1,000 was taxed at 15 per cent, provided your total net gains were no more than £5,000. If your total net gains were in the band from £5,000 to £9,500, your tax was £600 plus half of the excess over £5,000. For fuller details please refer to the 1984–85 and previous editions of this Guide.

18.6 Annual exemptions from 6 April 1980
(TCGA S3 & Sch 1)

The system for relieving small gains was changed from 6 April 1980. The following rules apply and the rates shown are for 1992–93:

(1) The first £5,800 of your net gains is exempted from capital gains tax. This applies no matter how high are your total gains for the year.
(2) Any set-off for losses from previous years (18.13) is restricted to leave £5,800 of gains to be exempted. In this way your exemption is protected and you have more losses to carry forward. All losses for the year must be deducted, however, in arriving at the net gains.
(3) These rules apply to personal representatives for the tax year of death and the next two years.
(4) The rules also apply to trusts for the mentally disabled and for those receiving attendance allowance.
(5) For other trusts set up before 7 June 1978 the first £2,900 of net capital gains each year is exempt (19.6).
(6) Trusts set up after 6 June 1978 by the same settlor each have an exemption of £2,900 divided by the number of such trusts. Thus if you have set up two trusts since that date, they each have an exemption of £1,450. In any event each trust obtains an exemption of at least £580.
(7) Any set off for trust losses from previous years is restricted so that the appropriate exemption (£2,900 etc) is not wasted.
(8) The above figures apply to future years subject to indexation in line with the increase in the Retail Prices Index in the December before the year of assessment, compared with the previous December. This applies unless Parliament otherwise directs.
(9) From 1990–91 onwards, husband and wife each have their own annual exemptions and the above rules apply to their own gains and losses alone. Previously, unless they were separated, only one annual exemption applied to their combined net gains.
(10) The corresponding annual exemption figures for previous years have been:

	Individuals, etc	Trusts
1980–81 & 1981–82	£3,000	£1,500
1982–83	5,000	2,500
1983–84	5,300	2,650
1984–85	5,600	2,800
1985–86	5,900	2,950
1986–87	6,300	3,150
1987–88	6,600	3,300
1988–89 to 1990–91	5,000	2,500
1991–92	5,500	2,750

18.7 What assets are liable?
(TCGA Ss21–27)

Subject to various exemptions (see below) all forms of property are treated as 'assets' for capital gains tax purposes including:

(1) Investments, land and buildings, jewellery, antiques, etc.
(2) Options and debts, etc.
(3) Any currency other than sterling.
(4) Any form of property created by the person disposing of it or otherwise coming to be owned without being acquired. (This would cover any article which you made or work of art created by you.)

18.8 What assets are exempted?
(TCGA—see below)

The following classes of assets are exempted from charge to capital gains tax subject to the relevant rules:

18.8.1 Table: Assets exempted from capital gains tax

(1) Private motor vehicles (S263).
(2) Certain gifts covered by an election (18.27).
(3) Your own home — this is known as your 'main private residence' (18.23).
(4) National Savings Certificates, Defence Bonds, Development Bonds, Save-as-you-earn, etc (S121).
(5) Any foreign currency which you obtained for personal expenditure abroad (S269).
(6) Any decoration for gallantry (unless purchased) (S268).
(7) Betting winnings including pools, lotteries and premium bonds (S51).
(8) Compensation or damages for any wrong or injury suffered to your person or in connection with your profession or vocation (S51).
(9) British government securities (S115). Disposals prior to 2 July 1986 were only exempt if the 'gilts' had been held for at least one year, or had passed to you on death or from a trust.
(10) Life assurance policies and deferred annuities provided that you are the original owner or they were given to you. If you bought the rights to a policy from its original owner you may be liable to capital gains tax on the surrender, maturity or sale of the policy, or death of the life assured (S210). Certain policies assigned after 25 June 1982 may give rise to income tax instead of capital gains tax, however (TA 1988 Ss540 & 544).
(11) Chattels sold for £6,000 or less (18.24).
(12) Assets gifted to charity (18.29.1).
(13) The gift to the nation of any assets (eg, paintings) deemed to be of national, scientific or historic interest; also land, etc, given to the National Trust (S258).

(14) The gift of historic houses and certain other property of interest to the public, provided they are given access — also funds settled between 2 May 1976 and 6 April 1984 for its upkeep (S258). (Now covered by the gifts exemption — 18.28.)
(15) Tangible movable property which is a wasting asset (ie, with a predictable life of 50 years or less). This includes boats, animals, etc, but not land and buildings (S45) nor assets qualifying for capital allowances.
(16) Disposals by a close company (12.17) of assets on trust for the benefit of its employees (S239).
(17) If you sell a debt this is not liable to capital gains tax provided you are the original creditor and the debt is not a 'debt on a security' (a debenture, etc). Otherwise capital gains tax applies. The 'debt on security' requirements do not apply, however, to certain business loans (excluding those from associated companies) made after 11 April 1978. Loss relief may be available on such debts and also on certain business guarantees made after that date (S251).
(18) Land transferred after 5 April 1983 from one local constituency association to another, which is taking over from it, as a result of the Parliamentary constituency boundaries being redrawn (S264).
(19) Certain corporate bonds issued after 13 March 1984 which you held for more than 12 months (18.19). Disposals after 1 July 1986 are exempt without time limit (Ss115–117).
(20) Transactions in futures and options in gilts and qualifying corporate bonds after 1 July 1986 (S115).
(21) Business expansion scheme shares issued to you after 18 March 1986, provided you are the first holder of those particular shares (10.25).
(22) Certain 'deep discount' (8.8) and from 14 March 1989, 'deep gain' securities (S117).

18.9 What constitutes a disposal?
(TCGA Ss21–26)

The following are examples of circumstances in which you will be treated as making a disposal or a part disposal of an asset:

(1) The outright sale of the whole asset or part of it.
(2) The gift of the asset or a part of it — the asset must be valued at the date of gift and this valuation is treated as the proceeds. An election for holding-over the gain is sometimes possible (18.28).
(3) If an asset is destroyed, eg, by fire, it is a disposal.
(4) If you sell any right in an asset, for example, by granting a lease, this is a part disposal although if you obtain a fair rent there is normally no capital gains tax liability.
(5) If any capital sum is received in return for the surrender or forfeiture of any rights, this is normally a disposal. For example, you may receive a sum of money for not renewing a

lease in accordance with a renewal option which you possessed.
(6) If you die, you are deemed to dispose of all of your assets at your date of death but no capital gains tax is payable. Whoever inherits your assets does so at their market value at your death.
(7) A part withdrawal from a life policy of the original owner and for which you gave money or money's worth (TCGA S210).

The following are not treated as disposals of assets for capital gains tax purposes:

(1) If you give or sell an asset to your spouse this is not treated as a capital gains tax disposal, provided he or she is living with you during the relevant tax year. In that case your spouse is charged to capital gains tax on any subsequent disposal that he or she makes of the asset as if bought when you originally acquired it at the actual cost to yourself (plus indexation allowance — 18.12).
(2) If you transfer an asset merely as security for a debt but retain the ownership this is not a capital gains tax disposal. This would apply, for example, if you mortgage your house.
(3) If you transfer an asset to somebody else to hold it as your nominee, this is not a disposal provided that you remain the beneficial owner.
(4) Gifts of assets to charities are effectively not treated as disposals (18.29.1).

18.10 How your chargeable gains are computed
(TCGA Ss15–20 & 37–40)

The following general rules should be followed:

(1) If the asset sold was originally acquired before 7 April 1965, special rules apply (18.17).
(2) Special rules also apply in the case of leases and other wasting assets (18.29.2).
(3) Ascertain the consideration for each of your disposals during the tax year — this will normally be the sale proceeds but in the following cases it will be the *open market value* of the assets (18.16):
 (a) Gifts of assets during the tax year (apart from those up to £100 in value to any individual prior to 6 April 1984).

(b) Transfers of assets (by gift or sale) to persons connected with you including your business partner and close relations other than your wife. This also applies to other disposals of assets not at arm's length. (Anti-avoidance rules operate to prevent losses being manufactured artificially in this way (13.9).)

(c) Transactions in which the sale proceeds cannot be valued, or where an asset is given as compensation for loss of office, etc to an employee. If, for example, you give your friend a picture from your collection on condition that he paints your house each year for the next ten years, then since this service cannot be accurately valued you are treated as disposing of your picture for its market value.

(4) Deduct from the disposal consideration in respect of each asset its original cost (or value at acquisition) together with any incidental expenses in connection with your original acquisition and your disposal of each asset. For disposals after 5 April 1988, if it gives a better result, you normally deduct the value at 31 March 1982 instead of the cost (18.11). Also deduct any 'enhancement' expenditure, ie the cost of any capital improvements to the assets not including any expenses of a 'revenue nature' (2.6).

(5) Deduct (if applicable) indexation allowance (see below).

(6) Your incidental costs of acquisition and disposal (see (4) above) include surveyors', valuers' and solicitors' fees, stamp duty, and commission in connection with the purchase and sale. Also the cost of advertising to find a buyer and accountancy charges in connection with the acquisition or disposal. No expenses are deductible, however, if they have already been allowed in computing your taxable revenue profits (2.6).

18.11 Re-basing to 31 March 1982 values
(TCGA Ss35–36 & Schs 3–4)

If you dispose of an asset after 5 April 1988, which you owned on 31 March 1982, its base value is automatically taken as its value at that date, provided this exceeds the cost. Thus, if you bought some shares for £1,000 in 1970 and they are worth £4,000 on 31 March 1982, you use £4,000 as their base value for capital gains tax purposes. Assuming you sell the shares for £10,000 in August 1992, your capital gain is £10,000 − £4,000 = £6,000 (ignoring indexation).

Re-basing to 31 March 1982 does not increase a gain or loss compared with what it would have been under the old rules. Furthermore, where there is a gain under the old system and a loss through re-basing, or *vice versa*, the transaction is treated as giving rise to neither gain nor loss. For example, if you sell an asset for £1,000 which had cost £500 and was worth £1,500 at 31 March 1982, ignoring indexation you had a gain of £500 under the old rules and a loss of £500 through re-basing; you are therefore treated as having no gain and no loss.

The existing rules for assets held at 6 April 1965 can themselves give rise to disposals being treated as producing no gain and no loss (18.17). This is not affected by re-basing.

Even if you did not hold an asset at 31 March 1982, it may still qualify for re-basing if you received it from someone else in circumstances that there was neither a gain nor loss under the rules and their acquisition was before that date. A particular example is where one spouse acquires an asset from another.

If you held assets at 31 March 1982, but subsequently realised them in circumstances such that your gain was deferred, re-basing does not apply. However, special relief is available regarding disposals after 5 April 1988 (excluding no gain/no loss disposals). Provided you make a claim to the Inland Revenue within two years of the end of the year of assessment in which the disposal is made, your original held-over, rolled-over or deferred gain is halved (TCGA S36 & Sch 4).

You have the right to elect that all of your assets are re-based as at 31 March 1982. There is a two year time limit for this irrevocable election (ie before 6 April 1990). However, this is extended to two years after the end of the tax year in which you make your first sale after 5 April 1988.

18.12 Indexation allowance
(TCGA Ss53–57)

If your disposal is after 5 April 1982 (31 March 1982 for companies) the original cost and enhancement expenditure may be increased by *indexation*. For disposals between 5 April 1985 (31 March for companies) and 6 April 1988, you had the option of basing indexation on the value of the asset sold, at 31 March 1982. After 5 April 1988, disposals are automatically re-based to their 31 March 1982 values if this is beneficial and so indexation is taken on the base value (18.11).

The expenditure is scaled up in proportion to the increase in the Retail Price Index from the month of acquisition (or March 1982, if later) until the month of disposal. For disposals prior to 6 April 1985, there was a one-year waiting period. Thus indexation ran from the later of 31 March 1982 and 12 months after the month of acquisition, until the month of disposal. Values for the *Retail Prices Index* are shown in 18.12.1 (p 281).

You obtain the full benefit of indexation relief, even to the extent that it creates or enlarges a loss. However, prior to 6 April 1985 (1 April 1985 for companies), indexation did not operate to create or increase a capital loss (18.13). Special rules apply regarding assets held on 6 April 1965 (18.17) and shares (18.14).

Transactions between husband and wife do not normally give rise to capital gains tax (18.9). Thus if you acquire an asset from your spouse, your deemed acquisition cost is taken to be his or hers, augmented by any indexation allowance attaching to it at the transfer date. When you sell the asset, you obtain full indexation allowance on your deemed acquisition cost, from the date you took over the asset from your spouse. Similar treatment applies to company intra-group transfers (12.15) and certain reconstructions. Legatees obtain indexation allowance as if they had acquired the assets at the date of death.

Regarding disposals after 5 April 1985 (31 March 1985 for companies) and before 6 April 1988 you had the option of electing for your indexation relief to be based on the market values at 31 March 1982 of the relevant assets, rather than the cost. Each election was needed within two years of the end of the tax year in which your disposal is made. (For companies, the time limit was two years from the end of the accounting period of disposal.) This applied not only to assets owned at 31 March 1982, but also to any that you obtained subsequently on a 'no gain no loss' basis from someone who had held them at that date.

18.12.1 Table: Retail prices index (adjusted)

	1982	1983	1984	1985	1986	1987	1988	1989	1990	1991	1992
January		82.6	86.8	91.2	96.2	100.0*	103.3	111.0	119.5	130.2	135.6
February		83.0	87.2	91.9	96.6	100.4	103.7	111.8	120.2	130.9	136.3
March	79.4	83.1	87.5	92.8	96.7	100.6	104.1	112.3	121.4	131.4	136.7
April	81.0	84.3	88.6	94.8	97.7	101.8	105.8	114.3	125.1	133.1	138.8
May	81.6	84.6	89.0	95.2	97.8	101.9	106.2	115.0	126.2	133.5	139.3
June	81.9	84.8	89.2	95.4	97.8	101.9	106.6	115.4	126.7	134.1	139.3
July	81.9	85.3	89.1	95.2	97.5	101.8	106.7	115.5	126.8	133.8	
August	81.9	85.7	89.9	95.5	97.8	102.1	107.9	115.8	128.1	134.1	
September	81.9	86.1	90.1	95.4	98.3	102.4	108.4	116.6	129.3	134.6	
October	82.3	86.4	90.7	95.6	98.5	102.9	109.5	117.5	130.3	135.1	
November	82.7	86.7	91.0	95.9	99.3	103.4	110.0	118.5	130.0	135.6	
December	82.5	86.9	90.9	96.0	99.6	103.3	110.3	118.8	129.9	135.7	

*Note: At January 1987 the index base was changed to 100.0 and the above table shows figures before that date adjusted to the same base.

18.12.2 Example: Computation of chargeable gain

Mr A sells a block of flats on 15 April 1992 for £250,000. The flats were bought in May 1981 for £100,000 and subsequent capital expenditure amounted to £17,000 (all pre-April 1982). Also £10,000 had been spent on decorations and maintenance. The legal costs on purchase were £1,500 and stamp duty was £1,000. Surveyors' fees prior to purchase amounted to £500. At 31 March 1982, the market value was £115,000*. £100 was spent in advertising the sale and agents' commission amounted to £6,000. Legal costs on sale were £900. Assuming that Mr A's profit will be taxed as a capital gain, what tax will he pay on it? Assume also that for 1992–93 Mr A has no other capital gains or losses and that his taxable income after all reliefs and allowances is £15,700.

Cost of block of flats		£100,000
Add:		
Enhancement expenditure		17,000
(decorations and maintenance not relevant)		
Legal costs on purchase		1,500
Stamp duty on purchase		1,000
Surveyors' fees on purchase		500
Total cost		£120,000*
Add:		
Indexation £120,000 × (138.8 − 79.4)/79.4		89,773
		£209,773
Proceeds		250,000
Less:		
Cost as above	£209,773	
Advertising	100	
Agents' commission	6,000	
Legal fees on sale	900	
		216,773
Chargeable gain		£33,227
Less: annual exemption		5,800
		£27,427
Capital gains tax at 25% (on £23,700 − £15,700 = £8,000)		£2,000.00
at 40% £19,427		7,770.80
		£9,770.80

*Note: if the market value at 31 March 1982 had been more than £120,000, the property would be re-based to this value and this would also be used in calculating indexation.

18.13 Capital losses
(TCGA Ss2, 16, 111 & 253–255)

If your capital gains tax computation in respect of any disposal during the tax year produces a loss, such loss is normally deductible from any chargeable gains arising during the year. Any remaining surplus of losses is then available to be carried forward and set off against any future capital gains. For 1989–90 and previous tax years, any unrelieved losses were offset against gains of your spouse in the same year. Any surplus losses were then carried forward to offset against your respective gains.

'Qualifying loans' made to traders which later prove irrecoverable rank as capital losses, subject to the rules. However, after 19 March 1990, any amounts subsequently recovered are taxed.

Your net capital gains are reduced by losses brought forward down to the tax free amount of currently £5,800 (18.6) and any balance of the losses is carried forward (TCGA S3(5)).

In computing your capital losses note the special rules for assets owned at 6 April 1965 (18.17) and that indexation allowance can both create and add to a loss (18.12). Also note that losses may be reduced by 1982 re-basing (18.11).

A result of indexation allowance creating capital losses was that *building society* share accounts could give rise to capital losses when closed down or reduced. This constitutes a capital gains tax disposal. No real loss is likely but for capital gains tax purposes, prior to 4 July 1987 indexation relief could produce a capital loss. However, from that date, countermanding legislation operates.

18.13.1 Relief for trading losses against capital gains
(FA 1991 S72)

For many years, companies have been able to set off trading losses against capital gains (12.15), but not *vice versa*. A similar relief operates from 1991–92 for individuals with losses from unincorporated businesses.

If you make a loss in your trade, profession or vocation and do not have enough income to cover it, you can elect for the unused losses for say 1992–93 to be set against your capital gains for that year. Any trading losses still unused would then be carried forward to

1993–94 and any not covered by your income for that year are available against 1993–94 capital gains. The relief does not cover 'hobby farming' and other businesses not carried out on a serious commercial basis.

18.14 Losses on unquoted shares in trading companies
(TA 1988 Ss573–576)

Beneficial rules apply to disposals after 5 April 1980 of shares in 'qualifying trading companies'. Provided you were the original subscriber, you can elect to obtain income tax relief (10.22) for any loss on a fully priced arm's length sale, liquidation, etc. The election is required within two years after the tax year in which the relief is to be used.

A 'qualifying trading company' is broadly one which has always been UK resident but never quoted and has traded for at least six years, or from within a year of incorporation if less. The company is permitted to have stopped trading within the previous three years provided it has not become an investment company in the meantime. 'Trading' excludes dealing mainly in shares, land or commodity futures with retrospective effect, qualified trading companies now exclude building societies and registered industrial and provident societies. The relief originally applied only to individuals, but was extended to certain investment companies regarding disposals of shares in 'qualifying trading companies' after 31 March 1981.

18.15 Assessment and payment of capital gains tax
(TMA S29 & TCGA Ss7, 48 & 279–281)

Assessments to capital gains tax are raised on the taxpayer concerned in respect of each tax year as soon thereafter as the Revenue obtain the necessary information. In the case of a company, however, its gains are included in its corporation tax assessment which is due for payment according to the special company rules (12.2).

Prior to 6 April 1990, in assessing the tax, the losses of one spouse could be deducted from the gains of another. Also, the wife's gains were assessed on the husband. Both of these rules ceased to have effect from 6 April 1990, with the introduction of independent taxation.

Your capital gains tax assessment for 1992–93 is due for payment on 1 December 1993 or 30 days after the assessment is issued, if later. For 1979–80 and previous years, your tax was due for payment three months after the end of the tax year in which the gains arose; or 30 days after the assessment was issued if later. For 1980–81 the due date was 1 December 1981 (or 30 days after the assessment was issued, if later) and this interval applies also for subsequent years.

The date on which a capital gain arises is the actual date of sale or gift, etc. In the case of a transaction in which a sales contract is used such as the sale of shares or property it is the date of the contract which applies. It is not the completion date if this is different. Similar considerations apply to fixing the date of acquisition for capital gains tax purposes.

Regarding certain disposals by gift, etc from 11 April 1972 to 5 April 1984 of land and buildings, non-quoted shares, or assets used exclusively in your business, you had the option of paying capital gains tax in eight yearly or 16 half-yearly instalments. If you pay by instalments you must pay interest on the overdue tax at the appropriate rate of $9\frac{1}{4}$ per cent, etc (14.7.2).

Controlling interests in companies are included (even if quoted). Disposals of any of the specified assets (except for land and investment companies, etc) qualify for relief from interest on the instalments unless they are overdue or the total market value of the assets exceeds £250,000.

Certain gifts after 13 March 1989, for which gifts relief is not available (18.28) qualify for the payment of any capital gains tax by instalments. The assets concerned are land, unquoted shares and controlling holdings of quoted shares. Subject to making an election, the tax becomes payable by ten equal yearly instalments. If the instalments are paid on time, the tax on gifts of agricultural property will carry no interest, otherwise, interest runs from the normal date when the total liability would have been due.

Normally, even if the sales consideration is paid by instalments over a number of years the gain is assessed for the tax year in which the sale arises. If, however, you can satisfy the Revenue that you would otherwise suffer undue hardship, payment of the tax can be spread over the period of the instalments (maximum eight years).

18.16 Valuations
(TCGA Ss272–274 & Sch 11)

It is necessary to value assets in various circumstances for capital gains tax purposes including gifts, transactions between connected persons, acquisitions on death and valuations at 6 April 1965. However, the most important date for valuations is 31 March 1982, for re-basing purposes (18.11).

The general rule for valuing assets for capital gains tax purposes is that you must take the 'market value' of the assets at the relevant time. 'Market value' means the price which the assets might reasonably be expected to fetch on a sale in the open market.

It is necessary to value only the assets actually being disposed of even though they form part of a larger whole. This is particularly important regarding the shares in a non-quoted company. Suppose you hold 90 per cent of the shares in such a company which are together worth £90,000. If you gift 10 per cent of the company's shares to your son you might assume that their value is £10,000. This would, however, probably not be true since your 90 per cent holding carried with it full control of the company whereas 10 per cent of the company's shares is a minority holding which would be normally worth considerably less than £10,000 in the circumstances mentioned. The true market valuation of the gifted 10 per cent holding might only be £1,000 depending on the profits of the company and dividends paid. Note that different valuation rules apply for inheritance tax and capital transfer tax purposes (20.12).

Unquoted share valuations must take account of all information which a prudent arm's-length purchaser would obtain.

Particular rules relate to the valuation of quoted securities such as shares and debenture stocks. (These apply in most cases, including 31 March 1982 valuations.) In this case you must normally take:

(1) the lower of the two prices shown in the Stock Exchange Official Daily List plus one-quarter of the difference between them, or
(2) halfway between the highest and lowest prices at which bargains (other than at special prices) were recorded in the shares or securities for the relevant day.

In valuing quoted shares at 6 April 1965, however, you must take the *higher* of:

(1) midway between the two prices shown in the Stock Exchange Official Daily List (ie the middle market price), and
(2) halfway between the highest and lowest prices at which bargains (other than at special prices) were recorded in the shares or securities for 6 April 1965.

Apart from quoted shares other valuations will normally require to be agreed with the Revenue valuation officers such as the district valuers who are concerned with valuing land and buildings.

18.17 Relief on sales of assets owned on 6 April 1965
(TCGA Sch 2)

Although a short term capital gains tax operated from April 1962 until April 1971 when it was repealed, the present-day system of capital gains tax only operates regarding sales after 6 April 1965. Rules were, therefore, introduced with the purpose of relieving such part of your capital gains as can be related to the period before 7 April 1965. Following the introduction of 1982 re-basing (18.11) these rules are of far less importance since in most cases, a lower gain (or greater loss) will result from re-basing. However, a better result sometimes results from applying the old rules and this is then used, unless you have elected for all of your assets to be valued as at 31 March 1982.

The general rule is that you assume that your asset increased in value at a uniform rate and you are relieved from capital gains tax on such proportion of the gain as arose on a time basis prior to 7 April 1965. This is known as the 'time apportionment' method. Thus if your total gain is G and you held an asset for A months prior to 6 April 1965 and B months after that date until the date of sale your taxable chargeable gain is $G \times B/(A + B)$. Your time apportionment benefit is limited to 20 years prior to 6 April 1965. Thus if you acquired an asset before 6 April 1945 you are treated as having acquired it on that date.

Instead of using 'time apportionment' you have the option of substituting for the cost of the asset its market value at 6 April 1965 (Sch 2(17)). In order to do this you must make an election to this effect to the Revenue within two years of the end of the tax year in which you make the disposal. (In the case of a company the election must be made within two years of the end of the accounting period in which the disposal is made.) It is very rare indeed that the market value of an asset at 6 April 1965 exceeds its value at 31 March 1982. Thus 6 April 1965 valuations are mainly relevant when you disposed of assets before 6 April 1988.

The rules do not allow you to increase a capital loss by means of a 6 April 1965 election. Also, if the effect of an election is to convert a gain into a loss, you are regarded as having no gain and no loss on the transaction.

Once you make an election it is irrevocable, even if it results in your paying more tax than on a 'time apportionment' basis. If you make an election, any indexation allowance to which you are entitled (18.12) is calculated on the 6 April 1965 value and not cost. This is now subject to your right to elect for indexation to be taken on the value at 31 March 1982 (18.11).

The 'time apportionment' basis *does not* apply to quoted shares and securities (18.18). Nor does it apply to land with development value when sold (or which has been materially developed after 17 December 1973). Such land is normally automatically dealt with on the 6 April 1965 valuation basis.

In the same way that your gain is reduced by the 'time apportionment' so any loss that you make on a disposal of an asset that you owned at 6 April 1965 is also reduced in this way. Thus if you bought an asset for £5,700 on 6 April 1945 and sold it for £1,000 on 6 April 1992 your total loss is £4,700, subject to indexation. Of this only £2,700 (£4,700 × 27/47) is an allowable capital loss.

18.18 Quoted shares and securities
(TCGA Ss104–117)

The following rules do not apply to *UK government securities* which are exempt from capital gains tax if sold (or otherwise disposed of). Prior to 2 July 1986 if you sold any such 'gilt edged' securities within a year of purchase you were liable to capital gains tax on your chargeable gain. Also, any compensation stock received on a nationalisation after 6 April 1976 will give rise to a gain or loss when sold. This includes the gain or loss on your original shares up to the date of issue of the compensation stock, together with the gain or loss on this stock if it is held for less than 12 months and sold before 2 July 1986. Any disposals of 'gilt edged' securities after 1 July 1986 are exempt from capital gains tax, nor do they create allowable losses, no matter how long they are held.

18.18.1 'Pooling'

All shares of the same company and class that you held prior to 6 April 1982 (1 April for companies) were put into a 'pool'. With the introduction of indexation allowance, however, pooling no longer applied to new purchases. However, pooling was reintroduced regarding share *disposals* after 5 April 1985 (18.18.4) for individuals and trusts, etc (after 31 March 1985 for companies). You now are treated as having one pool of shares purchased after 5 April 1982 and another before that time.

The 'pool' is considered indistinguishable regarding the various numbers of shares that it comprises. Thus if you bought 100 ordinary shares in A Limited on 1 May 1976 for £200 and another 200 ordinary shares in A Limited on 30 September 1980 for £1,000 your total pool cost is £1,200 (ie, £4 per share). If you then sell 100 shares they are not treated as being the original ones which you bought for £200; they are treated as coming from your 'pool' at the average pool cost of £4 per share giving a cost of £400.

'Pooling' does not apply to shares purchased on or before 6 April 1965 unless you elect for all your shares to be valued as at that date (18.18.8). In the absence of this election, you allocated any sales prior to 6 April 1982 first against your holdings at 6 April 1965 on a 'first in first out' basis. After these shares were eliminated you then went to the 'pool'.

Each separate purchase or sale of shares of the same company and class results in adjustments to the 'pool' except that if you buy and sell shares on the same day the respective sale and purchase are first matched against each other. Any surplus or deficit is then added to or deducted from your 'pool'. This rule ceased to apply for transactions from 6 April 1982 (1 April 1982 for companies — subject to a parallel pooling system), but was re-introduced from 6 April 1985.

18.18.2 Parallel pooling
(TCGA S112)

Parallel pooling applied only to companies. A formal and irrevocable election was needed which then applied to all disposals, from 1 April 1982 to 31 March 1985 of 'qualifying securities' (excluding gilts and 6 April 1965 holdings for which no market value election had been made). The election was required within two years of the end of the accounting period in which the first such disposal occurred. Disposals were first matched against acquisitions within the previous twelve months, taking the earliest first. Then, the pooled shares were regarded as being disposed of and finally non-pooled 6 April 1965 holdings. Two pools of costs were required, one indexed and one not. The costs of disposals were calculated in proportion to the shares sold, using the indexed pool. However, since it was not allowed to produce a loss, the indexation factor was reduced or eliminated as necessary.

18.18.3 Identification — Sales from 6 April 1982 to 5 April 1985
(FA 1982 Ss88 & 89 & Sch 13 & FA 1983 S34 & Sch 6)

If you disposed of quoted shares and securities between 5 April 1982 and 6 April 1985 special identification rules applied. Similarly, shares purchased between those dates were no longer pooled. (For companies, the dates are from 1 April 1982 to 31 March 1985.) Each of your existing share pools was treated as a separate asset with its own pool cost at 6 April 1982 and treated for indexation purposes as if acquired one year earlier.

Disposals after 5 April 1982 but before 6 April 1985 were taken in order and identified first against purchases in the previous 12 months taking the earliest first. Then, you looked at previous purchases, taking the latest first. Note, however, that purchases and sales in the same Stock Exchange account (or for settlement on the same day) were matched against each other. Each 'pool' holding was treated as a separate entity. However, an exception applied where certain dealings in the shares took place in 1981–82 (year to 31 March 1982 for companies).

18.18.4 Indexation and identification — Sales from 6 April 1985
(TCGA Ss104–114)

Revised rules apply to share disposals by individuals after 5 April 1985 and by companies after 31 March 1985. However, securities covered by the accrued income provisions to combat bond-washing (8.3) only came within the new indexation and identification rules after 27 February 1986.

As previously mentioned indexation now runs immediately (18.12). An exception is where you buy and then sell the same shares within 10 days, your transactions are matched and you obtain no indexation relief.

Under the revised rules, you must keep separate pools of shares acquired after 5 April 1982 and those obtained from 6 April 1965 to 5 April 1982. Furthermore, acquisitions prior to 6 April 1965 must be kept separately (18.18.1), unless there is a pooling election (18.18.8), in which case they are included in the 31 March 1982 pool.

If you sell shares after 5 April 1985, they are to be identified with your acquisitions of the same shares on a 'last in first out' basis. They are thus first identified with your post 5 April 1982 pool, then with your pre-6 April 1982 holdings and finally with your unpooled pre-6 April 1965 holdings. (For companies the pools run to and from 31 March 1982 and 1 April 1982.) If it produces a better result for you, disposals out of your pre-April 1982 and pre-April 1965 pools will be re-based (18.11), the market value at 31 March 1982 being taken.

From 19 March 1991, disposals of 'business start up scheme' (10.25) shares cannot be pooled with shares of the same type.

Indexation must be calculated separately on the different parts. Holdings acquired before 1 April 1982 can be valued at 31 March 1982 for indexation purposes if you make the required election (18.12). By a concession dated 25 May 1989, the Revenue will treat holdings of the same class held at 31 March 1982 as a single holding for re-basing and indexation. This applies whether the shares, etc were bought before or after 6 April 1965. Subsequent acquisitions cannot be treated in that way. However, every additional purchase will carry indexation relief from that date until sale and so a careful record is needed to calculate relief from the respective acquisition dates. This is done on a pooled basis by adding indexation relief to the pool prior to each purchase or sale. The total indexation relief in the pool is then found by deducting the total cost and the relief on the sale is simply the proportion appropriate to the number of shares sold.

18.18.5 Example: Share identification and indexation — Sales after 5 April 1985

Mr A carried out the following share transactions in the ordinary shares of quoted company B Ltd:

	Date	Number	Cost or Proceeds £
Purchases	20.6.78	2,000	3,000
	10.5.80	1,000	2,000
	10.7.83	2,000	4,000
	10.9.84	4,000	11,000
Sale	20.4.92	9,000	39,000

The value of B Ltd shares at 31 March 1982 was £1.80. Calculate Mr A's capital gain assuming the following indexation figures:—

March 1982 to April 1992	70%
July 1983 to September 1984	10%
September 1984 to April 1992	50%

(1) The shares sold are taken first out of the post 5 April 1982 pool:

Cost of 2,000 shares 10.7.83	£4,000
Indexation July 1983 to September 1984 10%	400
	4,400
Cost of 4,000 shares 10.9.84	11,000
	15,400
Indexation September 1984 to April 1992 50%	7.700
Cost and indexation for 6,000 shares	£23,100
Proceeds of 6,000 shares	26,000
Capital gain on 6,000 shares from post 5 April 1982 pool	£ 2,900

(2) The remaining shares sold are then identified against the pre-6 April 1982 pool:

Cost of 3,000 shares (£1.67 each)	£5,000
Re-based to £1.80 per share	5,400
Add indexation relief from March 1982 to April 1992 70%	3,780
	9.180
Proceeds of 3,000 shares	13,000
Capital gain on 3,000 shares	£3,820

TOTAL CAPITAL GAIN	£2,900 + £3,820	£6,720

18.18.6 Bonus issues, take-overs and company reorganisations
(TCGA Ss126–140)

If you receive a free scrip (or bonus) issue of shares of the same class as those that you already hold, you must treat the additional shares as having been bought when your original shares were bought. Thus if you bought 100 shares in A Limited for £2 each in 1960 and you now receive a bonus issue of 100 shares you will have 200 shares at a cost of £1 each which are all treated as having been bought in 1960. Note, however, the special rules for scrip dividend options (8.19).

Your company may have a capital reorganisation, in the course of which you receive shares of a different class either instead of or in addition to your original shares. You are not normally charged to capital gains tax on any old shares in your company which you exchange for new ones. Any capital gains tax is only payable when you sell your new holding. The rules for reorganisations including bonus issues hold good under the new 'indexation' system unless new consideration is given.

If you take up 'rights' to subscribe for additional shares in a company of which you are a shareholder, your rights shares are treated as having been acquired when your original shares were purchased and the cost of the rights shares is added to the original cost of your holding. If you sell your 'rights' on the market without taking up the shares this is considered to be a 'part disposal' of your holding and accordingly is charged to capital gains tax (18.21). (If the proceeds are small in relation to your holding, however, you can elect not to pay tax then but set off the proceeds against the original cost of your holding.) Under the indexation rules which now apply (18.18.4), however, any new consideration (for rights shares, etc) is treated effectively as a new acquisition so that indexation runs accordingly.

Regarding reorganisations taking place after 9 March 1981, anti-avoidance rules act to prevent you from obtaining capital gains tax loss relief artificially. Any increase in the capital gains tax acquisition value of shares which you obtain through the reorganisation is limited to the actual increase in value.

In the case of a take-over you may receive cash for your shares in which case this is taxed as an ordinary disposal. If, however, you receive shares or loan stock, etc in the acquiring company, you will not normally be liable to pay capital gains tax until you actually sell your new shares or loan stock, subject to certain conditions and anti-avoidance laws (13.9). One of the conditions is that the acquiring company already held, or obtains as a result of the take-over over 25 per cent of the ordinary share capital of the other company. All of the above rules concerning bonus issues, take-overs and company reorganisations apply equally to unquoted shares (18.20).

18.18.7 Investment trusts and unit trusts
(TCGA Ss99–103)

Special rules apply regarding all disposals both of shares owned *by* the trusts and of shares and units *in* the trusts by their shareholders and unit holders.

After 31 March 1980 authorised unit and investment trusts are exempt from tax on their capital gains. However, any disposals which you make of units and investment trust shares carry full capital gains tax with no credit (subject to your £5,800 annual exemption).

From 20 March 1990, capital gains tax indexation no longer applies to units in certain unit trusts and offshore funds. This mainly applies to gilt funds and sterling money funds, with at least 90 per cent invested in such funds or building society shares.

18.18.8 Holdings at 6 April 1965
(TCGA Sch 2)

'Time apportionment' (18.17) does not apply to quoted shares. Instead you must consider the mid-market price at 6 April 1965 (18.10). Subject to the election described below, your gain on any sales after 6 April 1965 of shares held at that date is the difference between the proceeds and the higher cost of the shares and their value at 6 April 1965. Similarly any allowable capital loss on such share sales is the difference between the proceeds and the lower of the cost of the shares and their value at 6 April 1965. However, for disposals after 5 April 1988, 1982 re-basing (18.11) is likely to occur. As a result, the value at 31 March 1982 is used.

If the price at which you sell the shares held at 6 April 1965 is between their value at that date and their cost then you are treated as having no gain and no loss for capital gains tax purposes (subject to the election described below). For indexation purposes, if the value at 6 April 1965 is used to compute a capital gain, then the allowance is calculated on that value (18.12). However, for disposals after 5 April 1985, you can elect for your indexation relief to be taken on the values at 31 March 1982 (18.12).

As regards disposals of quoted shares and securities which you held at 6 April 1965 you have the right to elect that any capital gains or losses on such disposals shall be calculated by substituting the 6 April 1965 values for the original costs in all cases. The election for each category is irrevocable, and has to be made within two years of the end of the tax year (or accounting year for a company) in which the first sale after 19 March 1968 is made (but see new rules below). Thus in most cases elections will have been made by now. Separate elections must be made for you and your wife and are required separately for ordinary shares and fixed interest securities (such as loan stock and preference shares). Full details are given in earlier editions of this book.

A further opportunity was introduced to allow you to elect to have pooled, quoted securities, which you acquired before 6 April 1965. The time limit is two years after the end of the year in which your first disposal occurs after 5 April 1985 (31 March 1985 for companies). The effect is that your various quoted securities become part of your respective pre-April 1982 share pools.

18.19 Exemption for corporate bonds
(TCGA Ss115–117 & 254–255)

The exemption for capital gains tax for gilt edged securities (18.8.1) was extended to certain corporate bonds satisfying the following conditions:

(1) The bonds were acquired or issued after 13 March 1984.
(2) They are debentures, loan stocks or similar securities, not necessarily secured but 'debts on security'.
(3) They are normal commercial loans, expressed in and redeemable in sterling.
(4) At least some of the shares or debentures of the issuing company are quoted.
(5) The bonds are capable of being marketed but are not issued by a company to another company in the same group.
(6) Disposals after 1 July 1986 are exempt regardless of the time for which the bonds have been held. Similarly losses have ceased to be available. Prior to that date, normally exemption only applied if you held the securities for at least one year before disposal.
(7) If you sustain a loss on a qualifying corporate bond held on or issued after 14 March 1989, you will obtain relief where part or all of the loan is irrecoverable.
(8) Regarding disposals after 18 March 1991, bonds convertible into other qualifying corporate bonds are exempt. However,

those convertible into shares or securities of the issuing company's quoted parent are not.

18.20 Unquoted shares
(TCGA S273 & Sch 2)

Many of the above points regarding quoted shares and securities apply also to unquoted shares but the following special rules should be noted:

(1) Regarding holdings of shares at 6 April 1965 the 'time apportionment' rule normally applies to sales after that date subject to the right of election for valuation at 6 April 1965 (18.17). This is not a 'blanket' election for all your non-quoted shares as is the case for quoted shares. (For disposals after 5 April 1988, 1982 re-basing is likely to prevail — 18.11.)

(2) If after 6 April 1965 there is a capital reorganisation or take-over regarding a non-quoted company in which you have shares 'time apportionment' normally stops at that time and on any future sales you have a time apportioned gain or loss to the date of reorganisation or take-over and the full gain or loss after that time. This does not apply, however, in the case of a bonus issue of the same class of shares (18.18.6).

(3) If a reorganisation or take-over as in (2) above occurred before 6 April 1965 any shares still held at that date must automatically be valued at 6 April 1965 and the time apportionment does not apply. You still consider, however, the cost of your original holding when computing any capital gain or loss on a future sale.

(4) Prior to 6 April 1982 (1 April for companies) the 'pooling' rules (18.18.1) applied to shares acquired after 6 April 1965 but not to acquisitions before that time which must be separately considered on a 'first in first out' basis.

(5) The indexing rules (18.18.4) apply to non-quoted shares as for quoted ones. The rule in (4) above regarding shares held at 6 April 1965 was modified, however, so that the 'last in first out' basis applied for disposals between 5 April 1982 and 6 April 1985.

(6) Any relief which you obtain against your income, for business expansion scheme investment (10.25) is not also available to create a capital loss. Thus if you eventually sell the shares at a profit, you will obtain full relief for the cost in calculating your capital gain, but not if you sell at a loss.

18.21 Part disposals
(TCGA Ss42 & 242–244 & Sch 3)

Where part of an asset is disposed of (including part of a 'pool' holding of shares in a particular company) it is necessary to compute the cost applicable to the part sold. This is normally done by multiplying the original cost by the fraction A/(A+B) where A is the consideration for the part disposed of and B is the market value of the remaining property at the date of the part disposal. If indexation applies (18.12), the cost apportionment formula is applied before computing the indexation allowance. No indexation is calculated on the costs attributable to the undisposed of part (until that is sold).

For part disposals after 5 April 1988, the fraction A/(A + B) is applied to the value at 31 March 1982 if more than the cost. If a part disposal has already taken place between 31 March 1982 and 6 April 1988, the gain on a further disposal after 5 April 1988 must be computed on the basis that 1982 re-basing applied to the earlier part disposal.

A special rule applies to small part disposals of land (only a small part of the whole being sold, etc). Provided that such proceeds during the tax year do not exceed £20,000 (£10,000 before 6 April 1983), you may deduct the proceeds from your base cost rather than pay tax now. For disposals after 5 April 1986, this rule applies where the proceeds do not exceed one-fifth of the total market value of the land.

18.22 A series of disposals
(TCGA Ss19 & 20)

Before 20 March 1985, if you acquired a series of assets (shares, etc) from one or more people connected (18.10) with you, all of the assets were valued together to find the relevant proceeds and your acquisition figure. After 19 March 1985, however, the rule operates only from the viewpoint of a person splitting up an asset or collection of assets by two or more transactions to connected persons. The transactions must be within a total period of six years.

18.23 Private residences
(TCGA Ss222–226)

The house or flat where you live is normally exempt from capital gains tax when you sell it, subject to the following rules:

(1) The house must have been your only or main residence during the time that you owned it subject to various allowable periods of absence (see below). You ignore all periods before 6 April 1965 for these purposes.
(2) You are allowed to be absent from the house for the following maximum periods without losing your exemption:
   (a) The last 36 months of ownership. For disposals before 19 March 1991, this period was 24 months.
   (b) Periods of absence totalling three years.
   (c) Any period throughout which you worked abroad.
   (d) Any periods up to four years in aggregate when you are prevented from living in your house due to your employment being elsewhere.
   (e) Any period during which you live in job-related accommodation, but intend to return to your main residence.

Provided you have no other residence which you claim to be exempt during the above periods they are taken cumulatively and so you could have a long period of absence and still not lose your exemption. You must, however, return to your main residence at the end of periods (b), (c) and (d) above or else you will lose part of your relief.

(3) Any periods of absence subsequent to 31 March 1982 in excess of the periods allowed (see above) result in the relevant proportion of your sale profit being charged to capital gains tax. (For disposals before 6 April 1988, all periods of absence after 6 April 1965 must be considered.) For example, if you bought your house in June 1983 and sold it in June 1991 at a profit of £8,000 having lived elsewhere for reasons unconnected with your employment for the middle six years, your chargeable gain is £8,000 × 1/8 = £1,000. (You are only allowed three years of absence and the last three in any event, leaving one year taxable.)
(4) If a specific part of your house is set aside for business purposes then that proportion of your profits on sale of the house will be taxable. Thus if you have eight rooms of which two are wholly used for business purposes you would normally claim 25 per cent of your house expenses against your business profits and when you sell your house you will pay capital gains tax on 25 per cent of your total gain (arising after 6 April 1965). If, however, you use no rooms exclusively for business purposes you will not normally be liable for any capital gains tax if you sell your house even though you claim part of your house expenses against your business profits.
(5) Regarding disposals before 6 April 1980 if part of your main residence was let, your capital gain on that part was not

covered by the exemption. (This restriction does not apply to periods mentioned in 2(a)–(e) above.) However, if your disposal is on or after that date and part has been let for residential purposes, you obtain further exemption. The extra amount is not to exceed the exemption on the part occupied by you, or £40,000 if smaller (£20,000 before 19 March 1991 and £10,000 before 6 April 1983).

(6) If you have two residences you can give written notice to the Revenue within two years as to which of the two should be treated as your main private residence and thereby be exempted from capital gains tax. The election should be given within two years of acquiring your second residence. If you do not elect then the Revenue will decide in the light of the time that you spend at each of your residences which of these is your main private residence.

(7) For the purposes of the exemption, your main residence is taken to include land of up to half of a hectare (including the site of the house). If the house is large and its character requires a larger garden, this is likely to be allowed. (Prior to 19 March 1991, the area was one acre.) Note that the exemption covers the disposal of part of your main residence; for example a strip of your garden. However, take care not to sell the house before the garden, since this would not then be part of your main residence.

Previously, you also obtained capital gains tax exemption on no more than one residence owned by you and occupied by a dependent relative (3.2.10), rent-free and without any other consideration. Relief was withdrawn for disposals after 5 April 1988 unless the dependent relative had remained in occupation from an earlier date (TCGA S226).

18.24 Chattels sold for £6,000 or less
(TCGA S262)

A chattel is an asset which is tangible movable property such as a chair, a picture, or a pair of candlesticks. For these purposes a set is treated as one chattel. If you dispose of a chattel for no more than £6,000 you pay no capital gains tax and if your proceeds exceed £6,000 your capital gain is restricted to five-thirds of the excess. Thus if you sell a set of antique chairs for £6,300 (original cost £500) your capital gain is restricted to $5/3 \times (£6,300 - £6,000) = £500$.

If you bought a chattel for more than £6,000, and sold it for less than £6,000, your allowable loss is restricted to the excess of the cost over £6,000.

For the years 1982–83 to 1988–89 inclusive, the exemption limit was £3,000. A £2,000 limit applied from 1978–79 to 1981–82, prior to which it was £1,000.

18.25 Replacement of business assets — roll-over relief
(TCGA Ss152–160)

You are liable for capital gains tax in respect of any sales of assets used in your business. Similarly a company is liable on any sales of its business assets. If further business assets are purchased within one year preceding and three years after the sale, 'roll-over' relief is obtained as a result of which the gain on the disposal is deducted from the cost of the new business assets. Thus, the gain is 'rolled over' and no tax is paid until the new business assets are sold, unless the latter are in turn replaced. (Note the special 50 per cent reduction for certain rolled-over pre-31 March 1982 gains — 18.11.)

Note, however, that regarding plant and machinery, roll-over relief is only available if it is fixed and so, for example, motor vans and fork lift trucks do not qualify.

To get the relief you must use the old and new assets in the same business. However, if you carry on several trades, they are treated as one for this purpose. (Relief is still available if you cease one trade and start another.) Also, roll-over relief applies regarding purchases and sales by you of personally owned assets used in your 'family company' (18.29).

If you are non-resident and replace a business asset chargeable to UK tax with one which is not, roll-over relief is generally no longer available. This covers the situation where you sell an asset used in your business in the UK and buy one overseas. This new rule normally applies where you dispose of the old asset or acquire the new one after 13 March 1989; but not if the new asset was acquired before that date and the old asset disposed of within one year.

Note that to obtain total relief, the entire proceeds must be invested, otherwise you pay tax on your capital gain up to the extent of the shortfall. Where the disposal takes place after 5 April

1988, the old asset only needs to have been used for business since 31 March 1982 for full relief to apply (if otherwise due).

If the new business asset is a wasting asset (18.29.2) it must be replaced by a non-wasting asset within ten years. Otherwise the rolled-over gain becomes chargeable. This also applies to assets which will become 'wasting' within ten years, such as a lease with 59 years to run. However, this clawback does not apply to a held-over gain arising before 31 March 1982 and becoming chargeable after 5 April 1988 (TCGA Sch 4).

'Roll-over' relief is applicable to companies (12.16). Also a special extension of the rules covers 'gilts' obtained by companies in exchange for group companies in the aircraft and shipping industries on compulsory acquisition through nationalisation. An election is required within four years of the exchange and then the normal new compensation stock rules do not apply.

For disposals or acquisitions after 13 March 1989, subject to transitional rules, dual-resident companies obtain no roll-over relief where they replace a UK business asset with one overseas. From 20 March 1990 roll-over relief is denied where the replacement asset is outside the UK tax charge and is acquired by a dual resident group member (13.9.15).

18.25.1 Roll-over relief on compulsory purchase
(TCGA Ss247 & 248)

From 6 April 1982 a form of roll-over relief, similar to that available on business assets (above) applies to certain non-business property which is sold to local authorities. The property must either be compulsorily bought from you or the purchasing local authority must have compulsory acquisition powers. The relief is not available if your replacement property qualifies for main residence relief (18.23).

18.26 Gifts of business assets

A form of 'hold-over' relief applied to certain transfers of assets, other than bargains at arm's length, made after 11 April 1978. The assets covered were any used in your trade or 'family company' (18.29); also shares in such a company. A claim was required from both the recipient and yourself, similar in effect to that for general gifts (below).

A more general relief applied for individuals after 5 April 1980 and for settlements after 5 April 1981 (below). The old relief still applied for gifts to companies. From 14 March 1989, the old rules for gifts of business assets are expanded (18.28), following the cancellation of the general relief for gifts (18.27).

18.27 General relief for gifts
(FA 1980 S79; FA 1981 Ss78 & 79, FA 1982 S82 & FA 1986 S101)

In general, transfers of assets which you made after 5 April 1980 and before 14 March 1989, other than bargains at arm's length, were covered by comprehensive 'hold-over' rules. Only UK resident or ordinarily resident individuals (15.3.1) were covered up to 5 April 1981 but after that date, gifts *to* UK trusts were included. From 6 April 1982 gifts *from* trusts were also included. There is a special 50 per cent reduction for certain held-over pre-31 March 1982 gains (18.11).

A claim is normally required from you both, whereupon your gain is reduced to nil and the recipient deducts your original capital gain from his acquisition value for the asset. (If your gift is to the trustees of a settlement, you alone need elect.) Should you receive some consideration the claim covers only the gift element, if this is less than your total gain. If you are entitled to retirement relief (below) this reduces the held-over gain.

Capital transfer tax may have been payable on the gift based on its market value. Following the introduction of inheritance tax (20.1) tax on gifts is less likely. If any capital transfer tax, or inheritance tax, is payable on the transaction, to the extent that this is no more than the original gain, the acquisition value is increased for the recipient. This even applies to inheritance tax eventually payable on 'PETs' (20.3).

Subject to certain exceptions, the following rule applies after 5 April 1981. If you have received a gift and made the election, then the held-over gain is assessed on you, should you become neither resident nor ordinarily resident in the UK before having sold the asset. However, this only applies if emigration is within six years of the end of the year of assessment of the gift.

The general gifts relief rules were cancelled regarding gifts made after 13 March 1989. However, you are still able to elect concerning gifts made earlier. The business asset gifts provisions are expanded from that date (18.28).

18.28 Gifts relief from 14 March 1989
(TCGA Ss165–169 & Sch 7)

With the removal of general gifts relief from 14 March 1989, the business gifts relief (18.26) has been expanded so that it now includes other items. The scope is now:

(1) Business assets used in a trade profession or vocation carried on by the giver or his family company, etc.
(2) Certain agricultural property (normally where the giver has vacant possession).
(3) Shares and securities in family trading companies or non-quoted trading companies. (These categories include the holding companies of trading groups.)
(4) Gifts of heritage property and to maintenance funds.
(5) Gifts to political parties which qualify for inheritance tax exemption.
(6) Gifts which give rise to an immediate charge to inheritance tax, for example, into a discretionary settlement (20.31.2). Potentially exempt transfers (20.3) do not qualify for this relief. However, if a gift is covered by the nil rate band and exemptions for inheritance tax but would otherwise be taxed, the gifts election is available.
(7) Distributions of capital from accumulation and maintenance settlements may also qualify for the election. However, the beneficiary must not obtain the capital later than the income entitlement.
(8) Subject to an election by donor and recipient, gifts to a housing association (TCGA S259).
(9) Certain assets not mentioned above, which are not eligible for gifts relief may qualify for the tax on disposal to be paid by instalments (18.15).
(10) The relief is only available if the donee is UK resident and/or ordinarily resident.
(11) A similar rule regarding recoupment of the relief on the emigration of the donee applies as previously (18.27).

18.29 Business retirement relief
(TCGA Ss163–164 & Sch 6)

If you are over 55 and dispose by gift or sale of the whole or part of a business which you have owned for the past ten years, you are exempted from capital gains tax on the first £150,000 of any gain arising in respect of the 'chargeable business assets' of the business. If you have several businesses your total relief is restricted to £150,000. To obtain retirement relief on disposals before 19 March 1991, you normally needed to be 60 and full relief applied on the first £125,000 of proceeds. For disposals before 6 April 1987 and after 5 April 1985, this figure was £100,000.

For disposals before 6 April 1985 £100,000 was available at age 65 with tapering relief between 60 and 65. Prior to 6 April 1983, this figure was £50,000, with £20,000 before 12 April 1978, and £10,000 before 3 July 1974. Note that you do not actually need to retire to obtain the relief. 'Chargeable business assets' include assets used for the trade, etc of the business, and also goodwill but not assets held as investments.

For disposals after 5 April 1988, not only is the first tranche of gains exempted from capital gains tax; the second tranche is given 50 per cent relief. From 19 March 1991, the second tranche is £450,000. (From 6 April 1988 to 18 March 1991, this tranche was £375,000). Thus if you are over 55 and sell your business, giving rise to a chargeable gain of £450,000, £150,000 of this is exempted from capital gains tax, as is 50 per cent × (£450,000 − £150,000) = £150,000. You are taxed on only £450,000 − (£150,000 + £150,000) = £150,000. (This example assumes that you have not used any retirement relief previously.)

After 5 April 1985, you are also able to obtain relief if you retire younger than the required age (55 after 18 March 1991 or otherwise 60) for reasons of ill-health. You must show that you are likely to remain incapable of performing your previous work and will require a medical certificate.

The above relief also covers any disposal of shares in a trading company which has been your 'family company' for at least the last ten years during which time you have been a full-time director of the company. A 'family company' is one in which you have 25 per cent of the voting rights or your immediate family has at least more than 50 per cent (at least 51 per cent before 6 April 1985) including 5 per cent held by yourself. Only the proportion of the gain on the shares attributable to the 'chargeable business assets' of the company compared with its total chargeable assets qualifies for the relief. Note that shares in subsidiary companies were not regarded as 'chargeable business assets' until after 5 April 1985.

Reduced relief is available concerning disposals after 11 April 1978, of the whole or part of a business which you have owned for less than ten years. You obtain 10 per cent of the full relief if you owned the assets for at least one year prior to disposal, 20 per cent relief for at least two years of ownership and so on.

If your wife complies with the requirements, she too will be eligible for the relief if she sells her business or shares in a 'family company'.

From 6 April 1985, the relief covers disposals by a settlement of assets used by a beneficiary for his own or his family company's business. Also shares in a family trading or holding company are covered. The beneficiary must have an interest in possession in the settlement, withdraw from the business and must retire.

18.29.1 Charities
(TCGA Ss256 & 257)

Charities are exempted from capital gains tax in respect of any gains on the disposal of assets provided that such gains are applied to charitable purposes.

If you make a gift of an asset to a charity you pay no capital gains tax on this disposal.

18.29.2 Leases and other wasting assets
(TCGA Ss45, 240 & Sch 8)

A 'wasting asset' is defined as an asset with a predictable life not exceeding 50 years, not including freehold land and buildings, etc. Leases with no more than 50 years still to run are a special kind of wasting asset and are separately treated for capital gains tax (see below).

'Wasting assets' which are also movable property (chattels) are normally exempted from capital gains tax. In the case of other wasting assets apart from leases, you must reduce their original costs on a straight line time basis over the respective lives of the assets. Thus if you buy a wasting asset for £10,000 with an unexpired life of 40 years and sell it after 20 years for £20,000, assuming the residual value after 40 years would have been nil, your allowable cost is £10,000 × 20/40 = £5,000; thus your chargeable gain is £20,000 − £5,000 = £15,000.

In the case of a lease with no more than 50 years of its original term unexpired (including leases for shorter terms) the original cost must be written off according to a special formula under which the rate of wastage accelerates as the end of the term of the lease is reached. If you sell such an interest in property and lease back the premises at a lower rent for less than 15 years, you may be taxed on all or part of the proceeds either as a trading receipt or under Schedule D Case VI (17.1.2).

18.30 Traded options
(TCGA Ss115, 143, 148 & 271)

Options to buy or sell quoted shares are now dealt with on the Stock Exchange and prior to 6 April 1980 were treated as wasting assets (above). From that day they are no longer so regarded which means that the entire cost is deductible on sale. Also from 6 April 1980 the abandonment of a traded option is treated as a disposal so that its cost is an allowable loss. From 6 April 1984, this treatment is extended to all traded options quoted on the London International Financial Futures Exchange and recognised stock exchanges. However, after 1 July 1986 transactions in futures and options in gilts and qualifying bonds are exempt from capital gains tax. A new rule provides that if you write a traded option and later extinguish this obligation by buying another option, the cost is allowable against the original sale.

18.31 Commodity and financial futures
(TCGA Ss72, 143 & 271)

Prior to 6 April 1985, profits from futures which are not part of a trade have been taxed under Schedule D Case VI (13.1). However, from that date, any profits less losses which you realise are normally covered by capital gains tax and not income tax. This rule applies to commodity futures or financial futures dealt in on a recognised futures exchange.

The 1987 Finance Act introduced broadly similar capital gains tax treatment for commodity and financial futures and qualifying options (18.30), which are dealt in 'over-the-counter'. From August 1990 income and gains from futures and options are exempt from tax in authorised unit trusts and pension schemes.

18.32 Overseas aspects
(TCGA Ss9–14, 25, 80–98, 159–160, 185–188, 275–279 & Sch 5 & F2A 1992 Ss35 & 44–50)

As already mentioned (18.3) provided you are resident and/or ordinarily resident in this country, you are liable to tax on capital

Capital gains tax 307

gains anywhere in the world. An exception is where assets are realised in a country which will not allow the proceeds to be remitted to the UK. You can then claim that your gain is deferred until the year when it becomes possible to remit the proceeds. If you are non-domiciled in the UK, you are only liable to capital gains tax on overseas gains to the extent that they are remitted here (16.1).

Non-residents carrying on a trade in the UK through a branch or agency are liable to capital gains tax on assets used in the business. From 14 March 1989, this also covers professions and vocations; however, assets are re-based to their values at that date. Furthermore from that date deemed disposals may take place for capital gains tax purposes. This happens if the assets are moved out of the UK or the trade, etc ceases.

If you are UK domiciled, the Revenue have powers to apportion to you the capital gains of certain overseas trusts from which you benefit (19.9) and companies. This extends to overseas companies owned by foreign trusts.

The *market value* rule (18.10) applies in general to gifts and other dispositions of overseas assets for less than full consideration involving neither resident nor ordinarily resident persons after 5 April 1983 (FA 1984 S66). From 10 March 1981 until 5 April 1983, however (and up to 5 April 1985, subject to an election), if you obtained an asset from such a person, your base cost is restricted to the actual consideration, if any.

Where a company is being 'exported' (15.3.3), there is a deemed disposal of all of its assets at market value for capital gains tax purposes. This broadly applies to companies migrating after 14 March 1988, from which time only those incorporated outside the UK will be able to become non-resident. Furthermore, roll-over relief (18.25.1) does not apply where assets are sold before and replaced after migration. If a company which migrates continues to trade in the UK through a branch or agency, any connected assets will be exempted from the deemed disposal.

If a foreign registered 75 per cent subsidiary of a UK company migrates, tax on the capital gains attributable to its foreign assets can be deferred. Parent and subsidiary must make a joint election and the tax becomes payable if any of the foreign assets are sold or if the parent–subsidiary relationship ceases.

After 13 March 1989, if a dual-resident company owns an asset which ceases to be within the UK capital gains tax charge through a double tax agreement, it is deemed to have disposed of the asset. Thus a capital gain may result. Also, for disposals after that date by a non-resident company, tax on the capital gains can be collected from other companies in the same group or from controlling directors. This applies if the original company does not pay within six months of the due date.

If you are a UK resident investor in an offshore 'umbrella fund' you will be subjected to a capital gains tax charge when you switch holdings. This applies to switches made after 13 March 1989.

With effect from 20 March 1990, non-resident companies may transfer their UK branch or agency business to UK resident companies without any immediate capital gains tax charge. This holdover relief applies if the companies are in the same world-wide group.

Sweeping changes operate from 19 March 1991 regarding the capital gains tax rules for overseas trusts. These are considered later (19.9.1).

With effect from 1 January 1992, various relieving provisions come into effect regarding cross-border reorganisations of businesses within the EC. As a result, capital gains tax may be deferred where there is a share exchange and on transfers of UK and non-UK trades, subject to the rules. For a share exchange, voting control must be acquired for shares with not more than 10 per cent of the nominal value in cash. Regarding a UK trade, this must be transferred from a company situated in one EC country to one situated in another, in exchange for securities.

19 The taxation of trusts and estates

19.1 Trusts

A trust is brought into existence when a person (the settlor) transfers assets to trustees for the benefit of third parties (the beneficiaries). Another word for a trust is a settlement. A trust may also be created under a will when a person (the testator) sets aside the whole or a portion of his estate to be administered (by trustees) for the benefit of his heirs or other beneficiaries. (Where an individual declares himself to be a trustee of certain of his assets a trust will also come into existence.)

19.2 Trusts where the settlor or testator is deceased

Where the settlor or testator has died, the taxation of trusts normally follows simple rules. The trust is assessed to basic rate income tax and sometimes additional rate (5.6) on its income. Some of this tax will have been deducted at the source (eg, taxed interest). Capital gains tax is charged on any capital gains of the trust (19.6).

The tax assessments are normally made in the joint names of the trustees who pay the tax out of the trust funds.

No higher rate tax is paid by the trustees but when the income is distributed to any of the beneficiaries this income is added to the beneficiaries' total income for tax purposes (5.2). The income distributions are normally treated as being net of income tax at the basic rate (25 per cent). Thus they carry a corresponding tax credit. In the case of discretionary trusts, etc (19.3.4) the additional rate (10 per cent) further increases the tax credit. Up to 5 April 1991, if part of the underlying income of the trust was building society interest, however, the appropriate portion of each income distribution was allocated to this interest and taxed in the beneficiary's hands in the same way as any income on his own building society investments (8.6). This 'see-through' rule did not apply to any UK resident with an absolute interest in the residue of an estate who could reclaim tax on the entire income distributions. After 5 April 1991, with the ending of the composite rate scheme, the 'see-through' rule is no longer relevant.

For example, suppose A has a life interest in a trust and received from it income for 1990–91 made up as follows:

	Total	Building society income	Other income
Gross	£1,375	£375	£1,000
Income tax at 25% (tax credit)	250	—	250
Actual payment to A	£1,125	£375	£750

A includes in his total income £1,500 (ie, £1,000 distribution from other income plus £375 × 100/75 grossed equivalent of building society income). If A is able to make an income tax repayment claim (14.6) he has £250 income tax credit from the trust available for repayment.

The trustees should issue with each payment a form R185E which sets out the amount paid and the relevant tax credit.

19.3 Trusts where the settlor is still living
(TA 1988 Ss660–685)

The taxation of trusts where the settlor is still living follows the general rules outlined above except that in certain circumstances the settlor himself is assessed to tax on the income of the trust. In order to avoid such assessment various rules should be observed including the following:

19.3.1 Period
(TA 1988 S660)

The settlement must be set up for a period which is capable of exceeding six years.

19.3.2 The settlor must not have an interest
(TA 1988 Ss673 & 683 & FA 1989 Ss108 & 109)

In the event that the settlor has retained an interest in the income or assets of the trust, he will be assessed to income tax on the income of the settlement to the extent that it remains undistributed. (The settlor has retained an interest in the trust if he or his wife can obtain some benefit from it.) Furthermore, if the income is distributed to others, subject to certain exceptions, the settlor and not the recipient will be charged to the excess of higher rate tax over the basic rate on the distribution. For trusts made after 13 March 1989, in which the settlor retains an interest, with some exceptions, he or she is taxed on all of the income at the basic and higher rates. (This applies to the income from existing settlements arising from 6 April 1990.)

For 1990–91 and subsequent years, simple outright gifts and pension allocations between husband and wife are not to be treated as settlements for the purposes of these rules. However, this does not apply to gifts of property which do not carry a right to all of the income or where a right to income alone is given.

19.3.3 The settlement must be irrevocable
(TA 1988 Ss671 & 672)

If the settlor or his wife has power to revoke the settlement or partially revoke it, he is assessed to income tax on its income.

19.3.4 Discretionary settlements
(TA 1988 S674)

Discretionary settlements are those under which the application of the income and/or capital of the trust is left to the discretion of the trustees. Under such a trust the settlor or his wife must not be able to benefit from the income, or else he will be assessed to income tax on that income, whether or not any of it is actually paid to him. This does not apply if only the widow or widower of the settlor may benefit.

19.3.5 Settlements for benefit of own children
(TA 1988 Ss663–670)

Under a trust created by the settlor, his own unmarried minor children (under 18 years of age) must not receive any income nor must it be used for their upkeep or education. Otherwise the settlor will be assessed to income tax on such income. This does not apply to income which is accumulated, however (see 19.4).

19.3.6 Capital sums paid to the settlor
(TA 1988 S677)

Where 'capital sums' from a settlement (including loans and loan repayments) are paid to the settlor, he is assessable to income tax. The assessments are limited to the undistributed trust income and the balance is carried forward for matching against future income. After 5 April 1981, the carry forward period is limited to 11 years from the 'capital sum' payment and no income is assessable for any period subsequent to the repayment by the settlor of a loan from the settlement.

The rules extend to companies connected with the settlement (normally where the trustees are participators and the company is close — 12.17). A 'capital payment' from the company to the settlor before 6 April 1981 gave rise to additional rate of trust income on the settlor. After 5 April 1981, this only applies if there is an associated capital payment or asset transfer within five years from the trust to the company.

Note: In all of the above cases there are rules to prevent the double taxation of the trust income so it will not be assessed both on the settlor and the beneficiaries. Usually, basic rate income tax is paid by the trust or it has already been deducted at the source as in the case of, for example, interest on government securities. Dividends received by the trust carry with them tax credits which are effectively transferred to beneficiaries who are given income distributions. Also, if the trust is subject to additional rate correspondingly higher tax credits attach to income distributions to beneficiaries (see below).

19.4 Accumulation settlements for the benefit of the settlor's children

If you wish to create a trust for the benefit of your minor (unmarried) children without being assessed to income tax on its income (see above) this can be done by means of an accumulation settlement. The income of the settlement should be accumulated for each child until at least the age of 18 and no payments should be made for their benefit until that age. (The trust deed normally states that the trustees are empowered to accumulate income.) If it is wished to distribute income to adult beneficiaries this can be done, but the income shares of the settlor's minor children must be accumulated, or else the settlor is liable to higher rate income tax on such income.

19.5 Income of discretionary trusts, etc
(TA 1988 Ss686–687 & 809)

Although it no longer applies to individuals (5.7), an additional rate of 10 per cent applies to all of the income of discretionary and accumulating trusts from 1988–89 to 1992–93. Previous rates have been 18 per cent for 1987–88, 16 per cent for 1986–87 and 15 per cent from 6 April 1973 to 5 April 1986. Thus if a discretionary trust receives dividends of £750 during 1992–93 these will be imputed with £250 tax to make a total of £1,000 on which additional tax of £100 will be payable by the trustees. If, however, allowable expenses of say £200 are incurred then only £1,000 − £200 = £800 is liable to the additional tax and so £800 × 10 per cent = £80 is payable.

The above applies to trusts where the income is accumulated or is payable at the discretion of the trustees but not where the income is treated for tax purposes as being that of the settlor; nor where a person is absolutely entitled to the income.

Where income distributions are made to beneficiaries, the amounts received by the latter are treated as being net of tax at 35 per cent (25 per cent basic rate plus 10 per cent additional rate). The recipients can reclaim part or all of this tax if their incomes are low enough. For example, if a discretionary trust pays £650 to your child (or for his maintenance) and he has no other income, there is a tax credit of £650 × 35/65 = £350 which is all reclaimable.

19.6 Trusts' capital gains tax
(TCGA Ss5, 68–76, 165–167 & Sch 7)

Regarding realisations by trusts after 5 April 1988, a 25 per cent capital gains tax rate applies, except for discretionary and accumulation trusts. Regarding the latter, a rate of 35 per cent applies. This is equivalent to the basic and additional rates. Where the settlor (or spouse) has an interest in or rights relating to a settlement, the 25 per cent rate may be increased to the settlor's top rate. Also, the settlor's annual exemption (£5,800) would apply if not used up (TCGA Ss77 & 78).

Prior to 6 April 1988, trusts were charged to capital gains tax at 30 per cent on all gains from the sales of chargeable assets (less capital losses) during each tax year (18.1).

For 1980–81 and 1981–82 the £3,000 annual exemption (18.6) applied to trusts for the mentally disabled and those receiving attendance allowance. (From 6 April 1981 only broadly half the property and income need be applied to the disabled.) Other trusts formed before 7 June 1978 obtained a straight annual exemption of £1,500 no matter how high their gains. Regarding trusts formed from that date the exemption of £1,500 was split between all those with the same settlor. Thus if you had settled four such trusts they each had an annual exemption of £375. If there were more than five, however, they each still had an exemption of £300.

For subsequent years the corresponding exemptions are:

	Disability trusts	Other trusts	Minimum
1982–83	£5,000	£2,500	£500
1983–84	5,300	2,650	530
1984–85	5,600	2,800	560
1985–86	5,900	2,950	590
1986–87	6,300	3,150	630
1987–88	6,600	3,300	660
1988–89			
1989–90 &			
1990–91	5,000	2,500	500
1991–92	5,500	2,750	550
1992–93	5,800	2,900	580

When any chargeable assets are introduced into the trust by the settlor this is a realisation by him on which he pays capital gains tax if applicable (18.10). For example, if A bought 1,000 shares in B Ltd for £1,000 in May 1983 and gifts them in June 1992 to a settlement that he created, the shares must be valued at that time. If the shares are then worth £2,000 he has a chargeable gain of £1,000 for 1992–93 (subject to indexation). If, however, the shares are worth only £600 at that time, he has an allowable loss of £400 (£1,000 − £600) which he can only set off against any capital gains resulting from other transactions between A and his trust. This is because they are treated as being 'connected persons' (18.10).

19.7 Trusts' capital gains tax — business assets, gifts, etc

Where, after 11 April 1978, business assets, including shares in 'family companies' were settled, the trustees and settlor could jointly claim for any gain on the assets to be rolled over (18.25). The effect was that the settlor had no capital gains tax to pay on the settled business assets, etc and the acquisition value for the trustees was correspondingly reduced. From 6 April 1981 to 13 March 1989, the general gifts relief (18.27) applied to disposals *to* trusts. Regarding gifts *by* trusts, the old business assets rules applied for 1981–82, after which the general gifts relief applied up to 13 March 1989. From 14 March 1989, the old business assets rules apply with some extensions (18.28), for instance concerning discretionary settlements.

From 6 April 1985 capital gains tax retirement relief was extended to cover certain trust disposals of business assets (or family company shares). This particularly applies where a beneficiary of the trust with a life interest in possession (other than for a fixed term), who previously carried on the business, withdraws from it and retires (18.29).

19.8 Trusts' capital gains tax — disposals of interests and distributions

The disposal of an interest in the trust by one of the original beneficiaries is normally exempt from capital gains tax. However, after 9 March 1981 this does not apply to non-resident settlements.

From 6 April 1982, where a *life interest* ends in a settlement otherwise than on death, capital gains tax no longer arises on the excess of its value over the base cost. However, on a subsequent disposal the original base value must be used. Where a *life interest* in a settlement ends on death, there is similarly no capital gains tax. However, the capital gains tax base value of the assets is adjusted to their market value at that time.

Where a capital asset of a trust is distributed to a beneficiary this is a chargeable event which can give rise to a capital gain in the trust. (This even applies for minors etc who are not yet able to legally own the property.) Thus if a trust bought 1,000 shares in B Ltd for £2,000 in April 1983 and it distributes them to beneficiary C in July 1992 when their market value is £3,000 the trust will have a capital gain of £1,000 (£3,000 − £2,000), which is assessable for 1992–93 subject to the annual exemption and indexation. (An exception to this rule is where a beneficiary under a will receives his entitlement — 19.10.3.) The beneficiary normally has a base value equivalent to the market value of the asset.

19.9 Foreign trusts
(TCGA Ss13, 80–90 & Sch 5)

For taxation purposes a trust is generally treated as being resident abroad if a majority of the trustees are so resident and its administration and management is carried out overseas. Such a trust was generally exempt from capital gains tax on realisations of assets in the UK and elsewhere. However, sweeping changes took effect from 19 March 1991 and that rule no longer applies in certain cases (19.9.1).

For income tax purposes, broadly, for 1989–90 (with some exceptions) and subsequent years if at least one trustee is UK resident and at least one is not, special rules apply (15.3.5), depending on the settlor's status when he introduces funds into the settlement. If the settlor was then resident, ordinarily resident or domiciled in the UK, the non-resident trustees are treated as UK resident for determining the trust's residence for income tax purposes. Otherwise, all of the trustees are treated as non-UK resident.

If the settlement arises on death, the residence, etc of the deceased at the date of death applies for deeming the residence of the trustees and a similar rule applies concerning the personal representatives.

There are rules under which the Revenue can sometimes assess UK resident beneficiaries with their shares of any capital gains (provided that the settlor is UK domiciled and resident or ordinarily resident either when he made the settlement or when the capital gain is made). Prior to 6 April 1981 this applied whether or not the beneficiaries received any part of the gains. However, in such circumstances, tax assessed prior to 6 April 1984 in respect of gains arising before 6 April 1981, can now be deferred until benefit passes. (This does not apply to tax already paid by 29 March 1983.)

Under the system which applies to the gains of overseas settlements after 5 April 1981 (UK domiciled and resident or ordinarily resident settlor), UK beneficiaries are only taxed to the extent that they receive *capital payments* attributable to such gains. Where the *capital payments* and trust capital gains are in different tax years the beneficiary is taxed in the later one. *Capital payments* made to beneficiaries after 5 April 1992 may attract a supplementary charge (19.9.1).

There are rules to prevent capital gains tax being avoided by transfers between settlements and by a trust changing its residence. For the purposes of the rules from 1984–85, the term 'settlement' is enlarged to include dispositions, arrangements and agreements; whilst 'settlor' takes in those making reciprocal arrangements or undertakings to provide funds indirectly. From 19 March 1991, there are rules to charge to tax, trust capital gains on settlors who have any interest in the settlement (19.9.1).

Where a beneficiary obtains an asset from a foreign trust after 5 April 1983, his base value is taken to be the market value of the asset, as a general rule. However, from 10 March 1981 to 5 April 1983, his base value was limited to the amount of any consideration which he actually gave for the asset, except in certain cases where the foreign trust was liable to UK capital gains tax.

UK income of foreign trusts is charged to income tax here along roughly the same lines as non-resident individuals are so charged. There is no higher rate liability, however, unless distributions are made to beneficiaries resident in this country or if the anti-avoidance provisions apply regarding transfers of assets abroad (13.9.2). In the latter event, in certain circumstances, the Revenue may charge any beneficiaries who are resident in this country with basic and higher rate income tax on the trust income.

19.9.1 Foreign trusts—Capital gains from 19 March 1991
(TCGA Ss80–87 & Sch 5)

New rules operate from 19 March 1991 aimed at increasing the application of UK capital gains tax to foreign trusts. These rules include a capital gains tax charge when the trustees of a settlement cease to be UK resident after 18 March 1991. This is based on the values of the assets which fall out of the UK capital gains tax net when the trustees change residence (not assets used in a UK trade). The trustees are not able to cover such gains by roll-over relief through buying new assets outside the UK tax charge.

As the settlor of a non-resident settlement, you will be charged to capital gains tax if certain conditions are satisfied including the following:

(1) You are UK domiciled and resident or ordinarily resident (15.2 and 15.3).
(2) You have an 'interest' in the settlement. This covers being able to benefit, now or in the future, from the income or property of the settlement. You are also caught if your spouse, children or their spouses can benefit.

(3) The rules apply to your settlement, if you set it up after 18 March 1991. Earlier settlements may also be caught, where, for example, property or income is provided otherwise than by way of arm's length bargains. Other instances include the trustees ceasing to be UK resident after that date and a member of your immediate family ((2) above) becoming a beneficiary for the first time.
(4) Any capital gains and losses made by your settlement before 19 March 1991 are not caught by the new rules. However, subject to the conditions being satisfied, you will be assessed on the subsequent net gains. Also, you will have an obligation to notify the Inland Revenue of events which may involve a charge to tax.

If you are a beneficiary of a non-resident settlement and receive a *capital payment* after 5 April 1992, you may be liable to pay a *supplementary charge* in addition to the normal capital gains tax. The rules include the following:

(1) You must be UK domiciled and resident or ordinarily resident (15.2 and 15.3). Also, the settlor has this status when you receive the payment or when the trust was established.
(2) Your capital payments will be matched with trust gains on a 'first-in first-out' basis.
(3) The supplementary charge runs from 1 December in the tax year following the one when the gain arose, to 30 November following the year of assessment in which your capital payment is made.
(4) You will not be charged if your capital payment falls to be matched with trust gains of the same or immediately preceding tax year.
(5) The supplementary charge will be 10 per cent of the tax for each year up to six. Thus, if the top rate remains 40 per cent, the maximum supplementary charge will be 24 per cent making a total of 64 per cent.

19.10 Estates of deceased persons

19.10.1 The tax liability of the deceased
(TMA Ss40, 74 & 77)

When a person dies, income tax and capital gains tax must be settled on all his income and capital gains up to the date of his death. Any of this tax that is not paid during his lifetime must be settled by his executors or administrators out of his estate.

If the deceased has not been assessed to tax on all his income or capital gains prior to his death, the Revenue are allowed to make assessments on such income and capital gains within three years after the end of the tax year in which death occurred. The Revenue may make assessments in this way in respect of any tax years ending within six years before the date of death in cases of fraud, wilful default or neglect of the deceased but no earlier years can be assessed (14.8.1).

19.10.2 Income tax during the administration period
(TA 1988 Ss695–720)

The administration period of an estate is the period from the date of death of the deceased until the assets are distributed to the beneficiaries according to the will of the deceased or according to the rules of intestacy. Where, however, a trust is set up under a will the administration period only normally lasts until the trust takes over the residue of the estate.

During the administration period, the executors or administrators pay any basic rate income tax assessments that arise on the income for that period. The tax paid by direct assessment or deduction at source is subtracted from the amounts of income paid to those entitled to the income of the estate. Non-trading expenses of the executors are also deducted, but normally, any trading expenses will have been deducted from trading income in arriving at its net taxable amount.

The beneficiaries include the income that they receive in their tax returns when the payments are made to them. They must return the gross equivalents allowing for income tax at the basic rate (25 per cent). Once the total income payable to each beneficiary has been ascertained, it is allocated to the respective tax years for which it arose and they pay (if applicable) higher rate tax on that basis.

19.10.3 Capital gains tax during the administration period
(TCGA Ss3 & 62)

Although before 31 March 1971 all of the chargeable assets of the deceased were considered for capital gains tax purposes to be disposed of at the date of his death, no such liability arises regarding deaths on or after that date. The executors or administrators of the estate are regarded as acquiring the assets at their market value at the date of death and if they later sell any of the assets during the administration period, the estate is assessed to capital gains tax on any surplus. The rate is 30 per cent up to 5 April 1988 and 25 per cent thereafter.

Thus if part of the estate of A deceased consisted of 1,000 shares in B Ltd whose value at his death on say 30 June 1989 was £2,000, if those shares are sold on 1 November 1992 for £3,000 (in order to pay inheritance tax for example), the estate is assessed to capital gains tax on £1,000 (£3,000 − £2,000) for 1992–93 (subject to indexation and annual exemption).

If, however, assets of the estate are given to beneficiaries in settlement of their entitlements under the will of the deceased, no capital gains tax is charged on the estate on such transfers of assets. Instead, each beneficiary is treated for capital gains tax purposes as if he had acquired the assets at the same time as the personal representatives acquired them and at the same value.

Thus in the example mentioned above, if instead of selling the 1,000 shares in B Ltd for £3,000 on 1 November 1992 the executors gave them to C on that day in satisfaction of a legacy provided by the will of A deceased, C is treated as having acquired the shares on 30 June 1989 for £2,000 only. (The value of £2,000 was the probate value of the shares at the date of death.) Thus no capital gains tax is payable by the estate in respect of the transfer. If, however, C then sells shares on 1 December 1992 for £3,500 his chargeable gain (subject to indexation) will be £1,500 (£3,500 − £2,000), although the shares have only gone up in value by £500 since he received them. This is because his entitlement to the legacy is considered for capital gains tax purposes to extend back to the date of death.

For the year of assessment in which death occurs and the next two years, the annual exemption is applied to the net gains (£5,800 for 1992–93, £5,500 for 1991–92, £5,000 for 1988–89, 1989–90 and 1990–91, £6,600 for 1987–88, £6,300 for 1986–87 and £5,900 for 1985–86, etc — 18.6).

See Chapter 20 (20.31) for guidelines to the inheritance tax rules concerning settlements.

20 Inheritance tax

20.1 Introduction

This chapter deals with what was originally known as capital transfer tax, but following sweeping changes in the 1986 Finance Act was renamed inheritance tax. The new name applies from 25 July 1986. However the new rules cover transfers on and after 18 March 1986.

The tax is highly complicated and technical. Although many of the basic capital transfer tax rules remain, important innovations such as potentially exempt transfers (PETs) were introduced (20.3). Many of its complexities are beyond the scope of this book. The following is thus only a brief outline.

The rules for capital transfer tax were originally contained in Sections 19 to 52 and Schedules 4 to 11 of the 1975 Finance Act which received Royal Assent on 13 March 1975. Substantial changes were made in subsequent Finance Acts which were consolidated into the 1984 Capital Transfer Tax Act, now known as the Inheritance Tax Act 1984 (ITA). The tax applies to lifetime gifts made after 26 March 1974, transfers on deaths occurring after 12 March 1975 and settled property. However, after 17 March 1986, lifetime transfers between individuals and to certain trusts are only taxed if death occurs within seven years (20.3).

Estate duty does not apply to deaths occurring after 12 March 1975 (20.14). Where property passed on deaths after 12 November 1974 and before 13 March 1975, estate duty applied at capital transfer tax rates (25.5). For details of estate duty, reference should be made to Chapter 19 of the 1974–75 *Hambro Tax Guide* and earlier editions.

20.2 Property chargeable
(ITA 1984 Ss1–3 & 103–114)

Subject to various exceptions and reliefs (20.16) inheritance tax will be charged on *chargeable transfers* which you make during your lifetime, as well as on the value of your estate when you die. However, since the introduction of the inheritance tax regime, the scope for tax on lifetime gifts has been much reduced by the rules concerning *potentially exempt transfers* (20.3). These escape tax unless death occurs within seven years. As a result, most inheritance tax is payable following death.

Chargeable transfers are evaluated by taking the decrease in your assets less liabilities brought about by the transfer and deducting certain exemptions (20.18). Normally, arm's length transactions are ignored if they are not intended to convey any gratuitous benefit. Any capital gains tax which you pay is ignored in calculating the decrease.

If you are domiciled (15.2) in the UK or deemed domiciled (20.4) here, inheritance tax applies to all of your property, wherever situated. Otherwise it only applies to your property in this country.

20.3 Potentially exempt transfers
(FA 1986 S101 & Sch 19 & F2A 1987 S96 & Sch 7)

If you make gifts after 17 March 1986 to other individuals, or to accumulation and maintenance settlements (20.31.1) or trusts for disabled persons, they are classed as 'potentially exempt transfers' (PETs). This means that inheritance tax will not be payable on these gifts unless you die within seven years. Should that happen, however, the PETs (less exemptions) become *chargeable transfers*. Your tax must then be recalculated as later indicated (20.5.1) but using the rate scale applying at death and subject to possible tapering relief (20.6).

From 17 March 1987, the scope of PETs includes lifetime transfers concerning interest in possession trusts. These are broadly trusts where one or more beneficiaries have the income or use of property as of right. Transfers into such trusts are PETs as are transfers out, except on death. If you make a PET, no inheritance tax return is required.

20.4 Deemed domicile
(ITA 1984 S267)

You are deemed to be domiciled in the UK if one of the following applies:
(1) You were domiciled here on or after 10 December 1974 and within the three years preceding the date of the chargeable transfer.
(2) You were resident here on or after 10 December 1974 and in not less than 17 of the 20 years of assessment ending with that in which you made the chargeable transfer.

20.5 Rate scale
(ITA 1984 S7; FA 1984 S101, etc & F2A 1992 S72)

Capital transfer tax was charged on the cumulative total of all your lifetime transfers after 26 March 1974 together with the property passing on your death. There was a ten year limitation on cumulation (20.7).

The inheritance tax scheme applying from 18 March 1986 only has a seven year limitation on cumulation. Also, as previously mentioned (20.3) lifetime transfers (excluding transfers to discretionary settlements, etc) are not cumulated unless you die within seven years. There are, however, various exemptions from the general rules (20.18).

Prior to 18 March 1986 the tax was charged at progressive rates shown in the appropriate tables (25.5). A lower scale applied to lifetime gifts and a higher one to property passing on death. If you died within three years of making a chargeable transfer, additional tax was payable to bring the charge on it up to the scale applicable on death. This rule still applied where death was within three years of a pre-18 March 1986 gift.

In general terms, if you made a chargeable transfer, you had two options. Either you paid the tax yourself, based on the value of the transfer plus the tax; or the recipient paid your tax, calculated on the transfer value excluding the tax. If you gave cash, however, you could deduct the tax from the amount given.

Inheritance tax is charged according to the following table (20.5.1) which applies to *chargeable transfers* and property passing on death after 9 March 1992. For 1991–92, the threshold was £140,000 for 1990–91 £128,000 and for 1989–90 £118,000, prior to which it was £110,000. (From 17 March 1987 to 14 March 1988 a far less favourable scale applied — 25.6.) There is only one scale but lifetime gifts which are not PETs (20.3) are charged at 50 per cent of the rate. This applies basically to transfers into discretionary settlements, charges on such settlements (20.31.2) and chargeable transfers arising from close company transactions. Tax is paid on such transfers soon after they are made, cumulating them with others within the previous seven years to calculate the amount. If death occurs within seven years, however, tax is adjusted using the full rates, with possible tapering relief (20.6) where death is later than three years after the transfer. However, the adjustment does not operate to reduce the original tax.

On death within seven years of a PET (20.3) inheritance tax must be calculated by treating it as a *chargeable transfer* and cumulating with any earlier chargeable transfers within seven years of the PET. Tax is calculated using the value of the gift when made but using the scale current at the date of death. On gifts more than three years before death, some tapering relief will be available (20.6).

20.5.1 Table: Inheritance tax rate after 9 March 1992

Slice of cumulative chargeable transfers	Cumulative total	% on slice	Cumulative total tax
The first £150,000	£150,000	Nil	£Nil
The remainder		40	

In general, the current rate scale applies to chargeable transfers and on deaths after 9 March 1992. Previously the rate scales have been modified periodically. Each time the burden has been slightly reduced. The full tables appear in Chapter 25.

On a death within three years of chargeable transfers at the old pre-18 March 1986 rates, the additional tax is found by taking the difference between the tax already paid and that payable at the new rates applying on death. Even if the tax on the new scale is less than that already paid no refund would be made in those circumstances.

20.6 Tapering relief
(ITA 1984 S7)

Where an individual dies within seven years of making a potentially exempt transfer (PET) (20.3) a proportion of the full tax is payable as follows:

Death in years	%
1–3	100
4	80
5	60
6	40
7	20

If a transfer is within the nil rate band, so that it attracts no inheritance tax, no benefit is obtained from tapering relief in that instance. Regarding those lifetime transfers which attract inheritance tax immediately at half the full rates (20.5), the tax is increased to full rates if death occurs within three years. Otherwise, the above tapering scale is applied to the rates current at death unless this produces a lower charge than that originally paid. In that case the original basis holds good.

20.7 The ten year cumulation period

FA 1981 introduced a ten year limitation on cumulations (superseded by a seven year limit from 18 March 1986). If you made a chargeable transfer it was added to all chargeable transfers which you made in the previous ten years and any made before that time dropped out. Thus suppose you gifted £50,000 in May 1974 and then nothing more until June 1984, your capital transfer tax on a gift then of £60,000 was calculated completely ignoring the earlier gift.

20.8 The seven year cumulation period
(ITA 1984 S3A)

Regarding chargeable transfers and deaths occurring after 17 March 1986, the cumulation period was reduced to seven years. This means that any transfers which you made in the three years to 17 March 1979 immediately fell out of cumulation regarding transfers after 17 March 1986.

Remember that only a limited category of transfers come into charge immediately (20.5). PETs (20.3) are only cumulated and charged to inheritance tax if you die within seven years. Then the PETs become *chargeable transfers* and are brought into cumulation with previous chargeable transfers within seven years of each PET (including the PETs within seven years of death). The estate left at death (20.15) is then added to the chargeable transfers in the last seven years in order to compute the inheritance tax on those assets.

20.9 Indexation of rate bands
(ITA 1984 S8)

For each year to 5 April, the inheritance tax rate or rates (20.5) are to apply subject to indexation. The threshold and the various rate-bands will be increased in proportion to the rise in the retail prices index from December to December and each new threshold will be rounded up to the nearest £1,000. This applies unless the Treasury otherwise directs.

20.10 Valuation
(ITA 1984 Ss160–170)

For inheritance tax purposes your assets are normally valued at their open market value at the transfer date. If the value of an asset which you keep is affected by the transfer, you will need to value your 'estate' both before and after the transfer in order to calculate its resultant fall. Your liabilities must be taken into account in valuing your total 'estate'.

20.11 Quoted securities passing on death
(ITA 1984 Ss178–189)

Relief is available where quoted securities are sold for less than their probate values within 12 months of death. This applies where any quoted shares or securities or holdings in authorised unit trusts are realised within one year of death. The persons liable to pay the inheritance tax can claim that the total of the gross sale prices should be substituted for the original probate values of the investments. Where, however, the proceeds are re-invested by those persons in quoted shares or unit trusts after the death and within two months after the last sale, the above relief may be reduced or lost.

20.12 Valuation of related property
(ITA 1984 S161)

Where the value of any of your property is less than the appropriate portion of the value of the aggregate of that and any 'related property' you must value your own property as the appropriate portion of the value of that aggregate.

'Related property' is property belonging to your spouse, which became so through an exempt transfer from you after 15 April 1976. Also included is property belonging to a charity, charitable trust, housing association, etc or which had belonged to them during the last five years which came from you or your spouse after that date.

This rule is particularly relevant to the valuation of unquoted shares. For example if you and your wife each have 40 per cent of the shares of an unquoted company, then the value of 80 per cent of the shares is normally much higher than twice the value of 40 per cent of the shares. This is because an 80 per cent holding carries with it full control of the company.

Thus the successful estate duty saving device of splitting a shareholding in a non-quoted company between your wife and yourself so that neither of you has control, is not effective (so far as the first transfer is concerned) in producing a lower aggregate value for inheritance tax purposes.

If you inherit any related property on a death after 6 April 1976, a special relief applies where you sell the property within three years of the death for less than the value on which tax was originally paid. Subject to various conditions including the requirement that the sale is at arm's length for a freely negotiated price, you can claim for the related property in question to be revalued at death on the basis that it was not related to any other property.

20.13 Land sold within three years of death
(ITA 1984 Ss190–198)

Where the person paying the capital transfer tax or inheritance tax arising on death on land or buildings sells them within three years of the death for less than their probate value, he can claim that the sale proceeds are substituted in the tax calculations. There are a number of conditions including the requirement that the shortfall is at least the lower of £1,000 and 5 per cent of the probate value of the land. Relief is extended beyond the three years regarding a compulsory purchase notified before the end of the three years.

20.14 Abolition of estate duty
(ITA 1984 Sch 6)

Estate duty does not apply for deaths occurring after 12 March 1975. For deaths prior to 13 November 1974 the old estate duty rules applied as did the rates (*Hambro Tax Guide* 1974–75, p 187). If the death occurred between those dates however, estate duty applied at the capital transfer tax rates (25.5); also the new exemption applied for transfers between husband and wife (20.18.1) and the new reliefs applied instead of the old for agricultural land (20.22) and timber (20.23).

20.15 Inheritance tax on death
(ITA 1984 S4 & FA 1986 Sch 19)

The general rule is that if you are domiciled (or deemed domiciled — 20.4) in the UK at the time of your death, all of your assets, wherever they may be situated, form part of the *gross value* of your estate for the purposes of determining the inheritance tax payable. The same applied for capital transfer tax.

If you are not domiciled in the UK at your death then the tax is only chargeable on those assets which are situated in the UK (20.29).

The *net value* of your estate is determined by making certain deductions (20.15.2) from the *gross value* of all the property passing on your death.

The tax on your death is charged as if immediately before your death you made a chargeable transfer equal to the *net value* of your estate, subject to certain adjustments and exemptions (20.16) if appropriate.

For deaths after 17 March 1986, the inheritance tax rules apply and the tax is calculated from the single scale taking account of your cumulative lifetime gifts within *seven* years of death. These gifts include PETs (20.3) on which no tax was previously paid. As previously explained, death may lead not only to tax on the estate but also on lifetime gifts (20.6).

Prior to 18 March 1986 the tax payable was calculated from the special rate scale which applied at death (25.5) taking account of cumulative lifetime gifts after 26 March 1974 and within *ten* years of death to ascertain the starting level on the scale. Your executors will need to apply for probate of your will. Otherwise, if you die intestate, letters of administration must be obtained. In either case, it will be necessary for an inheritance tax account to be completed (normally on CAP Form 202 or 200). At least a provisional amount of tax will need to be paid at that time. Further administrative rules appear later in this chapter (20.25).

20.15.1 Gross value of estate
(ITA 1984 S5)

The gross value of your estate includes all your property situated anywhere in the world, such as land, shares, the goodwill of a business, debts owing to you, etc; apart from *excluded property* (20.16).

Certain other amounts must also be included in your gross estate, even though they do not belong to you or only arise after your death, such as the proceeds of a life policy held by you on your own life, or any death benefit under a pension scheme which is payable to your estate (rather than under the more usual discretionary disposal clause contained in most pension schemes).

Other amounts to be included in your gross estate are various interests in trusts (20.31). In these cases the trustees may pay the appropriate tax but the rate is calculated by reference to the value of the estate including the trust funds.

20.15.2 Net value of estate

The more common deductions which are made from the gross value of your estate in order to arrive at its net value are as follows:

(1) Certain exempt transfers (20.18.3).
(2) Funeral expenses.
(3) Debts owing by you at the date of death which are payable in the UK. However, certain debts may be disallowed in whole or part if you had made connected gifts to the creditors, or the liability had not been incurred for full consideration for your benefit. This applies to post-17 March 1986 debts (FA 1986 S82).

(4) Debts due to persons outside the UK are normally only deductible from the value of assets situated outside this country.
(5) Whilst legal and other professional fees owing at the death may be deducted as debts, no deduction is given for probate and executors' expenses.
(6) Liabilities for income tax and capital gains tax up to the time of death, whether or not assessments were made before that time. No deduction can be made for capital transfer tax or inheritance tax payable on your death, however, nor can tax liabilities be deducted regarding income and capital gains arising for periods subsequent to your death.

20.16 Excluded property
(ITA 1984 S6)

The following 'excluded property' must be left out of the value of your estate for capital transfer tax and inheritance tax purposes, regarding both lifetime transfers and property passing on death:

(1) Property outside the UK if you are neither domiciled nor deemed domiciled in this country.
(2) A reversionary interest unless either you bought it or it relates to the falling in of a lease which was treated as a settlement (20.31). Certain anti-avoidance rules apply to prevent misuse.
(3) Cash options under approved retirement pension schemes (24.12.1), provided an annuity becomes payable to your dependants instead of the cash option itself.
(4) Certain UK government securities on which interest may be paid gross to non-residents (8.2), provided you are neither domiciled, deemed domiciled, nor ordinarily resident here.
(5) Certain overseas pensions from former colonies, etc including death payments and returns of contributions.
(6) Savings such as national savings certificates and premium bonds, if you are domiciled in the Channel Islands or the Isle of Man.
(7) Certain property in this country belonging to visiting forces and NATO headquarters staff.

20.17 Double taxation relief
(ITA 1984 Ss158 & 159)

Various other countries also operate systems of capital transfer tax/inheritance tax and the government of the UK is empowered to enter into agreements with them for the avoidance of the double payment of such tax both here and in the other country.

Concerning capital transfer tax or inheritance tax payable on death, relief is continued for estate duty payable on the same property in other countries if there was a 'double estate duty' agreement with the countries in question as at 12 March 1975. The following countries have agreements with the UK covering estate duty and/or capital transfer tax or inheritance tax:

France	Pakistan
India	South Africa
Ireland	Sweden
Italy	Switzerland
Netherlands	United States of America

Unilateral double taxation relief is available for overseas tax paid on death or a lifetime transfer. The tax must be of a similar nature to inheritance tax and if the property is situated in the overseas country, a credit is given against the UK tax of the amount of the overseas tax. If the property is either situated *both* in the UK and the overseas country, or in *neither* of those places, the credit against the UK tax is $C \times A/(A+B)$. A is the amount of capital transfer tax or inheritance tax, B is the overseas tax and C is the smaller of A and B.

20.18 Exempt transfers
(ITA 1984 Ss18–27)

Broadly, exempt transfers can be divided between those which apply both on death and during your life and those which are only exempt if the transfers are during your life. The first category includes transfers between your wife and yourself.

20.18.1 Transfers between husband and wife

Transfers between your wife and yourself both during your lives and on death were exempt from capital transfer tax and are exempt from inheritance tax. (Thus lifetime gifts are not even treated as PETs — 20.3). This exemption also applied for estate duty purposes on deaths after 12 November 1974. Similarly lifetime gifts between your wife and yourself prior to 27 March 1974 were outside the capital transfer tax net provided the donor survived 12 November 1974.

Full exemption does not apply, however, if the recipient of the property is not domiciled (or deemed domiciled) in this country (15.2) (unless the donor is also neither domiciled nor deemed domiciled here). In this case, only the first £55,000 (£50,000 prior to 9 March 1982 and £25,000 prior to 26 March 1980) transferred to the non-domiciled spouse is exempt. This resembles the previous estate duty relief.

Under the estate duty rules, if you left property in trust for your wife for life, when you died duty was paid; but none was payable on her subsequent death. (If her death is after 12 November 1974, no capital transfer tax or inheritance tax applies.) If, however, the first death occurs after 12 November 1974, the new relief applies and so no tax is payable on property passing to the surviving spouse. For this reason, when the latter dies, full inheritance tax is payable on the trust property.

20.18.2 Exempt transfers—Lifetime gifts

The following transfers are only exempt if made by an individual during his life. They do not normally apply to transfers made by trustees nor to assets passing on death. In any one fiscal year to 5 April, you can make all of these exempt transfers cumulatively and so can your wife. From 18 March 1986 the rules apply not only to chargeable transfers but also to PETs (20.3). Thus if a transfer which would otherwise be a PET is an exempt transfer, it will not attract inheritance tax, even if you die within seven years.

(1) *Transfers each year up to a value of £3,000.* (Prior to 6 April 1981 the limit was £2,000.) If you do not use up the full £3,000 allowance in one year, you can carry the unused part forward for one year only. If your transfers taken against this exemption reach £3,000 in one year, you have nothing available to carry forward, even though you may have had £3,000 carried forward from the previous year.
For example if you made no chargeable transfers in the year to 5 April 1992, you have £6,000 available for exempt

transfers under this category in the year to 5 April 1993. If, however, you transferred £500 in the year to 5 April 1992 you have £2,500 carried forward and so can transfer £5,500 in the year to 5 April 1993.

A special allocation rule (FA 1986 Sch 19) applies from 18 March 1986. In any year to 5 April, your annual exemption first reduces those lifetime transfers which are not PETs; and then your PETs. (Deaths within seven years may cause the re-allocation of your annual exemptions, particularly regarding amounts originally set against your 'non-PETs' for the following year.)

(2) *Small gifts.* Outright gifts to any one person not exceeding £250 for each year to 5 April are exempt. The £250 exemption cannot be used against gifts larger than that amount. Thus you can make an unlimited number of exempt gifts of £250 to different people but any gifts of £251 or more must be set against the £3,000 and other exemptions with the excess being potentially taxable (if the nil rate band has been exhausted).

(3) *Normal expenditure out of income.* To qualify under this exemption, a transfer must be part of your normal expenditure. This means that there must be an element of regularity. Life assurance premiums (24.4) are particularly suited for this. Further conditions are that the transfer is out of your after-tax income and you are left with enough income to maintain your usual standard of living.

Life policy premium payments will not qualify for this exemption, however, if they are made out of an annuity purchased on your life, unless you can show that the policy and the annuity were effected completely independently of each other. This rule even applies if you make gifts out of your annuity receipts and the donee pays the premiums on the policy on your life.

If you buy an annuity, and make transfers from it, only the income proportion of the annuity (24.14.2) is treated as your income for the purposes of the normal expenditure rule, the capital element is not.

(4) *Gifts in consideration of marriage* made to one of the partners of the marriage or settled on the partners and their children, etc. The limits are £5,000 if the donor is a parent of one of the marriage partners, £2,500 if a grandparent or great-grandparent or one of the parties themselves, or otherwise £1,000. (Eligibility for relief extends to marriage gifts from settlements where an interest in possession ends (20.31).)

20.18.3 Other exempt transfers

Subject to the particular rules, the following transfers are exempt both if made during your life and on death. They also apply to trusts (20.31).

(1) *Transfers in the course of trade, etc* are exempt if allowed as deductions in computing the profits for income tax purposes (10.3). This applies equally to professions and vocations, as well as allowable deductions against other forms of profits or gains for the purposes of income tax and corporation tax.

(2) *Gifts to charities* after 14 March 1983 are exempt without limit. If made before 15 March 1983 and on or within a year of death, however, the first £250,000 of gifts were exempt (£200,000 before 9 March 1982 and £100,000 before 26 March 1980). Gifts to settlements for charitable purposes are covered by the exemption, as are gifts to charities from other trusts.

(3) *Gifts to political parties* after 14 March 1988 (FA 1988 S137) are wholly exempt. Prior to 15 March 1988, the exemption was limited to £100,000 for gifts made within one year of death. For these purposes, a 'political party' is one with at least two members sitting in Parliament or one member and not less than 150,000 votes for its candidates at the last General Election.

(4) *Gifts for national purposes, etc* made to the National Trust, National Heritage Memorial Fund, National Gallery, British Museum and similar organisations including universities and their libraries as well as museums and art galleries maintained by local authorities or universities.

(5) *Gifts for public benefit* of property deemed by the Treasury to be of outstanding scenic, historic, scientific or artistic merit including land, buildings, pictures, books, manuscripts, works of art, etc.

(6) *PETs (20.3) of property held for national purposes, etc.* This exemption applies where, prior to the death of the recipient, the property is sold by private treaty (or gifted) to an organisation as mentioned in (4) above.

(7) *Gifts of shares* to an employee trust provided it will then hold at least half of the ordinary shares of the company (FA 1978 S67).

(8) *Gifts to housing associations* or sales of land to them at undervalue after 13 March 1989 (FA 1989 S171).

20.19 Relief for business property
(ITA 1984 Ss103–114, FA 1986 Ss105–106 & Sch 19, FA 1987 S58 & Sch 8 & F2A 1992 Sch 14)

In general, 'relevant business property' qualifies for business property relief. 'Relevant business property' includes a business or part of a business; shares owned by the controller of a company; unquoted minority shareholdings and land, buildings, plant and machinery used in your partnership or a company which you control. Control of a company for these purposes includes shareholdings which are 'related property' (20.12) in relation to your own shares.

In general, investment company and land or share-dealing company shareholdings do not qualify for the relief. However, UK stockjobbing and from October 1986 'market making' qualify for the relief. You must normally own the business property, or property which has directly replaced it for at least two years prior to the transfer or else it is not 'relevant business property' and so no relief is due.

The rates of relief are 100 per cent and 50 per cent. Prior to 10 March 1992 the relief was 50 per cent and 30 per cent.

Relief is available as follows (pre-10 March 1992 figures in brackets):

(1) The whole or part of a business — 100 per cent (50 per cent).
(2) Quoted company shares to be valued on a control basis — 50 per cent (50 per cent).
(3) Property transferred by you which is used in a trade by a company controlled by you or partnership in which you are a partner — 50 per cent (30 per cent).
(4) Holding in an unquoted trading company:—
     Over 25 per cent   100 per cent (50 per cent)
     25 per cent or less without
     control   50 per cent (30 per cent)
(5) Holding in a USM company:—
     Controlling   100 per cent (50 per cent)
     Over 25 per cent   100 per cent (nil).
     25 per cent or less without control   50 per cent (nil).

The 50 per cent relief category is extended to cover the transfer of land or buildings owned by a trust. Immediately before the transfer, the assets must have been used in his own trade by a person beneficially entitled to an interest in possession in the trust.

Business property relief is available against PETs which fall into charge following the donor's death within seven years. However, the relief is lost if the recipient disposes of the property before the donor's death. But relief is not lost if the gifted business property is disposed of, but replaced by other qualifying assets within one year. Also, the property must remain 'relevant business property' during the seven year period. If these conditions are satisfied for only part of the property, the relief is proportionately reduced. These rules also apply to other lifetime transfers within seven years of death.

Where part of an estate is left to the surviving spouse and thus attracts no tax, and part to others, the allocation of business property relief and relief for agricultural property (20.22) was open to abuse. However, from 18 March 1986 specific gifts of such property must be reduced by the relief. Otherwise, the relief is spread proportionately over the estate.

20.20 Waivers of dividends and remuneration
(ITA 1984 Ss14 & 15)

If you waive any remuneration to which you are entitled this normally does not produce any capital transfer tax or inheritance tax liability, provided the amount waived would otherwise have been assessable to income tax under Schedule E (9.1) and your employer obtains no income tax or corporation tax relief for the waived remuneration.

No inheritance tax (or capital transfer tax) accrues on the waiver of any dividend to which you have a right, provided you waive the dividend within the 12 months before it is due.

The above waiver rules apply from the inception of capital transfer tax.

20.21 Conditional exemption for certain objects and buildings, etc
(ITA 1984 Ss27, 78–79 Sch 4, FA 1985 Ss94–95 & Sch 26 & FA 1987 Sch 9)

Property similar to that mentioned in (4) and (5) above (20.18.3), is exempted from inheritance tax (and capital transfer tax) on death provided the recipient undertakes to keep it in the country, preserve it and allow reasonable access to the public. If it is later sold the tax is payable unless the sale is to an institution such as the British Museum, National Gallery or National Trust.

A similar relief applies to lifetime transfers subject to various conditions. The recipient must give the required undertaking. The relief extends to historical and artistic buildings and objects comprised in settlements. It also applies to settlements set up to maintain historic buildings and now objects historically associated with them, together with land of outstanding interest. Such settlements must tie up the capital for at least six years for maintenance purposes only. But after that funds may be withdrawn subject to inheritance tax in certain circumstances.

Special rules apply regarding maintenance settlements for approved objects and buildings etc. Provided the Board of the Inland Revenue (previously the Treasury) are satisfied that the trusts and trustees comply with certain requirements, transfers to such a settlement are exempt (20.18.3) for inheritance purposes. In general the trust funds must be used for the maintenance of approved assets for at least six years.

From 17 March 1987, the exemption applies where someone with a life interest in a trust dies and within two years the property goes into a heritage maintenance fund. Heritage property can be offered in lieu of inheritance tax and, from that date, there is the option of calculating the value of the property at the date of the offer instead of acceptance.

Land is exempted which is essential to a building of historic or architectural interest. Previously exemption depended on the land touching the building, but this is no longer necessary.

20.22 Relief for agricultural property
(ITA 1984 Ss115–124, FA 1986 S105 & Sch 19 & F2A 1992 Sch 14)

Under the rules which apply after 9 March 1981 you must have either occupied the property for the purposes of agriculture for at least two years before transferring it, or owned it for seven years up to that time, with others farming. The rules are relaxed where you inherit the property or where you have replaced one agricultural property by another. Agriculture now includes stud farming for the purposes of the relief (FA 1984 S107).

Before 10 March 1981, the relief applied to transfers on death and lifetime transfers by 'working farmers'. To qualify you must have been mainly or wholly engaged in agriculture as a farmer, farm worker or student in five of the seven preceding years. The relief applied to land including farmhouses and buildings occupied for farming by you for at least two years before the transfer.

The relief is 100 per cent if you enjoy the right to vacant possession or can obtain this within the next 12 months. Otherwise, the relief is normally 50 per cent, which applies to tenanted situations, etc. Prior to 10 March 1992, the rates were 50 per cent and 30 per cent. If you qualified for the higher relief under the old but not the new rules, you still obtain this regarding property held at 9 March 1981 and transferred after that date, up to the old limit of £250,000 or 1,000 acres if more valuable. The excess is then relieved at the lower rate which is now 50 per cent.

The grant of a tenancy of agricultural property is not to be treated as a transfer of value if it is made for full consideration (FA 1981 S97).

From 18 March 1986, similar new rules to those for business property relief apply regarding lifetime gifts within seven years of death and the allocation of relief to partially exempt estates (20.19).

20.23 Woodlands
(ITA 1984 Ss125–130)

Inheritance tax relief against the charge at death on growing timber is available, provided you either owned the woodlands for at least five years, or you acquired them by gift or inheritance.

Under the relieving provisions, provided the inheritor elects within two years of it, tax is not charged on your death. If, however, before the recipient dies, the timber is sold or given away, tax is charged on the proceeds or value of the gift. The tax rate is found by adding such proceeds to the estate at your death. Remember that the relief applies only to the timber and not the land on which it grows. However, the land may qualify for business property relief.

Where the disposal follows a change in tax rates the respective new rates (25.5) are applied, even if the death was before they took effect.

20.24 Quick succession relief
(ITA 1984 S141)

This relief applies to reduce the tax payable on death where the deceased himself received chargeable transfers on which the tax was paid within five years of his death. The deduction is broadly a proportion of the original tax, being 100 per cent, 80 per cent, 60 per cent, 40 per cent or 20 per cent, depending on whether the period between the transfer and the death is one, two, three, four or five years or less in each case. Where there are more than two transfers of the same property within five years of each other, special rules apply.

20.25 Administration and collection
(ITA 1984 Ss215–261, etc & FA 1986 Sch 18)

Inheritance tax (and capital transfer tax) are under the care and management of the Board of the Inland Revenue. Generally speaking the rules for administration, appeals and penalties resemble those for income tax (14.8.2).

Chargeable transfers must be reported to the Inland Revenue within 12 months from the end of the month of transfer or death.

As for estate duty, tax chargeable on death must be paid on at least an estimated figure before probate is granted (20.15). Inheritance tax (and capital transfer tax) on death are now payable out of the residuary estate unless there is a contrary direction in the will. However, property situated outside the UK continues to bear its own tax. Recipients of PETs are primarily responsible for the relevant tax.

Interest on unpaid tax runs from when the tax is due. The due date is six months after the end of the month in which death occurs. For lifetime transfers it is six months after the end of the month in which the transfer is made. In the case of transfers between 5 April and 1 October, the due date is 30 April in the following year. From 16 December 1986, there is a single rate of interest on overdue inheritance tax of 8 per cent reducing to 6 per cent from 6 June 1987 and increasing to 9 per cent from 6 October 1988. From 6 July 1989, the rate is 11 per cent, with 10 per cent applying from 6 March 1991, 9 per cent from 6 May 1991 and 8 per cent from 6 July 1991.

From 1 May 1985 to 16 December 1986, interest ran on overdue capital transfer tax at 9 per cent on death and 11 per cent on other transfers. These rates applied for inheritance tax purposes with 9 per cent for PETs. Between 30 November 1982 and 1 May 1985 the rate of interest was 6 per cent for transfers on death and 8 per cent otherwise. Prior to 1 December 1982 the respective interest rates were 9 per cent and 12 per cent, whilst before 1 January 1980 they were 6 per cent and 9 per cent. This interest is not deductible for income tax purposes. If you overpay inheritance tax or capital transfer tax you will get non-taxable interest at the same rates, up to the date on which the repayment of the excess tax is made.

20.26 Payment by instalments of tax on death
(ITA 1984 Ss227–229, FA 1986 Sch 19 & F2A 1992 Sch 14)

Capital transfer tax or inheritance tax on death on certain assets may be paid by annual instalments over ten years. (For deaths before 15 March 1983, instalments were yearly or half-yearly but limited to an eight-year period.) This applies to land and buildings, controlling holdings of shares in companies and certain other unquoted shares, as well as business assets. From 10 March 1992, shares dealt in on the USM are included. (PETs which become chargeable only qualify for the instalments basis if the recipient had kept the property until the death of the donor.)

Instalments paid on time concerning the shares and business assets mentioned above are free of interest. Land and buildings qualify for this relief only if they are held as business assets, otherwise interest is payable, currently at 9 per cent. A limit of £250,000 of assets qualifying for this relief existed before 10 March 1981 but was then removed completely. After 9 March 1981, tax in respect of property qualifying for the new agricultural relief may be paid in interest free instalments as above.

20.27 Payment of tax on lifetime gifts by instalments

The above provisions apply to lifetime transfers if the donee bears the tax and for settled property which is retained in a settlement. If interest is payable it is currently at 9 per cent. The interest free category is extended to include lifetime disposals of timber. In the case of minority holdings of unquoted shares, these must be worth at least £20,000, in order to qualify for the instalments option; also being at least 10 per cent holdings. The instalments basis may also be allowed where paying the tax in one sum would cause undue hardship and the recipient keeps the shares.

20.28 Inheritance tax and life assurance

If you effect a policy on your life for your own benefit, the proceeds payable on your death will be taxable as part of your net estate.

You may, however, effect a policy in a non-discretionary trust for some other person or persons, such as for example your wife and children. In this case the policy proceeds will not be paid into your own estate but will be paid to the trustees for the beneficiaries. Each premium payment, however, will constitute a separate potentially exempt transfer (20.3) by you. Thus they could be taxable if you die within seven years, unless an exemption applies such as the £3,000 or £250 reliefs (20.18.2), or the normal expenditure rule (20.18.2), or the policy is for your wife. If premiums are paid to a discretionary trust, each premium will be chargeable at the time and if no exemption applies, may give rise to recalculation of tax if death occurs within seven years.

Furthermore, for policies effected after 17 March 1986, the gifts with reservation rules (20.30.4) may apply. Broadly if you have a retained benefit in the policy the proceeds will form part of your estate at death.

If someone else effects a policy on your life and pays the premiums, then the proceeds are not taxable on your death. This is known as a 'life of another' policy. If the person who effects the policy predeceases you, however, then the surrender value of the policy at the date of death of that person is normally included in his taxable estate. Please refer to Chapter 24 for further details concerning this subject.

20.29 Property outside Great Britain

Since if you are neither domiciled nor deemed domiciled (20.4) in the UK, you will only normally pay inheritance tax (or capital transfer tax) on your assets situated here, it is important to ascertain the situation of particular property. The situation of property for inheritance tax purposes is normally deemed to be as follows:

(1) Cash — its physical location.
(2) Bank accounts — the location of the bank or branch (see also below).
(3) Registered securities — the location of the share register.
(4) Bearer securities — the location of the title documents.
(5) Land and buildings — their actual location.
(6) Business assets — the place where the business is conducted.
(7) Debts — the residence of the debtor.

Regarding deaths after 8 March 1982 foreign currency accounts with UK banks are exempted from capital transfer tax and inheritance tax if the deceased is not UK domiciled. This also applies if the deceased had an interest in possession (20.31) in a settlement with such an account, unless the settlor was UK domiciled, resident or ordinarily resident, when he made the settlement or the trustees were so situated immediately before the death. (ITA 1984 S158.)

20.30 Miscellaneous points

20.30.1 Close companies
(ITA 1984 Ss94–102 & FA 1986 Sch 19)

There are rules under which inheritance tax may be charged where a close company (12.17) makes a transfer of value. Broadly, tax may be charged on the company as if each of the participators (12.17.3) had made a proportionate transfer according to his or her interest in the company. The rules are extended to cover close companies being owned by trusts or being their beneficiaries.

Transfers of values arising as above from alterations in the capital and associated rights in a close company may attract inheritance tax at once. They are not PETs (20.3).

20.30.2 Free loans
(ITA 1984 S29)

From 6 April 1976 to 5 April 1981, subject to various exceptions, if you allowed someone else the use of money or property at no interest or less than the market rate, you were treated as making a chargeable transfer for each year to 5 April that the arrangement continued. The amount of the chargeable transfer was the shortfall of the interest (less tax), or other benefit which you got, compared with the market rate. These taxing provisions ceased to have effect after 5 April 1981 although interest-free loans for a fixed stated period can still be treated as a chargeable transfer under general principles.

20.30.3 Associated operations
(ITA 1984 S268)

Special rules enable the Revenue to treat two or more transactions related to a certain property as forming one 'chargeable transfer'. Where transactions at different times are treated as associated operations, the chargeable transfer is treated as taking place at the time of the last of these transactions.

20.30.4 Gifts with reservation
(FA 1986 S102 & Sch 20)

If you make a gift after 17 March 1986 but reserve some benefit, this will normally result in the property remaining yours for inheritance tax purposes on your death. (This could also apply if you later enjoy the benefit of the gifted property.) However, if you subsequently release the reservation, you will be treated as making a PET (20.3) or chargeable transfer at that time. In contrast to PETs, the Capital Taxes Office may require a return to be made for a gift with reservation.

A particular example is where you gift a house but remain living there. The rule does not apply if your benefit is minimal (eg you do not live in the house but only pay occasional visits). If you give full value for any benefit (eg pay a full rent for the house), the rule is also set aside. There is also an exception where the reservation represents reasonable provision by a relative for the care and maintenance of an elderly or infirm donor whose circumstances have changed since making the gift.

The rules do not normally catch regular premium insurance policies made before 18 March 1986 and not altered since then.

20.30.5 Family maintenance
(ITA 1984 S11)

If you make any of the following gifts during your life, they are exempt:

(1) For the maintenance, education, etc of your child, former wife or illegitimate child.
(2) For the maintenance or education of a child not in his parent's care, who has been in your care during substantial periods of his minority.
(3) For the care or maintenance of a dependent relative.

20.30.6 Deeds of family arrangement
(ITA 1984 S17)

Deed of variation

Inheritance tax is not charged on certain variations in the destination of property passing on death. Nor is it charged on the disclaimer of title to property passing on death. The variation or disclaimer must be within two years of the death. An election to the Revenue is required within six months of a variation.

This exemption operates similarly, but without time limit, where a surviving spouse's life interest under an intestacy is redeemed. It also applies if an interest in settled property is disclaimed unless there is some consideration in money or money's worth.

Disclaimers are effective for inheritance tax purposes. These involve one or more beneficiaries disclaiming their entitlement. As a result, the assets return to the estate and are dealt with according to the directions of the will or as on intestacy.

20.31 Settled property
(ITA 1984 Pt III & FA 1984 Ss102–104, FA 1986 Sch 19 & F2A 1987 S96 & Sch 7)

The rules concerning inheritance tax (and previously capital transfer tax) in relation to settled property are most detailed and the following are just a few guidelines:

(1) Broadly any settlement is subject to the inheritance tax rules on its world-wide assets, if at the time it was made the settlor was domiciled in the UK. Otherwise only assets situated in this country (20.29) are caught.

(2) The settlement of any property after 26 March 1974 is itself treated as a chargeable transfer by the settlor. However, after 17 March 1986, settlements on accumulation and maintenance trusts (20.31.1) or for the disabled are classified as PETs (20.3). Thus any property which you settle in this way only attracts inheritance tax if you die within seven years.

(3) If you have an interest in possession in any settled property for the time being (eg you receive the income as of right), the property itself is treated as yours for inheritance tax purposes. Thus if your interest ends, you will be treated as making a transfer of the value of the property concerned. The tax is calculated on the basis of your cumulative transfers to that time. You can deduct your £3,000 annual exemption (20.18.2) and marriage allowance if applicable (ITA S57).

(4) From 17 March 1987 lifetime transactions involving interest in possession settlements are classed as PETs. This covers gifts setting them up, transfers out and changes in the beneficial interests.

(5) No inheritance tax is payable if you obtain an absolute interest in property in which you previously had a life interest (or other interest in possession). Similarly, tax normally is not payable on the reversion to you in your lifetime (or your spouse within two years of your death) of property which you previously settled. However, after 8 March 1982 this rule normally no longer applies to discretionary settlements (20.31.2).

(6) Special rules apply to trusts where there is no interest in possession—particularly discretionary trusts, etc and accumulation and maintenance settlements (20.31.1).

(7) Quick succession relief is given if an interest in possession comes to an end within five years of a previous chargeable transfer of the settled property. The relief is now allowed against the tax due on the later transfer, etc but is calculated as a *percentage of the tax payable* on the first transfer. The percentage is 100 per cent, 80 per cent, 60 per cent, 40 per cent or 20 per cent where the interval is not more than one, two, three, four, or five years respectively.

(8) Superannuation schemes and charitable trusts are normally exempted from inheritance tax as are employee and newspaper trusts (ITA Ss76, 86 & 87); also certain 'protective trusts' and trusts for the mentally disabled (treated as having a life interest in property settled for them after 9 March 1981). Where property is held temporarily on such trusts, the tax charge is proportionately reduced on a time basis (FA 1984 S102).

20.31.1 Accumulation and maintenance settlements

Accumulation and maintenance settlements with no fixed interests in possession for one or more beneficiaries up to an age not exceeding 25 are not subjected to the periodic charge (20.31.2); nor is inheritance tax charged on the capital distributed to those beneficiaries. This relief covers for example a settlement under which your son obtains an interest in possession at the age of 25 and at 35 gets the capital, the income being accumulated up to 25 apart from various payments for his maintenance. No inheritance tax is payable during the currency of the trust, nor when your son becomes entitled to the income at 25 nor the capital at 35.

Relief broadly only applies if either not more than 25 years have passed since the original settlement date (or when it first became accumulating); or if all beneficiaries are grandchildren of a common grandparent (or their widows, widowers, children, step-children, etc).

Any payments into accumulation and maintenance settlements after 17 March 1986 are PETs (20.3). Thus no inheritance tax can be payable regarding their creation unless the settlor dies within seven years.

20.31.2 Discretionary trusts, etc

The following rules apply where there is no interest in possession in *all or part of the property*.

(1) The principal charge to inheritance tax (previously capital transfer tax) is the *periodic* charge. This usually falls on every tenth anniversary of the date of the settlement occurring after 31 March 1983. (Where a transfer requiring court proceedings was made in the year to 31 March 1983, the onset of the periodic charge was delayed until after that date.) The charge is at 30 per cent of the life-time capital transfer tax rate which would apply to the assets held on discretionary trusts (taking the N/40ths fraction for additions during the ten year period — see (3) below). For inheritance tax purposes you take 30 per cent of half the full rates. In calculating the rates of tax which apply, you must accumulate transfers made by the settlor in the seven years immediately prior to the creation of the settlement and other settlements made by him on the same day; but this does not apply to a pre-26 March 1974 trust. For periodic charges before 18 March 1986, you needed to accumulate transfers by the settlor in the *ten* years before the creation of the settlement.

(2) For a settlement made between 26 March 1974 and 9 March 1982, distributions of capital made in the preceding ten years are taken into account in calculating the rate of tax on the first periodic charge. An exemption applies for transfers to charities and benevolent funds for employees (this also applies to pre-27 March 1974 trusts).

(3) Interim charges are made on distributions of capital to beneficiaries between periodic charges, but only N/40ths of the full tax is charged on each distribution. (N is the number of completed three month periods for which the property has been held on discretionary trusts during the current ten year period — see (1) above.)

(4) Previously, tax was charged on the value of the trust property leaving the trust. However, after 8 March 1982, the charge is based on the reduction in the value of trust property, which could be greater.

(5) If property becomes settled under a will or intestacy it is taken to enter the settlement at death. Where the death is after 12 March 1984 any such property which is distributed within two years of death to a charity, employee trust, etc is treated as if distributed at the time of death (FA 1984 S103).

(6) Property passing directly from one discretionary settlement to another is treated as remaining in the first for the purposes of the discretionary settlement rules. However, after 14 March 1983 this does not apply to certain reversionary interests existing before 10 December 1981 (FA 1984 S104).

(7) Prior to 9 March 1982, special rules applied to non-resident trustees although these would not normally have come into force until after 31 March 1983. Now, however, the previously planned annual charge does not operate and non-resident trustees are liable for the periodic ten-year charge (see above).

(8) *Transitional relief* was given for capital distributions before 1 April 1983 out of pre-27 March 1974 settlements. A percentage only of the full tax was charged on such reorganisations or capital distributions.

(9) Transfers into discretionary settlements are charged to tax at half the rates applicable at death. If death occurred within three years and the original transfer was before 18 March 1986, the tax is increased by using the full rates at death (20.5.1). Subsequent to that date, if death occurs broadly within five years of a post-17 March 1986 transfer, the tax is likely to be increased, subject to tapering relief (20.6). 100 per cent of tax at full rates is due if death is within three years of the transfer, 80 per cent in the fourth year and 60 per cent in the fifth year.

20.32 Mutual and voidable transfers
(ITA 1984 Ss148–150 & FA 1986 Sch 19)

Complicated rules were introduced which referred back to periods before the 1976 Finance Act was passed, as well as after. Broadly, the object was to relieve both the giver and receiver from capital transfer tax where the receiver later returned the property, etc concerned to the original giver. (A similar rule is found in ITA 1984 S150 concerning voidable transfers.)

From 27 March 1980, anti-avoidance rules operated to prevent capital transfer tax being saved by *gifts back*, where the original gift had obtained business property (20.19) or agricultural property relief (20.22). Those reliefs were ignored in the calculations. Also savings from exploiting the rules for valuing life assurance policies in conjunction with gifts back were blocked.

The above rules concerning exemptions for mutual transfers have been abolished where the donee's transfer (the gift back) is after 17 March 1986.

20.33 Avoiding double charges
(FA 1986 S104)

Rules were introduced to prevent double charges to inheritance tax on transfers of value and other events occurring after 17 March 1986. The rules in part take the place of the previous rules (20.32) regarding mutual transfers. The situations covered include where a PET (20.3) becomes chargeable and immediately before the death the estate includes property acquired from the person who received the PET for less than full price.

20.34 Example: Calculation of inheritance tax payable

Mr A, having made no gifts relevant for capital transfer tax or inheritance tax, gives £56,000 to his son on 30 June 1989 and £100,000 to his wife on 15 September 1989. He dies on 31 May 1992 leaving an estate valued at £370,000, including £50,000 to his wife, £30,000 to charity and the remainder to his son, including his controlling interest in a family company valued at £120,000.

Inheritance tax is payable as follows:

30 June 1989 — gift to son		£56,000
Less Annual exemption 1988–89 brought forward	£3,000	
Annual exemption 1989–90	3,000	6,000
Potentially exempt (20.3)		£50,000
15 September 1989 — gift to wife is exempt provided she is UK domiciled (15.2)		
	£	£
Estate at death 31 May 1992		370,000
Less Bequests free of inheritance tax:		
To wife	50,000	
To charity	30,000	80,000
		290,000
Less business property relief (20.19)		
100% × £120,000		120,000
		170,000
Potentially exempt transfer 30 June 1989		50,000
		£220,000
Inheritance tax on £220,000 : £150,000	Nil	—
£70,000	40%	£ 28,000

21 An outline of VAT

21.1 Introduction

VAT was introduced into the UK on 1 April 1973 with an original rate of 10 per cent. A rate of 15 per cent replaced the previous 8 per cent standard rate and $12\frac{1}{2}$ per cent higher rate on 18 June 1979. The rate was increased to $17\frac{1}{2}$ per cent from 1 April 1991. All other countries now in the European Economic Community have introduced a similar tax and the coverage, but not the rates, has been (at least in theory) harmonised. It is beyond the scope of this book to give more than a brief outline of the provisions of VAT.

VAT in the UK is imposed:

(1) on imports of goods by any person into the UK;
(2) on the supply (such as sale, hire and HP) of goods and services (which together comprise virtually all supplies) by a business in the UK; and
(3) in certain circumstances the import of services by a business.

Hence the tax is payable whenever goods or services pass from one business to another or to a private consumer, although in the former case it is frequently refunded.

After the end of each accounting period for the tax (usually a period of three months) each business has to render a *return* to Customs & Excise of all its 'outputs', ie the supplies of goods and services it has made during the period to other businesses or to consumers; and has to account to Customs & Excise one month after the end of the period for VAT on the prices (before tax) of those outputs. Each business is, at the same time, normally allowed a credit for the VAT on its 'inputs' in that period, ie goods imported by it and goods and services supplied to it for the purposes of the business. Unlike income tax or corporation tax, no distinction is made between capital or revenue inputs; the credit generally extends to the tax on its capital purchases as well as on its purchases of stock in trade.

The total tax on the inputs of a business is ascertained from the tax invoices given to it by every other business which has supplied it with goods or services. Amongst other details a typical tax invoice shows:

Goods	£100.00
VAT at 17½%	17.50
Price payable	£117.50

At the end of each accounting period the business will total all the tax invoices it has received for its inputs in that period, which it must keep for production to Customs & Excise when required, together with its vouchers for tax imports; it will also total all its outputs for the period (keeping copies of all tax invoices it has rendered to other businesses) and a typical return for an accounting period will show:

Total outputs during the period	£50,000	
VAT thereon		£8,750
Total inputs for the period	£20,000	
VAT thereon		£3,500
Balance payable to Customs & Excise		£5,250

The effect of the credit mechanism is that although VAT is charged on each business in the chain of import, production and distribution, each business in the chain gets a credit for the tax on its inputs, so that the whole tax is passed on to the consumer on the final sale to him. This is best shown by an example which uses the original 10 per cent rate for simplicity:

	Price (ex-VAT)	VAT	
Manufacturer imports raw materials	£10	£1	
Manufacturer accounts to C & E on import			£1
Manufacturer sells product to wholesaler	£100	£10	
Manufacturer accounts to C & E for VAT			£9 (10−1)

Wholesaler sells product to retailer	£150	£15	
Wholesaler accounts to C & E for VAT			£5 (15−10)
Retailer sells to consumer	£200	£20	
Retailer accounts to C & E for VAT			£5 (20−15)
Consumer bears VAT of		£20	
Customs & Excise collect			£20

This example, however, only shows how VAT is collected and borne over a series of transactions; it is not necessary to trace each item in this way, as the return at the end of each accounting period will cover all the inputs and outputs of the period. Credit for the VAT on unsold stock will have been given on its purchase and it will therefore be held tax free until sale.

Because of the credit mechanism outlined above a business does not normally bear any tax; it merely acts as a collection agency. The ultimate consumer bears all the tax, which is why VAT is described as a sales tax. The difficulty of having a retail sales tax lies in determining when the final retail sale takes place. With VAT it does not matter; if the purchaser is a VAT registered business, he will generally get credit for the tax as input tax, and if he is not he will bear it. Another advantage of the credit mechanism is that the effect is neutral between supplies which go through a number of stages and those where the supplier is vertically integrated. In both cases the tax is on the amount of the final price to the consumer.

A turnover tax charges tax on tax and therefore encourages vertical integration which is not usually in the public interest.

As will be seen later (21.3), businesses which make some 'exempt' supplies do not get credit for the VAT on their inputs relating to these supplies.

21.2 VAT in practice

All businesses (21.4), except for the very small, are normally required to be registered with Customs & Excise and they have to make returns every three months. Some businesses which are likely to have repayments of tax, however, because they make zero-rated supplies, are allowed a one-month period. The return has to be completed and the tax paid by the end of the following month. Any amounts due to you will be paid but payments made to you in error may be recovered by assessment.

If Customs & Excise unreasonably delay any repayment to you, a repayment supplement of 5 per cent of the tax or £30 (if greater) will be due. Also, you have the statutory right to claim interest on your overpayment of VAT due to the error of Customs & Excise.

Businesses with annual turnovers under £300,000 which have been registered for at least one year are able to elect for annual VAT accounting. (Between 1 July 1988 and 9 April 1991, this figure was £250,000.) They make nine equal payments on account by direct debit and a tenth balancing amount with their annual return. Another arrangement open to businesses with outstanding VAT not more than £5,000 and turnovers under £300,000 is accounting for VAT on a cash rather than an invoice basis. Again, an election is needed.

From 1 October 1992, very large taxpayers will make monthly VAT payments. This applies to those with VAT of at least £2 million for their four quarters up to 31 March 1991 and they will make VAT payments on account of the first two months each quarter.

There are penalties which may be imposed by the Courts for overdue VAT returns and payments. The penalty is £100 plus £10 for each day that failure continues. This is increased to a daily penalty of $\frac{1}{2}$ per cent of the tax due, if it gives a higher figure. As a further penalty, repayments of VAT must be refused if previous tax or returns are overdue. Naturally, far heavier penalties apply in cases involving dishonesty.

The 1985 Finance Act contains much sterner provisions to counter VAT evasion and speed up tax payment. For example, failure to pay tax on time or submit returns may involve a 'default surcharge' of up to 30 per cent of the VAT involved. This has operated from 1 October 1986. From 1 April 1992, the maximum penalty is 20 per cent.

From 16 March 1988, the penalties on late registration for VAT are varied to 10 per cent, 20 per cent and 30 per cent of the tax. These rates apply where registration is late by no more than nine months, 18 months and more than 18 months respectively.

As from April 1990, a 'serious misdeclaration penalty' operated at 30 per cent of the tax. However, from 20 March 1991, the rate was reduced to 20 per cent, with 15 per cent applying from 11 March 1992. There is a 'period of grace' extending to the due date for the next return. Also, the penalty will not normally apply where disdeclarations are compensated for in the next return, nor where the undeclared tax is less than £2,000.

Furthermore, FA 1988 S16 introduces a 15 per cent penalty on 'persistent misdeclaration resulting in understatements or overclaims'. This penalty will only be used where a person has underdeclared or over-claimed tax twice within two years and a written warning has been issued. Giving incorrect certificates of entitlement to zero-rating regarding supplies of fuel and power, new buildings or construction services will be liable to a civil penalty.

There are rules determining into which period a supply falls. For goods it is normally the date when the goods are removed or made available, and for services it is the date of performance. (There are special rules where VAT rates change). There are two exceptions. If an invoice (which must contain specified information) is issued within 14 days after that time, the date of the invoice is taken. In practice this will usually apply and the advantage is that the VAT return can be made up from the copy invoices.

The other exception is for payments in advance when it is the date of invoice or payment which counts. This is the only time payment is relevant; normally it is the invoice which matters (see below under 'Special Cases' for the position of bad debts). An arrangement can also be made with Customs & Excise to use the last day of the calendar month or of a VAT accounting period as the time of supply.

The same rules apply for determining into which period the inputs fall. Consequently, relief for input tax will normally be available before the invoice has been paid. The invoices will need to be kept as proof. The VAT return will be a summary of invoices issued and invoices received. If tax is due to Customs & Excise, it will be paid with the return. Inputs of goods and services incurred prior to registration may subsequently be recovered in certain circumstances.

Although, strictly speaking, tax on *imports* by a business is due at the date of import, prior to 1 October 1984 a business was allowed to pay the tax with the next return. From that date, the VAT is payable by the 15th of the month following importation. (Payment must be by direct debit and covered by bank guarantee.) No tax is due so long as the goods are in a bonded warehouse. From 1 June 1985, taxable persons pay no VAT on temporary imports for repair, modification etc, provided ownership does not change. Where the reverse happens, VAT on the re-import only applies to the repairs, etc plus freight and insurance.

21.3 Zero-rating and exemption

So far we have assumed that all the inputs and outputs of a business are taxable at a positive rate. Certain types of supply are treated specially either because they are 'zero-rated' or because they are 'exempt'. Details of these types are set out in Schedules 5 and 6 to the Value Added Tax Act 1983 and summaries of these Schedules are given at the end of this chapter.

If a supply is *zero-rated* this means that no tax is charged on the supply but credit is given to the supplier for all tax on his inputs relating to that supply. *Exports* of goods, for instance, are zero-rated so that these leave the country free of VAT in the UK, although they may be liable to VAT in the country into which they are imported if that country imposes a VAT. Hence, a business which exports most of its products will probably find that its returns for an accounting period show more tax on its inputs than on its outputs (the majority being zero-rated). In that event, the business can claim back the difference from Customs & Excise. Zero rating also applies to goods shipped for use as stores on a voyage or flight to a destination outside the UK, or for retail sale in transit. However, after 26 July 1990, this does not apply to private voyages and flights.

The EC requires its members to have a VAT with a similar structure although different rates are allowed. One of the reasons is that the similar treatment of imports and exports ensures equality between home-produced and imported goods.

In addition to exports, food and many other items sold within the UK (21.14) are also zero-rated.

Exemption of a supply of goods or services is not so favourable as zero-rating, for whilst this means that there is no VAT on the supply (as with zero-rating), there is no credit allowed for the corresponding tax on the inputs of the business. Thus life assurance is one of the exempt items (21.16) so that there is no tax on a premium on a life policy but the life assurance company can get no credit for the tax on those inputs which it uses for its life assurance business. This introduces a hidden tax cost to its business.

A business which supplies both taxable (including zero-rated) and exempt goods and services is a 'partly exempt' business and will have an accounting problem. When claiming credit for the tax on the inputs from Customs & Excise, it is entitled to credit for the tax on those inputs which it uses for its taxable supplies but it is not entitled to credit for the tax on those inputs which it uses for its exempt supplies. Normally, a proportion of its input tax corresponding to its taxable supplies is allowed. However, many exempt items are ignored for this purpose.

From 1 April 1987 the position has been clarified. VAT is only recoverable if attributable to:

(1) business taxable supplies;
(2) supplies outside the UK which would have been VATable or zero-rated if made here;
(3) business supplies of certain warehoused goods disregarded for VAT;
(4) overheads supporting the above.

21.4 Business

Central to the working of VAT is the definition of 'business' because the credit mechanism is applied only to a business. It is defined to include any trade, profession or vocation. It also includes clubs and associations, such as sports clubs and members' clubs. The charging of admission fees, for example by the National Trust, is also taxable as a business. VAT is not charged on subscriptions to political parties, trade unions or professional bodies.

21.5 Small traders

From 11 March 1992 a person whose taxable (including zero-rated) supplies are not more than £36,600 (previously £35,000) per annum is not liable to be registered, although he can apply to be registered voluntarily. A business is required to register if the value of taxable supplies in the past 12 months exceeded £36,600. Alternatively, registration is required if there are reasonable grounds for believing that the value of taxable supplies will exceed £36,600 in the next 30 days. Prior to 21 March 1990, different rules applied. For example, there was a quarterly registration limit (£8,000), which has been abolished.

A small trader who is not registered is in the same position as a business making only exempt supplies. He does not charge tax to his customers and has to bear any input tax.

From 1 May 1992 *deregistration* is in general allowed if Customs & Excise are satisfied that the taxable supplies for the ensuing year will not exceed £35,100 (previously £33,600).

21.6 Zero-rated supplies

A person whose supplies are all zero-rated can apply to be exempted from registration. He will not then be able to claim a refund of his input tax but he will not have to make VAT returns.

21.7 Groups and divisions of companies

A group of companies may be registered as a single business and supplies between members of the group will be ignored. The requirement that the companies should be UK resident has now been widened to include overseas companies with an established UK place of business. One company in the group is responsible for making returns for all the members of the group. Alternatively, a company which is organised in divisions can register each division separately.

Rules were introduced in 1986 allowing the Commissioners of Customs & Excise to direct that separately registered entities are treated as one for VAT purposes. This applies for companies and other traders. The object is to combat artificially splitting a single business to avoid registration.

From 1 April 1990, capital items, such as computers, land and buildings over specified value limits are excluded from the VAT self-supply charge (21.11.3), which otherwise arises when assets are transferred to a partly exempt VAT group as part of the transfer of a going concern.

An outline of VAT   359

21.8 Local authorities

Local authorities are in the position of being both in business and also carrying on non-business activities, such as welfare services. Their business activities are treated in the normal way but the input tax on any non-business activities is refunded. In this way there is no hidden tax burden in the rates.

21.9 Charities

Sales in charity shops, fêtes, coffee mornings, etc of donated goods are zero-rated if the charity is established for the relief of distress. From 1 April 1991, this applies to all charities. Apart from this, business supplies of a charity are treated in the normal way; there is no exemption for charities. Non-business supplies such as distribution of free goods are outside the tax unless they are exported when they are zero-rated. Where a branch of a charity makes business supplies, for example sales at a fête, it may be treated as a separate entity from the charity and be entitled to the £36,600 limit before it is taxable. See Zero-rating (21.14) for certain reliefs applicable to charities. The list of zero-rated items related to charities is being increased over the years. Further details may be found in VAT leaflet 701/1/87.

21.10 Retailers

Because retailers often cannot record each sale separately there are special schemes for calculating the amount of the tax which they pay. The schemes also deal with the difficulty of retailers which sell both zero-rated goods (eg, food) and standard-rated goods (eg, kitchen equipment). Details of the schemes are contained in Customs & Excise Notice No 727 and supplements describing each scheme.

21.11 Special cases

21.11.1 Motor cars

No deduction of input tax on motor cars is allowed on cars acquired for use in the business. This also applied to the acquisition of hire cars and taxis, except London-type taxis. However, from 1 August 1992, VAT is recoverable for vehicles used in their businesses by private taxi and self-drive firms and driving schools. The hire charge is available for credit as input tax. A car dealer is not affected and can claim a credit for input tax in the normal way, but if he takes a car out of stock and uses it in his own business, tax must be paid and it is not available for credit (see 'Self-supply', below). The definition of 'motor car' for this purpose excludes commercial vehicles, vans without rear side windows and vehicles accommodating only one or more than 11 persons.

Petrol supplied at below cost by companies and partnerships etc for private journeys is not allowable for VAT purposes so far as the input tax is concerned. This creates problems in computing the disallowance and from 6 April 1987 a quarterly scale corresponding to the income tax figures (9.6.5) is used for each person concerned. The company, etc is charged VAT on the scale figures which effectively cancels the appropriate input tax. The basic scale figures are as follows:

Cylinder capacity	Scale 6.4.87– 5.4.92 £	Accounting periods beginning on or after 6.4.92	
		Petrol	Diesel
Up to 1400 cc	120	125	115
1401–2000 cc	150	158	115
over 2000 cc	225	235	148

If a car is wholly used for business purposes, the scale charge does not apply; nor does it apply where a car is used entirely for private purposes, in which case input tax is not deductible.

21.11.2 Business entertainment

Input tax on business entertainment (except reasonable entertainment for overseas customers) is not deductible. From 1 August 1988, input tax on entertaining overseas customers also ceases to be deductible. Entertainment includes meals, accommodation, theatres and sporting facilities. This does not, however, prevent deduction of input tax on subsistence expenses refunded to employees.

21.11.3 Self-supply

It is advantageous for a business which makes exempt supplies to produce its own goods since no input tax will be charged for which

An outline of VAT 361

it will be unable to obtain a credit. To prevent distortion, an order charging printed stationery to tax even though supplied to oneself has been made. Thus a bank, which is exempt, printing its own stationery would be charged tax on the value of the stationery and it could not obtain relief for the tax. An order also applies to cars to prevent avoidance of the non-deduction of input tax mentioned above.

Regulations may be made to restrict the recovery of input tax on self-supplies by partly exempt businesses. Recovery will only be allowed to the extent governed by the business's partial exemption method.

Developers of certain non-residential *buildings* may be treated as making self-supplies in various circumstances. This applies where, for example, a lease is granted which is an exempt supply; also, when the developer is not a fully taxable person and occupies the building.

In such cases VAT is chargeable based on the land and taxable construction costs, subject to certain exclusions. These include where the value is less than £100,000 and where the construction was completed before 1 August 1989; also, if the freehold had already passed and the non-residential building is new.

21.11.4 Second-hand goods

Second-hand goods are chargeable to tax in the normal way, except that there are special provisions relating to cars, motorcycles, caravans, boats and outboard motors, original works of art, antiques over 100 years old, collectors' pieces, electronic organs and aircraft, which provide that VAT is payable only on the dealer's mark-up. Except in the case of cars these provisions apply only when no tax was charged on the dealer's acquisition or when tax was charged on another dealer's mark-up. Where goods are taken in part-exchange, full VAT is still payable on the new goods supplied.

21.11.5 Sales on credit

A separately disclosed credit charge is exempt from VAT.

21.11.6 Gifts

Business gifts of goods are taxable on the cost price but items costing under £10 (in aggregate) can be ignored. Gifts of services are not taxable.

21.11.7 Personal use

If a person acquires goods in the course of business and uses them for his own personal use, eg, a shopkeeper who takes goods off the shelf, tax is payable on the cost price of the goods.

21.11.8 Accommodation for directors

From 26 July 1990, VAT on repairs, refurbishments and other expenses relating to domestic accommodation provided for directors and their families will not rank as deductible input tax. This applies where the accommodation is provided by a business for domestic purposes but not to any rooms used specifically for business where a proportion of the total VAT would be deductible.

21.11.9 Bad debts

A limited relief for bad debts exists where the debtor goes bankrupt or goes into liquidation after 1 October 1978. The amount excluding VAT is claimed from the liquidator, etc and the VAT from Customs & Excise. Retailers in effect obtain bad debt relief as the special schemes are based on payments. (Relief extends beyond cases of formal insolvency.)

From 1 April 1991, the relief has become more comprehensive. Automatic bad debt relief will become available on debts which are more than one year old and have been written off in the accounts.

21.11.10 Tour operators

Previously, the services of tour operators regarding overseas package holidays were not liable to VAT in the UK. However, FA 1987 S16 introduced a special VAT margin scheme. UK based tour operators buying in services pay VAT on the margin between their buying and selling prices. This applies if the services are used in the EC, including the UK. Furthermore they are not able to recover any VAT charged by suppliers for those services.

21.12 Documentation

The legislation contained in FA 1972 and nearly all the subsequent Finance Acts is now consolidated into the Value Added Tax Act 1983. FA 1985 contains various provisions, particularly regarding enforcement, penalties and interest. Legislation in FA 1986

An outline of VAT   363

includes the private petrol rules, whilst F2A 1992 contains important provisions relating to various matters within the EC including removing fiscal frontiers (21.17). Also a large number of statutory instruments have been made under powers contained in the Acts, all of which are available from HMSO.

Detailed information is contained in the following Notices issued by Customs & Excise which are available free from any Customs & Excise VAT office:

Number
- 41 Trade Classification
- 101 Deferring duty, VAT and other charges
- 197V VAT on goods delivered from wet warehouses
- 200 Temporary importations into the European Community
- 201 Temporary imports from the European Community
- 480 Special import entry procedures: period entry
- 700 The VAT Guide
- 702 Imports and warehoused goods
- 703 Exports
- 704 Retail Exports
- 705 Personal exports of new motor vehicles
- 706 Partial Exemption
- 711 Second-hand Cars
- 712 Second-hand Works of Art, Antiques and Scientific Collections
- 713 Second-hand Motor-cycles
- 714 Young Children's Clothing and Footwear
- 717 Second-hand Caravans and Motor Caravans
- 719 Refund of VAT to 'Do-it-yourself' Builders
- 720 Second-hand Boats and Outboard Motors
- 721 Second-hand Aircraft
- 722 Second-hand Electronic Organs
- 723 Refunds of VAT in the European Community and other countries
- 724 Second-hand Firearms
- 726 Second-hand Horses and Ponies
- 727 Special Schemes for Retailers
- 731 Cash accounting
- 732 Annual accounting
- 741 International Services
- 742A Property ownership
- 742B Property development
- 744 Passenger Transport, International Freight, Ships and Aircraft

748 Extra-statutory concessions
749 Local Authorities and similar bodies

It should be emphasised that these Notices are guides, and, with the exception of No 727 and the parts of the Notices relating to second-hand goods which deal with keeping records, they do not have any legal force. Several of the Notices are supported by numerous leaflets on specific topics.

21.13 Appeals

Independent VAT tribunals deal with appeals about the matters listed below. There are tribunals in London, Edinburgh, Belfast and Manchester. The tribunal consists of a chairman who can sit alone or with one or two other members. The procedure is explained in a leaflet printed by the President of VAT Tribunals which is available from Customs & Excise VAT offices. The 1985 Finance Act (S27 & Sch 8) contains certain rules about VAT Tribunals. For example chairmen must be barristers or solicitors (advocates in Scotland) of seven years' standing.

The matters over which the tribunals have jurisdiction are as follows:

(1) Registration.
(2) Registration of groups of companies.
(3) Assessment of VAT by Customs & Excise.
(4) The amount of VAT chargeable.
(5) The amount of the deduction of input tax.
(6) Apportionment of input tax by a partly exempt person.
(7) Special schemes for retailers.
(8) The value of certain supplies.
(9) The provision of security.
(10) Repayment of VAT on certain imports.
(11) Refunds to do-it-yourself builders.
(12) Bad debt relief.
(13) Voluntary registration of a person whose turnover is below the limit.
(14) Appeals against certain Commissioners' decisions which in turn depend upon prior unappealable decisions which they made.

There is an appeal from the tribunal on a point of law (there is no appeal on a question of fact) to the High Court and from there to the Court of Appeal. There is a final appeal to the House of Lords if leave to appeal is obtained. In Scotland appeals go to the Court of Session and thence to the House of Lords.

21.14 Zero-rating

The following is a list of the important items. Full details are contained in the General Guide (VAT Notice No 700) available from Customs & Excise:

Group 1: Food   All food except pet foods, alcoholic drinks and certain food products (such as ice cream, chocolate, confectionery including cereal bars, soft drinks and potato crisps). Meals out are, however, taxable and from 1 May 1984 this includes hot take-away food and drink.
Group 2: Sewerage Services and Water   Water except for distilled water and bottled water; emptying cesspools. (Standard rated from 1 July 1990 if for industrial use — 21.15.)
Group 3: Books etc   Books, newspapers, magazines, music, maps. But diaries and stationery are taxable.
Group 4: Talking Books and tape recorders for the Blind and Handicapped and Wireless Sets for the Blind, including (from 1.4.92) their repair and maintenance.
Group 5: Newspaper Advertisements   From 1 May 1985, however, all of these items are fully taxable.
Group 6: News Services   News services supplied to newspapers. However, these are fully taxable from 1 April 1989.
Group 7: Fuel and Power   Coal, gas, domestic heating oil, electricity. (But now standard rated unless for domestic use — 21.15.)
Group 8: Construction of Buildings, etc   Sale of the freehold or grant of a lease for more than 21 years of a building by a builder; construction, and demolition of buildings but not repairs. Sales by a builder's merchant, and architects' and surveyors' fees are, however, taxable. A person building his own house (not merely conversions and alterations) can reclaim tax paid on items purchased. (But see 21.15 concerning non-residential buildings and civil engineering works now standard rated.) After 31 May 1984 conversions, reconstructions, alterations and enlargements are standard rated and sales of reconstructed buildings are exempt.
Group 8A: Protected Buildings   This includes alterations and reconstructions of listed buildings, ancient monuments and listed churches.
Group 9: International Services   Exports of services, such as professional advice to non-residents (except individuals resident in the

EEC) and overseas insurance. In some cases the 'import' of professional services is charged to VAT.

Group 10: Transport Passenger transport (inland and international) including travel agents (except in relation to hotels in the UK or package tours), and international freight transport. Taxis and hire cars are, however, taxable, as are pleasure boats and aircraft. From 1 May 1990, lifeboats and slipways, etc are all included and from 1 April 1992, spare parts etc for lifeboats.

Group 11: Caravans and Houseboats Caravans which are too large to be used as trailers on the roads (22.9 feet in length or 7.5 feet in breadth). But smaller caravans are taxable.

Group 12: Gold Transactions on the London Gold market.

Group 13: Bank Notes

Group 14: Drugs, Medicines, Medical and Surgical Appliances Drugs dispensed by a registered pharmacist on a doctor's prescription. Other drugs purchased without a prescription are taxable. Medical and surgical appliances for the disabled. Donated computer equipment is zero-rated and lifts and distress systems for the handicapped and necessary work on bathrooms, etc in private homes. From 1 April 1987 zero rating is extended to bathrooms etc for the handicapped in charity residential homes. From 1 May 1990, more general relief is available for medical equipment, ambulances, etc purchased out of charitable funds or donated. This extends to the sale of donated goods and printed media advertising costs.

Group 15: Imports, Exports, etc This group has limited application.

Group 16: Charities (21.9). This includes non-classified advertising, medical video or refrigeration equipment and motor vehicles with from seven to fifty seats. Also, drugs and chemicals used in medical (and veterinary) research by a charity are zero-rated, also welfare vehicles for the terminally ill and certain rescue equipment. The sale of donated goods is now fully included, as is fund-raising and educational advertising on television, radio and cinema. From 1 April 1992 toilet facilities in charity-run buildings and boats adapted for the handicapped are covered.

Group 17: Clothing and Footwear Clothing for young children, industrial protective clothing and motor-cyclists' crash helmets. (Protective boots and helmets are standard-rated if supplied to employers for their employees — 21.15.)

Export of Goods This does not include exports to Northern Ireland, which is part of the UK, or to the Isle of Man.

Note: Zero-rating has priority over exemption if a supply falls into both categories.

An outline of VAT 367

21.15 Important changes to zero-ratings

On 21 June 1988, the European Court of Justice ruled that certain zero-ratings did not comply with European Community Law. As a result, the following items are *standard-rated* (*15 per cent*) no earlier than 1 April 1989, details being in the 1989 Finance Act:

(1) construction of buildings for industrial and commercial use;
(2) supplies after 31 March 1989 of fuel and power other than to final consumers for domestic use;
(3) sewerage services and water supplies to industry after 30 June 1990;
(4) supplies after 31 March 1989 of news services insofar as they are not provided to final consumers;
(5) protective boots and helmets supplied to employers after 31 March 1989 for use by their employees.

All contracts entered into before 21 June 1988 continue to be zero-rated. Owners of non-domestic property have the option to elect to charge VAT on rents, and on sales of certain used buildings, from 1 August 1989. If you elected before 1 November 1989, it could go back to 1 August 1989. Otherwise the election can take effect no earlier than the date when made. Owners can obtain no input tax relief before the election has effect, subject to transitional relief. Certain transactions in non-residential buildings may be treated as self-supplies giving rise to VAT.

Where the rent is payable by someone who was in occupation immediately before 1 August 1989, only half of the rent for the year to 31 July 1990 carries VAT. However, for charities, greater relief starting at 80 per cent and tapering over five years is available.

Exempt businesses will be adversely affected by the new rules but some relief will be obtained by phasing in VAT on rents over a period of time.

21.16 Exemptions

The following is a list of the more important items. Full details are contained in the General Guide (VAT Notice 700) available from Customs & Excise:
Group 1: Land Sales, leases and hiring out of land and buildings (unless within zero-rating Group 8). But hotels (excluding

conference facilities), holiday accommodation, camping, parking, timber, mooring, exhibition stands and sporting rights are taxable. (The sale and construction of new non-residential buildings and civil engineering works from 1 April 1989 is standard rated — 21.15.)

Group 2: Insurance All types of insurance and insurance brokers and agents. Both premiums and the payment of claims are exempt.

Group 3: Postal Services Post, except telegrams. But telephones and telex are taxable.

Group 4: Betting, Gaming and Lotteries Bookmakers, charges for playing bingo. But admission or session charges, club subscriptions and takings from gaming machines are taxable.

Group 5: Finance Banking, buying and selling stocks and shares and charges from credit card companies to retailers etc. accepting the cards. But stockbrokers' commissions and unit trust management fees are taxable.

Group 6: Education Schools, universities, non-profit-making institutions teaching pupils of any age, or providing job training; private tuition by an independent teacher.

Group 7: Health Doctors, dentists, dental workers, nurses, midwives, registered health visitors, registered opticians (including spectacles supplied in the course of treatment), chiropodists, dieticians, medical laboratory technicians, occupational therapists, orthoptists, physiotherapists, radiographers and remedial gymnasts, hearing aid dispensers, registered pharmaceutical chemists, medical and surgical treatment (except health farms, etc).

Group 8: Burial and Cremation Undertakers, crematoria.

Group 9: Trade Unions and Professional Bodies

Group 10: Sports Competitions

Group 11: Certain Works of Art, etc.

Group 12: Fund-Raising Events Supplies of goods and services by charities and other qualifying bodies (including certain subsidiaries) in connection with fund-raising events (from 1 April 1989).

Note: Zero-rating has priority over exemption if a supply falls into both categories.

21.17 Trading within the EC

F2A 1992 Sch 3 contains detailed provisions related to the introduction of the Single Market from 1 January 1993. From that date, import procedures will be abolished for movements of goods within the EC. Instead there will be a concept of 'acquisition'. Supplies of goods between persons registered for VAT in EC countries continue to be zero-rated. However, the acquirer will account for VAT in the member state to which the goods are sent.

Private individuals will normally bear VAT at the appropriate rate in the member state of the supplier. However, VAT in the member state of the purchaser (and not the supplier) applies to mail order purchases, new motor vehicles, motor cycles, boats and aircraft; also supplies to non-VAT registered businesses and non-taxable institutions.

21.18 Optional rate for farmers
(F2A 1992 S15)

From 1 January 1993, farmers can choose whether to register for VAT or opt to become flat rate farmers. If your taxable supplies are below the registration level (£36,600) you will still have the option of not registering for VAT, nor will you have to become a flat rate farmer.

As a flat rate farmer, you will be outside the VAT system and so obtain no relief for purchases. However, to compensate you, a fixed rate is to be added to your sales and retained by you. The actual rate will be fixed by the Treasury later in 1992.

22 Stamp duty

22.1 Introduction

Stamp duty is perhaps the most modest of capital taxes. However, even though the rates are very low, stamp duty is likely to arise on some of your major capital transactions and could involve significant sums. Therefore a brief outline is given below. This concentrates on the *ad valorem* duties, which are charged according to the value of a transaction, rather than the less important *fixed duties*.

The stamp duty rules are contained in the Stamp Act 1891, Stamp Duties Management Act 1891 and subsequent Finance Acts. The 1984 Finance Act (S105) halved the rates of some of the main *ad valorem* duties to 1 per cent from 20 March 1984 (12 March 1984 for most Stock Exchange transactions). The 1985 Finance Act removed certain fixed duties (S79) and abolished contract note duty. Also, *gifts* ceased to be liable to *ad valorem* duty; along with deeds of family arrangement (20.30.6) and divorce transfers. The duty on share transfers was further reduced to $\frac{1}{2}$ per cent by the 1986 Finance Act (S58). Also, a new stamp duty reserve tax was introduced (22.6). The 1990 and 1991 Finance Acts are abolishing stamp duty on share transactions and property other than land and buildings from a date to be announced (22.7).

Stamp duty is essentially a charge on documents (instruments). It is not charged on the transactions and so if you carry out a transaction without documenting it, no duty should be chargeable. Furthermore if you later make a separate written record of an oral contract, this should not involve stamp duty. However, the Inland Revenue are re-appraising their attitude towards stamp duty avoidance and certain rules regarding shares are being changed. For example bearer letters of allotment are no longer exempted.

The payment of stamp duty is confirmed by a stamp being impressed on the document. The stamp office may need to adjudicate the value of a transaction for duty purposes and you could need to supply balance sheets and other details. If documents are not stamped, you will not always be open to action by the Revenue but the instruments will not be admitted in evidence in court. Also, you may be liable for fines if you present the instrument late for filing—in practice after 30 days from when the instruments are first executed (or brought into the UK).

22.2 Exemptions

The following table lists some of the more important exemptions from stamp duty:

22.2.1 Table: Exemptions from stamp duty

Transfers of Government Stocks ('Gilts')
Transfers of units in certain authorised unit trusts invested in UK government securities, etc
Transfers of short term loans (no more than five years)
Transfers of certain fixed rate non-convertible loan stocks
Transfers of bearer loan capital
Transfers of certain non-sterling loans raised by foreign governments or companies
Conveyances, transfers or leases to approved charities (FA 1982 S129)*
Conveyances, transfers or leases to the National Heritage Memorial Fund*
Transactions effected by the actual operation of law
Documents regarding transfers of ships (or interests in them)
Transfers brought about by will (testaments and testamentary instruments)
Articles of apprenticeship and of clerkship
Customs bonds, etc
Certain legal aid documents
Contracts of employment
Certain National Savings documents
Deeds of Covenant and bonds
Policies of insurance and related documents (excluding life assurance up to 31 December 1989)
One life assurance policy which is substituted for another according to the rules (FA 1982 S130)
Transfers (and issue) of certain EC Loan Stocks
Transfers of Treasury guaranteed stock (eg, British Electricity 3% 1968–73)
Property put into unit trusts ($\frac{1}{4}$% prior to 16 March 1988) (FA 1988 S140).
Agreement pursuant to Highway Acts

Appointment, procuration, revocation
Letter or power of attorney
Deeds not liable to other duties no longer liable to 50p duty
In Scotland, resignation, writ, etc
Warrants to purchase Government stock, etc (FA 1987 S50)
Transfers to a Minister of the Crown or the Treasury Solicitor (FA 1987 S55)

*Not treated as duly stamped unless they have a stamp denoting not chargeable to duty

22.3 Capital duty
(FA 1973 Ss37 & 48 & Sch 19 & FA 1988 S141)

Prior to 16 March 1988, capital duty applied to companies which are managed in Great Britain or outside the European Community with the registered office in Great Britain, including UK limited companies, limited partnerships and EC companies. These were known as 'capital companies'. The duty was levied on 'chargeable transactions', which include the formation of a 'capital company' and the increase of its capital by the contribution of assets, including the capitalisation of a debt. Capital duty was abolished as from 16 March 1988.

Duty was charged at £1 on every £100 of the amount on which duty is chargeable with parts of £100 counting as £100. The amount on which duty was charged on the formation of a company or the increase of its capital was the consideration contributed by the members. This was normally cash but could be other assets taken at open market value. Where the registered office, etc, was transferred from abroad, the duty was charged on the net asset value of the company.

22.4 Relief for take-overs

Prior to 16 March 1988, relief from capital duty applied where an existing 'capital company' or one being formed, acquired share capital of another 'capital company' so that it owned 75 per cent of it. Relief also applied if the whole or part of one 'capital company's' undertaking was acquired by another. In order to obtain the relief, the consideration must have consisted of no more than 10 per cent cash and the rest, shares in the acquiring company. The relief was lost if within five years the shareholding in the acquired company fell below 75 per cent.

Similar relief applied from *ad valorem* stamp duty (FA 1985 S78) up to 24 March 1986. The exemption applied where a company issued shares, etc, in exchange for those of another company, in the course of obtaining control. It also applied if the first company already had control. Relief normally remained, however, where there was a company reconstruction with no real change in ownership.

22.5 *Ad valorem* duties

The most important stamp duties with which you may be involved are those which increase according to the consideration involved. These are known as *ad valorem* duties. Normally, *ad valorem* duties are charged at a fixed percentage but this is sometimes expressed in bands, so that the $\frac{1}{2}$ per cent on share transfers, etc, is 50p for every £100 or part thereof. Also, for some duties, sliding scales apply for small transactions.

In general, the rate for land and buildings is 1 per cent, but there is normally a £30,000 threshold, at or below which no duty is payable. However, for documents executed from 20 December 1991 to 19 August 1992 the threshold is £250,000, following which it reverts to £30,000. (Once the threshold is passed, the entire value is charged to duty.)

The following table gives the basic percentage rates of various *ad valorem* duties:

22.5.1 Table: *Ad valorem* stamp duties

	Rate
Capital duty (1% before 16 March 1988)	Nil
Conveyance or transfer on sale other than share transfers*	1%
Share transfers (generally including unit trusts)	
from 27 October 1986	$\frac{1}{2}$%
Certain non-exempt loan transfers after 31 July 1986	$\frac{1}{2}$%
Exchanges or partitions of freehold land	1%
Inland bearer instruments (3% before 27 October 1986)‡	$1\frac{1}{2}$%
Overseas bearer instruments‡	$1\frac{1}{2}$%
Conversion of UK shares into depositary receipts (22.6)	$1\frac{1}{2}$%
Lease premiums	1%

Leases: *Ad valorem* **duty on rents**

Term	Annual rent	Duty for every £50 or part thereof
Not exceeding 7 years or indefinite	Not exceeding £500 exceeding £500	Nil 50p
7–35 years	—	£1
35–100 years	—	£6
over 100 years	—	£12

(Where the rent does not exceed £500 a sliding scale applies.)

Life assurance policies—up to 31 December 1989	Amount assured: Up to £50	Nil
	£50–£1,000	5p per £100 or part
	Over £1,000	50p per £1,000 or part
After 31 December 1989		Nil
Superannuation annuity contract or grant	—	5p per £10 annuity or part
After 31 December 1989		Nil

*Includes land, etc. For most categories including houses, no duty is payable if the value is certified at no more than £30,000 (£250,000 from 20.12.91 to 19.8.92).

‡Bearer loan capital exempt.

22.6 Stamp duty reserve tax
(FA 1986 Ss86–99)

A charge called stamp duty reserve tax applies at $\frac{1}{2}$ per cent on certain transactions in securities otherwise not liable to stamp duty. The charge broadly operates from 27 October 1986 but does not apply to securities exempt from sale duty (eg, gifts) or traded options, etc. Examples of when the tax applies are renounceable letters of allotment and sometimes where there is no transfer document (eg, closing transactions within Stock Exchange accounts). A special rate of $1\frac{1}{2}$ per cent applies to the conversion of UK shares into depositary receipts after 18 March 1986.

22.7 Abolition of stamp duty on shares, etc
(FA 1990 Ss107–111 & FA 1991 Ss110–117)

All stamp duties on shares will be abolished from a date to be announced. This is to coincide as far as possible with the introduction of paperless dealing under the new Stock Exchange share transfer system. At the same time, stamp duty charges on property other than land and buildings will go, including on patents, goodwill and debt. (Duty on Northern Ireland banknotes will be abolished from 1 January 1992.)

The duties to be abolished include the $\frac{1}{2}$ per cent stamp duty on individual share transfers, 1.5 per cent where UK shares are transferred into clearance services or converted into depositary receipts, stamp duty reserve tax (22.6), stamp duties on bearer shares and unit trust unit transfers. The 50p fixed duty on share transfers other than sales also will go.

23 Social security

23.1 Introduction

The main social security legislation is now comprised in the Social Security Acts of 1975, 1985 and 1986. The subject is a wide one and only an outline is given below.

Arguably, social security contributions are not a tax but their effect is very similar. Although ultimate benefits such as retirement pensions are secured, when you pay the contributions, you must normally do so out of your after-tax income. Social security contributions payments do not reduce your taxable income any more than do income tax payments. An exception is that from 6 April 1985, half of your Class 4 contributions are deductible (10.28).

23.2 National Insurance contributions

Contributions are payable under four categories known as 'Class 1' (employees), 'Class 2' (self-employed), 'Class 3' (voluntary) and 'Class 4' (self-employed earnings related). Classes 2 and 3 are flat rate contributions and Class 4 is dealt with subsequently (23.5). The following points should be noted regarding Class 1:

(1) Contributions are graduated according to earnings up to a certain level and are collected together with income tax under the PAYE system (9.14). They are not allowable for income tax purposes.
(2) Your employer supplements your contributions. Your employers' contributions are deductible for tax purposes.
(3) No contributions are payable if the weekly earnings are less than £54 but once this level is reached, your entire wages (up to £405) carry percentage contributions.

(4) From 6 October 1985 there is no upper earnings limit for employers. They pay contributions on the total earnings of employees.
(5) If your employers operate an approved pension scheme which is contracted out of the state scheme, lower contributions will be due. If you contract out via a Personal Pension Plan, you still pay full National Insurance contributions. The rebate is paid direct to the pension plan.
(6) You will not have to pay contributions if you have retired and passed normal retirement age (60 for a woman and 65 for a man). If you are still working beyond age 65 you will not be liable for contributions. Your employer remains liable, however.
(7) If you have a company car and earn no less than £8,500 annually, your employer will pay Class 1A National Insurance contributions at 10.4 per cent on your taxable benefits. These comprise both your car scale benefit and fuel benefit, where applicable. This is an annual charge, first payable for 1991–92 in June 1992.

The following tables give details concerning the rates of contribution.

23.2.1 Table: National Insurance contributions

	Tax year			
	1992–93		1991–92	
	Employee	Employer	Employee	Employer
'Class 1' — employees aged 16 & over:				
Lower earnings limit (LEL) pw	£54·00		£52·00	
Upper earnings limit (UEL) pw	£405·00		£390·00	
(a) earnings less than LEL:	Nil	Nil	Nil	Nil
(b) earnings LEL or more and contracted out: up to LEL on balance up to UEL	See Table 23.4			
(c) earnings at least LEL and contracted in: on earnings up to UEL				
'Class 2' — self-employed pw	£5·35		£5·15*	
'Class 3' — voluntary pw	£5·25		£5·05	

| 'Class 4' — self-employed earnings related | 6.3% on annual earnings between £6,120 & £21,060 | 6.3% on annual earnings between £5,900 & £20,280 |

*Lower earnings limit £3,030

23.2.2 Table: Class 1 National Insurance contributions

1991–92 Employee	Not contracted-out	Contracted-out	1992–93 Employee	Not contracted-out	Contracted-out
Weekly earnings below £52	Nil	Nil	Weekly earnings below £54	Nil	Nil
Earnings above £52			Earnings above £54		
0–£51.99	2%	2%	0–£53.99	2%	2%
£52–£390	9%	7%	£54–£405	9%	7%
£390 or more	No further liability		£405 or more		No further liability

1992–93 Employer	Not contracted-out %	Contracted-out %		
Weekly earnings		First £54	Excess over £54	
Under £54.00	Nil	Nil	Nil	
£54.00– 89.99	4.6	4.6	0.8	
90.00–134.99	6.6	6.6	2.8	
135.00–189.99	8.6	8.6	4.8	
190.00–405.00	10.4	10.4	6.6	
over £405.00	10.4% on all earnings	10.4	{ 6.6 on £351 { 10.4 on excess	

1991–92 Employer				
Weekly earnings	Not contracted-out %	Contracted-out % First £52	Excess over £52	
Under £52.00	Nil	Nil	Nil	
£52.00– 84.99	4.6	4.6	0.8	
85.00–129.99	6.6	6.6	2.8	
130.00–184.99	8.6	8.6	4.8	
185.00–390.00	10.4	10.4	6.6	
over £390.00	10.4	10.4	{ 6.6 on £338 { 10.4 on excess	

23.3 Social security benefits

A wide range of benefits is payable. These are summarised below and split between those which are taxable and those which are not.

23.3.1 Table: Taxable social security benefits

	From 6.4.91 to 5.4.92 £	From 6.4.92 £
Retirement pension		
— Single	52.00	54.15
— Wife (or other adult dependant)	31.25	32.55
Old person's pension (extra 25p payable if over 80)	31.25	32.55
Invalid care allowance		
— Single	31.25	32.55
— Wife (or other adult dependant)	18.70	19.45
Invalidity allowance (only taxable if paid with retirement pension)		
— Higher rate	11.10	11.55
— Middle rate	6.90	7.20
— Lower rate	3.45	3.60
Widow's benefit		
— Lump sum (death after 10.4.88)	1,000	1,000
— Pension — basic (variable below 55)	52.00	54.15
— Widowed mother's allowance	52.00	54.15
Unemployment benefits — Standard rate under pension age		
— Single	41.40	43.10
— Wife (or other adult dependant)	31.25	32.55
Income support		various

23.3.2 Table: Non-taxable social security benefits

	From 6.4.91 to 5.4.92 £	From 6.4.92 £
Sickness benefit — Standard rate: under pension age		
— Single	39.60	41.20
— Wife (or other adult dependant)	24.50	25.50

Maternity allowance	40.60	42.50
Invalidity pension		
— Single	52.00	54.15
— Wife (or other adult dependant)	31.25	32.55
Severe disablement allowance		
— Single	31.25	32.55
— Wife (or other adult dependant)	18.70	19.45
Attendance allowance		
— Higher rate	41.65	43.35
— Lower rate	27.80	28.95
Child benefit		
First child		
— to 5 October	8.25	9.65
— from 6 October	9.25	9.65
Each other child		
— to 5 October	7.25	7.80
— from 6 October	7.50	7.80
One parent benefit		
— addition for first child	5.60	5.85
Increases for children — child's special allowances and guardian's allowances — each child	10.70	10.85
Mobility allowance	29.10	Nil
Disability allowance (replaces mobility allowance)		
— mobility component — higher	—	30.30
lower	—	11.55
Industrial disablement benefit (maximum)	84.90	88.40
— unemployability supplement	52.00	54.15
— constant attendance allowance (normal maximum)	34.00	35.40
— exceptionally severe disablement allowance (addition)	34.00	35.40

Housing benefits — various

War pension — death benefit, disablement, widow's pension, widower's pension—various

Note: In addition, earnings related unemployment benefit supplement is exempt from income tax.

23.4 Statutory sick pay

Employers generally pay up to 28 weeks statutory sick pay for each employee in any tax year. (The employee does not need to have paid National Insurance contributions.) Only after that is any sickness benefit paid direct by the State. Employers can deduct their statutory sick pay payments in any month from the total National Insurance contributions payable to the authorities.

Statutory sick pay is paid at the following weekly rates (daily rates are calculated proportionally):

Normal weekly earnings	1992–93	Normal weekly earnings	1991–92
Less than £54.00	Nil	Less than £52.00	Nil
£54.00–£189.99	£45.30	£52.00–£184.99	£43.50
£190.00 or more	£52.50	£185.00 or more	£52.50

23.5 Class 4 National Insurance contributions

Self-employed persons and others liable to Schedule D income tax under Cases I and II may be charged, in addition to their normal flat-rate Class 2 contributions, an earnings related amount under Class 4. The following should be noted.

(1) The contribution rate for 1992–93 is 6.3 per cent which applies to your Cases I and II income between £6,120 and £21,060. The maximum is thus 6.3 per cent × £14,940 = £941.22.

(2) The rates, etc for previous years were as follows:

Year	% rate	From £	To £	Maximum payable
1975–76	8	1,600	3,600	160.00
1976–77	8	1,600	4,900	264.00
1977–78	8	1,750	5,500	300.00
1978–79	5	2,000	6,250	212.50
1979–80	5	2,250	7,000	237.50
1980–81	5	2,650	8,300	282.50
1981–82	5.75	3,150	10,000	393.87
1982–83	6	3,450	11,000	453.00
1983–84	6.3	3,800	12,000	516.60
1984–85	6.3	3,950	13,000	570.15

Year	% rate	From £	To £	Maximum payable
1985–86	6.3	4,150	13,780	606.69
1986–87	6.3	4,450	14,820	653.31
1987–88	6.3	4,590	15,340	677.25
1988–89	6.3	4,750	15,860	699.93
1989–90	6.3	5,050	16,900	746.55
1990–91	6.3	5,450	18,200	803.25
1991–92	6.3	5,900	20,280	905.94

(3) Prior to 6 April 1975, the charge did not apply.
(4) Class 4 is payable on your Schedule D assessments under Cases I and II for the tax year; after capital allowances, but with no deduction of personal allowances, pension contributions, etc. Your share of partnership income is thus included.
(5) If your wife has self-employed earnings, these are also charged to Class 4 as if her earnings were separate from yours.
(6) Class 4 does not apply to men over 65 at the end of the previous year of assessment and women then over 60.
(7) Your contributions for each year of assessment are normally collected through your income tax assessment on your self-employed earnings. Thus it is payable in two instalments (14.7.1).
(8) It is possible to defer your Class 4 payments in certain cases, such as where you also pay Class 1 contributions.
(9) If you are not resident in the UK (15.3) Class 4 will not apply.

24 Tax aspects of life assurance, pensions, annuities and PHI
by VINCE JERRARD

24.1 Types of contract

This chapter looks at four categories of contract:

(1) Life policies (eg, whole-life policies, endowment policies, term assurances).
(2) Pension contracts (eg, occupational pension schemes, personal retirement annuity plans and Personal Pension Plans.
(3) Purchased general annuities (immediate and deferred annuities).
(4) Permanent health insurances.

Each of these enjoys a different tax treatment, and will be looked at separately, both from the life company's position (to see what benefits the company is able to offer) and from your point of view, as a policyholder, to see how your premiums and proceeds are treated.

24.2 Life policies
24.3 The company's tax position
(TA 1988 Ss76, 432 et seq & FA 1989 Ss82–89 Sch 8 FA 1990 Ss41–48 & Schs 6–9 & F2A 1992 S65)

In respect of their life assurance business, companies are generally taxed on the excess of their investment income and realised capital gains over management expenses (the 'I–E basis'). In June 1988 the Inland Revenue issued a Consultative Document on the taxation of the life assurance industry. The results of the consultations were enacted in the Finance Acts of 1989 and 1990.
The Revenue decided against the more radical proposals as suggested in the Consultative Document and in favour of reforming the existing regime. Accordingly, the basis of life company taxation remains unchanged: while a policy is held intact there is no

tax liability on the policyholder and the income and gains attributable to the policy are taxed in the hands of the life company.

The key changes applicable to life assurance business (which came into effect on 1 January 1990) were:

(1) The erection of a 'ring fence' around pensions business to stop pensions business expenses being set off against life business profits.
(2) A reduction in the tax rate charged on policyholders' income and gains. The new rate is 25 per cent, replacing the previous rates of 35 per cent for income and 30 per cent for gains. As life companies are generally able to defer realisations of assets, it is likely that they will pass on this benefit by making deductions for tax on policyholders' gains at a rate lower than 25 per cent, particularly in the case of unit-linked policies.
(3) There is a new formula for determining the proportions of a company's income and gains which should be allocated respectively to policyholders and shareholders. The company's profits (as opposed to the profits of the funds maintained for its policyholders) are chargeable to corporation tax at the usual rates.
(4) The expenses of acquiring new business, currently available for tax relief in full when they are incurred, are to be spread forward and allowed over a period of seven years. This spreading of relief over seven years will not come fully into force until 1994; in the meantime there will be transitional relief so that, for example, five-sevenths of 1990 expenses were allowed immediately in that year. Three-sevenths are allowable in 1992.
(5) The introduction of new rules to tax unrealised gains in a life company's holding of unit trusts.
(6) Finance (No 2) Act 1992 contains a provision confirming the Revenue's view of the existing position to the effect that a life company can be taxed on investment income accruing for the benefit of policyholders even where it is making trading losses.

24.4 The tax treatment of your premiums and proceeds
(TA 1988 Ss266 et seq, 539 et seq Schs 14 & 15)

Life assurance policies are divided into two classes for tax purposes. These are:

(1) Qualifying policies.
(2) Non-qualifying policies.

This distinction is relevant only for the individual policyholder's tax position as discussed below (24.5–24.7); there is no differentiation between the two types of policy as far as life company taxation is concerned.

Various changes to the rules were introduced by FA 1975 and in general these took effect from 1 April 1976, 'the appointed day'. An older qualifying policy will not be subject to the changes unless its terms have been significantly varied after that date.

The 1989 Budget announced the Inland Revenue's intention to consult with the industry in respect of simplification of the tax treatment of policyholders. Although changes were expected to be announced in the 1990 Budget, none has materialised, and the prospects for radical reform of the policy tax regime appear to have receded, at least in the short term.

The three main types of policy — whole of life assurances (where the sum assured is payable on the death of the life assured, at any time); term assurances (where the sum assured is payable on death during the policy term); and endowment assurances (where the sum assured is payable on death during the policy term, or survival to the end of the term) — can all be qualifying or non-qualifying policies depending on whether they satisfy the appropriate qualifying rules for that type of policy.

24.5 Qualifying policies

These are regular premium policies, ie whole life, term or endowment policies which satisfy the qualifying conditions set out in TA 1988 Sch 15 and do not fall foul of 'anti-avoidance' provisions.

For company-owned policies see 24.7.14.

24.5.1 Qualifying rules

The main features of the qualifying rules are as follows:

Premiums:

(1) must be payable for a period of ten years or more, annually or more frequently. Term assurances may be written for shorter periods; and

(2) must be fairly evenly spread so that premiums payable in any one period of 12 months should neither be more than twice the amount of premiums paid in any other 12 month period, nor more than 1/8th of the total amount of premiums payable over the first ten years (in the case of whole life policies) or over the term of the policy (in the case of an endowment).

The sum assured:
(1) for an endowment policy, must not be less than 75 per cent of the total premiums payable during the term of the policy. This percentage is reduced by 2 per cent for each year by which the life assured's age exceeds 55 years at the issue of the policy;
(2) for a whole of life policy, must not be less than 75 per cent of the total premiums payable if death were to occur at the age of 75 years;
(3) for a term policy, which has no surrender value and ends before the life assured's 75th birthday, need not satisfy any minimum requirement.

Benefits:
(1) may include the right to participate in profits, the right to benefits arising because of disability or the right to a return of premiums on death under a certain specified age (not exceeding 16 years); but
(2) may not include any other benefits of a capital nature.

The rules for certain special types of policy may vary from those referred to above, eg, mortgage protection policies, family income policies and industrial assurances.

24.5.2 Options

Where a policy issued after the appointed day gives options to the policyholder (eg to increase the sum assured, or the premium, or extend the policy term) these options will be tested at the outset to decide whether every one of the possible permutations would still leave the policy as a qualifying policy. If so, the policy qualifies and will remain qualifying on any subsequent exercise of the option; if not, the presence of the option will mean that, from outset, the policy cannot be qualifying. Options in policies in respect of contracts made before 1 April 1976 will be disregarded until they are exercised. If they are exercised, the policy will then be tested under the current rules to decide whether or not the policy remains qualifying.

24.5.3 The advantages of qualifying policies

(1) You may be eligible for tax relief on your premiums (pre-14 March 1984 policies only — see 24.5.4).
(2) While the policy is in force, all income and gains attributable to your policy and the tax thereon are the responsibility of the life company.
(3) Gains made under the policy are not liable for basic rate tax when realised by the policyholder.
(4) The proceeds are usually entirely free of tax, provided premiums are kept up for at least ten years (or three-quarters of the term of an endowment policy, if shorter).

24.5.4 Tax relief on your premiums
(TA 1988 Ss 266 & 274)

(a) Insurances made after 13 March 1984

No tax relief is available for premiums paid under policies issued in respect of contracts made after 13 March 1984.

For these purposes a policy issued on or before 13 March 1984 is treated as being issued after that date if the benefits it secures are increased or its term is extended (either by the exercise of an option built into the contract, or by an agreed variation outside the contract terms) after that date.

(b) Insurances made before 14 March 1984

You are entitled to tax relief on premiums paid by you under such qualifying policies (or other life assurance policies issued in respect of contracts made before 20 March 1968) up to the greater of £1,500 or 1/6th of your total income (see 3.2.8). This is usually known as Life Assurance Premium Relief (LAPR).

In order to be eligible for relief the policy must be one issued on your own life or that of your spouse, the premium must be paid by you or your spouse, and the payer must reside in the UK when the payment is made.

The relief will normally be obtained by deducting the tax relief from the premiums payable to the life office, resulting in a premium payment net of tax relief. The life office will recover the deficiency from the Inland Revenue. Should you over-claim (ie, deduct in excess of both the £1,500 and the

1/6th of income limit) the Revenue have the right to recover the excess relief by assessment and disallow the future payment of net premiums on particular policies.

If the benefits secured by such a policy are increased or its term extended after 13 March 1984, the relief on premiums paid subsequently will be lost (see above).

For the year 1992/93 the relief is given at the rate of 12.5 per cent.

24.5.5 Tax relief claw-back—Qualifying policies

(a) Claw-back on early surrender
(TA 1988 Ss 268 et seq & Sch 14)

(1) If a qualifying policy was surrendered or made paid-up (or a bonus became payable in cash) during the first four policy years, the Revenue could 'claw-back' some or all of any LAPR previously obtained, subject to a ceiling. This provision is now 'spent' as any policy benefiting from LAPR must have completed its fourth year by 14 March 1988. Details of these clawback rules can be found in previous editions of this book.

(b) Premiums paid out of a partial surrender
(TA 1988 Ss 266 & 269)

(1) If a policyholder pays a premium on a qualifying policy eligible for LAPR (ie, a pre-March 1984 policy) and effectively recoups himself in whole or in part by withdrawing money from that policy by way of a partial surrender of policy rights (or a surrender of a bonus) no LAPR will be allowed. The life assurance company will be required to claw-back out of the sum payable to the policyholder an amount equal to a percentage of the current year's premium (or of the amount withdrawn, if less, in which case, if any further surrender is taken, an additional claw-back will be made until the total claw-back is reached). The percentage is the rate of LAPR for the year in which the surrender happens.

(2) The legislation applies to qualifying policies issued in respect of insurances made after 26 March 1974.

24.5.6 Proceeds of qualifying policies
(TA 1988 Ss539–552, TCGA 1992 S210)

(1) A policyholder will have no personal liability to CGT on a disposal of the policy if he is the original beneficial owner of

the policy or if he is an assignee and acquired the policy other than for money or money's worth.
(2) The possible income tax consequences in respect of the proceeds of a qualifying policy depend on the operation of the 'chargeable event' rules (see 24.7). Generally, if premiums are kept up for at least ten years (or three-quarters of the term, if shorter) or until earlier death, the entire policy proceeds will be free of all income tax in the policyholder's hands, whether they are paid by way of surrender, maturity or death. In any event, no basic rate tax liability will arise in respect of a gain made in connection with a UK life assurance policy.

24.6 Non-qualifying policies

All other policies are non-qualifying policies. The most important category of these is single-premium investment policies, frequently described as single-premium bonds. (Bonds issued in respect of assurances made before 20 March 1968 are, however, treated in effect as qualifying policies.) With the removal of LAPR in the Finance Act 1984, some regular premium non-qualifying policies were introduced in order to take advantage of the flexibility available through not having to satisfy the qualifying rules but these were more likely to cause a tax charge in respect of the policy proceeds and did not prove to be particularly successful.

In addition, policies that may commence initially as qualifying policies, can subsequently become non-qualifying policies if certain significant variations occur causing a breach of the qualifying rules — eg, substantial changes to premium levels or reductions in sums assured etc.

24.6.1 Connected policies
(TA 1988 S267 & Sch 15(13) & (14))

There are special provisions designed to prevent the exploitation of the qualifying rules by artificial combinations of policies, such as short term bonds. A policy cannot be qualifying if it is connected with another, and either:

(1) one policy must lapse when the other does, and taken together the policies would constitute a non-qualifying policy; or

(2) the terms of either policy provide benefits greater than would otherwise reasonably be expected.

24.6.2 Tax treatment of non-qualifying policies (including single premium bonds)
(TA 1988 Ss267 and 539–552, TCGA S210)

(1) No tax relief is available in respect of the premium. (Note, however, that where a policy was initially a qualifying policy and later became non-qualifying, because its terms were varied, past tax relief obtained does not have to be repaid unless the policy was made paid-up in the first few years (24.5.5). In such cases only future relief will not be allowed.)
(2) The income and gains attributable to the policy while it is in force receive exactly the same tax treatment as qualifying policies—the income and gains are those of the life company whose responsibility it is to pay the taxes and submit returns, etc.
(3) The policy proceeds will be free of capital gains tax in the hands of the original beneficial owner of the policy, or in the hands of an assignee who did not give consideration for the assignment. In respect of CGT the rules are identical for qualifying and non-qualifying policies.
(4) The income tax consequences of a disposal of the policy will depend on the chargeable event rules (see 24.7). No basic rate liability will arise on a chargeable event but higher rate tax will be payable if the policyholder's income plus the relevant proportion of the gain made under the policy is sufficiently high.
(5) Until its abolition (for individuals) by FA 1984, gains realised in respect of such policies were also liable to the investment income surcharge, where applicable. For details of the effect of the investment income surcharge on life assurance policy gains, see previous editions of this book.

24.7 Chargeable events
(TA 1988 Ss539–552)

Chargeable events in the case of non-qualifying policies are:

(1) Death of the life assured.
(2) The maturity of the policy.
(3) The total surrender of the policy.
(4) The assignment of the policy for money or money's worth.

(5) Excesses arising on partial surrenders in any policy year commencing after 13 March 1975 (see 24.7.6).

Chargeable events in the case of qualifying policies are the same as those listed above but with the following amendments:

(a) Death or maturity will be a chargeable event only if the policy has previously been made paid-up within the first ten years (or three quarters of the term of an endowment policy, if shorter).
(b) A surrender, an assignment for money or money's worth or an excess will be a chargeable event only if it occurs before the expiry of ten years (or three quarters of the term of an endowment policy, if shorter) or if the policy was made paid-up within that period.

Assignments between spouses living together or as security for debts are not chargeable events.

The surrender of a right to a bonus or the taking of a bonus is now treated in the same way as any other partial surrender if it gives rise to an excess. Also, loans made by the insurer against policies issued in respect of contracts made after 26 March 1974 are treated as partial surrenders, except where the loan is made under a qualifying policy and either interest is charged at a commercial rate or the sum is lent to a full-time employee of the insurance company for the purpose of house purchase or improvement.

A development in the UK life assurance market in recent years has been the ability to include 'dread disease' benefits in many policies, both qualifying and non-qualifying. This benefit pays a capital sum on the diagnosis of the life assured as suffering from any of the dread diseases specified in the policy. Typically, these will include heart attack, stroke, cancer, heart by-pass surgery, etc. In general, the receipt of such benefit will be tax free in the hands of the policyholder as the occasion of its payment will not constitute a chargeable event.

24.7.1 Calculating the gain on the happening of a chargeable event
(TA 1988 S541)

Where a chargeable event occurs the gain arising on the event must be computed. The calculation depends on the nature of the event but, broadly speaking, it is the investment profit made under the policy, taking into account previous relevant capital benefits enjoyed and the total premiums paid.

Any extra amount received at that time by way of death benefit is treated as a mortality profit and is not included in the gain for tax purposes.

For example, consider a non-qualifying policy under which £5,000 is paid as premium. No partial surrenders are made but the life assured dies and the sum assured paid out is £10,000. If, immediately prior to the death of the life assured, the policy's surrender value was £6,000, the chargeable gain on the death is £6,000 – £5,000, ie, £1,000. The mortality profit of £4,000 is not included in the chargeable gain.

The rules for calculating the gain as a result of a withdrawal or partial surrender are somewhat different (see 24.7.6).

24.7.2 Taxing gains on chargeable events

(1) As mentioned, no liability arises to basic rate tax in respect of life policy gains, nor will there usually be any capital gains tax liability (but neither will there be any refund in respect of tax paid by the life company where the policyholder is a non-taxpayer or pays tax at a lower rate). The gain is treated as the top part of the taxpayer's income and may attract higher rate income tax, where applicable. The taxpayer will usually be the policyholder (but see 24.7.12).
(2) As the gain has accrued over the life of the policy, it would be rather harsh to treat the total gain as the taxpayer's income in the year of receipt, as this could push him into an unrealistically high band in that year. A measure of relief is therefore afforded by a process known as 'top slicing'.

24.7.3 Top slicing

The top slicing calculation set out in the legislation requires a three stage operation.

(1) The tax on the whole gain is calculated as if it were the top part of the individual's total income.
(2) Tax is calculated by reference to an 'appropriate fraction' of the gain, usually referred to as the 'slice'. This calculation is as follows:
    (a) The gain is divided by the number of complete years the policy has been held to the date of the chargeable event.

For example, if a single-premium bond was purchased for £5,000, and was cashed in five years later for £7,000, the chargeable gain would be £2,000. The 'slice' of the gain would be £2,000 divided by five, ie, £400.
(b) The 'slice' is added to the taxpayer's other taxable income of the year in which the chargeable event occurs, and is treated as the top part of his taxable income in order to determine whether the 'slice' is subject to any higher rate tax, and if so at what effective rate of tax.
(c) The appropriate tax rate applicable to the 'slice' is then applied to the whole gain (ie, £2,000 in the above example). The appropriate rate is the difference between:
 (i) the taxpayer's average rate of tax on the 'slice' when added to his other taxable income, and
 (ii) the basic rate (currently 25 per cent in tax year 1992/93).
(3) The relief due under these rules is equal to the difference between the two amounts of tax calculated under (1) and (2) above and is given as a reduction of the tax computed under (1).

It can be seen that a 'shorthand' method of determining the tax payable is to apply just the calculation involving the slice ((2) above) and for simplicity this method is used in the examples in this chapter.

Notes:
 (i) The whole gain (without top slicing) is counted as income for the purposes of determining whether any age allowance should be reduced (see 3.2.15).
 (ii) Top slicing is not available where the taxpayer is a company (5.9).
 (iii) Any available relief in respect of investment in a Business Expansion Scheme is left out of account when calculating top slicing relief (10.25).
 (iv) The taxpayer's total income for top-slicing purposes is computed without reference to amounts chargeable in respect of loss of office (S148) (9.12) or lease premiums chargeable as rent (Ss34–36) (7.7.1).
 (v) The examples shown in this chapter assume no reliefs or amounts as mentioned in (iii) and (iv) are present.

24.7.4 Example: No tax on the gain

An individual buys a bond for £20,000 in May 1987 and cashes it in 5 years later for £27,500. The gain is therefore £7,500 and the 'slice' is £1,500.

Taxable income (excluding policy gain)	15,000
'Slice'	1,500
Taxable income	£16,500

The tax on the 'slice' is therefore 25% less 25% = 0.

24.7.5 Example: Slice falling into the two rate bands

A man purchases a bond for £12,000 in May 1987. Five years later he cashes it in for £17,000. The gain is £5,000. In that year his taxable income after reliefs is £23,000.

Tax calculation on gain:

Gain ÷ years held	=	slice of £1,000
Taxable income + 'slice'	=	£24,000
Rate on slice		
On £700 (ie £23,000 to £23,700) at 25%	=	£175
On £300 (ie £23,700 to £24,000) at 40%	=	£120
Therefore total tax on slice	=	£295
Therefore average rate on slice		
$\frac{295}{1000} \times 100\%$	=	29.5%
Rate applied to gain is 29.5% − 25%	=	4.5%

The tax payable is £5,000 × 4.5% = £225.

24.7.6 Partial surrenders — 'Excesses'

A partial surrender will be a chargeable event if it is too large. At the end of each policy year an allowance is given of 1/20th (5 per cent) of the premium. If this allowance is not used it is carried forward to the next policy year, and so on, on a cumulative basis (the limit being 100 per cent of the premium). If a partial surrender is made the amount withdrawn will be compared, at the end of the policy year, with the cumulative allowances. If the total of the partial surrenders is less than the cumulative allowance, no chargeable event will be deemed to have occurred and the amount withdrawn will also be carried forward.

If in any policy year the amount withdrawn, plus previous cumulative withdrawals carried forward, exceeds the cumulative allowances, a 'chargeable event' will occur. The *excess* will be treated as a gain and will be subject to higher rate tax, if applicable, regardless of the actual performance of the policy.

Once an excess has occurred, all cumulative withdrawals and allowances up to that date will be deemed to have been used up and the process of allowances (subject to the overall limit of 100 per cent of the premium) and withdrawals will start afresh, until the next excess, being the next chargeable event.

When the final chargeable event occurs (eg, death, maturity, final surrender, assignment for value), the total profit on the policy will be brought into account, the profit being the final proceeds plus previous partial surrenders from which will be deducted the premiums paid and any gains on past chargeable events (ie, past excesses).

For 'top slicing' the periods of spread are the number of complete policy years since the start of the policy in the case of the first chargeable event and final termination; and the number of policy years since the previous chargeable event in the case of the second and subsequent excesses. Gains will be charged to tax in the income tax year in which the relevant policy year *ends* or, in the case of the final chargeable event, the tax year in which it occurs.

If, on final termination, the overall gain on the policy is less than the excess previously chargeable to tax, the difference can be deducted from the policyholder's taxable income in that year for the purposes of *higher rate tax only*.

24.7.7 Example: Total encashment following 5 per cent regular withdrawals

Original investment £10,000.
For 10 years draws £500 pa paying no tax, as allowances not exceeded. In year 11 cashes in bond for £12,000.
Assume bondholder's taxable income = £24,000.
Gain = £12,000 + £5,000 − £10,000 = £7,000
(Slice = £7,000 ÷ 10 = £700).
Income + slice = £24,700 (whole slice falls into 40% rate)
Tax on gain = 15% (40% − 25%) × £7,000 = £1,050.

24.7.8 Example: Postponing withdrawals

Use allowances later — eg, to pay school fees.
£10,000 bond.
Years 1–10 no withdrawals. 10 × 5% (= 50%) cumulation of allowances.
Years 11–15 withdrawals of up to 15% pa (total 75%) possible, tax-free at the time, eg, £1,500 pa for 5 years, totalling £7,500.
If bond cashed in after 16 years having balance of, say, £18,000, gain equals £18,000 + £7,500 − £10,000 = £15,500.
'Top-slice' by 16 to find rate of tax on gain.

24.7.9 Example: Cumulation of allowances and withdrawals

A £10,000 bond: £1,200 withdrawn after four policy years; a further £4,500 withdrawn after six policy years; £1,000 after eight, and the balance of the bond, say £10,400, is surrendered after ten policy years.

Years	A Cumulative allowances £	B Surrender £	C Cumulative surrender between chargeable events £	D Gain (C−A) £
1	500	0	0	0
2	1,000 (2×500)	0	0	0
3	1,500 (3×500)	0	0	0
4	2,000 (4×500)	1,200	1,200	0
5	2,500 (5×500)	0	1,200	0
6	3,000 (6×500)	4,500	5,700	2,700
7	500	0	0	0
8	1,000	1,000	1,000	0
9	1,500	0	1,000	0
10		10,400		

Final gain = (£10,400 + £1,200 + £4,500 + £1,000) − £10,000 − £2,700
= £4,400

Notes:
(i) Gain of £2,700 after six years is divided by six for top-slicing.
(ii) Final gain of £4,400 is divided by ten for top-slicing.

24.7.10 Partial surrender of old policies (issued before 14 March 1975)

The rules relating to excesses apply to all policies whenever they were issued. The current system, however, applies only from the

Tax aspects of life assurance, pensions, annuities and PHI

first policy year falling wholly after the passing of FA 1975 (ie, after 13 March 1975) and the system of 5 per cent allowances runs only from then. Withdrawals made before the first policy anniversary after 13 March 1975, are governed by the old system and no 5 per cent allowances apply to these policy years — indeed the allowances for these years are lost altogether.

Until FA 1975 a partial surrender of rights under a policy was automatically a chargeable event and the gain element in the proceeds received by way of partial surrender received the same treatment as a gain on a total surrender.

24.7.11 Example: Old policy

£10,000 bond taken out on 1 July 1972. 8 per cent withdrawals of £800 per annum taken on 30 June 1973, 1974 and 1975. Profit element in each of these withdrawals was subject to treatment on old basis and 5 per cent allowances do not apply to any of these withdrawals, including that on 30 June 1975.

If £800 was withdrawn in new policy year commencing 1 July 1975, £500 (5%) would have represented the allowance for policy year ending 30 June 1976; and the excess of £300 would have been subject to higher rate tax and investment income surcharge, if applicable, in the year of assessment ending on 5 April 1977.

24.7.12 Persons liable for the charge
(TA 1988 Ss547 & 551)

(1) Where a policy is held by an individual absolutely, or is held as security for a debt owed by him, the tax charge, if any, will fall on him.
(2) Where a policy is held on trust, the charge falls upon the settlor, if he is then alive, who can recover the tax from the trustees.
(3) If, immediately before the chargeable event, the rights under the policy were held in the beneficial ownership of a company or on trust created by or as security for a debt owed by a company, the charge falls on the company (see 24.7.14).
(4) If a policy is assigned for value and subsequently re-assigned to the original policyholder and a chargeable event occurs subsequently, the original policyholder is liable for the higher rate tax charge, if any.
(5) Where a policy is assigned as a gift, any chargeable excesses arising due to partial surrenders made from the policy during that policy year but prior to the assignment are taxed on the

assignor; any further gains are taxed on the new beneficial owner.
(6) Since the introduction of independent taxation for tax year 1990/91, husbands and wives are taxed separately in respect of their policy gains. Previously the wife's gains were assessed on the husband.

24.7.13 Certificates of chargeable event
(TA 1988 S552)

When a chargeable event occurs, it is the duty of the life assurance company to submit a certificate to the Inland Revenue with details of the policy and the amounts payable and previously paid by way of partial surrender.

24.7.14 Life assurance policies taken out by companies

In certain circumstances, a company may take out life assurance policies on the lives of its directors or other key executives — 'key man' policies — or other policies, eg, to provide funds to repay loans or other indebtedness.

In general, if the policy that is effected is term assurance for a short period (usually not more than five years), without a surrender value and is effected solely to provide protection against a loss of profits likely to result from the key man's death, the premiums will be tax-deductible and the proceeds would be taxable in the company's hands. If, on the other hand, the policy is for a longer term, is one that will have a surrender value, is effected for a 'capital' purpose, or where the life assured has a material shareholding in the company, the premiums will not be tax-deductible and the proceeds are unlikely to be charged to Corporation Tax in the company's hands other than by virtue of the life assurance chargeable event rules.

Until the Finance Act 1989 qualifying policies owned by companies were treated in much the same way as those held by individuals, ie, they provided tax-free proceeds on maturity or surrender after the required policy term. Gains from non-qualifying policies were also tax-free in the hands of companies save only where the company was 'close', in which case any chargeable gain was deemed to be part of the company's distributable income. The Finance Act 1989 Sch 9 made two significant changes which apply to policies effected on or after 14 March 1989 (or effected prior to that date and subsequently varied to increase the policy benefits or increase the policy term) where, immediately prior to the chargeable event the rights conferred by the policy were owned by a company or were held on trusts created, or as security for a debt owed by a company.

The changes are that:

(1) The policy is to be treated as if it were non-qualifying for the purpose of the chargeable event rules even if it satisfies the qualifying rules.
(2) Chargeable gains from such policies are treated as the company's income and are chargeable under Schedule D Case VI.

There is an exception to this charge in respect of policies used to secure company debts incurred in purchasing land to be occupied by the company for the purposes of its trade (or in constructing, extending or improving buildings so occupied). Broadly speaking, providing that the policy has been used in this way since its inception, the chargeable gain will only be the amount by which the policy proceeds exceed the lowest amount of the loan while secured by the policy.

For close investment-holding companies, chargeable gains on pre-14 March 1989 policies are taxable (as previously).

24.8 Inheritance tax and life policies

The provisions of the Finance Act 1986 radically amended certain aspects of capital transfer tax and renamed it 'inheritance tax'. While these changes clearly have an effect on the use of life assurance policies for tax planning (in particular the 'reservation-of-benefit' rules which seriously affect the efficacy of certain widely-used 'flexible' trusts) life assurance remains one of the best ways of providing for such tax liabilities.

See Chapter 20 for details of inheritance tax. The following is a very brief summary of a complex and detailed area.

24.8.1 Death of policyholder

A life assurance policy beneficially owned by the deceased is property that is subject to inheritance tax in the same way as any other property owned by him (20.15.1).

24.8.2 Gifts of policies

Gifts of policies may generally be made in two ways:

(1) Writing the policy in trust or making a subsequent declaration of trust.
(2) Assignment of the policy.

In either case subsequent premiums may be paid: (*a*) by the donor direct; (*b*) by the beneficiary out of cash gifts from the donor; (*c*) by the beneficiary out of his own resources; (*d*) by a combination of the above.

In general, if the gift is to an individual, an accumulation and maintenance trust, a trust for the disabled or (with effect from 17 March 1987) a trust in which there is an interest in possession, it will constitute a 'potentially exempt transfer' (PET) and will only be taxable if the donor dies within seven years of making the gift. Gifts to other trusts such as discretionary trusts may attract lifetime inheritance tax.

If any of the usual inheritance tax exemptions apply (20.18) neither the gift of the policy nor any gifts of premiums that have been made will be taxable, eg:

(1) The gift of the premium or policy falls within the annual exemption — currently £3,000 (note that if the policy is a qualifying policy and premiums are payable net of life assurance relief then it is the net premium that constitutes the gift; if the premium is paid gross, it is the gross premium that constitutes the gift).
(2) The premiums come within the donor's normal expenditure out of income exemption (note that this applies to payment of premiums not to the gift of an existing policy).
(3) The gifts fall within the marriage settlement exemption.
(4) The gifts fall within the small gifts exemption — outright gifts of not more than £250 per donee (for example a premium on a policy written in trust for the absolute benefit of a child).
(5) Policies written by husband or wife in trust for the other.

If none of the exemptions applies, inheritance tax may be payable in respect of the gift of the policy or the payment of subsequent premiums (unless they fall within the first £150,000 of non-exempt gifts in respect of which a nil rate is payable).

If inheritance tax is payable, the chargeable transfers are the premiums paid by the donor; or, if a gift of an existing policy is made by assignment or declaration of trust, the chargeable transfer is generally the greater of the total gross premiums paid or the market value of the policy (usually the surrender value).

If cash gifts have been made to enable the premiums to be paid by the beneficiary, the amount of the cash gifts will usually be PETs. The proceeds of the policy on death, maturity or surrender will not be subject to inheritance tax in the hands of the recipient of the assignment or a beneficiary having an interest in possession in the trust.

24.8.3 Life of another policies

On the death of the life assured the proceeds are totally free of inheritance tax (20.28). Clearly they do not form part of the life assured's estate, as the policy is not owned by him. The surrender value will, however, be potentially chargeable in the policyholder's estate if he dies before the life assured.

If the policyholder is enabled to pay the premiums by virtue of cash gifts from the donor, the cash gifts will be taxable for the donor, unless the exemptions mentioned above apply, but the proceeds will be free of inheritance tax in the policyholder's hands.

24.8.4 Use of policies

Life assurance policies can be used in two main ways in inheritance tax planning:

(1) as a vehicle for making gifts to your beneficiaries; and
(2) to create a fund for the eventual payment of the tax.

Thus they help both to minimise the amount of tax payable and offer a means of paying any unavoidable liability whenever it arises.

24.9 Pension business

24.9.1 Introduction

In recent years, the structure of pensions provision in the UK has undergone considerable reform. Over the period between October 1987 and July 1988 quite radical changes took place with the replacement of one form of individual pension plan with another, the widening of the scope of some existing forms of pension and the introduction of a new way for members of company pension schemes to top-up their benefits.

The changes have been designed:

(1) to reduce the cost of the State Earnings Related Pension Scheme (SERPS) and to encourage employees to leave the scheme;
(2) to increase flexibility in pension planning and freedom of choice for the individual;
(3) to allow other institutions (such as banks and building societies) to offer pensions in addition to the traditional pension providers, the life assurance companies.

The Finance Act 1989 also introduced further changes designed, *inter alia*:

(1) to enable employers to offer pension benefits higher than those previously permissible;
(2) to restrict the maximum contributions payable to (and in some cases the maximum benefits receivable from) pension plans and schemes which receive favourable tax treatment;
(3) to simplify the administration of schemes which enable employees to top-up the benefits from their employer's scheme;
(4) to end the practice of some pension providers of setting pension business expenses against life assurance profits.

For some years pensions have been separated into three categories:

(1) those provided by the State;
(2) individual (or 'personal') pension arrangements; and
(3) occupational pension schemes.

Until recently, occupational and personal schemes were clearly distinct. They had different tax regimes, were subject to different methods of Inland Revenue control and could also be differentiated by the involvement or otherwise of the individual's employer. These distinctions have been blurred somewhat by the new framework but the structures of the occupational and personal pension regimes remain separate for tax purposes and this distinction continues to be used in this chapter as the means of differentiating the two regimes.

The whole subject of pensions is a complex one and is likely to be subject to continued change over the next few years as the Government responds to the pressures of an aging population, much publicised pension scheme defaults and the requirements of the European Community. Accordingly, what follows is an overview rather than an exhaustive analysis.

24.9.2 Tax position of the life company
(TA 1988 S438, FA 1989 Ss82–89 & Sch 8)

The investment income and capital gains referable to a company's pensions business are totally exempt from tax so that pension funds provide what is often referred to as a 'gross roll-up'.

These tax exemptions apply to pension funds irrespective of whether the funds relate to personal plans or occupational schemes, provided the plan or scheme has the necessary approved or exempt approved status.

The Finance Act 1989 has introduced the concept of the 'ring fence' around companies' pensions business to stop the practice of some offices who set some of their pensions business expenses against their life assurance business profits to obtain tax relief for those expenses.

24.10 The State pension scheme

The State scheme provides three types of pension:

(1) *The basic pension*

> This is a contributory scheme which aims to provide a pension of approximately 20 per cent of national average earnings. It is not related to salary but to obtain the maximum pension you must have paid (or have been credited with) National Insurance contributions for about 90 per cent of your expected working life. The pension (which is taxable as earned income if attributable to your own contributions) is increased each year in line with the Retail Prices Index.
>
> The earnings limit which led to the pension being reduced if the pensioner had earnings of more than a certain amount (£75 in 1989) was abolished from 1 October 1989.

(2) *The graduated pension*

The graduated pension scheme ran from April 1961 until April 1975 and provided a supplement to the basic pension. Both contributions and benefits were related to earnings.

(3) *The State Earnings Related Pension Scheme (SERPS)*

SERPS was introduced in 1978 and is based on National Insurance contributions made by employers and employees on earnings between the lower and upper earnings limits (currently £54 pw and £405 pw respectively). The earnings between these two figures are often called 'band earnings'. The self-employed neither contribute towards, nor benefit from, SERPS.

Originally, SERPS was intended to provide a pension of 25 per cent of band earnings, based on the best 20 years earnings. However, in recent years it has become clear that to support this level of SERPS pension would place a considerable burden on earners in subsequent years. As a result, for those reaching State Retirement age (65 for males, 60 for females) after 5 April 1999, SERPS benefits will be reduced. In such cases earnings will be based on an average over the whole of your working life and not the best 20 years and the percentage of those earnings will be reduced on a sliding scale from 25 per cent, for those retiring in 1999/2000 to 20 per cent for those retiring in 2009/2010 or later.

State pensions do not provide any cash lump sum at retirement or any opportunity of retiring and receiving benefits before State Retirement age. Benefits can be postponed for up to five years, in which case the pension will be increased.

The main benefit from the state scheme is a lifelong pension for the individual but SERPS can also, in certain circumstances, provide a widow's pension which will be of a reduced amount unless the widow is aged over 40 and has dependent children (or over 50 with no dependent children).

24.10.1 Contracting-out of the State Earnings Related Pension Scheme

Since its introduction it has been possible to forgo SERPS benefits in return for a reduction, for both employer and employee, in National Insurance contributions.

Until 6 April 1988, this 'contracting-out' was only possible through an employer-sponsored occupational pension scheme which guaranteed to provide a broadly equivalent level of benefits to the SERPS benefits being lost. Since 6 April 1988, employers have been able to offer contracting-out on a 'money purchase' basis without having to provide the guarantee previously required.

However, this change still left the decision whether to offer contracted-out status firmly in the employer's hands. Further changes which took effect on 1 July 1988 gave the individual employee the right to contract out of SERPS on an individual basis, without his employer's consent. The new plans which enable this are also money-purchase arrangements.

Contracting-out through personal pension plans, involves the payment of 'protected rights contributions' to the relevant personal pension contract. The contributions are identified separately from any other contributions paid and create a 'protected rights fund'; it is the 'protected rights benefits' paid out of this fund at retirement which replace the SERPS benefits lost through the decision to contract out.

The protected rights contributions are made up of the National Insurance rebate given in respect of those who contract out, an 'incentive' payment made to those who are, broadly speaking, contracting-out for the first time and tax relief on the employee's share of the National Insurance rebate, where appropriate. The original incentive payment of 2 per cent will cease from April 1993 from when a 1 per cent payment will be payable for personal pension plans for those over 30.

Contracting-out via a Personal Pension Plan is an annual decision and the individual can contract back into SERPS for the purposes of future benefits.

In general, contracting-out will be of benefit to younger employees but may not match the likely SERPS entitlement for older people. For those contracting out in 1992/93, the cut-off ages are approximately 50 (males) and 43 (females) if the 2 per cent incentive applies in full. In other cases the cut-off ages are approximately 46 and 40, respectively.

Contracting-out is not always a simple decision and expert advice should be sought.

24.11 Personal pension plans and retirement annuity contracts
(TA 1988 Ss618 et seq, FA 1989 Sch 7)

Personal Pension Plans (PPPs) were introduced on 1 July 1988 and superseded the Retirement Annuity Contracts (often called 'section 226 contracts') which ceased to be available for new business after 30 June 1988.

In most respects the legislation governing the two types of arrangement is the same but there are some important differences:

(1) Employers may pay contributions to an employee's PPP but were not allowed to contribute to a S226 contract.
(2) Employee's contributions to a PPP are paid net of basic rate tax under a system known as pension relief at source (PRAS).
(3) Under a PPP a maximum of 25 per cent of the fund being used to provide benefits for the member may be taken as a tax-free cash lump sum. Under S226 contracts cash commutation was based on a multiple of the remaining annuity, usually a more generous method of computing the cash lump sum.
(4) An employee's PPP which is able to receive (or even one which is funded entirely by) protected rights contributions will enable the employee to contract out of SERPS, something which could not be achieved through a S226 contract.
(5) Benefits may be taken between ages 50 and 75 under a PPP. Under a S226 contract benefits could not commence until age 60 (but in both cases earlier retirement ages are possible for specific occupations which the Revenue acknowledge as having a short working life, or in the case of ill-health). No benefits can be taken from a PPP protected rights fund until State Pension Age (males 65, females 60).
(6) PPPs can be offered by a greater range of pension providers than could S226 contracts. Banks, building societies and unit trust groups can offer PPPs, in addition to the more traditional approach of investing contributions in pension policies offered by life companies. At least one personal pension management scheme has been set up to provide the legal framework and administrative support to individuals wanting a greater say in the running and investment of their pension. Where the PPP is fully invested in life and pension policies it need not be set up under a trust but such a trust is necessary if the other types of PPP investment are used.

(7) The Finance Act 1989 enabled most individuals to make greater contributions to PPPs (as a percentage of their earnings) but also introduced a 'cap' of £60,000 (indexed to £75,000 for 1992–93, £71,400 in 1991–92) in respect of earnings which can be taken into account for contribution purposes. Neither of these changes applies to S226 contracts.

24.11.1 Personal pension plans

Eligibility

(1) You will be eligible to make contributions to one of these plans if you are in receipt of 'relevant earnings'. This means either earnings from non-pensionable employments, or from businesses, professions, partnerships, etc. Thus, if you have any Schedule D Case I or II earnings, you normally qualify for relief from income tax in respect of premiums paid under a PPP approved by the Revenue, to provide an annuity at your retirement. This relief is also available if you have a non-pensionable employment, eg with a firm which does not provide a pension scheme. You are not eligible if you belong to an approved pension scheme operated by your employers, but you are eligible if you are not a member of such a scheme.
(2) If your employer's pension scheme provides only a sum assured payable on your death while in the employer's service, your earnings from that employment will still be regarded as 'relevant earnings'.
(3) Where you have two sources of income, one being relevant earnings, and the other arising from pensionable employment, you are eligible to contribute to a PPP in respect of your non-pensionable earnings, subject to certain limits.
(4) In two cases it is possible for an individual to have a PPP even though he is not eligible to make contributions to it. The first is that it is possible for an employee who is a member accruing pension benefits under his employer's occupational pension scheme to effect a PPP in order to contract out of SERPS. Such a PPP may not receive any contributions other than protected rights contributions. The second is that a PPP can be established in order to accept a transfer payment from another approved pension scheme or arrangement, even though the individual is not then eligible to make contributions to the PPP.
(5) Controlling directors of investment companies are not eligible for any form of PPP in respect of earnings from such

a company nor are certain other controlling directors who are in receipt of benefit from their employer's occupational scheme.

Tax relief on premiums and limits

(1) If you have relevant earnings, and pay either single or annual premiums to a PPP within the limits mentioned below, you enjoy full tax relief on those premiums in the relevant years. Employees pay premiums net of basic rate tax and any higher rate relief is claimed through the PAYE coding. The new 20 per cent tax band does not affect the rate at which the employee can deduct tax, which remains the 25 per cent basic rate. The self-employed can set off premiums against earned income.

(2) The current annual limits for contributions to PPPs are shown in (4) below and are expressed as a percentage of your 'net relevant earnings' (NRE). This means relevant earnings from your non-pensionable employment or business, etc, less certain deductions such as expenses, trading losses, capital allowances, etc. Personal charges such as interest or payments under deeds of covenant are not deducted.

(3) Contributions may be paid to a PPP and a S226 contract at the same time but contributions to a S226 contract reduce the amounts that can be paid to a PPP and can restrict the overall contributions in some cases.

(4) The PPP contribution limits since 1989/90 are as follows (for S226 limits see 24.12 and for the limits for previous years see earlier editions of this book):

Age at beginning of year of assessment	%
below 36	$17\frac{1}{2}$
36–45	20
46–50	25
51–55	30
56–60	35
61 or more	40

For example, a 48 year-old with net relevant earnings of £20,000 can contribute up to £5,000 pa to a PPP. A 58 year old with the same NRE could contribute £7,000.

(5) For tax year 1989–90, a limit was introduced for the first time to restrict the maximum amount of net relevant earnings which could be taken into account in determining the contributions payable to a PPP. The original limit was £60,000 but

it was introduced so as to be increased in subsequent years in line with the Retail Prices Index, rounded up to the nearest multiple of £600. The figure for 1992/93 is £75,000. For example, in 1992/93 an individual aged 48 with net relevant earnings of £75,000 can contribute up to £18,750 to a PPP. No greater contribution would be possible no matter how far net relevant earnings exceeded £75,000.

(6) If you have two sources of income, one from pensionable employment, and the other being net relevant earnings, you may contribute to the above limit in respect of your relevant earnings regardless of the level of your pensionable earnings. For example, a 58 year old has pensionable earnings as a company executive of £25,000 per annum. He also has net relevant earnings from a part-time consultancy of £8,000 per annum. He can pay premiums to a PPP of 35 per cent of £8,000 = £2,800.

(7) An amount not exceeding 5 per cent of your net relevant earnings can be used to provide a lump sum payable from the PPP, in the event of your death before age 75. Premiums used to provide this life cover must be included as part of the contributions you are permitted to pay to your PPP.

(8) If your employer pays contributions to your PPP, these too must be taken as part of the maximum contribution which can be made to your plan. Employer's contributions are not treated as the employee's income.

(9) Protected rights contributions paid to your PPP to enable you to contract out of SERPS can be paid in addition to the maximum permissible contribution calculated as the appropriate percentage of your net relevent earnings.

(10) Married couples who each have relevant earnings are entitled to pay separate premiums based on their respective net relevant earnings. It is important that the spouse paying the premiums has sufficient taxable earnings to be able to take full advantage of the relief available. For example, a wife with an income of less than her personal allowances and reliefs will be paying no tax so that, effectively, no relief will be available on the premiums paid by her, unless her salary is increased (although it appears that relief granted under the PRAS system would not be reclaimed by the Revenue in such cases).

(11) For tax years prior to 1990/91 provided the spouse paying the premiums had sufficient taxable earnings to make use of the available relief, the relief for a couple taxed jointly, in effect, was given at the highest rate(s) paid on their joint earnings. Spouses who had elected for separate taxation were given

relief against their separate earnings. For tax years 1990/91 and later, independent taxation removes this apparent anomaly in giving relief for couples who were jointly taxed.
(12) It is important to bear in mind that there are three separate aspects here: eligibility to pay premiums; ability to utilise relief available as a result of paying such premiums; and the method of giving that relief.

Year for which relief granted and 'carry-back'

Relief for premiums is only given against net relevant earnings of the tax year in which premiums are paid, but you can elect to have any premium you pay treated for tax purposes as if it had been paid during the preceding tax year; or, if you had no relevant earnings for the premium to be relieved against in that year (eg, because of losses or retirement), then in the tax year before that; ie there is a 'carry-back' period of one or two years. When electing to obtain relief in this way it does not matter whether you have any net relevant earnings in the year in which you actually pay the premium but if you do not have any prospective tax liability you may not be able to utilise the tax relief available. The maximum relief available in any year is the amount of net relevant earnings for that year (or, where carry back is used, the relief available in the year in which the premium is treated as being paid).

Eligibility to pay premiums and 'carry-forward'

To the extent that premiums paid in any year fall short of the permitted maximum of net relevant earnings, it is possible to carry forward the shortfall on unused eligibility for up to six years and use the shortfall (on a first-in first-out basis) to obtain entitlement to pay a premium in a subsequent year, where that premium exceeds the maximum percentage limit of net relevant earnings for the year in which it is paid. (This is subject to a modification where the assessment of relevant earnings for a year is not determined until more than six years after the end of that year.)

Thus the earliest year's unused entitlement to pay premiums which may be utilised to permit payment of a premium paid in 1992/93 is that for 1986/87. The maximum payable by way of premiums in any tax year will be $17\frac{1}{2}$ per cent (or the appropriate higher figure for those over 35 years old) of the net relevant earnings for that year plus any unused entitlement for the previous six tax years. Thus, for example, if you are 35 or under and pay a premium of £3,000 in respect of the net relevant earnings of the current year, say £15,000, the first £2,625 ($17\frac{1}{2}$ per cent of £15,000) is permitted because of those relevant earnings, and the remaining £375 only by virtue of any unused entitlement brought forward. The Revenue's interpretation of the legislation is that the maximum contribution payable in any year is the amount of relevant earnings for that year (even where 'carry forward' would have suggested a greater eligibility to pay contributions).

Benefits payable and age at which they may be taken

(1) The PPP scheme established by the pension provider can allow the individual to make more than one 'arrangement' under it. The advantages of this are that, as benefits from an arrangement can, generally, only be taken once if they are to include a cash lump sum, multiple arrangements can give the opportunity to take benefits in stages.
(2) Your pension may start being paid at any age between 50 and 75. It is not necessary for you actually to retire before the annuity may commence. In certain occupations, the Revenue allow an annuity to start earlier than the age of 50 (eg, jockeys, motor racing drivers, cricketers, etc). Under no circumstances may the annuity start later than the age of 75.
(3) The annuity payable to you can take one of many forms: sterling or unit-linked, guaranteed or non-guaranteed, etc. In most contracts there is a provision that if you die before the beginning of the annuity, an annuity is payable to your widow or dependants nominated by you or, alternatively, a lump sum could be paid, not exceeding the amount of the contributions plus a reasonable amount of interest or bonuses (this generally would include capital growth and income attributable to the premiums paid under a unit-linked plan).
(4) Should your PPP incorporate a sum assured, on your premature death the lump sum would be paid and this can be arranged to be free of inheritance tax by writing it in trust where the PPP scheme itself is not set up under trust.
(5) Any annuity payable to the widow, widower, or dependant would be free of inheritance tax (ITA 1984 S152).
(6) The whole of any annuity payable either to you, your spouse or your dependants will be treated and taxed as income (and not, as is the case with purchased life annuities, partly as income and partly as a return of capital, see 24.14.2). However, the annuity will be treated as earned income to the extent to which contributions have been allowed for tax relief.
(7) A lump sum may be taken from the PPP, between the ages of 50 and 75, up to a maximum of 25 per cent of the fund then being used to provide you with retirement benefits. For PPPs effected prior to 27 July 1989, the value of any Protected

Rights Fund incorporated in the plan could be taken into account in calculating the cash lump sum available but any fund used to provide benefits for a widow(er) or dependants had to be excluded. For PPPs effected on or after that date these rules are reversed, ie, the Protected Rights Fund must be excluded but funds for widow(er)s' and dependants' benefits can be included.

(8) Instead of taking the annuity from the life company with whom you hold the contract, you can use the fund built up for your annuity in order to purchase an annuity from any other company, thus obtaining the best terms then available ('open market option'). If your PPP is provided by an organisation which is not a life assurance company, your pension (and life assurance) must be provided by a life company.

24.11.2 Contracting-out via a PPP

If a PPP has an 'appropriate scheme certificate' from the Occupational Pensions Board it will be able to receive protected rights contributions (and may be funded by them entirely) and so enable the individual employee to contract out of SERPS.

A PPP which receives only protected rights contributions (a 'PPP(PRO)') can be effected by an employee who is a member of a contracted-in occupational scheme but wishes to contract out on an individual basis.

Contributions

Protected rights contributions are made up of the National Insurance rebate, the incentive (where applicable) and tax relief on the employee's share of the rebate (which grosses it up at the basic rate). The rebate is equal to the difference between the contracted-in and contracted-out National Insurance rates on the individual employee's band earnings (the earnings between the upper and lower earnings limits). Both employer and employee continue to pay full National Insurance but the rebate is paid by the DSS to the individual's plan after the end of the relevant tax year.

The incentive is 2 per cent of band earnings and is payable for up to six tax years commencing 1987/88, but will continue for many at 1 per cent from April 1993, see 24.10.1. Until 5 April 1989, a plan could be 'backdated' to receive the incentive and rebate for tax year 1987/88.

Broadly speaking, the incentive is payable to those who contract out for the first time and those who have been in contracted-out employment for less than two years.

Benefits

No cash lump sum can be taken from a protected rights fund but, for plans effected prior to 27 July 1989, the value of the fund can be included for the purposes of the calculation of the maximum cash sum from a non-protected rights fund forming part of the same pension arrangement, if benefits are being taken from both funds at that time. For plans effected on or after that date the value of the protected rights fund cannot be included in the lump sum calculation.

The pension must commence between State Pension age (65 males, 60 females) and the age of 75. It must increase at 3 per cent pa or the rate of the Retail Prices Index, whichever is lower, and must not discriminate between males and females, married or single people in terms of the annuity rates offered.

A protected rights pension must continue for the benefit of a widow/widower or dependant on the individual's death, at a rate not less than one half of the individual's pension.

On death before retirement age the protected rights fund can be paid to the deceased's estate or nominees but no life assurance sum assured can be included in the protected rights benefits.

24.12 Retirement annuity contracts (S226 contracts)

No new S226 contracts can be entered into after 30 June 1988 but contracts in existence by that date can continue much as before. Contributions can continue to be paid to such contracts and regular contributions can be increased in the future.

Several of the key differences between these S226 contracts and the new PPPs have already been highlighted, eg, no employer's contributions; contributions paid gross and the tax reclaimed; no facility for an employee to contract out through a S226 contract; and no general entitlement to take benefits before age 60. The more favourable rules for determining the maximum lump sum cash which can be taken from a S226 contract, which have been referred to already, are that the cash can equal three times the annual annuity payable after the cash has been taken. Contracts entered into on or after 17 March 1987 are subject to a maximum cash lump sum of £150,000 per contract.

S226 contracts are not subject to the capping of earnings to be taken into account when determining maximum contributions but do not benefit from the increased percentages set out at 24.11.1. The S226 contribution limits as percentages of net relevant earnings are now:

Age at beginning of year of assessment	%
up to 50	$17\frac{1}{2}$
51–55	20
56–60	$22\frac{1}{2}$
61 or more	$27\frac{1}{2}$

It should be noted that, although many S226 contracts contain an open market option to allow the annuity to be purchased from a life company other than the one with which the pension plan has been effected, exercising such an option after 30 June 1988 will have the effect of transferring the policy proceeds to a new PPP (unless the policyholder has a second S226 contract already in existence with that other life company). Thus, in the absence of another S226 existing contract, the benefits will be paid out of a PPP with the resulting less favourable calculation of the maximum cash lump sum compared to the S226 contract.

24.12.1 Occupational schemes
(TA 1988 Ss590 et seq and Sch 23, FA 1989 Sch 6)

These are schemes provided by an employer for the benefit of some or all of his employees but they are not available to directors of investment companies.

In the 1989 Budget the Chancellor introduced the concept of unapproved 'top up' pension schemes. These schemes offer none of the usual occupational scheme tax benefits but allow an employer to provide benefits greater than those allowed under an approved occupational scheme.

A recent decision of the European Court of Justice has given rise to considerable concern over occupational pension schemes. The Court held that such a pension constituted pay and so came under the scope of Article 119 of the EEC Treaty and that the principle of equal pay applied to each element of remuneration. The case in question (*Barber v GRE*) appears to have far-reaching consequences for occupational schemes, eg in respect of the current different retirement ages for men and women, but has caused considerable uncertainty as to its full scope. A second case is expected to be heard by the Court in 1992 and it is hoped that this will bring much needed clarification of the effect of the *Barber* judgment.

Approved schemes

Approval of such schemes is given by the Pension Scheme Office (PSO) which is a branch of the Inland Revenue. The PSO was previously called the Superannuation Funds Office (SFO).

'Approval' will prevent contributions paid by the employer being taxed in the employees' hands as a benefit in kind.

'Exempt Approval' will give the additional benefits of the gross roll-up in the fund and tax relief for the employee in respect of regular contributions he makes to the scheme. Exempt Approval will also mean that the employer's contributions will be deductible business expenses without relying on the normal rules for deductibility applying to Schedule D income.

In most cases approval is given under the PSO's discretionary powers which are extremely wide-ranging.

The conditions include requirements that:

(1) The scheme be set up under irrevocable trusts for the sole purpose of providing 'relevant benefits' in respect of service as an employee. Relevant benefits, broadly speaking, include most types of financial benefit given in connection with the termination of an employee's service with a particular employer.
(2) The scheme is recognised by employer and employee and that the employee is given written particulars of its essential features.
(3) The employer contributes to the scheme (except in the case of free-standing AVC schemes — see 24.13).
(4) Pension benefits are payable on retirement at a specified age not earlier than 60 (or 55 in the case of women) and not later than 70, up to a maximum permitted benefit calculated by reference to the employee's final remuneration and the length of service with that employer. (See section on Benefits.) Benefits may be available in respect of early retirement

after age 50 (45 in the case of women) or at any age where retirement is due to ill health. Taking benefits can be postponed but for those subject to the capping of income (see later) benefits must be taken no later than age 75. There is also a maximum to the permitted pension which can be provided for widows and dependants.

(5) No pension may be surrendered, commuted or assigned, save for commutation on retirement up to a maximum lump sum again calculated by reference to length of service and final remuneration (see section on Benefits).

A scheme may also provide for a lump sum payment of up to four times the employee's final remuneration on death in service and for a return of the employee's contributions in certain cases.

Since 6 April 1988 it has not been possible for an employer to make membership of an occupational scheme (other than one providing death-in-service benefits only) compulsory. Employees are also able to opt out of their employer's scheme and so become eligible to effect their own PPP, independent of the employer. In general, leaving a good occupational scheme is unlikely to be wise except where its benefits are poor and expert advice should be sought if this is contemplated.

(i) Contributions

The employer must make some contribution to the scheme although the employee may indirectly provide the necessary funds by agreeing to a reduction in salary, 'a salary sacrifice'. Contributions by the employer to an exempt approved scheme are deductible business expenses, although relief in respect of non-regular contributions may be deferred by being spread over a maximum of five years.

The employee may make personal contributions of up to 15 per cent of his remuneration. Personal contributions attract tax relief at the highest rate paid by the individual.

Unlike PPPs there are no specific limits on the amount of contributions which may be made to an occupational scheme instead (subject to the 'income capping' rules referred to below), the controls operate on a level of benefits which is allowed. If a scheme becomes 'over-funded' (ie, where the scheme has more capital than is necessary to meet its prospective liabilities), payment of further contributions may be restricted or capital may have to be returned to the employer or the employee may be subject to a tax charge.

Finance Act 1986 (now TA 1988 Sch 22) provided machinery for determining what constitutes over-funding and what action should be taken if it occurs. If a refund is made to the employer it is taxable at a special rate of 40 per cent. Where a surplus arises from an employee's voluntary contributions any refund to the employee will have tax deducted at 35 per cent under the provisions of the Finance Act 1989. An employee who is a higher rate taxpayer will be subject to a further charge taking the total to 48 per cent.

(ii) Benefits

Many schemes provide a pension of one-sixtieth of final remuneration for each year of service so that the maximum pension of two-thirds of final salary is reached after 40 years' service.

In recent years changes in legislation have created different sets of benefit rules, according to when the scheme was established or when the member joined it. The key categories are pre-17 March 1987 members, post-16 March 1987 members and those affected by the 'capping' of income under the Finance Act 1989.

Pre-17 March 1987 members
An 'uplifted sixtieths' scale may be used to provide the maximum benefit after only ten years (taking into account benefits from previous employments). Final salary or final remuneration may be calculated in either of the ways permitted by the PSO:

(1) the remuneration in any of the five years preceding the normal retirement date (remuneration includes the average of fluctuating emoluments earned over at least three years ending with the year in question); or
(2) the highest average of total emoluments over any period of three consecutive years ending within ten years before the normal retirement date.

Benefits in kind taxable under Schedule E may be included when calculating final salary. Company directors with substantial shareholdings may only calculate final salary using the definition quoted in (2) above.

Past years may be permitted to be 'dynamised' when computing final salary, ie, increased by reference to the rise in the Retail

Prices Index (RPI) between the year in question and the normal retirement date. Pensions in payment may be increased on a discretionary basis, by reference to the RPI or by a fixed percentage, typically 3 per cent or 5 per cent per annum compound.

For those retiring after 16 March 1987 'final salary' excludes certain income and gains from shares, etc acquired through share option, share incentive or profit sharing schemes. In addition those with final salaries of over £100,000 pa will have to use definition (2) above, subject to transitional reliefs for those retiring before 6 April 1991. As an alternative they may use £100,000 as final salary for benefit purposes.

The employee is often given the right to commute a part of his pension for a tax-free cash lump sum up to a maximum of $1\frac{1}{2}$ times final remuneration (three-eighths of final salary for a maximum of 40 years service). An 'uplifted eightieths' scale may be used to provide the maximum lump sum after 20 years' service.

The scheme may provide a lump sum of up to four times final remuneration on the death of the employee in service, together with a refund of the employee's personal contributions. Such payments are usually made by the trustees of the scheme who have a discretion as to selection of the recipient, from a class of potential beneficiaries. Such payments are usually free of inheritance tax.

Pensions may be paid for a spouse or dependant, of up to two-thirds of the maximum pension to which the deceased would have been entitled at the normal retirement date.

On death in retirement a pension may be provided for a spouse or dependant in the same way as for death in service.

Post-16 March 1987 members
The rules are broadly the same as those above but the 'uplifted sixtieths' scale can now provide maximum pension benefits only after 20 years' service. The 'uplifted eightieths' scale for lump sums can only be used in conjunction with the use of the uplifted sixtieths scale for the pension. In addition, the maximum final salary figure for calculating lump sums is £100,000 (subject to increase by Treasury order).

Those affected by income capping
The Finance Act 1989 introduced new rules for members of schemes established on or after 14 March 1989 and for members

joining pre-14 March 1989 schemes after 31 May 1989. For such members, no benefits can be provided in respect of any remuneration which exceeds a specified amount. For the tax year 1989/90 this figure was set at £60,000 but, as with PPPs, the figure is to be indexed in future years in line with the Retail Prices Index and for 1992/93 is £75,000.

Early retirement benefits for such members are also improved so that the maximum pension (two thirds of final salary) can be provided at any time on retirement between the ages of 50 and 70, subject to the member having 20 years of service with the employer.

There is also a slightly simplified method of calculating the allowable tax-free cash lump sum at retirement: this can be 2.25 × the pre-commutation pension available or three-eighths of final remuneration for each year of service (up to a maximum of 40), whichever is the greater. The cash lump sum is still subject to a maximum of one and one-half times final salary capped where appropriate.

It is possible that members not caught by these rules would prefer to be subject to them, eg, to enjoy a more favourable lump sum calculation. Such members may elect (with the scheme trustees' consent in the case of pre-17 March 1987 members) to become subject to these rules but they will then apply as a package, ie, it is not possible to elect to become subject to only some of them and not to others.

The 1989 Budget proposals would have meant that personal contributions to an approved occupational scheme would also be subject to the remuneration cap for all members of all schemes (no matter when the individual joined or the scheme was established). This proposal was modified as the Bill passed through Parliament and personal contributions are only affected by the remuneration cap where the scheme was established on or after 14 March 1989 or the member joined a pre-14 March 1989 scheme after 31 May 1989.

(iii) Pension provision for company directors

Since FA 1973, controlling directors of close companies are eligible for inclusion in an approved pension scheme established by their company, either as a group scheme or as an individual pension arrangement for the director concerned. Thus, they can obtain benefits with premiums paid by their company being deductible for corporation tax and personal contributions up to 15 per cent of their incomes being allowed for income tax. They may obtain potential benefits within the general pension limits, including a pension of up to two-thirds of their final salary (if they have been employed by their company for 10 years or more — 20 years for post-March 1987 members), the right to commute a portion of their pension up to a maximum of $1\frac{1}{2}$ times final salary, after 20 years' service; a widow's pension of two-thirds of the individual's pension; and, in the case of death-in-service life cover, four times salary plus a widow's pension of 4/9ths of salary.

In general, the same rules apply to 'controlling' directors as to any individuals in an occupational pension scheme, however, because a director of a family company is in a rather different position from an ordinary employee, the Revenue have imposed some limitations on directors with at least 20 per cent control, eg, the measurement of final salary is more stringent than for non-controlling directors.

An employee who has since March 1987 been a 'controlling director' or at any time during the ten years before retirement is subject to the more restrictive definition of final remuneration which applies to those who are still controlling directors at retirement.

Directors with 20 per cent control and those who are members of families controlling over 50 per cent of the company may not join a company's approved pension scheme, if it is an investment company.

(iv) Unapproved schemes

Unapproved occupational pension schemes may be established by employers to provide benefits greater than those allowable under the legislation relating to approved schemes and so can top-up benefits to more than the maximum two-thirds of final salary, and can provide additional benefits for employees with insufficient service and benefits in respect of employees' earnings in excess of the capped figure, as appropriate.

Such schemes may be funded (ie, contributions set aside in order to fund the promised benefits) or unfunded (ie, at retirement the benefits will be paid by the company out of current income or investments).

If the scheme is funded, the employer will obtain tax relief on the contributions as a normal business expense but the employee will be taxed on those contributions as if they were emoluments. Any employee's contributions will not be tax deductible.

The investment of contributions receives no special tax treatment but is taxed as appropriate to the investment medium used for the investment.

Any pensions paid from unapproved schemes and lump sums from unfunded schemes are taxable in the hands of the employee but lump sum benefits from funded schemes may be paid free of tax.

24.12.2 Contracting-out via an approved occupational scheme

In the past, only 'defined benefit' schemes were able to contract out of the State Earnings Related Pension Scheme (SERPS) because of the requirement that the scheme must provide a guaranteed minimum pension. In recent years the approach has changed: due to the increasing burden of SERPS on future generations the Government proposes to restrict the benefits provided and encourage people to opt out of SERPS in favour of individual pension arrangements. At the same time flexibility and transferability are key objectives of the proposals now being implemented.

As already mentioned, money-purchase schemes can now be used to contract out of SERPS without the previous requirement of a guarantee attaching to the benefits which are, in effect, replacing SERPS.

A contracted-out money purchase (COMP) scheme will receive protected rights contributions by way of National Insurance rebate and incentive payment, where appropriate, as is the case with a PPP. However a COMP will receive the National Insurance payments monthly, direct from the employer, and not as a lump sum, a year in arrears, as does a PPP. COMPs will usually require a small personal contribution from the employee in order for him to obtain tax relief on his share of the National Insurance rebate paid into the pension scheme.

An occupational scheme can contract out all of its members or can specify which categories of occupations are to be contracted-out. In either case individual members of the scheme can elect to stay contracted-in to SERPS in relation to the occupational scheme (but they could still contract out on an individual basis through a PPP(PRO) or a free-standing AVC scheme).

With a COMP, the Inland Revenue's limits on maximum benefits apply to the aggregate of the protected rights and non-protected rights benefits; a contracted-in occupational scheme member may obtain the maximum benefits from the occupational scheme, in addition to the protected rights benefits, from a PPP(PRO) effected to contract out of SERPS.

24.12.3 Simplified approved occupational schemes

These are schemes which can be established using standard documentation provided by the Inland Revenue and the DSS. Created primarily for the new pension providers (banks, building societies and unit trust groups) they are easier to administer but are restricted in the benefits they can provide compared to 'full' occupational schemes.

24.13 Free-standing AVC schemes

From October 1987 all occupational scheme members are entitled to top-up their pensions by making contributions to a separate pension scheme of their own. Such a 'free-standing' Additional Voluntary Contribution (AVC) scheme may not be commuted into a cash lump sum and must be aggregated with the occupational scheme to determine the maximum permitted benefits. The overriding limit on personal contributions, 15 per cent of salary, remains.

Although regulated by the occupational pension scheme tax legislation, free-standing AVC schemes also have similarities to PPPs in that they are individual arrangements independent of the individual's employer. They can also be used by a member of a contracted-in occupational scheme to receive protected rights contributions and so contract out of SERPS in much the same way as a 'protected rights only' PPP. The main differences are that: no tax relief is allowed on the employee's share of the National Insurance rebate paid to a free-standing AVC scheme; and that, if an occupational scheme member contracts out of SERPS by means of a free-standing AVC scheme, the Revenue's maximum benefits limits apply to the aggregate of the benefits from both schemes.

An employee's contributions to such schemes must be paid net of tax relief at the basic rate.

Following proposals in the 1989 Budget, the administrative requirements of such schemes were simplified, particularly for members making contributions of no more than £2,400 pa, for whom the liaison required at outset with the members' occupational scheme (a source of considerable difficulty in the past) is no longer required.

Rules were also introduced in the Finance Act 1989 to allow overfunding caused by personal contributions to be returned to the member at retirement (previously such overfunding merely relieved the occupational scheme from having to meet its full commitment). Repayments to the member are subject to tax at 35 per cent (an effective 48 per cent is paid by higher rate taxpayers) to recoup the tax relief allowed on the contributions and the tax-free nature of the pension fund.

24.13.1 Inheritance tax and pension policies

Although a policyholder may not alienate his right to a retirement pension, it is possible to assign any death benefits provided under retirement annuity or personal pension plans, whether provided as a sum assured or as a return of the retirement fund. The inheritance tax rules broadly are similar to those applicable to life policy assignments except that:

(1) discretionary trusts of these assignable benefits will not be subject to the usual inheritance tax charging regime of ten-yearly and exit charges, provided the benefits are distributed within two years of the individual's death;
(2) the right to a pension is not treated as giving rise to an interest in possession in the pension fund;
(3) the gift of a 'return of fund' death benefit will usually be regarded as having no value, provided the individual is in good health. Similarly, subsequent contributions to the pension will be treated as being attributable to the provision of the pension benefits and not the death benefit, providing the individual is in good health at the time the contribution is made.

Occupational schemes are usually written under discretionary trusts and also achieve the same inheritance tax exemptions on payment of contributions and distribution of benefits.

24.14 General annuity business

24.14.1 The company's position
(TA 1988 Ss 436, 437 & FA 1991 S48 & Sch 7)

At present, if the annuities paid by the company to general annuitants during the tax year exceed or equal the investment income and realised gain of the general annuity fund, the fund is not taxed on the income and gains. Companies, therefore, try to balance the income of the fund against their annuity payments, which explains the special rates that are sometimes offered for different classes or ages. Annuity rates are, as a result, generally based on gross income and tend to be high at times of high interest rates.

The Budget of 1991, however, announced proposals to change the taxation of general annuity funds in order to move it onto a similar basis to ordinary life assurance, with effect for accounting periods commencing after 31 December 1991. The change applies to existing business, subject to transitional relief.

24.14.2 The individual annuitant
(TA 1988 Ss656 & 685(4A))

(1) If you purchase an annuity from a life company the annuity paid is regarded as consisting of a capital element (representing a return of premium) and an income element. The ratio between the two depends on actuarial mortality tables: the older the age of the annuitant, the higher the capital content. The capital content is fixed from the outset.

The effect is that the capital content is tax-free, while the income element is treated as ordinary investment income, subject to income tax at the basic and higher rates, if applicable. The company pays the annuity after deduction of basic rate tax.

(2) An immediate annuity is one that starts immediately. A deferred annuity is one that runs from some time in the future. Some annuities are for the annuitant's lifetime; others are for a limited period (temporary annuity) ceasing at the end of the period or on death, if earlier. Some annuities are, however, guaranteed to run for a minimum period, and will continue to be paid after death to the annuitant's personal representatives or assignees.

(3) It is the Revenue's view that the right to an annuity is a right to property which is 'wholly or substantially a right to

income'. Accordingly, it is not possible to effect income tax savings by assignment of an annuity from one spouse to another, in an effort to take advantage of independent taxation.

24.14.3 Guaranteed income bonds

These are most often structured as a series of endowment or term policies, but they may also be a combination of two separate purchased annuity contracts: a temporary immediate annuity and a deferred lifetime annuity. Your lump sum investment is split between the two according to the premium for each type of contract. For example:

(1) If you are a male aged 65 and purchase a ten-year guaranteed income bond for a total price of £10,000 an amount of, say, £5,200 might be the price of the temporary annuity and £4,800 the price of the deferred annuity contract. The net temporary annuity could be as high as, say, £1,000 per annum for ten years, representing a gross yield on a £10,000 outlay of 10 per cent per annum. The capital content of the temporary annuity instalments would be approximately £700 and the income element £300. The income element would be paid subject to deduction of income tax at the basic rate and treated as investment income in your hands.

(2) At the end of the ten years, the temporary annuity ceases and you then have the option of taking either a deferred lifetime annuity under the deferred contract of, say, £1,700 per annum or a lump sum equal to your initial outlay (ie £10,000). If you take the deferred annuity, the capital content will be relatively low; in the above example it might be £470 per annum, and the income element £1,230 per annum. The latter is fully chargeable to income tax.

(3) *Guaranteed income bonds issued on or before 26 March 1974.* If in the case of a guaranteed income bond issued on or before 26 March 1974, you opt to cash in the deferred annuity and take the lump sum, the difference between the lump sum of £10,000 and the purchase price of the deferred annuity (£4,800) is treated as a gain chargeable to higher rate tax (but not to basic rate tax) in a similar way to the gain under a single premium bond (24.6.2). In this case, the gain would be £5,200, (ie £10,000 cash option less £4,800 purchase consideration) realised after ten years. A slice of £520 (£5,200 divided by ten) would be added to your other taxable income in the year of cashing-in and the appropriate rate or rates applicable

to the slice applied to the total gain of £5,200 (Ss542, 543 & 547).
(4) If you choose to surrender your guaranteed income bond after, say, three years, the same principle applies, but in calculating the gain under the temporary annuity contract you deduct the capital elements of all the annuity payments you have received to that stage under the temporary annuity from the purchase price for that annuity thereby inflating the gain (S543).
(5) *Bonds issued after 26 March 1974*. In the case, however, of guaranteed income bonds and guaranteed growth bonds (deferred annuity bonds) issued after 26 March 1974, any gain arising on surrender or the taking of a cash option (£5,200 in the example mentioned in (3) above) will be subject to basic rate tax in addition to the higher rate. Moreover, the proceeds on death under an annuity contract made on or after 10 December 1974 granting a death benefit will be treated in the same way as surrender proceeds.
(6) Loans taken against these bonds will be treated as total or partial surrenders and any gains deemed to have been realised will be subject to tax as in (3) and (5) above.

24.15 Permanent health insurance (PHI)

PHI policies are designed to provide a replacement income for the individual if he is unable to work through illness or disability. Contracts are usually available to those aged between 16 and 60 but will terminate on the insured reaching his normal retirement date. Contracts, once entered into, cannot be terminated by the provider of the cover, except in the case of non-disclosure or other breach by the insured.

Structure

PHI contracts can be written as life assurance policies (usually non-qualifying policies to avoid having to provide a substantial sum assured on death) but payment of disability benefits is not treated as a surrender of rights for the purposes of life policy taxation.

Tax position

Premiums will usually not be deductible expenditure for income tax purposes although for some years the industry has argued for a measure of relief. The exception to this is that if an employer effects a PHI policy on a member of his staff, in order to enable him to continue to pay the employee's salary during period of disability or illness, or if the PHI policy is to cover a revenue loss during such period, the employer might be able to claim the premiums as a business expense, in some circumstances.

The benefits from PHI policy are taxable as unearned income in the hands of the policyholder, under Schedule D Case III. Where the individual receives benefit for his own disablement, he can take advantage of an Inland Revenue concession which gives him a 'tax holiday'. This means that he will not be taxed on the benefit until it has been paid for a complete tax year; for example, if benefit commences in May 1991 it will not become taxable until the tax year commencing 6 April 1993. Policies owned by someone other than the insured do not benefit from this tax holiday.

Typical provisions

Payment of benefit will usually commence after a deferred period. This will be between, typically, one and 12 months and is used to avoid claims for short term disabilities or illnesses. The longer the deferred period, the cheaper the cover will be. In hazardous occupations and those where relatively small illnesses are common and disabling, short deferred periods may not be offered.

Policies will usually limit benefits to a percentage (frequently 75 per cent but often with a lower percentage for particularly high incomes) of pre-disability earnings. This is frequently reduced by other benefits received during the period of disability and provides an incentive to the individual to return to work as soon as possible.

The definition of 'disability' is key to the working of the policy. Some contracts will not treat the individual as disabled if he is capable of doing any part of his former job. Others may not treat a person as disabled if he can do another job for which he is reasonably suited even if he is completely unable to do the former job.

Benefits

The benefit is usually a regular payment, commencing at the end of the deferred period, and payable weekly, monthy or quarterly in arrears. The level of benefit will be determined by the amount of cover purchased and the maximum benefit determined by reference to pre-disability earnings. Partial benefit may be paid where the individual can continue in work but with reduced earning capacity and some policies may include a rehabilitation benefit to help the individual back to work after a period of disability by means of a continuing reduced benefit.

Most flexible PHI policies will allow the cover to be increased as the individual's salary increases and some will offer this as an automatic indexation in line with, for example, the RPI or AEI (Retail Prices or Average Earnings Indices, respectively). Some policies also offer the option of an increasing benefit (again in line with an appropriate index) during a period of disability although such contracts are, or course, more expensive.

In some cases the policy may even offer a cash lump sum on termination of the contract.

25 Tax tables

25.1 Income tax table for 1992–93

Income	Single person	Married man
£3,000	—	—
4,000	111	—
5,000	311	—
6,000	539	167
7,000	789	367
8,000	1,039	609
9,000	1,289	859
10,000	1,539	1,109
12,000	2,039	1,609
14,000	2,539	2,109
16,000	3,039	2,609
18,000	3,539	3,109
20,000	4,039	3,609
25,000	5,289	4,859
30,000	6,967	6,279
40,000	10,967	10,279
50,000	14,967	14,279
70,000	22,967	22,279

Notes:
(1) Single personal and married couple's relief have been taken into account.
(2) Other reliefs have been ignored.
(3) The tax for a married man has been calculated on the assumption that he obtains the married couple's allowance.

25.2 Tax rates and allowances for 1976–77 to 1991–92

	76–77	77–78	78–79	79–80	80–81	81–82	82–83	83–84
Income tax basic rate	35%	34%	33%	30%	30%	30%	30%	30%
Investment income surcharge			(see 25.4)					
Single personal allowance	735	945	985	1,165	1,375	1,375	1,565	1,785
Married personal allowance	1,085	1,455	1,535	1,815	2,145	2,145	2,445	2,795
Married couple's allowance								Nil
Wife's earned income allowance (maximum)	735	945	985	1,165	1,375	1,375	1,565	1,785
Child relief								
Under 11	300	‡170*	‡100					
11–15	335	‡205*	‡135					
16 and over and studying	365	‡235*	‡165	Nil	Nil	Nil	Nil	Nil
Dependent relative relief								
female claimant	145	145	145	145	145	145	145	145
other	100	100	100	100	100	100	100	100
Life assurance relief — normal percentage of premiums allowed as deduction from tax payable (deducted from premiums from 1979–80)	17.5%	17%	16.5%	17.5%	17.5%	15%	15%	15%

*£26 more for the first child for 1977–78.

	84–85	85–86	86–87	87–88	88–89	89–90	90–91	91–92
Income tax basic rate	30%	30%	29%	27%	25%	25%	25%	25%
Single personal allowance	2,005	2,205	2,335	2,425	2,605	2,785	3,005ø	3,295ø
Married personal allowance	3,155	3,455	3,655	3,795	4,095	4,375	Nil	Nil
Married couple's allowance	Nil	Nil	Nil	Nil	Nil	Nil	1,720	1,720
Wife's earned income allowance (maximum)	2,005	2,205	2,335	2,425	2,605	2,785	Nil	Nil
Child relief	Nil	Nil	Nil	Nil	Nil	Nil	Nil	Nil
Dependent relative relief								
female claimant	145	145	145	145	Nil	Nil	Nil	Nil
other	100	100	100	100	Nil	Nil	Nil	Nil
Life assurance relief — normal percentage of premiums (deducted from premiums)	15%*	15%*	15%*	15%*	15%*	$12\frac{1}{2}$%*	$12\frac{1}{2}$%*	$12\frac{1}{2}$%*

ø Available separately for husband and wife from 1990–91.
* Only on pre-14 March 1984 policies.
‡ Relief at 1976–77 levels for certain children living abroad and students (3.2.5).

Note: Allowances for 1992–93 are detailed in Chapter 3 (3.0.1); income tax rates for 1992–93 are given in Chapter 5 (5.0.1).

25.3 Income tax rates

	1976–77				1977–78		
Slice of income	Rate %	Total income	Total tax	Slice of income	Rate %	Total income	Total tax
£5,000	35	£5,000	£1,750	£6,000	34	£6,000	£2,040
500	40	5,500	1,950	1,000	40	7,000	2,440
1,000	45	6,500	2,400	1,000	45	8,000	2,890
1,000	50	7,500	2,900	1,000	50	9,000	3,390
1,000	55	8,500	3,450	1,000	55	10,000	3,940
1,500	60	10,000	4,350	2,000	60	12,000	5,140
2,000	65	12,000	5,650	2,000	65	14,000	6,440
3,000	70	15,000	7,750	2,000	70	16,000	7,840
5,000	75	20,000	11,500	5,000	75	21,000	11,590
Remainder	83			Remainder	83		

for 1978–79

Slice of income	Rate	Total income (after allowances)	Total tax
£ 750 (0–750)	25%	£ 750	£ 187.50
7,250 (750–8,000)	33%	8,000	2,580
1,000 (8–9,000)	40%	9,000	2,980
1,000 (9–10,000)	45%	10,000	3,430
1,000 (10–11,000)	50%	11,000	3,930
1,500 (11–12,500)	55%	12,500	4,755
1,500 ($12\frac{1}{2}$–14,000)	60%	14,000	5,655
2,000 (14–16,000)	65%	16,000	6,955
2,500 (16–18,500)	70%	18,500	8,705
5,500 ($18\frac{1}{2}$–24,000)	75%	24,000	12,830
Remainder	83%		

for 1979–80

Slice of income	Rate	Total income (after allowances)	Total tax
£ 750 (0–750)	25%	£ 750	£ 187.50
9,250 (750–10,000)	30%	10,000	2,962.50
2,000 (10–12,000)	40%	12,000	3,762.50
3,000 (12–15,000)	45%	15,000	5,112.50
5,000 (15–20,000)	50%	20,000	7,612.50
5,000 (20–25,000)	55%	25,000	10,362.50
Remainder	60%		

for 1980–81 and 1981–82

Slice of income	Rate	Total income (after allowances)	Total tax
£11,250 (0–11,250)	30%	£11,250	£3,375
2,000 (11,250–13,250)	40%	13,250	4,175
3,500 (13,250–16,750)	45%	16,750	5,750
5,500 (16,750–22,250)	50%	22,250	8,500
5,500 (22,250–27,750)	55%	27,750	11,525
Remainder	60%		

Tax tables

for 1982–83

Slice of income	Rate	Total income (after allowances)	Total tax
£12,800 (£0–12,800)	30%	£12,800	£3,840
2,300 (12,800–15,100)	40%	15,100	4,760
4,000 (15,100–19,100)	45%	19,100	6,560
6,200 (19,100–25,300)	50%	25,300	9,660
6,200 (25,300–31,500)	55%	31,500	13,070
Remainder	60%		

for 1983–84

Slice of income	Rate	Total income (after allowances)	Total tax
£14,600 (£0–14,600)	30%	£14,600	£4,380
2,600 (14,600–17,200)	40%	17,200	5,420
4,600 (17,200–21,800)	45%	21,800	7,490
7,100 (21,800–28,900)	50%	28,900	11,040
7,100 (28,900–36,000)	55%	36,000	14,945
Remainder	60%		

for 1984–85

Slice of income	Rate	Total income (after allowances)	Total tax
£15,400 (£0–15,400)	30%	£15,400	£4,620
2,800 (15,400–18,200)	40%	18,200	5,740
4,900 (18,200–23,100)	45%	23,100	7,945
7,500 (23,100–30,600)	50%	30,600	11,695
7,500 (30,600–38,100)	55%	38,100	15,820
Remainder	60%		

for 1985–86

Slice of income	Rate	Total income (after allowances)	Total tax
£16,200 (£0–16,200)	30%	£16,200	£4,860
3,000 (16,200–19,200)	40%	19,200	6,060
5,200 (19,200–24,400)	45%	24,400	8,400
7,900 (24,400–32,300)	50%	32,300	12,350
7,900 (32,300–40,200)	55%	40,200	16,695
Remainder	60%		

for 1986–87

Slice of income	Rate	Total income (after allowances)	Total tax
£17,200 (£0–17,200)	29%	£17,200	£4,988
3,000 (17,200–20,200)	40%	20,200	6,188
5,200 (20,200–25,400)	45%	25,400	8,528
7,900 (25,400–33,300)	50%	33,300	12,478
7,900 (33,300–41,200)	55%	41,200	16,823
Remainder	60%		

for 1987–88

Slice of income	Rate	Total income (after allowances)	Total tax
£17,900 (£0–17,900)	27%	£17,900	£4,833
2,500 (17,900–20,400)	40%	20,400	5,833
5,000 (20,400–25,400)	45%	25,400	8,083
7,900 (25,400–33,300)	50%	33,300	12,033
7,900 (33,300–41,200)	55%	41,200	16,378
Remainder	60%		

for 1988–89

Slice of income	Rate	Total income (after allowances)	Total tax
£19,300 (£0–19,300)	25%	£19,300	£4,825
Remainder	40%		

for 1989–90 and 1990–91			
£20,700 (£0–20,700)	25%	£20,700	£5,175
Remainder	40%		
for 1991–92			
£23,700 (£0–23,700)	25%	£23.700	£5,425
Remainder	40%		

25.4 Investment income surcharge

	Age up to 65		Age over 65	
1976–77	£1,000	Nil	£1,500	Nil
	1,001–2,000	10%	1,501–2,000	10%
	over 2,000	15%	over 2,000	15%
1977–78	1,500	Nil	2,000	Nil
	1,501–2,000	10%	2,001–2,500	10%
	over 2,000	15%	over 2,500	15%
1978–79	1,700	Nil	2,500	Nil
	1,701–2,250	10%	2,501–3,000	10%
	over 2,250	15%	over 3,000	15%
1979–80	5,000	Nil	5,000	Nil
	over 5,000	15%	over 5,000	15%
1980–81	5,500	Nil	5,500	Nil
& 1981–82	over 5,500	15%	over 5,500	15%
1982–83	6,250	Nil	6,250	Nil
	over 6,250	15%	over 6,250	15%
1983–84	7,100	Nil	7,100	Nil
	over 7,100	15%	over 7,100	15%

25.5 Capital transfer tax rates

Slice of cumulative chargeable transfers	Total	Capital transfer tax payable			
		Lifetime scale		On death	
		% on slice	Cumulative total tax	% on slice	Cumulative total tax
before 27 October 1977					
The first £15,000	£15,000	Nil	£Nil	Nil	£Nil
The next					
5,000	20,000	5	250	10	500
5,000	25,000	7.5	625	15	1,250
5,000	30,000	10	1,125	20	2,250
10,000	40,000	12.5	2,375	25	4,750

10,000	50,000	15	3,875	30	7,750
10,000	60,000	17.5	5,625	35	11,250
20,000	80,000	20	9,625	40	19,250
20,000	100,000	22.5	14,125	45	28,250
20,000	120,000	27.5	19,625	50	38,250
30,000	150,000	35	30,125	55	54,750
50,000	200,000	42.5	51,375	60	84,750
50,000	250,000	50	76,375	60	114,750
50,000	300,000	55	103,875	60	144,750
200,000	500,000	60	223,875	60	264,750
500,000	1,000,000	65	548,875	65	589,750
1,000,000	2,000,000	70	1,248,875	70	1,289,750
Remainder		75		75	

from 28 October 1977 to 25 March 1980

The first					
£25,000	£25,000	Nil	£Nil	Nil	£Nil
The next					
5,000	30,000	5	250	10	500
5,000	35,000	7.5	625	15	1,250
5,000	40,000	10	1,125	20	2,250
10,000	50,000	12.5	2,375	25	4,750
10,000	60,000	15	3,875	30	7,750
10,000	70,000	17.5	5,625	35	11,250
20,000	90,000	20	9,625	40	19,250
20,000	110,000	22.5	14,125	45	28,250
20,000	130,000	27.5	19,625	50	38,250
30,000	160,000	35	30,125	55	54,750
50,000	210,000	42.5	51,375	60	84,750
50,000	260,000	50	76,375	60	114,750
50,000	310,000	55	103,875	60	144,750
200,000	510,000	60	223,875	60	264,750
500,000	1,010,000	65	548,875	65	589,750
1,000,000	2,010,000	70	1,248,875	70	1,289,750
Remainder		75		75	

from 26 March 1980 to 9 March 1981

The first					
£50,000	£50,000	Nil	£Nil	Nil	£Nil
The next					
10,000	60,000	15	1,500	30	3,000
10,000	70,000	17.5	3,250	35	6,500
20,000	90,000	20	7,250	40	14,500
20,000	110,000	22.5	11,750	45	23,500
20,000	130,000	27.5	17,250	50	33,500
30,000	160,000	35	27,750	55	50,000
50,000	210,000	42.5	49,000	60	80,000
50,000	260,000	50	74,000	60	110,000
50,000	310,000	55	101,500	60	140,000
200,000	510,000	60	221,500	60	260,000
500,000	1,010,000	65	546,500	65	585,000
1,000,000	2,010,000	70	1,246,500	70	1,285,000
Remainder		75		75	

from 10 March 1981 to 8 March 1982

The first					
£50,000	£50,000	Nil	£Nil	Nil	£Nil
The next					
10,000	60,000	15	1,500	30	3,000
10,000	70,000	17.5	3,250	35	6,500
20,000	90,000	20	7,250	40	14,500
20,000	110,000	22.5	11,750	45	23,500
20,000	130,000	25	16,750	50	33,500
30,000	160,000	30	25,750	55	50,000
350,000	510,000	35	148,250	60	260,000
500,000	1,010,000	40	348,250	65	585,000
1,000,000	2,010,000	45	798,250	70	1,285,000
Remainder		50		75	

from 9 March 1982 to 14 March 1983

The first					
£55,000	£55,000	Nil	£Nil	Nil	£Nil
The next					
20,000	75,000	15	3,000	30	6,000
25,000	100,000	17.5	7,375	35	14,750
30,000	130,000	20	13,375	40	26,750
35,000	165,000	22.5	21,250	45	42,500
35,000	200,000	25	30,000	50	60,000
50,000	250,000	30	45,000	55	87,500
400,000	650,000	35	185,000	60	327,500
600,000	1,250,000	40	425,000	65	717,500
1,250,000	2,500,000	45	987,500	70	1,592,500
Remainder		50		75	

from 15 March 1983 to 12 March 1984

The first					
£60,000	£60,000	Nil	£Nil	Nil	£Nil
The next					
20,000	80,000	15	3,000	30	6,000
30,000	110,000	17.5	8,250	35	16,500
30,000	140,000	20	14,250	40	28,500
35,000	175,000	22.5	22,125	45	44,250
45,000	220,000	25	33,375	50	66,750
50,000	270,000	30	48,375	55	94,250
430,000	700,000	35	198,875	60	352,250
625,000	1,325,000	40	448,875	65	758,500
1,325,000	2,650,000	45	1,045,125	70	1,686,000
Remainder		50		75	

from 13 March 1984 to 5 April 1985

The first					
£64,000	£64,000	Nil	£Nil	Nil	£Nil
The next					
21,000	85,000	15	3,150	30	6,300
31,000	116,000	17.5	8,575	35	17,150
32,000	148,000	20	14,975	40	29,950

37,000	185,000	22.5	23,300	45	46,600
47,000	232,000	25	35,050	50	70,100
53,000	285,000	27.5	49,625	55	99,250
Remainder		30		60	

from 6 April 1985 to 18 March 1986

The first					
£67,000	£67,000	Nil	£Nil	Nil	£Nil
The next					
22,000	89,000	15	3,300	30	6,600
33,000	122,000	17.5	9,075	35	18,150
33,000	155,000	20	15,675	40	31,350
39,000	194,000	22.5	24,450	45	48,900
49,000	243,000	25	36,700	50	73,400
56,000	299,000	27.5	52,100	55	104,200
Remainder		30		60	

25.6 Inheritance tax rates

Slice of cumulative chargeable transfers	Cumulative total	% on slice	Cumulative total tax
from 18 March 1986 to 16 March 1987			
The first			
£71,000	£71,000	Nil	£Nil
The next			
24,000	95,000	30	7,200
34,000	129,000	35	19,100
35,000	164,000	40	33,100
42,000	206,000	45	52,000
51,000	257,000	50	77,500
60,000	317,000	55	110,500
Remainder		60	
from 17 March 1987 to 14 March 1988			
The first			
£90,000	£90,000	Nil	£Nil
The next			
50,000	140,000	30	15,000
80,000	220,000	40	47,000
110,000	330,000	50	102,000
Remainder		60	
from 15 March 1988 to 5 April 1989			
The first			
£110,000	£110,000	Nil	£Nil
Remainder		40	

from 6 April 1989 to 5 April 1990

| The first £118,000 | £118,000 | Nil | £Nil |
| Remainder | | 40 | |

from 6 April 1990 to 5 April 1991

| The first £128,000 | £128,000 | Nil | £Nil |
| Remainder | | 40 | |

from 6 April 1991 to 9 March 1992

| The first £140,000 | £140,000 | Nil | £Nil |
| Remainder | | 40 | |

Glossary

The following are a selection of terms which are explained in more detail where indicated.

Ad valorem duties	Duties which are charged as a percentage of the subject matter—particularly stamp duty (22.5)
Advance corporation tax	Tax payable by companies on dividend payments, etc, which is offset against the full (mainstream) corporation tax liability (12.6)
Back duty	Under-assessed tax for previous years, normally due to evasion (14.8)
Basic rate tax	Income tax at 25 per cent (2.2)
Business Expansion Scheme	Government scheme for encouraging investment in smaller companies by giving tax relief on money subscribed (10.25)
Claw-back	The loss of relief previously obtained, eg, stock relief (10.6) or life assurance relief (24.5.5)
Close companies	Companies closely controlled by generally no more than five shareholders and their associates (12.17)
Close Investment Holding Company (CIC)	A close company which is neither a trading company nor a property investment company, nor a member of a trading group (12.18)
Current use value	The value of property on the basis that its use is limited to existing planning consents
Domicile	The country which you regard as your natural home (15.2)
Earned income	Income derived from an individual's personal, mental or physical labour and some pensions (3.1)

General Commissioners	Lay people appointed to hear tax appeals (14.4)
Higher rate tax	Income tax at the higher rates, currently 40 per cent (5.1)
Indexation allowance	Capital gains tax relief for inflation (18.12)
Interest in possession	Entitlement to receive the income of a settlement (20.31)
Mainstream corporation tax	A company's main corporation tax liability based on its accounts (12.6.5)
Partnership	The relationship existing between two or more persons in business together with the object of making profits (11.1)
Personal allowance	Certain deductions from your total income for tax purposes (3.2)
Personal equity plan (PEP)	Share purchase scheme under which up to £9,000 can be invested each year with income tax and capital gains tax advantages (8.10)
Potentially exempt transfers (PETs)	Gifts between individuals or to certain trusts which are only considered for inheritance tax if the donor dies within seven years (20.3)
Profit related pay (PRP)	Incentive payments to employees which attract limited income tax relief, subject to the rules (9.15)
Relevant base value	Main deduction in computing realised development value on which development land tax was chargeable
Residence	Where you are treated as living for tax purposes (15.3)
Special Commissioners	Full-time professionally qualified civil servants appointed to hear tax appeals (14.4)
Tax avoidance	Legally arranging your affairs to reduce your tax liability (13.9)
Tax evasion	Illegal tax saving (13.9)
Tax exempt special savings account (TESSA)	Savings account with bank or building society offering tax-free interest (8.11)
Trust	Otherwise known as a settlement—assets held by one or more trustees

Unearned income	for the benefit of others (19.1) Income from investments as opposed to earned income such as salaries and pensions (3.1)
Year of assessment	Year ending 5 April, for which tax is payable (2.8)

Index

Abatement, 12.17.2
Accommodation—
  company house occupied rent free, 9.6.3
  directors, 21.11.8
  furnished lettings, 7.5, 7.14
  holiday lettings, 7.6
  provided for employees, 1.2.6, 4.6, 9.6.12
Accounts basis of assessment, 9.13
Accounting periods—
  advance corporation tax, 12.6.2
  corporation tax, 12.4
Accrued income, 8.3
Accumulation and maintenance settlements, 1.2.17, 1.4.2, 1.4.5
  inheritance tax, 20.31.1
  settlor's children, 19.4
Ad valorem duties, 22.5
Additional personal relief, *see* Children
Additional voluntary contributions, 5.3, 24.12.1, 24.13
Administration of estates, *see* Estates
Advance corporation tax, *see* Corporation tax
Age allowance, 1.7.7, 3.2.15
  married couples, 3.2.2
Agriculture—
  agricultural property relief, 1.4.2, 1.4.7, 20.22
  buildings, capital allowance on, 10.14
  farming profits, 13.6
  land, 7.11
  VAT, 21.18
Alimony, 4.1, 6.8.3
  See also Husband and wife
Allowances—
  age, 1.7.7, 3.2.15
  capital, *see* Capital allowances
  entertainment, 9.6.4
  income tax saving, 1.2.1

Allowances—*contd*
  personal, 3.2
  additional (for children), 3.2.12
  married couple's, 3.2.2
  married (pre-1990), 3.2.3, 6.2
  single, 3.2.1, 6.1
  wife's earned income, 3.2.4
  tax return, 14.1.4
  travelling, 9.6.4
  widow's bereavement, 3.2.16
  See also Personal reliefs
Annual payments—
  apart from interest, 4.1
  deductions at source, 4.1
  defined, 4.2
  See also Interest; Loans
Annuities—
  company's position, 24.14.1
  generally, 24.14
  guaranteed income bonds, 24.14.3
  individual annuitant, 24.14.2
  inheritance tax planning, 1.4.6
  retirement annuity contracts, *see* Pensions
Anti-avoidance—
  artificial transactions in land, 7.11, 13.9.5
  bank lending, 13.9.12
  capital allowances—leasing, 13.9.6
  capital gains tax, 13.9.9, 13.9.18
  commodity futures, 13.9.10
  companies—
    controlled foreign, 13.9.13
    dual resident, 13.9.15
    group relief transactions, 13.9.7
    migration of companies, 13.9.16
    sales of subsidiaries, 13.9.18
  evasion distinguished, 13.9
  generally, 13.9
  interest schemes, 13.9.8
  Lloyd's underwriters, 13.9.17
  non-resident trusts, 13.9.19

Anti-avoidance—*contd*
  offshore funds, 13.9.14
  rent between connected persons, 13.9.11
  sale and leaseback, 13.9.5
  sale of income derived from personal activities, 13.9.4
  sales at undervalue or overvalue, 13.9.3
  transactions in securities, 13.9.1
  transfer of assets abroad, 13.9.2
Appeal—
  against assessment, 14.3
  hearings, 14.5.4
  value added tax, 21.13
Armed forces—
  allowances, bounties and gratuities, 2.6.1
Artificial transactions in land, 7.10, 13.9.5
Assessable profits—
  computation of, 10.4
    example, 10.4.1
Assessments—
  appeals against, 14.3
  basis, 9.13
  capital gains tax, 18.15
  discovery, 14.2.3
  due dates for payment, 14.2.2
  error in 14.2.5
  fraud, 14.8.1
  income tax, 5.7
  mechanism, 14.2.1
  neglect, 14.8.1
  partnership, 11.2
  period less than full year, 2.9
  remission, 14.2.5, 14.2.6
  Schedule A, 7.1, 7.4
  Schedule D—
    basis of, 10.7, 10.26
    closing years, 10.7.3–10.7.4
    opening years, 10.7.1–10.7.2
  Schedule E, 9.13
  time limits, 14.2.4
  period less than full year, 2.9
  wilful default, 14.8.1
  year of, 2.8
Assets—
  at employee's disposal, 9.6.3, 9.6.7
  business, gift of, 1.4.1, 18.26
  equalisation of, 1.4.4
  reduction by gifts, 1.4.1
  security, 10.9.9
  short-life, 10.9.6

Assets—*contd*
  use by employee, 9.6.7
  wasting, 18.29.2
Associated—
  companies, 12.8
  operations, 20.30.3
Assured tenancies—
  business expansion scheme, 10.25
  capital allowance on acquisition, 10.16
Attendance allowance, 2.6.1
Author—
  copyright sales and royalties, 13.4
Avoidance, *see* Anti-avoidance

Back duty investigations, 14.8
  See also Investigations
Bad debts, 21.11.9
Balancing allowances and charges, 10.9.4, *see also* Capital allowances
Bank—
  interest, 1.2.19, 2.7
    composite rate scheme, 8.7, *see also* Interest
  lending, 13.9.12
  TESSAs, 1.2.12, 8.11
Bankruptcy, 13.8
Beneficial loan arrangements, 9.6.8
Benefits—
  child, 3.2.6
  fringe, 1.2.6, 9.6, 9.7
  permanent health insurance, 24.15
  social security—
    non-taxable, 23.3.2
    taxable, 23.3.1
Blind person's relief, 3.2.14
Board and lodging, 9.6.3
Bond washing, 8.3
Building societies—
  interest, 2.7, 5.5, 8.6
  special arrangements, 13.7
  TESSAs, 1.2.12, 8.11
Buildings—
  agricultural, 10.14
  hotels, 10.15
  industrial, 1.2.3, 10.11
  loan for purchase and improvement, 4.6
  small workshops, 10.13
Business—
  assessment, basis of, 10.7
  assets—
    gifts of, 1.4.1, 18.26

Index 447

Business—*contd*
assets—*contd*
relief—
on compulsory purchase, 18.25.1
on replacement, 18.25
See also Capital gains tax
capital allowances, *see* Capital allowances
cars, *see* Cars
cessation rules, 1.2.8, 8.5.3, 8.5.4, 10.7.3, 10.7.4, 12.17.4
post-cessation receipts, 10.27
earnings basis of assessment, 10.26
entertainment, *see* Entertainment
expansion scheme, 10.25
expenses, 1.2.2., 10.3
allowable, 10.3.1
not deductible, 10.3.2
gift of assets, 18.26
interest paid for purpose of, 4.4
losses, 1.2.8, 5.3, 10.22–10.24
National Insurance, 10.28
new, 1.2.8, 10.23
non-resident, liability to tax, 17.1.1
opening year assessment, 1.2.8
pensions, *see* Pensions
profits, 10.1, 10.4
property relief, 1.4.2, 1.4.7, 1.4.8, 20.19
purchase of—
annual payments to former owner, 4.1, 5.3
relevant business property, 20.19
retirement relief, 1.3.5, 1.7.7, 18.29
small, 10.4, 21.5
stock—
relief, 10.6, 12.22
valuation, 10.5
trading defined, 10.2
value added tax, 21.4
See also Schedule D

Canteens—
for employees, 1.2.6, 9.6.3
Capital—
allowances, *see* Capital allowances
duty, 22.3
expenses, 2.6
profits distinguished from revenue profits, 2.5
transactions, 2.5.1
Capital allowances—
agricultural buildings, 10.14
anti-avoidance, 13.9.6

Capital allowances—*contd*
assured tenancies, 10.16
base period, 10.8.1
cars for business, 9.6.6, *see also* Cars
companies, 12.10
computer software, 10.9.14
de-pooling, 10.9.6, 10.9.7
dredging, 10.19
enterprise zones, 1.2.3, 10.12
films, 10.21
generally, 10.8
hotel buildings, 10.15
industrial buildings, 1.2.3, 10.11
know how, 10.18
mineral extraction, 10.20
patent rights, 10.18
plant and machinery—
balancing allowances and charges, 10.9.4, 10.20
example, 10.9.5
cars, 10.9.10
example, 10.9.11
examples of, 10.9.5
first year allowances, 10.9.1
fixtures, 10.10
generally, 10.9
hire purchase, 10.9.12
leasing, 10.9.13
motor vehicles, *see* cars
safety at sports grounds, 10.9.8
sales, 10.9.4
security assets, 10.9.9
ships, 10.9.3
short-life assets, 10.9.6
writing down allowance, 10.9.2
scientific research, 10.17
small workshops, 10.13
tax saving, 1.2.3
Capital gains tax—
administration period, during, 19.10.3
annual exemptions, 18.6
anti-avoidance, 13.9.6, 13.9.9
assessment, 18.15
assets—
exempt, 18.8
table, 18.8.1
liability, 18.7
owned on 6 April 1965, 18.17
wasting, 18.29.2
base value, 18.11
business assets—
gifts of, 18.26
replacement of, 18.25
business retirement relief, 18.29

448 *Index*

Capital gains tax—*contd*
  chargeable gain—
    computation, 18.10, 18.12
    defined, 18.2
  charities, 1.3.8, 18.29.1
  chattels sold for £6,000 or less, 18.24
  collection, 14.7
  commodity futures, 18.31
  company, 12.15
    sales of subsidiaries, 13.9.18
    computation, 18.12.2
  compulsory purchase, 18.25.1
  corporate bonds, exemption for, 18.19
  dealing in property, 7.9
  disposal—
    part, 18.21
    series of, 18.22
    what constitutes, 18.9
  financial futures, 18.31
  generally, 18.1
  gifts—
    business assets, 18.26
    from 14 March 1989, 18.28
    general relief for, 1.3.1, 1.3.3, 1.4.1, 18.27, 18.28
  gilt edged securities, 18.18.1
  indexation allowance, 1.3.7, 18.12, 18.18.4
  investment trusts, 18.18.7
  leases, 18.29.2
  liability, 2.1, 2.2, 18.3
  losses—
    capital, 18.13
    company, 12.15
    group relief, 12.11, 12.13
    relief for trading, 18.13.1
    unquoted shares in trading companies, 18.14
  loss relief, 1.3.2, 10.22
  overseas aspects, 18.32
  part disposals, 18.21
  partnership, 11.6
  payment, 18.15
  PEPs, 1.2.11
  pooling, 18.18
  private residence, 1.3.9, 18.23
  quoted shares and securities—
    bonus issues, 18.18.6
    company reorganisations, 18.18.6
    generally, 18.18
    holdings at 6 April 1965, 18.18.8
    identification—
      sales from 6 April 1982 to 5 April 1985, 18.18.3

Capital gains tax—*contd*
  quoted shares and securities—*contd*
    identification—*contd*
      sales from 6 April 1985, 18.18.4
      example, 18.18.5
    indexation, 18.18.4
      example, 18.18.5
    investment trusts, 18.18.7
    pooling, 18.18.1
      parallel, 18.18.2
    take-overs, 18.18.6
    unit trusts, 18.18.7
  rates, 2.2, 18.4
  re-basing to 31 March 1982 values, 18.11
  relief—
    moderate total gains before 6 March 1980, 18.5
    retirement, 18.29, *see also* Retirement
    sale of assets owned on 6 April 1965, 18.17
  retail prices index, 18.12.1
  roll-over relief, 18.25
    groups of companies, 12.16
  savings, 1.3
    £5,800 net gains exemption, 1.3.1
    bed and breakfast transactions, 1.3.1
    charities, 1.3.8, 18.29.1
    discretionary settlements, 1.4.2
    gifts election, 1.3.3, 18.28
    husband and wife, 1.3.1, 1.3.4
    loss relief 1.3.2
    indexation, 1.3.7
    private residence, 1.3.9, 18.23
    retirement relief, 1.3.5
    timing, 1.3.6
  tax return, 14.1.3
  traded options, 18.30
  trusts—
    business assets, 19.7
    disposal of interests, 19.8
    distribution, 19.8
    foreign, 19.9.1
    gifts, 19.7
  unit trusts, 18.18.7
  unquoted shares, 18.20
  valuations, 18.16
  wasting assets, 18.29.2
Capital transfer tax—
  rates, 25.5
  See also Inheritance tax

Cars—
  business use, 1.2.2, 1.2.6
  capital allowances, 10.9.10
    higher priced, example, 10.9.11
  directors', 9.6.5
  form P11D, 9.6.3
    particulars, 9.7
  higher paid employees, 9.6.5
  mileage allowance, 9.6.6
  National Insurance contribution, 23.2
  P11D particulars, 9.7
  scale charge, 1.2.6, 9.6.5
  taxation of, 9.6.3, 9.6.5
  value added tax, 21.11.1
Cash basis, 10.26
Cash vouchers, 9.6.3, 9.6.11
Cessation of business, 1.2.8, 8.5.3–8.5.4, 10.7.3–10.7.4, 12.17.4
Chargeable gains, see Capital gains tax
Charges on income, 5.4
Charities—
  capital gains tax,
    saving, 1.3.8
    relief, 18.29.1
  deeds of covenant, 1.2.16, 4.1, 5.3, 6.5, 13.2.1
  exempt transfers, 20.18.3
  exemption from tax, 13.2.1, 18.29.1
  gift aid, 13.2.1
  gifts to, 1.2.16, 1.3.8, 1.4.3, 1.7.7, 20.18.3
  income tax saving, 1.2.17, 13.2.1
  inheritance tax, 20.18.3
  non-charitable use of funds, 13.2.1
  value added tax, 21.9
Child benefit, 2.6.1, 3.2.6
Childcare facilities, 1.2.6, 9.6.3, 9.6.14
Children—
  accumulation settlements, 19.4
  additional personal relief, 3.2.12, 6.8.2
  child benefit, 3.2.6
  child relief, 3.2.5
  deeds of covenant, 6.5
  income, 6.6
  maintenance payments, 6.8.3
    small, 6.8.4
  scholarships, 9.6.13
  settlement for, 19.3.5
  tax planning, 1.7.1
  trust for benefit of, 19.3.5
Class 4 National Insurance Contribution, 10.28

Close companies—
  abatement, 12.17.2
  apportionment of income, 12.17.1
  cessations, 12.17.4
  defined, 12.17
  distributions, 12.17.3
  inheritance tax, 20.30.1
  imputation system, 12.17.1
  investment holding, 1.2.4, 12.18
  liquidations, 12.17.4
  loans, 12.17.3
Clothing, 9.6.3
Code number, 9.14.3
Collection of tax—
  generally, 20.25
  interest on overdue tax, 14.7.2
  payment on account, 14.7.1
Collectors of taxes, 14.2
Commissioners, General and Special, 14.4
Commodity futures, 13.9.10, 18.31
Companies—
  accommodation for employees, see Accommodation
  accounts, future changes, 12.25
  associated, 12.8
  capital allowances, 1.2.3, 12.10
  capital gains, 12.15
  close, see Close companies
  controlled foreign, 12.21
  corporation tax, see Corporation tax
  demergers, 12.23
  directors, see Directors
  dividends, see Dividends
  dual resident, 13.9.15
  family, 1.4.8
  future administrative changes, 12.25
  imputation system, 12.3
  groups of companies—
    general provisions, 12.16
    group loss relief, 12.13
    interest on overdue tax 14.7.2
    relief, anti-avoidance restriction, 13.9.7
    VAT, 21.7
  incorporation, 1.2.4
  liability for tax, 2.2, 2.3.1
  losses—
    capital, 12.15
    generally, 12.11
    group loss relief, 12.13
    terminal, 12.14
  migration of, 13.9.16
  non-resident, trading in UK, 12.19
  overseas, dividends from, 8.1.3

Companies—*contd*
  overseas income, with, 12.20
  reconstructions, 12.12
  residence, 15.3.3
  small, corporation tax rate, 1.2.4, 12.7
  stock relief, 12.22
  tax saving by incorporation, 1.2.4
  unquoted, purchasing own shares, 12.24
  See also Corporation tax
Compensation for loss of office, 1.2.6, 9.6.16
  general, 9.12
  tax treatment, 9.12.1
Composite rate scheme, 8.6, 8.7
Computer software, 10.9.14
Contract—
  life policy, *see* Life assurance
  permanent health insurance, 24.15
  purchased general annuities, *see* Purchased general annuities
  retirement annuity, *see* Pensions
Controlled foreign companies, 12.21
Controlling directors—
  pension scheme, 1.2.14
Copyright—
  sales, 3.1, 13.4
  top slicing relief, 5.9, 13.4
Corporate bonds—
  capital gains tax exemption, 18.19
Corporation tax—
  accounting periods, 12.4
  advance—
    accounting periods, 12.6.2
    carry back, 12.6.6
    carry forward, 12.6.6
    distributions, 12.6.1
    dividends, 12.6
    franked investment income, 12.6.4
    franked payment, 12.6.3
    set off against mainstream tax, 12.6.5
  application of, 12.2
  associated companies, 12.8
  collection, 14.7
  computation of assessable profits, 12.9
  groups of companies, 12.16
  imputation system, 12.3
  profits, 12.2
  rates, 2.2, 12.2.1
  repayment supplement, 12.5
  small companies' rate, 1.2.4, 12.7
Covenants, *see* Deeds of covenant

Crèches, *see* Childcare facilities
Credit—
  cards, 9.6.3, 9.6.11
  sales on, value added tax, 21.11.5
  tax, 2.4
  tokens, 9.6.11

Daughter's services, 3.2.13
Dealing in property, 7.9
Death—
  deed of family arrangement, 1.4.9
  husband, 6.7.1
  inheritance tax, *see* Inheritance tax
  wife, 6.7.2
Debts—
  bad, value added tax, 21.11.9
Deceased Persons, *see* Estates; Inheritance tax
Deduction of tax at source, 2.4
  See also Composite rate scheme
Deductions—
  business, *see* Expenses
  tax payable, from, 5.5
  total income, 5.3
Deeds of covenant—
  charities, 1.2.16, 4.1, 13.2.1
  husband and wife, 6.5
  income tax savings, 1.2.16
  no tax relief, 4.1
  pre-1965, 4.1, 5.3
Deeds of family arrangement, 1.4.9, 20.30.6
Deep discount securities, 8.8
Deep gain securities, 8.8
Demergers, 12.23
Dependent relative relief, 3.2.10, 18.23
  home purchase loan, 4.6
De-pooling, 10.9.6, 10.9.7
Development land tax, 7.13
Diplomats—
  visiting, position of, 17.5
Directors—
  accommodation for, 9.6.12, 21.11.8
  assessment basis, 9.13
  cars, 9.6.5
  controlling, pension scheme for, 1.2.15
  expenses, 9.7
  fringe benefits, 1.2.6, 9.6.2, 9.6.3
  medical insurance, 9.6.10
  PAYE, 9.6.9
  return, 9.6.16
  scholarships, 9.6.13
Disability pensions, 2.6.1

Index 451

Discovery, 14.2.3
Discs—
  capital allowances, 10.21
Disposals, *see* Capital gains tax
Distributions—
  advance corporation tax, 12.6.1, *see also* Corporation tax
  close company, 12.17.3
Dividends—
  advance corporation tax, 12.6
  deep discount securities, 8.8
  non-residents, payments to, 17.1.5
  overseas companies, 8.1.3
  return, 8.1.1
  scrip dividend options, 8.9
  subsidiary companies, 12.16
  tax credits, 2.4, 5.5
  tax deduction vouchers, 8.1.2
  taxation, 8.1
  waiver of, 20.20
  See also Interest
Divorce—
  additional personal relief, 6.8.2
  alimony, 6.8.3
  during tax year, 6.8.1
  effect of, 6.8
  foreign, 6.8.5
  maintenance payments, 6.8.3
  tax status, 6.8
  See also Husband and Wife
Domicile—
  change of, 1.5, 15.4
  choice, of, 15.2.2
  deemed, 1.5, 20.4
  defined, 15.2
  dependency, of, 15.2.3
  importance of, 15.1
  origin, of, 15.2.1
  tax effects of, 15.1.1
  See also Residence
Double taxation relief—
  income tax, 16.6
  inheritance tax, 20.17
Dredging—
  capital allowance for, 10.19
Dual resident companies, 13.9.15
Dwelling house—
  capital gains tax savings, 1.3.9, 18.23
  dependent relative relief, 4.6
  expenses of running, 1.7.3
  income tax savings, 1.2.11
  joint ownership, 1.4.4
  main private residence, 1.3.9, 18.23
  purchase, 1.2.11
  tax planning, 1.1.2

Earned income, 3.1
Earnings—
  basis, 10.26
  overseas employment, 16.5
  profit related pay scheme, 1.2.6, 9.15
  waiver of, 20.20
  wife's, 1.2.9, 6.4
Earnings-related supplement, 2.6.1
Employees—
  business cars, 1.2.6
  childcare facilities, 1.2.6, 9.6.14
  compensation for loss of office, 9.12
    tax treatment, 9.12.1
  fringe benefits, 1.2.6, 9.6.2, 9.6.3
  golden handshake, 1.2.5, 9.6.16, 9.12
  higher paid—
    cars, 9.6.5
    expenses payments, 9.7
    fringe benefits, 1.2.6, 9.6.2, 9.6.3
    return, 9.6.16
    scholarships, 9.6.13
  interest-free loans, 1.2.6
  living accommodation provided, 1.2.6, 4.6, 9.6.12
  luncheon vouchers, 1.2.6, 9.6.3
  pension schemes, 1.2.6, 9.6.3
  personal pensions, 1.2.14, 24.11
  P11D particulars, 9.7
  profit related pay schemes, 1.2.6, 9.15
  recreation facilities, 1.2.6, 9.6.3
  saving tax for, 1.2.6
  share owning—
    acquisition at under value, 9.9.5
    profit sharing schemes, 9.9.6,
    setting-up costs, 9.9.7
    share ownership plans (ESOPs), 9.10
  retirement pension schemes, 9.11
  young, tax planning for, 1.7.3
Employers—
  change of, 9.14.5
  PAYE returns, 9.14.4
Employment—
  abroad, 1.2.19, 9.1, 9.5, 16.3
    travelling expenses, 9.6.4
  allowable expenses, 1.2.5
  childcare facilities, 9.6.14
  early working life, 1.7.3
  income from—
    amounts included, 9.6
    beneficial loan agreement, 9.6.8
    compensation for loss of office, 9.12
    credit tokens, 9.6.11

Employment—*contd*
  income from—*contd*
    deductions, 9.8
    directors' PAYE, 9.6.9
    employees' shareholdings, 9.9.5
    entertainment allowances, 9.6.4
    expense payments, 9.8
    form P11D, 9.7
    fringe benefits, 9.6.2
    living accommodation, 9.6.12
    medical insurance, 9.6.10
    motor cars, 9.6.5
    non-resident, liability to tax, 17.1.17
    profit related pay, 9.15
    profit sharing schemes, 9.9.6
    retirement pension schemes, 9.11
    return, 9.6.16
    scholarships, 9.6.13
    share option schemes, 9.9.6
    share ownership plans, 9.10
    travelling allowances, 9.6.4
    typical items, 9.6.1
    use of assets, 9.6.7
    vouchers, 9.6.11
  overseas earnings—
    100% deduction, 16.5.1
    remittances, 16.5.2
  tax planning, 1.2.5
  See also Schedule E
Enterprise Zones, 10.12
Entertainers—
  visiting, 17.6
Entertainment—
  allowances, 9.6.4
  P11D particulars, 9.7
  value added tax, 21.11.2
Entry warrant to obtain documents, 14.5.2
Equalisation of assets, 1.1.2, 1.4.4
ESOPs (Employee Share Ownership Plans), 9.10
Estates—
  deceased person—
    capital gains tax during administration, 19.10.3
    gross value of estate, 20.15.1
    income tax during administration, 19.10.2
    net value of estate, 20.15.2
    estate duty, abolition of, 20.14
    tax liability, 19.10.1
  See also Inheritance tax

European Community—
  European economic interest groupings, 11.8
  VAT on trading within, 21.17
Exempt transfers, 20.18
Expenses—
  allowable, 1.2.5
  business, *see* Business
  capital, 2.6
  deductions, 9.8
  directors', 9.7
  higher paid employees, 9.7
  overseas employment, 16.5.3
  return, 9.6.16
  revenue, 2.6
  Schedule A, 7.1.2, 7.2

Family—
  credit, 2.6.1
  deeds of arrangement, 1.4.9, 20.30.6
  income supplement, 2.6.1
  maintenance, gifts for, 20.30.5
  protection of company, 1.4.8
Farming, 13.6, 21.18, *see also* Agriculture
Films—
  capital allowances, 10.21
Financial futures, 18.31
Financial planning, 1.1
Financial year, 12.2
First year allowances, 10.9.1
Fixtures—
  capital allowances, 10.10
Fluctuating income, 5.9
Foreign—
  divorce, 6.8.5
  trusts, 19.9
  See also Overseas
Fraud, 14.8.1
Friendly societies, 13.2.2
Fringe benefits, 1.2.6, 9.6.2
  table, 9.6.3
Furnished lettings, 7.5, 7.6.1, 7.14
Futures—
  capital gains tax, 18.31
  commodity, 13.9.10

Gallantry awards, 2.6.1
Gambling profits, 2.6.1
General commissioners, 14.4
German compensation payments, 2.6.1
Gift Aid, 13.2.1

Gifts—
  back, 20.32
  business assets, 1.4.1, 18.26, 18.28
  capital gains tax, 1.3.1, 1.3.3
    general relief, 18.27
    from 14 March 1989, 18.28
  charities, to, 1.2.17, 1.4.3, 20.18.3
  exempt transfers, 1.4.1, 20.18
  inheritance tax, see Inheritance tax
  life policies, 24.8.2
  larger, 1.4.2
  lower rate taxpayers, 1.2.17
  marriage, on, 1.1.2, 1.4.1, 20.18.2
  normal expenditure, 1.4.1
  potentially exempt transfers (PET), 20.3
  reduction of assets by, 1.4.1
  tax savings, 1.2.17
  third parties, from, 9.6.4
  value added tax, 21.11.6
Gilt edged securities, see Government securities
Golden handshakes, 1.2.6, 9.6.16, 9.12
Government bonds, 2.6.1
Government securities—
  interest paid on, 8.2
  non-residents, 17.2
Group loss relief, 12.13
Groups of companies, see Companies

Health insurance, see Medical insurance
Higher paid employees, see Employees
Higher rate income tax, 5.0.1, 5.7
  non-residents, 17.1.8
Hire purchase—
  capital allowances, 10.9.12
Holiday lettings, 3.1, 7.6
Hotel buildings, 10.15
House, see Dwelling house
Housekeeper relief, 3.2.11
Housing—
  benefit, 2.6.1
  grants, 2.6.1
Husband and wife—
  alimony under court order, 5.3, 6.8.3
  capital gains tax saving, 1.3.4, 1.7.4
  death—
    husband, 6.7.1
    wife, 6.7.2
  deeds of covenant, 6.5
  divorce, 6.8
    additional personal relief, 6.8.2
    alimony, 6.8.3
    during tax year, 6.8.1

Husband and wife—*contd*
  divorce—*contd*
    foreign, 6.8.5
    house purchase loan, 4.6
    maintenance payments, 6.8.3, 6.8.4
  equalisation of assets, 1.1.2, 1.4.4
  exempt transfer, 20.18.1
  independent taxation, see Independent taxation
  inheritance tax, 1.4.1
  marriage after 5 April 1990, 6.2
    tax return, 6.2.1
  married couple's allowance, 3.2.2, 6.1
  married personal allowance, 3.2.3
  newly-married, tax planning for, 1.7.4
  returns, 6.2.1
  separate assessment, 6.3
  separate taxation, 6.4
  separation, 6.8
    house purchase loan, 4.6
  tax returns, 6.2.1
  wife's earnings—
    earned income allowance, 1.2.9, 3.2.4
    separate assessment, 6.3
    separate taxation, 6.4
  wills of, 1.4.5
  See also Children

Immigrants, 17.8
Improvements—
  property, 4.6
Imputation system, 12.3
  close companies, 12.17
Income—
  accrued, 8.3
  amounts included, 9.6
    typical items, 9.6.1
  business, see Business
    cessation, 8.5.3
  charges on, 5.4
  children's, 6.6
  classes of, 2.3.1
  dividends, see Dividends
  earned, 3.1
  employment, from, see Employment
  discretionary trusts, 19.5
  fluctuating, 5.9
  fresh, 1.2.8, 8.5.1, 16.2.1
  fringe benefits, 9.6.2
    table, 9.6.3
  interest, see Interest
  land, from, see Land

Income—*contd*
  non-residents, *see* Non-residents
  overseas, 1.2.17, 2.3, 16.1–16.6
  partnership, 11.2
  personal activities, derived from, 13.9.4
  property, from, *see* Property
  support, 2.6.1
  tax free, 2.6.1
    at basic rate only, 2.6.1
  taxable, 2.3
  total—
    deductions, 5.3
    defined, 5.2
  unearned, 3.1
  visitors', 17.3
Income tax—
  administration period, during, 19.10.2
  allowances, 3.2, 25.2
  assessment, 5.7
  charges on income, 5.4
  classes of 2.3
  collection, 14.7
  computation, 5.0.1–5.9
  deduction at source, 2.4
  deductions from tax payable, 5.5
  due date for payment, 14.2.2
  fluctuating income, 5.9
  higher rate, 5.0.1, 5.7, 17.1.8
  husband and wife, *see* Husband and wife
  indexation of bands, 5.1
  interest on overdue, 5.8, 14.7.2
  investment income surcharge, 5.6, 25.4
  PAYE, *see* PAYE
  payment, 5.7
  rates, 2.2, 5.0.1, 25.2, 25.3
  return, *see* Tax return
  savings—
    business expenses, 1.2.2
    capital allowances, 1.2.3
    controlling directors' pension scheme, 1.2.15
    deeds of covenant, 1.2.16
    employees, for, 1.2.6
    employments, 1.2.5
    gifts, 1.2.17
    house purchase, 1.2.11
    incorporation, 1.2.4
    independent taxation, 1.2.10
    life assurance, 1.2.13
    new businesses, 1.2.8
    overseas income, 1.2.19

Income tax—*contd*
  savings—*contd*
    personal pensions, 1.2.14
    personal reliefs, 1.2.1
    repayment claims, 1.2.7
    Schedule D income, fresh source of, 1.2.8, 8.5.1, 16.2.1
    settlements, 1.2.17
    tax-free investments, 1.2.12
    wife's earnings, 1.2.9
    work overseas, 1.2.19
  Schedules, *see* Schedules A, B, C, D, E, F
  table for 1992–93, 25.1
  tax credits, 2.4
  total income—
    deductions, 5.3
    defined, 5.2
  year of assessment, 2.8
Independent taxation—
  divorce, and, 6.8.1
  effect of, 6.2
  generally, 6.1
  return, 6.2.1, 14.1
  tax planning, 1.1.2, 1.2.10
Indexation—
  capital gains tax, 1.3.7, 18.12
  capital losses, 18.13
  income tax bands, 5.1
  inheritance tax, 20.9
  personal relief, 3.3
Individual—
  liability for tax, 2.1
  overseas trading by, 16.4
  residence of, 15.3.2
Industrial buildings—
  capital allowances, 1.2.3, 10.11
Information—
  returns of, 14.5.3
Inheritance tax—
  abolition of estate duty, 20.1, 20.14
  accumulation and maintenance settlements, 20.31.1
  administration, 20.25
  agricultural property relief, 1.4.7, 20.20
  associated operations, 20.30.3
  avoiding double charges, 20.33
  business property relief, 1.4.7, 20.19
  calculation example, 20.34
  capital transfer tax, 20.1
  chargeable transfers, 20.2
  close companies, 20.30.1
  collection, 20.25
  conditional exemption, 20.21

Inheritance tax—*contd*
cumulation period—
  seven year, 20.8
  ten year, 20.7
death, on, 20.15
deemed domicile, 20.4
discretionary trusts, 20.31.2
dividends, waiver of, 20.20
double charges, avoiding, 20.33
double taxation relief, 20.17
estate duty, abolition of, 20.1, 20.14
excluded property, 20.16
exempt transfers—
  charities, 20.18.3
  conditional exemption, 20.21
  employee trust of shares, 20.18.3
  generally, 20.18
  housing associations, 20.18.3
  husband and wife, 20.18.1
  in course of trade, 20.18.3
  lifetime gifts, 20.18.2
  national purposes, 20.18.3
  political parties, 20.18.3
  public benefit, 20.18.3
family—
  arrangement, deeds of, 20.30.6
  maintenance, 20.30.5
free loans, 20.30.2
generally, 20.1
gifts with reservations, 20.30.4
gross value of estate, 20.15.1
indexation of rate bands, 20.9
instalment payments—
  on death, 20.26
  on lifetime gifts, 20.27
insurance for, 1.1.2
land sold within three years of death, 20.13
larger gifts and settlements, 1.4.2
life policies, 1.4.9, 20.28, 24.8
marriage gifts, 1.1.2
mutual transfers, 20.32
net value of estate, 20.15.2
nil rate, 1.1.2
overseas property, 20.29
payment, 20.26, 20.27
periodic charge, 20.31.2
planning—
  agricultural relief, 1.4.7
  annuities, 1.4.6
  business relief, 1.4.7
  charitable gifts, 1.4.3
  deeds of family arrangement, 1.4.9
  equalisation of assets, 1.4.4
  family companies, 1.4.8

Inheritance tax—*contd*
planning—*contd*
  funds for payment, 1.4.10
  generally, 1.4
  larger gifts, 1.4.2
  reducing assets by gifts, 1.4.1, 20.18
  settlements, 1.4.2
  wills, 1.4.5
potentially exempt transfers, 20.3
property chargeable, 20.2
property outside Great Britain, 20.29
quick succession relief, 20.24
quoted securities passing on death, 20.11
rate scale, 20.5, 25.6
  after 5 April 1991, 20.5.1
related property, 20.12
remuneration, waiver of, 20.20
settled property, 20.31
tapering relief, 20.6
trust property, 20.31
valuation, 20.10, 20.12
  gross estate on death, 20.15.1
  net estate on death, 20.15.2
voidable transfers, 20.32
waivers, 20.20
woodlands, 20.23
Inland Revenue—
  appeals to, 14.3
  approval of occupational pension scheme, 9.11.1
  Board of, 14.2
  Commissioners of, 14.4
  generally, 14.1–14.8
  powers of, 14.5
Insolvents, 13.8
Inspectors of Taxes, 14.2
Insurance—
  medical, 9.6.10
  permanent health, 24.15
  See also Life assurance
Interest—
  annual, 4.3
  anti-avoidance, 13.9.8
  back duty investigation, 14.8
  bank—
    arising basis, 1.2.19
    composite rate scheme, 8.7
    grossing up, 2.7
    payment of gross interest, 8.7
  building society, 2.7, 8.6
  buildings, loan for purchase and improvement, 4.6
  business purposes, loan for, 4.4

Interest—*contd*
  deep discount and deep gain
    securities, 8.8
  government securities, 8.2, 17.2
  interest-free loans, 1.2.6
  land, loan for purchase and
    improvement of, 4.6
  mortgage, 4.7
  non-residents, 17.1.3, 17.1.4
  not taxed at source, 8.4 to 8.5, *see
    also* Schedule D Case III
  overdue tax, on, 5.8, 14.7.2
  payments—
    annual, 4.3
    business loan, 4.4
    deduction of tax, 4.3
    mortgage, 4.7
    tax relief, 4.5
      table, 4.5.1
  Personal Equity Plan (PEP), 8.10
  Schedule D, 8.4, 8.5
  Schemes, anti-avoidance provisions,
    13.9.8
  TESSAs, 8.11
  underpaid tax, 14.8.2
  See also Dividends
Investigations—
  accountants' papers, 14.5.1
  appeal hearings, 14.5.4
  back duty
    fraud and negligence, 14.8.1
    generally, 14.8
    interest, 14.8.2
      previous rules, 14.8.3
      new rules, 14.8.3
  entry warrants, 14.5.2
  powers of Revenue, 14.5
  returns of information, 14.5.3
Investment income—
  children, 6.6
  close investment holding companies
    (CICs), 12.18
  franked, 12.6.4
  overseas—
    generally, 16.1
    remittance basis, 16.1.1, 16.1.2
    remittances, 16.1.3
  separate taxation, 1.2.9
  surcharge, 5.6, 25.4
Investment managers—
  acting for non-residents, 17.1.6
Investment trusts—
  Capital gains tax, 18.18.7

Job release schemes, 2.6.1

Keith Committee, 12.25
Know how—
  capital allowances, 10.18

Land—
  agricultural, 7.11
  artificial transactions in, 7.10,
    13.9.5
  dealing in property, 7.9
  Development Land Tax, 7.13
  furnished lettings, 7.5, 7.14
  holiday lettings, 7.6
  income from, *see* Schedule A
  lease premiums, 7.7
  loan for purchase and improvement,
    4.6
  non-resident, liability to tax, 17.12
  profits or gains from, 7.1
  sale and lease back, 7.12, 13.9.5
  Schedule A—
    assessment under—
      example, 7.4.1
    expenses allowed against, 7.1.2
    special rules regarding, 7.2
    income falling within, 7.1
    leases at full rent, 7.2
    losses, 7.3
    See also Schedule A
  sold within three years of death,
    20.13
  woodlands, 7.8
  See also Property
Leases—
  at full rent, 7.2
  capital gains tax, 18.29.2
  premiums, 7.7
  top slicing relief, 7.7.1
Leasing—
  anti-avoidance, 13.9.6
  machinery for, 10.9.13
Lettings—
  furnished, 7.5, 7.6.1, 7.14
  holiday, 7.6
Liability for tax—
  capital—
    expenses, 2.6
    profits, 2.5.1
  capital gains tax, 2.1, 2.2, 18.3
  deduction of tax at source, 2.4
  income free of tax, 2.6.1
  non-residents, 2.1, 17.1
  period of assessment less than full
    year, 2.9
  planning, *see* Tax planning

Liability for tax—*contd*
  revenue—
    expenses, 2.6
    profits, 2.5.2
  tax credits, 2.4
  taxable income, 2.3
    classes of, 2.3.1
  taxes payable, 2.2
  who is taxable, 2.1
  year of assessment, 2.8
Life assurance—
  chargeable events, 24.7
    certificates of, 24.7.13
    gain on happening of, 24.7.1
    taxing gains on, 24.7.2
    top slicing, 24.7.3
  company—
    'key man' policies, 24.7.14
    tax position, 24.3
  cumulation of allowances and withdrawals, 24.7.9
  death of policyholder, 24.8.1
  excesses, 24.7.6
  family protection, 1.1.2
  gifts of policies, 24.8.2
  house purchase, 1.2.11
  income tax savings, 1.2.13
  inheritance tax, 20.28
    funds for, 1.4.2, 1.4.10
    planning, 24.8.4
  liability for charge, 24.7.12
  life of another policies, 24.8.3
  mortgages, and, 1.2.11, 1.2.13
  non-qualifying policies
    connected policies, 24.6.1
    generally, 24.6
  partial surrenders, 24.7.6
    old policies, 24.7.10, 24.7.11
  pre-1984 policies, 3.2.8
    example, 3.2.9
  postponing withdrawals, 24.7.8
  qualifying policies—
    advantages of, 24.5.3
    benefits, 24.5.1
    options, 24.5.2
    premiums, 24.5.1
    proceeds, 24.5.6
    rules, 24.5.1
    sum assured, 24.5.1
    tax relief on premiums, 24.5.4
      claw-back, 24.5.5
  relief, 1.2.11, 1.2.13, 3.2.7–3.2.9, 5.5
    pre-1948 policies, 3.2.8
  single premium bonds, 24.6.2

Life assurance—*contd*
  tax gains on—
    no tax on gain, example, 24.7.4
    partial surrenders, 24.7.6
    slice falling into two rate bands, 24.7.3
    total-encashment, 24.7.7
  tax treatment of premiums and proceeds, 24.4
    liability for charge, 24.7.11
    top slicing of non-qualifying, 5.9
  use of policies, 24.8.4
Liquidation, 12.17.4
Living accommodation, *see* Accommodation
Lloyd's underwriters, 13.9.17
Loans—
  bank, 13.9.12
  beneficial, 9.6.8
  building, purchase of, 4.6
  close company, 12.17.3
  free, 20.30.2
  interest free for employees, 1.2.6, 9.6.3
  land, purchase of, 4.6
  See also Mortgages
Local authorities—
  value added tax, 21.8
Long service awards, 9.6.3
Losses—
  capital gains tax, *see* Capital gains tax
  company, 12.11
    group loss relief, 12.13
    terminal, 12.14
  furnished lettings, 7.6.1
  holiday lettings, 7.6.1
  new business, 10.23
  partnership, 11.3
  relief for, 10.22
  Schedule A, 7.3
  Schedule D, 1.2.8, 10.22
  terminal, 10.24
Lottery prizes, 2.6.1
Luncheon vouchers, 1.2.6, 9.6.1, 9.6.3

Machinery—
  capital allowances, *see* Capital allowances
  leasing, 10.9.13
  sale of, 10.9.4
Main private residence, *see* Dwelling house

Maintenance payments—
  divorce—
    additional personal relief, and, 6.8.2
    court order, under, 4.1, 5.3, 6.8.3
    small, 6.8.4
    tax deduction, 6.8.3
    voluntary, 6.8
      post-14 March 1988, 6.8.3
  See also Husband and wife
Market gardening, 13.6
Marriage—
  gifts on, 1.1.2, 20.18.2
  married couple's allowance, 3.2.2, 3.2.15
  personal allowance, 3.2.3
  post-5 April 1990, 6.2
  See also Husband and wife: Independent taxation
Married couples—
  allowance, 3.2.2, 3.2.15
  See also Husband and wife
Maternity allowance, 2.6.1
Medical insurance, 9.6.3, 9.6.10, 24.15
Middle age—
  tax planning, 1.7.6
Mineral extraction—
  capital allowances, 10.20
Miscellaneous profits, 13.1
Mobile telephones, 9.6.3, 9.6.15
  car telephones, 9.6.5
Mobility allowance, 2.6.1
Mortgage—
  income tax saving, 1.1.2
  interest only, 1.2.11
  interest payments, relief for, 1.2.11
    deduction of tax from, 4.7
  repayment, 1.2.11
  See also Loans
Motor cars, *see* Cars

National Insurance—
  categories, 23.2
  Class 1, 23.2
  Class 4, 1.2.9, 10.28, 23.5
  contributions, 23.2
  earnings limit, 1.2.9
  non-residents, 23.5
National purposes—
  gifts for, 20.18.3
National Savings Bank, 2.6.1
National Savings Certificates, 2.6.1
Negligence, 14.8.1

Non-residents—
  business profits in UK, 17.1.1
  company trading in UK, 12.19
  dividend payments, 17.1.5
  earnings, 9.2
  employment in UK, income from, 17.1.7
  entitlement to reliefs, 17.7
  higher rate income tax, 17.1.8
  income from property and land in UK, 17.1.2
  interest—
    from UK sources, 17.1.3
    from UK securities, 17.1.4
    gross on government securities, 8.2.1, 17.2
  investment managers acting for, 17.1.6
  liability for tax, 2.1, 17.1
  NI contribution, 23.5
  Schedule E Case II, 9.2
  UK tax reliefs, entitlement to, 17.7
  See also Overseas; Residence; Visitors

Occupational pension schemes, 1.2.6, 24.12.1
  See also Employee, Pensions; Retirement
Office—
  compensation for loss of, 9.12
  tax treatment, 9.12.1
Offshore funds, 13.9.14
Organisations—
  tax-free, 13.2
Outings for employees, 9.6.3
Overdue tax—
  interest on, 5.8
Overseas—
  capital gains tax, 18.32
  company dividends from, 8.1.3
  divorce, 6.8.5
  earnings, 9.1
    100% deduction, 16.5.1
    expenses, 16.5.3
    remittances, 16.5.2
  employment, 1.2.17, 9.5, 9.6.4, 16.5
  income, 1.2.19, 16.1–16.6
    assessment, 16.2. *See also* Schedule D Cases IV and V
  double taxation relief, 16.6
    table of countries, 16.6.1
    generally, 16.1

Overseas—*contd*
  income—*contd*
    remittance basis, 16.1.1
      application of, 16.1.2
      examples, of remittances, 16.1.3
    UK companies, 12.20
  partnership, 11.7
  professions conducted partly abroad, 16.3
  property and inheritance tax, 20.29
  trading by individuals, 16.4
  transfer of assets, 13.9.2
  See also Non-residents

P11D—
  particulars on, 9.6, 9.7
PAYE—
  code number, 9.14.3
  deductions from tax payable, 5.5
  directors' 9.6.9
  employer—
    change of, 9.14.5
    returns, 9.14.4
  generally, 9.14
  payment, 9.14.1
  profit related pay, 9.15
  records, 9.14.2
Parenthood—
  daughter's services, 3.2.13
  son's services, 3.2.13
  tax planning, 1.7.5
  See also Children
Partnership—
  assessments, 11.2.1
  capital allowances, *See* Capital allowances
  capital gains, 11.6
  changes of partners, 1.2.8, 11.4
  defined, 11.1
  election for continuing basis, 11.5
  European economic interest groupings, 11.8
  husband and wife, 1.2.9
  liability for tax, 2.1
  losses, 11.3
  overseas, 11.7
  residence, 15.3.4
  retirement payments, 4.1, 5.3
  taxation of income, 11.2
  valuation of, 1.4.8
Patent holders—
  capital allowances, 10.18
  earned income, 3.1
  generally, 13.3
Pay, *see* Earnings

Payment of tax—
  capital gains tax, 18.15
  due dates for, 14.2.2
  income tax, 5.7
  interest on overdue tax, 14.7.2
  late, 12.25
  on account, 14.7.1
  PAYE, *see* PAYE
Penalties, 14.8.2–14.8.4
  previous rules, 14.8.3
Pensions—
  additional voluntary contributions, 24.13
  contracting out—
    state pension, 9.11, 24.10.1
    via approved occupational scheme, 24.12.2
    via personal pension plan, 24.11.2
  contributions as deduction, 9.8, 9.11
  controlling directors, 1.2.15
  earnings limit, 24.10
  free-standing AVC schemes, 24.13
  fringe benefit, as, 1.2.6, 9.6.3, 9.11
  generally, 24.9.1
  occupational schemes, 1.2.6, 9.11, 24.12.1
    simplified, 24.12.3
  personal plans, 1.2.14, 24.11, *see also* Personal pension schemes
  policy, inheritance tax, 24.13.1
  retirement annuity contacts, 24.11, 24.12
  retirement schemes, 9.11
    conditions for Revenue approval 9.11.1
  section 226 contracts, 24.11, 24.12
  state scheme—
    basic pension, 24.10
    contracting out, 24.10.1, 24.11.2, 24.12.2
    graduated, 24.10
    State Earnings Related Pension Scheme (SERPS), 24.10
  tax position of life company, 24.9.2
  war widows', 2.6.1
Permanent health insurance, 9.6.3, 9.6.10, 24.15
Personal equity plans (PEPs), 1.2.11, 1.2.12, 8.10
Personal pension schemes, 1.1.2, 1.2.10, 1.2.14, 24.11
  benefits payable, 24.11.1
  contracting out of SERPS, 24.11.2
  eligibility, 24.11.1
  generally, 24.11

Personal pension schemes—*contd*
  limits, 24.11.1
  tax relief, 24.11.1
  year for which granted, 24.11.1
Personal reliefs—
  additional, 3.2.12, 6.8.2
  age allowance, 1.7.7
  at a glance, 3.0.1
  blind person, 3.2.14
  child, 3.2.5, 3.2.6
    additional, 3.2.12
  daughter's services, 3.2.13
  dependent relative, 3.2.10
  earned income, 3.1
  general illustration, 3.3.1
  housekeeper, 3.2.11
  indexation, 3.3
  life assurance, 3.2.7–3.2.9
  son's services, 3.2.13
  tax saving, 1.2.1
  unearned income, 3.1
  See also Allowances
Place of abode in UK, 15.3.6
Plant—
  capital allowances, *see* Capital allowances
  sale of, 10.9.4
Political element in tax planning, 1.8
Political parties—
  gifts to, 20.18.3
Post-cessation receipts, 10.27
Post-war credits, 2.6.1
Premium Bond winnings, 2.6.1
Private sickness insurance, 9.6.3, 9.6.10, 24.15
Profession—
  capital allowances, *see* Capital allowances
  computation of assessment, 10.4
  conducted partly abroad, 16.3
  defined, 10.1
  profits from, 10.1
  subscriptions, 9.6.16
  See also Schedule D
Profit—
  business, *see* Business
  capital distinguished from revenue, 2.5
  company, *see* Corporation tax
  computation of assessable, 10.4, 12.9
  miscellaneous, 13.1
  related pay scheme, 1.2.6, 2.6.1, 9.15
  Schedule D Case VI, 13.1
  sharing schemes, 9.9.6

Property—
  dealing in, 7.9
  furnished lettings, 7.5, 7.14
  holiday lettings, 7.6
  improvements, 4.6
  lease premium, 7.7
  non-resident, liability to tax, 7.1.2
  outside Great Britain, 20.29
  rent a room relief, 7.14
  rent between connected persons, 13.9.11
  See also Land; Schedule A
Public benefit, gift for, 20.18.3
Purchased general annuities—
  company's position, 24.14.1
  guaranteed income bonds, 24.14.3
  individual annuitant, 24.14.2
Purchased life annuities, 2.6.1

Quick succession relief, 20.24
Quoted shares, *see* Capital gains tax; Shares

Reconstruction of companies, 12.12
Records—
  PAYE, 9.14.2
Registered friendly societies, 13.22
Reliefs—
  capital gains tax, *see* Capital gains tax
  Class 4 National Insurance contributions, 10.28
  non-resident's entitlement to, 17.7
  overseas trading by individual, 16.4
  personal, *see* Personal reliefs
  roll-over, 18.25
  stock, 10.6, 12.22
Remission of tax—
  limits from 14 March 1990, 14.2.6
  official error, 14.2.5
Remittances of foreign income, 1.2.19, 16.1–16.6
  remittance basis—
    application of, 16.1.2
    defined, 16.1.1
    examples, 16.1.3
Remuneration, *see* Earnings
Rent a room relief, 7.14
Rent between connected persons, 13.9.11
Repayment—
  claims, 1.2.7, 1.2.16, 1.7.7, 14.6
    example, 14.6.1
  supplement, 12.5, 14.6.2

Residence—
 change of, 1.5, 15.4
 companies—
  determination of, 15.3.3
  dual resident, 13.9.15
  migration of, 13.9.16
 defined, 15.3
 house purchase, 1.1.2
 immigrants, 17.8
 importance of, 15.1
 individual, 15.3.2
 main private, 1.3.9
 non-resident companies trading in UK, 12.19
 non-resident trusts, 13.9.19
 ordinary, 15.3.1
 partnership, 15.3.4
 place of abode in UK, 15.3.6
 private, see Dwelling house
 tax effects, 15.1.1
 trust, 15.3.5
 visitors to UK, 17.4
 visits abroad, 15.3.7
 See also Domicile; Non-resident
Retail prices index, 18.12.1
Retailers—
 value added tax, 21.10
Retirement—
 age for men and women in occupational pension schemes, 24.12.1
 annuity contracts, 24.11, 24.12
 capital gains tax relief, 1.3.5, 1.7.7, 18.29
 pension schemes, 9.11
  conditions for revenue approval, 9.11.1
 tax planning, 1.7.7
 See also Pensions
Return, see Tax return
Revenue—
 expenses, 2.6
 profits distinguished from capital profits, 2.5
 transactions, 2.5.2
Roll-over relief, 18.25
Royalties, 13.4

SERPS, 24.10
Safety at sports grounds, 10.9.8
Sale—
 and lease back, 7.12, 13.9.5
 at undervalue or overvalue, 13.9.3
 income derived from personal activities, 13.9.4

Save-as-you-earn contracts, 2.6.1
Savings related option scheme, 9.9.3
Schedule A—
 assessment under, 7.1, 7.4
 exceptions, 7.1.1
 expenses allowed, 7.1.2, 7.2
 income falling within, 2.3.1, 7.1
 lease premiums, 7.7
 losses, 7.3
Schedule B—
 woodlands, 2.3.1, 7.8
Schedule C—
 deduction of tax at source, 2.4
 income falling within, 2.3.1
Schedule D—
 assessment—
  basis of, 10.4, 10.7
  closing years, 10.7.3
   example, 10.7.4
  opening years, 10.7.1
   example, 10.7.2
 basis of charge, 8.5
 cases, 2.3.1
 Case I, 7.8, 7.9
  assessable profits, 10.1
  basis of assessment—
   closing years, 10.7.3
    example, 10.7.4
   generally, 10.7
   opening years, 10.7.1
    example, 10.7.2
  computation, 10.4
  distinguished from Schedule E, 9.4
  expenses—
   allowable, 10.3.1
   not deductible, 10.3.2
  trading defined, 10.2
 Case II—
  assessable profits, 10.1
  basis of assessment—
   closing years, 10.7.3
    example, 10.7.4
   generally, 10.7
   opening years, 10.7.1
    example, 10.7.2
  computation, 10.4
  distinguished from Schedule E, 9.4
  expenses—
   allowable, 10.3.1
   not deductible, 10.3.2
 Case III, 8.4, 8.5
  basis of charge, 8.5
  cessation of income, special rules, 8.5.3
   example, 8.5.4

Schedule D—*contd*
  Case III—*contd*
    fresh income, special rules, 8.5
      example, 8.5.1
    interest not taxed at source, 8.4
      example, 8.4.1
  Case IV—
    basis of assessment, 1.2.19, 16.2
    cessation of income, 16.2.2
      example, 16.2.3
    fresh income, 16.2.1
  Case V—
    basis of assessment, 16.2
    cessation of income, 16.2.2
      example, 16.2.3
    fresh income, 16.2.1
  Case VI, 7.5, 13.1
    miscellaneous profits, 13.1
  cash basis, 10.26
  dealing in property, 7.9
  earnings basis, 10.26
  income falling within, 2.3.1
  interest not taxed at source, 8.4
  losses—
    new business, 10.23
    relief, 10.22
      example, 10.22.1
    terminal, 10.24
  new business, 1.2.8, 10.23
  overseas income, 1.2.17, 16.2
  post-cessation receipts, 10.27
  source of income—
    cessation, 8.5.3, 8.5.4
    fresh, 8.5.1, 8.5.2
  sub-contractors, 13.5
  woodlands, 7.8
Schedule E—
  Case I, 9.1
  Case II, 9.2
  Case III, 9.3
  deduction of tax at source, 2.4
  distinction between Schedule D Case I or II, 9.4
  income falling within, 2.3.1
Schedule F—
  deduction of tax at source, 2.4
  income falling within, 2.3.1
Scholarships, 2.6.1, 9.6.3, 9.6.13
Scientific research allowance, 10.17
Scrip dividend options, 8.9
Season tickets, 9.6.3, 9.6.11
Second-hand goods—
  value added tax, 21.11.4
Securities—
  accrued income 8.3

Securities—*contd*
  bond washing, 8.3
  capital gains tax, *see* Capital gains tax
  chargeable, 8.3
  deep discount, 8.8
  deep gain, 8.8
  government, interest paid on, 8.2, 17.2
  quoted, passing on death, 20.11
  transactions in, 13.9.1
  See also Shares
Security assets, 9.6.3, 9.6.7, 10.9.9
Self-employment—
  Class 4 National Insurance contributions, 10.28
Separate assessment, 6.3
Separate taxation, 6.4
Separation—
  additional personal relief, 6.8.2
  alimony, 6.8.3
  during tax year, 6.8.1
  effect of 6.8
  maintenance payments, 6.8.3
  See also Husband and wife
Servicemen and servicewomen—
  travelling expenses, 9.6.4
Settlements—
  accumulation and maintenance, 1.2.17, 1.4.2, 1.4.5, 19.4, 19.6, 20.31.1
  child, for, 19.4
  discretionary, 1.4.2, 1.4.5, 5.5, 19.3.4, 19.5, 20.31.2
  fixed trusts, 1.4.2
  inheritance tax, 20.31
  larger, 1.4.2
  periodic charge, 1.4.2
  tax saving, 1.1.2, 1.2.17, 1.4.2
  See also Trusts
Share incentive schemes, 9.9.4
Share option schemes—
  approved, 9.9.2
  savings related, 9.9.3
  unapproved, 9.9.1
Shares—
  capital gains tax, *see* Capital gains tax
  employee shareholdings, 9.9.5, *see also* Employees
  ESOPS, 9.10
  gifts of, 1.3.3, 20.18.3
  personal equity plans, 8.10
  profit sharing schemes, 9.9.6
  quoted, passing on death, 20.11
  stamp duty, 22.1
  transactions in, 13.9.1

Shares—*contd*
  unquoted—
    capital gains tax on, 18.20
    company purchasing own, 12.24
    losses on, 18.14
  See also Dividends; Securities
Ships—
  capital allowances, 10.9.3
Short-life assets, 10.9.6
Sick pay, statutory, 23.4
Sickness benefit, 2.6.1
Small—
  companies corporation tax, 1.2.4, 12.7
  gifts, 20.18.2
  maintenance payments, 6.8.4
  workshops, 10.13
Social security—
  benefits—
    non-taxable, 2.6.1, 23.3.2
    taxable, 23.3.1
    statutory sick pay, 23.4
  See also National Insurance
Son's services, 3.2.13
Special Commissioners, 14.4
Sports grounds, safety at, 10.9.8
Sportsmen—
  visiting, 17.6
Stamp duty—
  ad valorem, 22.5
  capital duty, 22.3
  exemptions, 22.2.1
  generally, 22.1
  relief for take-overs, 22.4
  reserve tax, 22.6
  share transfers, 22.1, 22.7
Statutory sick pay, 23.4
Stock—
  relief, 10.6, 12.22
  valuation, 10.5
Student—
  tax planning, 1.7.2
Sub-contractors, 13.5

TESSAs, *see* Tax exempt special savings accounts
Takeovers—
  capital gains tax, 18.18.6
  stamp duty, 22.4
Tapes, 10.21
Tax accountants' papers, 14.5.1
Tax avoidance, *see* Anti-avoidance
Tax bands—
  indexation, 5.1

Tax bands—*contd*
  lower rate—
    expansion of, 1.8
    gifts and settlements, 1.2.17
Tax bill—
  computing, 5.0.1–5.9
Tax credits, 2.4, 5.5
Tax evasion—
  tax avoidance distinguished, 13.9
  tax planning compared, 1.1
  See also Anti-avoidance
Tax exempt special savings accounts, (TESSA's) 1.2.12, 2.6.1, 8.11
Tax-free income, 1.2.12, 2.6.1, 2.7
Tax-free organisations—
  charities, 13.2.1
  friendly societies, 13.2.2
  trade unions, 13.2.2
Tax liability, *see* Liability for tax
Tax planning—
  basic plan, 1.1.2
  change of residence and domicile, 1.5
  don'ts, 1.1.1
  income tax saving, *see* Income tax
  inheritance tax, *see* Inheritance tax
  political element, 1.8
  seven ages of, 1.7
    childhood, 1.7.1
    early working life, 1.7.3
    middle age, 1.7.6
    newly married, 1.7.4
    parenthood, 1.7.5
    retirement, 1.7.7
    student days, 1.7.2
  way ahead, 1.8
  year end planning, 1.6
Tax rates, 5.0.1
Tax return—
  capital gains, 14.1.3
  claim for allowances, 14.1.4
  dividends, 8.1.1
  employment income, 9.6.16
  generally, 14.1
  husband, 6.2
  income, 14.1.1
  independent taxation, 6.2.1, 14.1
  outgoings, 14.1.2
  request for, 14.1
  wife, 6.2, 14.1
Tax saving, *see* Capital gains tax; Income tax
Tax tables—
  capital transfer tax, 25.5
  income tax 1992–93, 25.1

Tax tables—*contd*
  inheritance tax, 25.6
  investment income surcharge, 25.4
  rates and allowances, 25.2, 25.3
Tax year—
  divorce during, 6.8.1
  separation during, 6.8.1
Taxes payable, 2.2
Tenancies, assured, 10.16
Terminal losses, 10.24
Timing—
  capital gains tax saving, 1.3.5
Total income—
  deductions, 5.3
  defined, 5.2
Top-slicing relief, 5.9, 7.7.1
Tour operators—
  value added tax, 21.11.10
Trade—
  defined, 10.2
  overseas trading by individual, 16.4
  profits from, 10.1
  taxation of, 10.1
  transfers in course of, 20.18.3
  See also Schedule D
Trade unions, 13.2.2
Traded options, 18.30
Travelling allowances, 9.6.4, *see also* Cars
Trusts—
  accumulation for children, 19.4
    inheritance tax, 20.31.1
  capital gains tax—
    business assets, 19.7
    disposal of interests, 19.8
    distributions, 19.8
    generally, 19.6
    gifts, 19.7
  defined, 19.1
  discretionary, 19.3.4
    income of, 19.5
    inheritance tax, 20.31.2
  disposals, 19.8
  foreign, 19.9
    capital gains from 19 March 1991, 19.9.1
  inheritance tax, 20.31
  liability for tax, 2.1
  non-resident, 13.9.19
  residence, 15.3.5
  settlor or testator—
    deceased, 19.2
    still living, 19.3
  See also Settlements

Unearned income, 3.1, 5.6
Unit trusts, 18.18.7
Unmarried couples—
  mortgage interest, 4.6
Unquoted company purchasing own shares, 12.24

Valuation—
  capital gains tax, 18.16
  inheritance tax, 20.10, 20.12
  stock, 10.5
Value added tax—
  accommodation for directors, 21.11.8
  appeals, 21.13
  bad debts, 21.11.9
  business defined, 21.4
  business entertainment, 21.11.2
  charities, 21.9
  deregistration, 21.5
  documentation, 21.12
  European Community, trading within, 21.17
  exemption, 21.3, 21.16
  flat rate farmers, 21.18
  generally, 21.1
  gifts, 21.11.6
  groups and divisions of companies, 21.7
  in practice, 21.2
  local authorities, 21.8
  motor cars, 21.11.1
  personal use, 21.11.7
  retailers, 21.10
  sales on credit, 21.11.5
  second-hand goods, 2.11.4
  self-supply, 21.11.3
  small traders, 21.5
  tour operators, 21.11.10
  zero-rated supplies, 21.6
  zero-rating, 21.3, 21.14, 21.15
Visitors—
  becoming residents, 17.4
  diplomats, 17.5
  entertainers, 17.6
  income, taxation rules, 17.3
  sportsmen, 17.6
Vocational training, 3.2.17
Vocations—
  capital allowances, *see* Capital allowances
  profits from, 10.1
  See also Schedule D
Vouchers—
  income from employment, 9.6.11

Vouchers—*contd*
  income tax deduction, 8.1.2
  luncheon, 1.2.6

Waiver of dividends and remuneration, 20.20
Wasting assets, 18.29.2
Wedding presents, 2.6.1, 20.18.2
Widow—
  bereavement allowance, 3.2.16
  war pension, 2.6.1
Wife, *see* Husband and wife
Wilful default, 14.8.1
Wills—
  deeds of family arrangement, 1.4.9
  inheritance tax planning, 1.4.5, 1.7.7

Woodlands—
  assessable value, 7.8
  basis of assessment, 7.8
  inheritance tax, 20.23
  occupying, meaning, 7.8
  Schedule B, 7.8
  Schedule D, 7.8
Work, *see* Employment
Working clothes, 9.6.3, 9.8
Workshops—
  small, 10.13
Wound pensions, 2.6.1
Writing down allowance, *see* Capital allowances

Year of assessment, 2.8
Year-end planning, 1.6

Other titles in the Allied Dunbar Library

Allied Dunbar Tax Guides

- Allied Dunbar Business Tax and Law Guide — WI Sinclair & John McMullen
- Allied Dunbar Capital Taxes and Estate Planning Guide — WI Sinclair & PD Silke
- Allied Dunbar Expatriate Tax and Investment Guide — David Phillips
- Allied Dunbar Investment and Savings Guide 1992–93 — General Editor. Harry Littlefair
- Allied Dunbar Retirement Planning Guide — Barry Bean, Dr Beric Wright & Bill Tadd
- Allied Dunbar Pensions Guide — AM Reardon

All of these titles in the Allied Dunbar Library are available from leading bookshops

For more information please contact: Longman Law, Tax and Finance, 21–27 Lamb's Conduit St, London WC1N 3NJ Tel: (071) 242 2548

Other titles in the Allied Dunbar Library

Allied Dunbar Money Guides

- Buying and Selling Your Home — Richard Newell
- Buying and Selling Your Home in France — Henry Dyson
- Buying and Selling Your Home in Spain — Per Svensson
- Financial Care for your Elderly Relatives — Beverley Chandler
- Financial Planning for the Over 50s — Robert Leach
- Insurance: Are you Covered? — Mihir Bose
- Investing in Shares — Hugh Pym & Nick Kochan
- Leaving Your Money Wisely — Tony Foreman
- Making Your Job Work — David Williams
- Managing Your Finances — Helen Pridham
- Planning School and College Fees — Danby Block & Amanda Pardoe
- Planning Your Pension — Tony Reardon
- Running Your Own Business — David Williams
- Tax and Finance for Women — Helen Pridham
- Tax for the Self-Employed — David Williams
- Your Home in Italy — Flavia Maxwell
- Your Home in Portugal — Rosemary de Rougemont